SCOTLAND : SHOWING MAJOR RIVER SYSTEMS

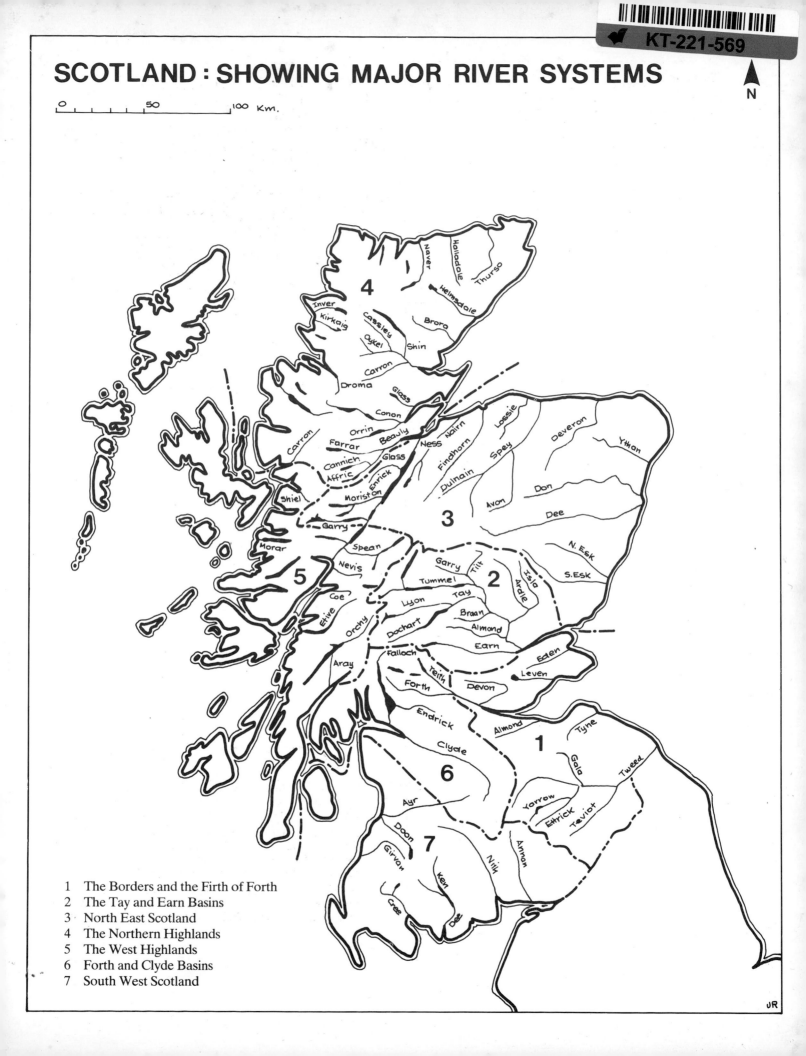

1   The Borders and the Firth of Forth
2   The Tay and Earn Basins
3   North East Scotland
4   The Northern Highlands
5   The West Highlands
6   Forth and Clyde Basins
7   South West Scotland

THE
WATERFALLS
— OF —
SCOTLAND

THE WATERFALLS —OF— SCOTLAND

Worth gaun a mile to see

Louis Stott

maps by James Renny

AUP

Aberdeen University Press

First published 1987
Aberdeen University Press
A member of the Pergamon Group

British Library Cataloguing in Publication Data
Stott, Louis
   The waterfalls of Scotland.
   1. Waterfalls — Scotland — Guide-books
   2. Scotland — Description and travel — 1981–
   — Guide-books
   I. Title
   914.11′04858   GB1487

ISBN 0-08-032424-X

Printed and bound in Great Britain by
A. Wheaton & Co. Ltd, Exeter

For Leila Stott; Janet Kean; Katherine Stott;
Alison and Emma Smith

(on p i) **Alltnambeathac (Ossian's Showerbath),** *West Highlands.* COLIN ALSTON

(on p ii) **De'il's Cauldron, Falls of Lednock,** *near Comrie.* PETER DAVENPORT

Contents

Illustrations

INTRODUCTION

Here, foaming down the skelvy rocks,
    In twisting strength I rin;
There high my boiling torrent smokes,
    Wild-roaring o'er a linn;
Enjoying large each spring and well
    As Nature gave them me
I am, although I say't mysel
    Worth gaun a mile to see.
Robert Burns
The Humble Petition of Bruar Water

Waterfalls are focal points of river scenery. Their appeal is universal. Some people are impressed by the sheer height of a fall, others by the volume of water contained in it. Others find delight in the cascading water itself or in the beauty of the setting.

Some falls can be seen at a distance across the glen; others, secret places where the setting is all, must be seen close at hand. Waterfalls are rich in associations. Often there are folk-tales of fairies, witches and water sprites associated with them. More prosaically, they are known as places to catch fish, as the sites of water-mills and of early industries; and in recent years some Scottish falls have provided sites for impressive hydro-electric projects.

The first literary visitors to Scotland – Gray, Johnson, the Wordsworths – wrote accounts of falls. Native writers – Burns, Boswell, Scott, Hogg – praised waterfalls, and drew visitors from all over the world to see them. Painters – Turner, Thomson, Millais – found, in the waterfalls of Scotland, sublime subjects for well-known works.

The Victorians were excited by waterfalls and their guide books drew attention to some Scottish falls, which, for one reason or another, are neglected nowadays. The increase in travel abroad, and the discovery, in Africa and America, of the great waterfalls of the world, have qualified the superlatives used by early travellers. In comparison with the waterfalls of Europe, the waterfalls of Scotland are thought to be modest. At the beginning of the twentieth century, water power schemes and water supply schemes began to diminish the flow of water in a number of falls which had figured prominently in the most popular itineraries. In particular, the establishment, as early as 1896, of an aluminium factory at Foyers detracted greatly, in the minds of guide book writers, from its importance as a tourist attraction.

Some well-known falls have been changed, but many more, equally celebrated, have not. Many of those affected by water-power schemes can still be seen in spate. Several hundred falls in Scotland provide local tourist attractions: of these, more than seventy merit the attention of every visitor who really wishes to know Scotland well. Some waterfalls are especially attractive on days marred by rain. Some have equal if opposite merit in dry weather, for few pleasures excel the discovery of a hidden cascade on a hot day, and it is sometimes possible on a dry day to approach close to a waterfall which cannot easily be approached in spate.

This book distinguishes more than 750 waterfalls in Scotland, each of which is attractive in its own way. Some of the most picturesque are readily accessible and have always been stopping places for tourists. The grandest route from Carlisle to Edinburgh passes the Grey Mare's Tail. Beside the Great North Road, the A9, lie the Hermitage, the Falls of the Bruar, and the Falls of Truim, and, at a little distance from it, the Linn of Tummel, Black Spout and the Falls of Urrard. The A82 from Glasgow to Inverness provides a cavalcade of cataracts – the Falls of Inversnaid across Loch Lomond, the Falls of Falloch, the Falls of Glencoe, the Falls of Invermoriston and the Falls of the Allt Sigh. The National Trust for Scotland, the Scottish Wildlife Trust and the Forestry Commission have established guided walks and forest trails close to main roads.

Some falls provide fine short walks from the principal tourist resorts. From Aberfeldy everyone must visit the Falls of Moness. In Killin are the Falls of Dochart and, at a little distance, the Falls of Lochay. Near Crieff are the Falls of Turret and the Falls of Monzie. At Talnotry in Galloway there is a fine fall, another Grey Mare's Tail. From Fort William the Falls of Glen Nevis, in aggregate the most impressive in Scotland, make a notable excursion.

Other falls are further afield. Glen Feshie is for connoisseurs. The Fall of Glomach is just one of a number of highly attractive waterfalls in Kintail.

The Falls of Kirkaig and Eas Coul Aulin in Sutherland are impressive. At the head of Glen Esk and of Glen Tilt are remote mountain falls in the hidden recesses of the Grampians. To reach falls like these, longer expeditions are necessary, but they provide great rewards.

In his *Tales of Travel* Lord Curzon considered the appeal of waterfalls:

There is something in the setting and movement of falls that presents a variety of effect, both sensational and aesthetic, with which even the greatest mountain cannot vie.

Waterfalls are a quintessential component of Scottish scenery. This book is designed to provide the visitor with a key to their enjoyment.

Varieties of Falls

Waterfalls commonly occur where rivers and streams encounter relatively hard rocks. Where the gradient is sufficiently steep the body of water in a river falls forward in rapids. When the gradient is steeper the whole mass of water topples in a waterfall. The distinction between the two is difficult to define because the volume of water in a particular stream varies from time to time. However, where the water falls vertically away from the rocks what is generally called an unsupported fall occurs. Many would assert that only unsupported falls are true waterfalls. A mountain torrent tumbling helter skelter down a hillside forms what is sometimes called a waterslide. The term cataract is used to describe a single great fall, and the term cascade is used to describe a series of linked falls. Where the topmost rocks overhang it can be said that a curtain fall occurs. An apron fall is formed where the underlying rocks are resistant. When rocks are tilted upstream the fall is sometimes described as a waterchute. In some cases the falling water all vapourises before it reaches the valley floor, in which case a bridal-veil fall is formed. This kind of fall, the product of great height – epitomised by the falls in the Lauterbrunnen Valley in Switzerland – does not occur in Scotland, but Eas Coul Aulin exhibits this characteristic to some extent.

The archetypal waterfall is Niagara which crosses almost horizontal sediments. A cap-rock of relatively hard limestone causes the fall and the water tumbles into a deep plunge-pool. In the case of Niagara this pool is deeper than that part of the fall above the water. Underneath the limestone are softer sandstones and shales which are much more rapidly worn away. The cap-rock is undermined and collapses, which means that the site of the fall migrates upstream. This is a characteristic of all waterfalls. It means that they tend to eliminate themselves. Below the fall is a gorge which marks the former positions of the fall. Below the Falls of Kirkaig there are twenty-one former plunge pools in the well marked gorge cut by the river. The pools are well-known to salmon fishermen and mark the former positions of these falls which, from the geological point of view, are relatively recent. Other falls, like the Linn of Dee, have almost succeeded in eliminating themselves.

Where the river bed is exposed the mechanism by which it cuts through rock shelves can be examined. Stones carried by the stream grind potholes in the bed which becomes honeycombed with them. Nowhere is this process better exemplified than in the Falls of Massan which are, in fact, a series of linked potholes several metres deep. Sometimes two are linked where the wall between them has collapsed, but in other cases it is only at the bottom of two potholes that a breach has occurred and a natural bridge across the stream is formed. In spate these are submerged.

Where falls occur in succession the possibilities for rock sculpture are increased. Double falls, linked by a short pool, are common, one of the finest instances being provided by the Eas Chia-aig beside Loch Arkaig. Twin falls, caused where the water finds its way round an obstacle in a rock shelf, are also highly picturesque. Where such falls persist an island of rock, a rock stack, is left in the gorge below the falls. A good example of this type of rock sculpture occurs in the gorge of the Cuinneag close to Braemore in Ross. Sometimes the situation is more complicated, and a second fall is formed over the side of the channel occupied by the main stream. In other cases the water divides below the lip of the fall. The falls in Glen Feshie exhibit this characteristic in low falls; the Falls of Glomach are high falls of this complex type. The rock sculpture of Scottish waterfalls is infinitely varied. Taken in conjunction with the number of different rock types in which falls occur, it accounts for the individual character and special charm of many falls.

Natural conditions which favour the development of waterfalls are widespread in Scotland. Geographers generally divide the country into three main regions: the Scottish Highlands, composed largely of metamorphic rocks; the Central Lowlands, composed of relatively undisturbed sedimentary rocks; and, the Southern Uplands made up of strongly folded sedimentary rocks. In all three regions there are intrusions of igneous rocks like granite, and widespread outcrops of volcanic rocks like basalt. Within each region, too, there are marked variations in altitude, even in the Central Lowlands. These differences in relief, due either to the structure of the rocks or to the effects of former glaciation, give rise to an abundance of possible sites for waterfalls.

Distribution of Falls

In Scotland most waterfalls are due to the effects of former glaciation and it is to be expected that they will be most widely distributed in those places where glacial erosion has been most marked. A number of different features associated with glacial erosion give rise to waterfalls and it is useful to distinguish between them.

The fundamental landform of glaciated highlands is the corrie, the hollow in which the snow accumulated and consolidated before moving downhill. Corries are roughly semi-circular in plan and in cross-section and are characterised by a steep headwall, formed by the plucking action of the ice, and a hollow or basin enclosed by the corrie walls sometimes occupied by a corrie lochan. Waterfalls occur at the corrie headwall – notably the Falls of Dee in Garbh Choire between Braeriach and Cairn Toul in the Cairngorm Massif – and at the lip of the corrie where the burn draining it falls into the valley below as, for example, in the falls on the Allt Coire Mhic Fhearchair in Torridon. Glaciated valleys are steep-sided and flat-bottomed with truncated spurs, hanging valleys – tributary valleys which fall steeply into the main valley – long straight stretches, ribbon-lakes and fiords. They are called glacial troughs and are characterised by irregular, stepped profiles, most noticeably at their heads where one or more corries fall steeply into them. The spectacular falls at the head of Loch Avon in the Cairngorms occur at the end of such a glacial trough. Many of Scotlands best-known falls occur in hanging valleys. Eas Coul Aulin is an outstanding example. At the outfall of many ribbon lakes there are fine river falls, of which the Falls of Leny below Loch Lubnaig and the Falls of Morar are perhaps the best-known. Other river falls like the Falls of Tummel occur where there is a break in the 'long profile' of a glacial trough.

While many falls can be attributed almost exclusively to the erosive power of ice, a number of highly distinctive falls are caused by the effects of glaciation manifesting themselves in a different way. As the ice retreated, river erosion began again and many rivers were swollen by melt-waters, and in some instances cut completely new channels or rapidly deepened their existing valleys, giving rise to highly spectacular gorges. The gorges of the Droma, the Glomach, the Spean, the Nevis and the Leven almost certainly originated in this way. In other instances notable ravines have been formed where post-glacial rivers have begun to cut back into gorges formed by glacial action, as is the case at Eagle's Fall in Glen Fyne and elsewhere. At other places there are falls which are caused by glacial deposition. The old course of the Clyth Burn in Caithness was blocked by boulder clay and it was forced to find its way to the sea by another, more spectacular, route.

Coastal waterfalls are similar to waterfalls caused by glacial action in that the normal sequence of river erosion has clearly been interrupted: this is due to a change in sea level which leaves streams hanging above the coast. In Skye and elsewhere in North and West Scotland there are numerous falls of this type indicating very youthful coasts which, from the geological point of view, are very recent. Changes in sea level of this kind are complex and have affected the coasts of Britain in various ways. It is sufficient here to note that falls will result where there has been a change involving the uplift of the land. Coastal falls of the kind found in Skye are obvious examples of this, as are falls which occur where

Falls of Turret, near Crieff. A noteworthy example of falls affected by man, in this case by the creation of the Turret Reservoir, one of the largest public water supply undertakings in Scotland. PETER DAVENPORT

Hermitage Falls, Dunkeld. These are rich in literary and artistic associations. The pioneer Scottish photographer, George Washington Wilson, made the Hermitage the subject of picture postcards and stereoscopic cards in Queen Victoria's reign. PETER DAVENPORT

there are old lines of cliffs some little· distance inland. However, this kind of movement of the land relative to the sea increases the erosive power of all rivers, and falls which can be attributed to this cause are found a great distance inland. The Falls of Clyde are of this type. The upper basin of the river represents an old river system: the lower basin of the Clyde is graded with reference to a sea level at or about the level of the sea today.

The last group of falls are also due to earth movements of a different kind. Faults place different kinds of rocks next to one another and frequently account for areas of high land. Because they are abrupt they tend to give rise to waterfalls. Indeed many falls which can, in a more general sense, be attributed to other causes are often found where there are faults. The Highland Boundary Fault and the Ochil Fault are two outstanding examples. It must be remembered, of course, that the sites of falls tend to migrate upstream and the fall may be found at a distance from the fault.

While it is possible to advance these general explanations for waterfalls it is essential to remember that particular falls will have particular explanations. In any valley there may be a number of unremarkable mountain torrents and one distinctive fall.

Rivers and Streams

If the site and shape of a particular fall is determined by geology at least part of its appeal is likely to be determined by the water which it discharges. Streamflow is influenced by two sets of factors: climatic factors and catchment factors, which are broadly related but can be usefully distinguished from one another.

In Scotland the amount of water entering streams as a proportion of the amount of water falling as rain and snow varies from over 80% in the north and west to about 50% in the Lothians. Thus the pattern of streamflow is controlled by climate. The river regimes which are found in Scotland are described as oceanic and, as might be expected, they tend to be highest in winter and lowest in summer. However, where snow melt is a significant factor there is a maximum in December and a secondary maximum in April or even May. The lowest flows occur in June and begin to increase again in the Autumn. This characteristic is most marked in the West and, in a belt from Kintail to Argyll, it is in the six months from February to July that there are the lowest flows. In the east – in the Grampian and Lothian regions – the six months from May to October are the driest. There are considerable variations from year to year in these patterns and the influence of particularly wet or dry months is very marked.

Catchment factors include area, relief and aspect, geology and vegetation cover. Area is by far the most significant factor and generally speaking there is a broad agreement between catchment size and mean flow. However there are variations from one part of the country to another: the Clyde drains a much bigger basin than the Spey, but it has a smaller discharge. Nevertheless the falls with the greatest discharges will occur on the rivers with the largest basins. In respect of volume of

water, Campsie Linn on the Tay is the largest waterfall in Great Britain. Variations in altitude influence rainfall: altitude is significant in determining the amount of snow cover. In northern Scotland there are significant daily variations in stream flow due to snow melt. Geology is a more significant catchment factor in England where there are many more permeable rocks than in Scotland. However it is probably geology, combined with land use, that accounts for the difference between the Clyde and the Spey.

In most of Scotland, run-off (the surface water discharged from the land into a river) is very direct: water flows off the old, hard rocks of Scotland straight into her rivers and streams. Peat cover, which tends in itself to enhance the impermeability of rocks, the occurrence of bogs and the widespread distribution of lochans all help to even out discharges to some extent. It is not certain what exact effect afforestation has on river discharges: it tends to even out discharges but it may well reduce the amount of water available altogether.

An insight into the effects of all these factors can be obtained from a study carried out on the Allt Uaine in Argyll. It drains a tiny basin west of the Arrochar Alps where there is a rainfall of some 3454 mm. The underlying rocks are mica schists covered with morainic drift, with a peat overlay. Its basin is about 1.5 square kilometres in extent. The study found that the main discharge was 0.3 cubic metres per second. In dry conditions the discharge was about one tenth of that and when the ground was saturated the burn would rise in about an hour to a discharge of 3.0 cubic metres a second, ten times greater than its average discharge and one hundred times greater than its discharge in dry conditions. After rain the burn would fall to a discharge of about 2.0 cubic metres a second in three hours and about one cubic metre a second after seven hours. If conditions did not alter it would fall to its average discharge in about sixteen hours.

Some people seem to believe that waterfalls should only be visited in spate, but there is a good deal to be said for visiting falls in a variety of conditions. The conditions observed in the basin of the Allt Uaine are exaggerated by the confined nature of the catchment and it can safely be said that most falls will be reasonably full between twelve and thirty-six hours after heavy rain. At high spate it may well be dangerous to attempt to visit many falls and the best features are frequently obscured. Flood water surging over the lip of a fall so that it presents a single wall of brown liquid is awe-inspiring, but the absence of white water and of the highlights provided by intermediate ledges renders most falls less attractive in this state.

Heights and Discharges

The height of falls is generally taken to be of greater interest than their discharge, and there is more information available about heights than there is about discharges.

Most heights are estimates. There are considerable differences between the figure given for various falls.

Linn of Quoich, *near Braemar. Falls of great beauty, also of geological interest. The Quoich stream flows over schists forming a series of deep potholes – from which the name of the river is derived. Tradition has it that in 1715 the Earl of Mar used one pothole here to mix punch for Jacobite supporters.* PETER DAVENPORT

This is due in part to the fact that it is difficult to be precise. The height of even a straightforward fall may vary from one part of the river to another. At the Pot of Gartness there is a fall of 1.2 metres in the main channel in midstream, but the river also tumbles over other rock ledges 1.5 metres and 1.8 metres above the pool below. There is one point where the fall is 2.1 metres close to the left bank of the stream. These differences occur in all falls and depend to a certain extent on the state of the water. Curiously, the height of certain falls is reduced in spate. The water becomes confined in the gorge below the fall and the height of the surface of the plunge pool is

raised. Some low falls may be eliminated in flood. In the case of high falls it is generally considered that the height of the unsupported part of the fall is what counts, but in the case of Eas Coul Aulin, this also varies according to the amount of water in the fall.

The combined height of linked falls may be impressive, but it is difficult to determine when they should be considered to be a single fall and when they should be distinguished from one another. One useful concept is that of 'head': this is always much greater than the apparent height of a fall and is the difference between one level and another. It is a term used by engineers to

Linn of Muick, *near Ballater. A fish pass has been hewn into the rocks on the west bank to enable salmon to climb against the heavy fall of water.*
PETER DAVENPORT

determine the fall of water for purposes of hydro-electric power generation: it measures the difference between a level above the fall and the level below it. In the case of the Falls of Clyde the combined head is 87 metres whereas the height of the falls is 62 metres. Information about the height of falls is always interesting, but ultimately it is not necessary to be absolutely precise about it.

Discharges vary considerably. The mean discharge of the Clyde at the falls is about 25 cubic metres a second. In December the mean discharge is over 80 cubic metres a second and in June not much more than 8 cubic metres a second. The highest recorded discharge is in excess of 500 cubic metres a second, more than twenty times the mean. The potential power and fury of Stonebyres, the steepest of the falls, is striking. Nowhere else in the British Isles is there the possibility of generating any quantity of hydro-electric power without storage. The Falls of Clyde are great falls in this respect.

Estimated Heights and Discharges of Certain Waterfalls in Scotland

Name of Fall	Area of Basin sq km	Height metres	Mean Discharge cumecs
Eas Coul Aulin	3.4	200	0.25
Fall of Glomach	20.4	112	1.60
An Steall Ban	5.0	105	0.50
Reekie Linn	152.0	24	5.80
Falls of Braan	200.0	25	6.00
Fall of Kirkaig	115.0	18	7.00
Falls of Clyde	932.0	55*	25.00
Falls of Moriston	486.0	8	20.90
Falls of Shin	495.0	4	15.79
Campsie Linn	4590.0	2	155.60

Reekie Linn, *near Alyth. In ordinary conditions there is a fall of six metres followed by a fall of 18 metres. In spate these unite to form a single fall. The apron of water is precipitated into a plunge pool 36 metres deep. At the bottom of the fall is a cave called the Black Dub.* PETER DAVENPORT

One or two other falls have a greater discharge than the Falls of Clyde but none of such great height. Campsie Linn has by far the greatest discharge. Next were the Eilan Aigas Falls on the Beauly which were about four metres high. The Falls of the Inverness-shire Garry, severely affected by hydro-electric works, come next; then the Falls of the Spean. All these have a greater discharge than the Falls of Clyde. The Invermoriston Falls are of the same order as the Falls of Clyde and the only other falls in this league are the Falls of Conon. At the outlet of Loch Luichart the Conon falls 38 metres in less than a kilometre. It has a discharge of some 16 cubic metres per second and was the site in 1929 of the Ross-shire Electric Supply Company's early hydro-electric power scheme.

There are two broad groups of falls, those with a relatively low discharge but of great height and those with high discharges of no great height. Of the latter the Falls of Clyde are clearly the finest. Of the former the

Falls of Glomach have a much greater discharge than Eas Coul Aulin and have rightly been considered the finest of the great falls. Excluding corrie headwall falls and other doubtful cases, the highest falls are Eas Coul Aulin (200 metres high), Glomach (112), Measach (82.5), An Steall (105), Bruar (60), Grey Mare's Tail (60), Falls of Kinlochmore (45), Foyers (36), Ben Glas Fall (36), and Black Spout (36).

If the Falls of Clyde – Bonnington Linn, Cora Linn, Dundaff Linn and Stonebyres Linn – are taken together they are as high as the Grey Mare's Tail at 62 metres. The head at Foyers is 108 metres although the principal fall is only 30 metres in height. It nevertheless drains a basin of more than 250 square kilometres and probably had a mean discharge of about 12.5 cubic metres before the hydro-electric plant was set up. It justified the epithet 'strikingly awful' applied to it in the Statistical Account because it would discharge ten times that quantity in flood.

Four falls which fail to get into either of these two categories deserve mention. They are relatively high falls on well known rivers of the second rank. They are Reekie Linn on the Isla, Cauldron Linn on the Devon, the Falls of Kirkaig and the Lower Falls of the Nevis.

Plants and Animals

It is the setting of a fall which singles it out. In the case of the Fall of Glomach it is the character of the remote moorlands between Glen Affric and Kintail which gives this fall at least part of its atmosphere. And in the case of the Falls of Braan it is the richly wooded countryside above Dunkeld which contributes so greatly to the feel of the place. It is useful to try to isolate one or two of the highly characteristic features of these and other interesting environments.

The boisterous mountain torrents on which many waterfalls occur are difficult places for plants or animals to live. But in spite of the difficulties – the force of water, the variations in discharge and the cold temperature – there are a number of advantages: the water itself is sometimes highly mineralised and at falls it is highly charged with oxygen. Some plants or animals are properly adapted to hang on. Waterfalls are places where mosses and liverworts which cling to the rock and enjoy the damp conditions thrive. The water milfoil, myriophyllum, is an example of a plant found in swift flowing larger streams whose leaves absorb the carbon dioxide dissolved in the water to form sugars and discharge oxygen. Willow moss, Fontinalis pyretica, and Rhocomitrium aciculare are examples of plants found at most waterfalls.

The banks of the ravines and gorges in which most falls are found are more or less densely wooded. Some falls in the north west – even those close to sea level – and corrie headwall falls are bereft of trees, but generally birch is found associated with either pine or oak and alder and rowan. In some cases there is such a varied collection of trees and ground plants that the gorge is designated as a nature reserve, as is the Corrieshalloch Gorge.

Birch is perhaps the most attractive of all our trees. Its wonderful variety of form means that it can add many different qualities to a scene. Sometimes it resembles a sturdy shrub, as at the Fall of Glomach where there are four or five birches perched on the natural platform above the abyss into which the fall tumbles. At the Black Linn of Blairvaich there is a natural birch wood and fully grown trees frame the fall, clinging to the mossy banks of the gorge while another tree perched on the pinnacle of a rock ledge above the Forth gives perspective to the scene. The birch can reach twenty four metres in height, but trees of eight to ten metres in height are very common and provide a means of estimating the height of falls.

Grey Mare's Fall, Kinlochleven. A formidable fall, always breathtakingly beautiful because of its scale and striking because of the confined nature of the gorge. PETER DAVENPORT

The ground flora of these riverside woodlands includes a rich variety of plants. There is a loving account of the Plant Life of the Scottish Highlands by Alexander Holden (1952) which refers often to such woods. Here is his description of the water avens:

I first became acquainted with this plant near the head of beautiful Glen Nevis, where it was growing in a marshy patch at the bottom of the deep boulder-strewn gorge of the Nevis, and whenever I review my specimens this romantic spot comes back to me with its black precipices, its huge rough boulders, its swirling waters and its beauty and peace. Its rocky sides are a perfect rock garden with yellow saxifrage, wood geranium, melancholy thistle, rose-root and butterwort watered by the little streams that tumble down from the high summit of Aonach Mor.

The yellow saxifrage is particularly found colonising those shingle banks in the middle of swift salmon rivers where the debris brought down has accumulated in mid stream. The yellow mountain saxifrage, Saxifraga aizoides, is another of Holden's favourites:

I first made acquaintance with this beautiful saxifrage at the head of Glen Nevis, where I have found many interesting mountain plants. A small waterfall came tumbling down the steep mountain side, dashing itself against rocks and boulders in clouds of spray as it rushed down from springs near the summit of Ben Nevis. I climbed beside this glistening cascade, where my eye was caught by several bright golden patches at the waters edge. Scrambling down I found that the patches were several large tufts of the yellow mountain saxifrage, their leaves bedewed with spray.

This rich variety of trees, shrubs and ground herbs adds greatly to the charm of waterfalls. The same cannot be said for the insects. Waterfalls, or more particularly the enclosed pools below them, are closely associated with midges, but these are troublesome everywhere and no more likely to spoil a visit to a waterfall than any walk in the country. In a heavy atmosphere in the summer months the only advice is to avoid visits between six o'clock at night and dusk or to put up with them as best you can. However, it is almost as infuriating to be indoors on a fine night as it is to be pestered by these unloved little creatures.

The larvae of many flies are aquatic; some Mayfly larvae, for example, are specially adapted for clinging to stones in strong currents. Water beetles and dragonflies are also found near waterfalls. Of freshwater molluscs the pearl mussels, for which the Kerry and other west coast rivers are noted, are the most interesting.

Fish associated wth the middle and upper reaches of rivers include the eel which invades rivers like the Kirkaig. Brown trout are particularly associated with the upper reaches of many Scottish streams, but it is the sea trout and, above all, the salmon which are the fish most associated with waterfalls. They were once so abundant that in the middle of the seventeenth century it was observed that the city fathers of Stirling were compelled to re-inforce an ancient statute that commanded masters not to force apprentices to feed on salmon more than three times a week. The Spanish Ambassador was astonished to find that on the Ericht the inhabitants used neither rod nor spear to catch salmon. The obliging fish jumped into a pot set on the rocks, presumably at the Falls of Keith.

The leaping behaviour of salmon at waterfalls is the subject of a fascinating study by T. A. Stuart (1962). He found that while the progress of salmon seems to be dependent on the temperature of the water the fish makes its leap under the stimulus of the impact of the water falling in the pool below. Astonishingly the salmon makes a 'standing' leap and does not accelerate towards the surface as one might expect. The highest leap is supposed to be under five metres (16') and fish surmount higher falls by using intermediate pools. The smallest fish leap in the driest conditions. Fish migrate throughout the year, but it is the spring and, particularly, the autumn runs which give rise to the spectacle of leaping fish which draws crowds to such places as The Pot of Gartness, Buchanty Spout, and the Falls of Shin.

Birds particularly associated with the faster flowing rivers and streams include the heron, the osprey and the goosander, all of which prey on salmon. In Galloway kingfishers are found, too. However the two birds most likely to be encountered are grey wagtails and dippers. David Knowlton (1974) in another very useful general account covering the whole of Scotland describes this bird well:

> If there is one bird more than any other which the nature lover associates with the fast-flowing mid and upper reaches of Scottish streams from the Borders to Sutherland it is the dipper.
> As he stands on a mid stream boulder jerking himself up and down, and even more as he indicates his mastery of his environment by walking under the water on the rocky bed, he is the river personified.

The three mammals most closely associated with the river bank are the water vole, which lives in the dense bank vegetation, the watershrew and the otter. However it is much more likely that a visit to a fall will be enlivened by a herd of deer seen on a distant hillside or a mountain hare louping away from you than by an encounter with any of these three.

Man and Waterfalls

Waterfalls are frequently associated with crossing places. Immediately below a fall, in the shallows at the exit from the plunge pool, there is often a good site for a ford and the boulders arrested at the foot of the fall make admirable stepping stones. Falls themselves occur at places where the river is narrow enough to bridge making use of the natural abutments provided.

It is thought that the Roman garrisons on Hadrian's Wall had a few water-driven corn mills. It was, however, in the middle ages that water power became essential to the village economy and the presence of a waterfall became a real asset. The building of weirs and the harnessing of falls has meant that many lowland falls are now unrecognisable as such. John Hume's Regional Archeology of Scotland lists many mill sites. They are intrinsically interesting places, but comparatively few of them are directly associated with falls which are tourist attractions.

Falls which were well hidden were often the haunt of cattle receivers and hermits. In Galloway and Carrick particularly they were hiding places for Covenanters. Fugitives throughout the ages seem to have found waterfalls attractive. Many notable 'leaps' – places where men jumped for their lives across brawling rivers – are close to waterfalls.

Man's closest association with waterfalls, established since the very earliest times, has been as a fisherman. Eels and salmon and sea trout have always been taken from Scottish rivers and they are nowhere easier to catch than at waterfalls. The best account of the salmon fisheries is perhaps that of the Reverend Dugald Stewart Williamson of Tongland in the New Statistical Account of 1843. He describes the Doaches, the elaborate salmon weirs erected on the Dee connected by stone batteries, and indicates the various methods used to take fish. Stake nets erected at the mouth of the river were common. Hang nets, or bag nets drawn across the lower end of a pool were also used, but, in Tongland at least, by far the greatest number of fish were taken by shoulder-nets, "a net fixed to a semicircular bow of wood attached to a pole twenty feet in length". The skill and strength required to take fish by this method can be appreciated if it is considered that on one occasion thirty five salmon were taken with a single throw. Drag nets, worked by two men, were similar to shoulder nets. Other methods included draught nets, used in tidal pools, the gaff and the rod. Nothing if not thorough, Williamson also describes grappling, used by poachers. Until comparatively recent times salmon was the principal source of protein in Scotland.

The cottages and farmhouses, fields and hedgerows and even the roads in Scotland represent a reorganisation of the countryside which was inspired by the improvers of the eighteenth century. At this time large scale industry began to be established in the countryside. Some isolated industries – the furnaces of Wester Ross, for example – were set up earlier than this, but during the eighteenth century waterfalls were harnessed on a much larger scale than before. Arkwright used Dundaff Linn, the most tractable of the Falls of Clyde, to provide motive power for New Lanark in 1784. At Catrine on the Ayr, at Deanston on the Teith, and at Stanley on the Tay, large textile mills were established at similar sites. These four used plentiful supplies of water in considerable rivers to drive highly efficient systems. More erratic streams were also used, but in spite of the disadvantages of their country sites, Deanston and Stanley, for example, persisted much longer than, say, the textile mills in Blairgowrie.

At the same time as the Industrial Revolution was beginning to transform parts of the Scottish countryside, a number of distinguished literary and scientific visitors were drawing attention to the principal sights to be seen in the cities and towns and in the countryside.

Charles Dickens visited the Falls of Lochay in July 1841. He wrote enthusiastically to John Forster about them:

We left Lochearnhead last night and went to a place called Killin, eight miles from it, where we slept. I walked six miles with Fletcher after we got there, to see a waterfall: and it was a magnificent sight, foaming and crashing down three great steps of riven rock; leaping over the first as far as you could carry your eye, and rumbling and foaming down into a dizzy pool below you, with a deafening roar.

Dickens is, perhaps, the least likely waterfall enthusiast among Victorian literary men, but he was simply continuing a long tradition.

William Gilpin in 1776 noted the absence of trees beside the Bruar in his 'picturesque tour', but it was Robert Burns who immortalised Bruar in 1787. Burns was acquainted with Cauldron Linn on the Devon as well as with a number of linns in Ayrshire. Those pioneers, Johnson and Boswell, commented on a number of falls, notably those at Talisker. Thomas Gray (1716-71) noted the Devil's Cauldron at Glamis, while James MacPherson (1736-96) lent abiding interest to the falls of Glen Etive.

However, it was the Wordsworths and Coleridge, Walter Scott and John Wilson – 'Christopher North' – who brought Victorian tourists flocking to the waterfalls of Scotland. Scott used Whistler's Glen (Rhu), the Falls of Ledard, the Falls of Glenfinglas, the Falls of Bracklinn and Campsie Linn as settings in his works. Wordsworth will always be associated with the Falls of Inversnaid and the Falls of Glen Falloch. Coleridge put the Fall of Foyers on the map.

James Hogg followed Scott in his admiration for waterfalls. Two Gaelic poets – Duncan Ban MacIntyre and William Smith – are also associated with falls. Later poets who write about falls are Andrew Young (the Falls of Glomach) and Iaan Crichton Smith (Lower Falls of Nevis).

Waterfalls have always had a fascination for the writers of adventure stories. John Buchan and Alastair Maclean have used them and perhaps the most famous such description is that in 'Kidnapped' where Stevenson describes the crossing of a fall in Glencoe, a crossing which, on inspection, turns out to be topographically unnecessary, but which sticks in the memory.

The countryside itself changed in the eighteenth and nineteenth centuries. The depredations on the Caledonian Pine Forest in the Highlands were to some extent compensated by the works of improving landlords who planted different conifers and broadleaved trees. During the nineteenth century there were radical changes in the economy of the Highlands and the cheviot and the stag came to dominate a deserted land. In the Lowlands, water supply schemes like Robert Thom's schemes for Bute and Greenock became more elaborate. Improved roads and railways made the countryside more accessible, Joseph Mitchell, one of the great improvers of communications, records how, in addition to constructing roads and bridges, he made the first safe access to the Falls of Foyers. Spas like Moffat, Ballater and Strathpeffer numbered waterfalls among their attractions.

There was no more dedicated tourist than Queen Victoria whose journals convey her sense of wonder at the beauties of Scotland. Balmoral is typical of the country estates which the upper classes acquired, away from the growing industrial burghs in the Lowlands. The tradition of 'improvement' was continued and access to many falls was further enhanced. The more enlightened landlords encouraged visitors and, by the end of the nineteenth century, in Cowal and the Campsies for example, working people could visit romantic dells provided with paths and bridges and embellished with follies. It is probable that Scotland's countryside was more developed at this period than it has been until very recent times. A post-card of the waterfalls at the Waterworks in Dunoon indicates the kind of attraction which the diligent tourist might be expected to visit, an early twentieth century equivalent of the Cruachan Hydro Electric Power Scheme.

In relation to the widespread changes which have taken place since the First World War these developments were isolated and Scotland's mountains and glens were, in the modern mind, unspoiled. As far as waterfalls are concerned the most dramatic of these changes has been the development of hydro-electric power. Water-mills are comparatively local and, if some schemes did involve weirs and lades, their effect on rivers was restricted. The first hydro-electric schemes were on the same scale – with the exception of Foyers – and water wheels were replaced by turbines. The first scheme known in Britain was installed at Cragside in Northumberland in 1879/82 and the first commercial scheme dates from 1883 when two 52 horse power turbines were installed at Salmon Leap Falls, Portrush in Northern Ireland. Early Scottish schemes included one established in the Inchnacardoch Forest in 1890 for St. Benedicts Abbey, Fort Augustus, the Blarmachfoldach scheme at Fort William of 1896, and the Ravens, Ben Wyvis scheme in 1903. Many schemes for country houses were installed at about this time. However with Foyers in 1896, Kinlochleven in 1907-9 and Lochaber from 1924 to 1943, the British Aluminium Company instituted schemes which had an altogether more radical effect on the landscape. They transformed existing lochs into reservoirs, built dams which made two lochs into one and created entirely new lochs, diverted water from rivers through penstocks and built factories and power stations. The Foyers scheme brought forth one of the earliest public campaigns on grounds of amenity with Canon H. D. Rawnsley, a founder of the National Trust, and Ruskin playing a leading part.

Although the Highlands afforded the greatest potential for hydro-electrical power it was in the South of Scotland that the first two major public schemes were instituted. The Falls of Clyde were harnessed in 1927. In 1936 the Galloway Water Power Company completed the first scheme which involved a whole river basin and the diversion of water from an adjacent catchment. In the Highlands the Grampian Electric Supply Company built their Rannoch Power Station in 1930 and Tummel Bridge in 1933. The Ross-shire Electric Supply Company established their Loch Luichart Power Station in 1929.

This transformation has been extended and developed by the North of Scotland Hydro Electric Board. In some instances – Affric and Glen Nevis are two outstanding examples – schemes were successfully opposed on amenity grounds and modified or abandoned. The most significant victory of this kind led to the exclusion of the Falls of Glomach from the Affric scheme. In other instances schemes have been implemented and have brought about all-embracing changes. Falls have been obliterated, river beds have been deprived of water and a great deal of damage has been done, but in some places amenity has been improved and, although there has been change, what has been established – as at Pitlochry and at Cruachan – is interesting and attractive in itself.

Characteristic of the second half of the twentieth century have been the development and conservation of the countryside by public and quasi-public bodies: the Scottish Tourist Board, the Hydro Electric Board, the Forestry Commission, the Nature Conservancy Council and the National Trust for Scotland, together with local authorities and other organisations. All of these bodies have played their part in improving access to falls and, in some cases, opening up previously little-visited falls. The Forestry Commission have played a singularly important part; a notable example is the Forest Walk which leads to the Allt na Cailliche Falls in Glen Garry.

The development of nature trails and waymarked paths is deprecated by some, but it has brought a wider public to the countryside and, in places, restricted access where it might be harmful. These devices serve to remind us what a crowded island we live in and how easy it is for a thoughtless society to destroy its heritage. Some falls are as remote and inaccessible as ever they were and the wilderness in which they are situated is unspoiled, but others are situated in places where man's artifice may not be apparent, but where the natural landscape has been substantially modified by improvers and by visitors themselves.

Waterfalls are wild places where nature is dominant and man is an observer. Much of their interest derives from their natural history, and an interest in their natural history on the part of every visitor is most likely to conserve them.

Words and Waterfalls

The pronunciation of the names of many Scottish waterfalls is perplexing, the spelling is often uncertain, and the meanings are frequently obscure. But they are a delight: interesting and frequently redolent with atmosphere. No one can dispute that MacLean's Towel is a splendid name for a waterfall which forms a great white patch on a hillside above Loch Linnhe visible for miles.

In the Highlands the Gaelic word for waterfall is Eas *(Ess)*. The Scandinavian word is Fors *(Force)* which occurs occasionally. The Norsemen made an interesting distinction between a waterfall and a ravine or torrent, the word for which is Gill. There is no such distinction in Gaelic and Eas is applied to both waterfalls and helter-skelter mountain streams. In the Lowlands the commonest word for a waterfall is Linn, which is usually derived from a Celtic word for a pool. It is easy to see how the name for a pool became transferred to the fall itself. In Welsh the name can mean 'noisy'.

Variations include the Gaelic Sput, or Spout, which is

quite common, and Steall which also means spout. Loup has at least two meanings. It is applied to places where the water leaps and to places where fish leap. It is also sometimes used for places where the stream is narrow enough to jump across: such places are often found where there are waterfalls. Slug is another word for a narrow place, as in the Slug of Achrannie: slog, as in the Slog of Dess is a variant of this.

Sometimes the name of a river or stream will suggest that it will have waterfalls on it. Garvald, a very common name, is Garbh Allt, rough stream. It occurs in a variety of other forms: Garrawalt, Garabal, Garvel and Garrel. The Leanach, the angry burn, forms the Ess of Glenlatterach. Braan means roaring river and Bruar means boiling. Garnock means noisy, and Levern talkative. The Mad Cataract and the Clattering Burn speak for themselves.

An even more fascinating group of names describe the character of the river bed. Pot is a generic term for waterfall which refers to the potholes in the river bed, as does cauldron in the Deil's Cauldron. Pattak means full of potholes, and Quoich means drinking cup. The Falls of Measach, Easan na Miasaich, means the fall of the place of the platters, a reference to the potholes worn in the river bed. Eas nan Cuinneag, in Applecross, is the waterfall of the buckets.

Of descriptive names the best known is the Grey Mare's Tail. Few of the falls with this name resemble a mare's tail at all, but it has been very widely applied. One writer suggests that it is a corruption of the Gaelic, but this is unlikely. Eas Coul Aulin is called the Maiden's Tresses. Other names are more commonplace, but are equally revealing. Of colour names the most frequent is Black, or Dubh, because waterfalls are often gloomy places or because the deep plunge pools at the foot of waterfalls on peaty rivers are notably inky. Black appears in Black Spout, but also in the Falls of Divie. White occurs in White Falls in Glen Roy, in the Falls of Fender and in the numerous cases of Sput Ban and Eas Ban. It is held by some authorities that Glomach may be

An Steall Ban, at the head of the Nevis Gorge, which results from various effects of glaciation. GEOLOGICAL MUSEUM

derived from the Norwegian for White, and no one who has seen that most spectacular of falls in spate would dispute the appropriateness of the name. Green, that most appealing of colours in water occurs in Glas Allt and in the various examples of Easain Uaine.

Sometimes common terms, for example Dubh, black, and Ban, white, and Mor, great, and Beag, small, are used to distinguish between pairs rather than to describe falls. Eas Mor is also used to describe the first real obstacle for salmon. Among the most widespread of simple descriptive names are the names of animals and plants. These may refer to the flora or fauna of the district, or they may ascribe the character of an animal, for example, to the watercourse, or they may have folklore connections. Astonishingly there is only one Birch Linn. Among the names of plants and animals found are Derry (oak), Tromie (elder), Leven (elm), Cuileann (holly), Chaorainn (rowan) and Each (horse), Fiadh (deer), Damh (stag) and Fitheach (raven). The two most famous animal falls are Dog Fall and Badger Fall in Glen Affric. Muckle Alicompen, the fall in Campsie Glen, is almost certainly named after the medicinal herb, Elicampane.

A further group of descriptive names include Roaring Mill in Glen Nevis, Roaring Linn in the Borders and Rumbling Bridge Falls. The Devil and Witches also occur widely. Fairy Linn near Paisley, Witches' Linn at Talla, Alltnacallich in Sutherland and Eas Pheallaidh in Glen Lyon are all connected with folktales.

Which Waterfalls?

If waterfalls are focal points of river scenery it might be thought to be a relatively simple matter to identify the principal falls.

There is an almost infinite number of waterfalls and it is quite impractical to attempt to describe them all. The problem is partly one of definition, but, if it is accepted that it is the setting of a waterfall which makes it an attractive place, then no entirely satisfactory definition can ever be reached.

It might be argued that the same is true of mountains, and that, by adopting a single criterion, this problem was solved by Sir Hugh Munro. He listed all the separate mountains and tops over three thousand feet. Complexities arise in the case of waterfalls which do not arise in the case of hills. Both mountain falls and river falls must be included. It would be tedious to try to identify every burn which tumbles three hundred metres down a mountainside in wet weather, and it would be pointless to try to determine whether it was, in fact a true waterfall. Equally a tiny stream falling a short distance can form an attractive fall provided the setting is right, whereas another burn which apparently fulfils the same criteria may be considered commonplace.

What constitutes a waterfall? It has been pointed out that the Falls of Leny are rapids rather than waterfalls and there is much truth in this. However, the Leny at this point closely resembles the most famous of the Falls of Clyde, Cora Linn. Purists may insist that only 'unsupported falls' count, but this would eliminate many well-known falls. What may appear to be an unbroken cataract in spate can become a cascade in dry weather. The problem is perfectly illustrated by what might be supposed to be a question long since resolved. What is the highest waterfall in Scotland?

It is generally agreed that the highest unsupported fall is Glomach, 113 metres in height. Eas Coul Aulin is a cascade of 201 metres. Some authorities assert that it has an unsupported fall of 156 metres, others that it falls sheer for as little as 46 metres. The first authoritative account of Eas Coul Aulin was given in the Scottish Mountaineering Club's Guide Book 'The Northern Highlands' (1953):

On the south side of the valley, just three quarters of a mile (1.2 km) south west of the Stack of Glencoul, the well-named Eas a'Chual Aulinn (Splendid Waterfall of Coul) falls over the open cliff face from a height of 825 feet (252 metres) above sea level. Its stream, which is about the size of the Glomach Burn of Kintail falls some 500 feet (152 metres) – measured twice by aneroid – in three or four closely linked vertical leaps and then steeply cascades another one hundred and fifty (46 metres).

Campbell Steven debates this in his interesting account in Enjoying Scotland (1971).

The initial drop, although in wildly turbulent flood, was relatively short, measuring perhaps fifteen or twenty feet (4.5 – 6.0 metres). There followed three truly splendid leaps more or less equal in height and interrupted by two explosive white cauldrons. At the foot, where the angle lessened to a roof top tilt, the fall split into a delta of minor cataracts and rivulets. The crux was, of course, the central section and I tried to be as fair in my measurement as I could. In the end, I decided that each of these plunges must measure approximately 150 feet (46 metres), an estimate which agreed with the contour lines of the map and also with the known aneroid figure for the whole fall. This meant that in ordinary conditions the Eas Coul Aulin could not be acclaimed the waterfall with the highest single drop; only after quite exceptionally heavy rain was it conceivable that the two intruding cauldron ledges might be eliminated thus allowing the water a free fall of 400 feet (122 metres) or more.

Apart from measurements of this kind there is very little information about the height of waterfalls. Guide books give estimates of the heights of the better known falls but the Ordnance Survey does not record the heights in the same authoritative way that it gives the heights of hills. It may be possible in some instances to get a fairly accurate picture by means of counting contours, but this is not the same.

Height, by itself, must be rejected as a sole criterion for judging a fall. Most will be content to leave the final word on this matter with MacCulloch:

It cannot be disputed that Foyers is the first in order of all our cascades: but it is vain to attempt to compare it in respect of beauty with that of Tummel or those of Clyde, as it would be to compare a landscape of Cuyp with one of Rubens, or the bay of Naples with Glenco. Such pictures are not comparable; and to draw comparisons, is to compare names not things; it is only in the word cascade that there is a resemblance.

Consideration must be given to whether or not a fall has a name. Falls of more than usual interest are generally named. In the Ordnance Survey map there are notable omissions. Until recently Eas a'Chual Aulinn was unnamed. This defect has been remedied on the new 1:50,000 map. It is, however, symptomatic that this fall should have been omitted from the Seventh Series of the One Inch Map. The Six Inch and 1:10,000 maps are better, but, generally speaking, they do not add greatly to the information given on the up-to-date 1:25,000 maps where they are available. An obscure, but long-standing example illustrates the problem. In his book The Cairngorm Hills of Scotland, Seton Gordon (1925) whose knowledge of these hills was unrivalled describes a corrie waterfall which, as he points out, is of considerable interest.

> I have so far written little of the burn of clear icy water that drains Loch Coire an Lochain. It flows a short distance, then disappears below ground – to emerge a few hundred yards beyond as a foaming milky torrent thet can be clearly seen from the valley of the Spey. Allt Coire an Lochain – to give it its Gaelic name – in reality has its head-springs on the Brae Riach plateau only a few hundred yards north of one of the sources of the Dee. Its waters flow north and quickly increasing in volume reach the edge of the precipice and in a series of cascades fall into Loch Coire an Lochain below. It is curious that this waterfall – Easan Coire an Lochain – should be neither named nor drawn on any map. It is frequently visible from Aviemore – 10 miles away and I have never seen it dry. Thus its absence from even the 'six-inch' dry map is inexplicable. Only during a time of winter frost is Easan Coire an Lochain stilled.

It is only recently that the Survey has acknowledged the Falls of Dee which, of course, constitute a doubtful case in themselves.

Some indication of the coverage given by the Ordnance Survey can be gathered by examining particular maps, although the coverage itself is variable. The work of the Survey in revising and updating information is always going on. The Quarter-Inch Map which shows most falls is that of the Firth of Clyde: it names Falls of Lora, the Falls of Cruachan, the Falls of Lochay, Spout Rolla, the Deil's Cauldron, the Falls of Acharn, the Falls of Moness and the Falls of Falloch. At this scale, this is a very reasonable number of falls to show. What is surprising is the choice of falls. Both Spout Rolla and the Deil's Cauldron are relatively obscure in comparison with a number of falls which are omitted. If the Falls of Falloch are included, surely the Falls of Leny should be named. It may be argued that it is not possible satisfactorily to include both the Pass of Leny and the Falls of Leny. At this scale it may also be difficult to show the Falls of Clyde which are also omitted. However, Bracklinn Falls, the Falls of Ledard, the Falls of Braan and the Falls of Inversnaid are all quite as well known as the Falls of Lochay and all occur within the confines of this sheet. It could be argued, with rather less justification, that Eas Fors on Mull, the Spout of Ballagan, the Loup of Fintry and the Falls of Devon should find a place. Some of these defects are made up on the one inch and 1:50,000 maps.

However, these maps have their defects. The Loup of Fintry and Cauldron Linn are both omitted even at this scale. It is not practical to give the names of all falls and it will be readily accepted that showing the word 'Waterfall' above the farm of Ledard is a sufficient indication of the Falls of Ledard. Neither of the two aforementioned falls even have the word Waterfall to show where they are. Both are considerable falls on important streams. There are further complications in the case of unnamed falls. In Glen Falloch the Garabal Fall is indicated by the word Waterfall on the 1:50,000 map, but the falls on the Allt Arnan and the Ben Glas Burn are not. The Ben Glas Falls are outstanding and easily the most significant of the three on a number of grounds. All this suggests that those maps need to be treated with caution in efforts to identify falls.

Obviously the six-inch and 1:10,000 maps must be consulted to resolve questions of detail. The 1:25,000 maps are useful in that they cover a good deal more ground, but they are unlikely to be sufficiently informative in case of difficulty. Some indication of the coverage can be gained by considering particular maps. Neither the one-inch nor the 1:50,000 map shows any falls in the Kilpatrick Hills. The 1:25,000 map shows two falls, The Spout of the Three Marches and The Spout of the White Horse. Both of these delightfully named falls are worth visiting for their wild moorland setting, but neither of them is significant and there are a number of other falls of considerably more importance in these hills. Of these the most significant is Ishneich, a thirty metre fall on Gallangad Burn. There is no reference to this fall on the 1:25,000 map. The falls named on the six-inch map include Spardie Linn, Black Linn, Bow Linn, The Grey Mare's Tail, Lady's Linn, Annies Linn, Auchineden Spout, Dualt Spout, Ladies' Linn and Ishneich as well as the other two. The location of some two dozen other falls which are unnamed is also given. The six-inch map is thus an admirable source, in this instance, although very few people would consider it worth while to seek out Annie's Linn, while the Pot of Gartness, which is a widely visited salmon leap on the Endrick is indicated simply as fall and not named.

The survey may show waterfalls, but clearly does not attach great significance to them. I am nevertheless greatly indebted to Survey maps which, remain, in this field as in others, a first point of reference.

If the Ordnance Survey map can be inconvenient, other sources are infuriating. The New Statistical Account is good in parts. The sections on the Hydrology of the Parishes are sometimes conscientiously written. At other times it is clear that the incumbent had little or no interest in the subject and either skimped it or omitted it. Many falls, of course, occur on the edge of parishes and may be omitted by two ministers on the grounds that each believed that the other would refer to it. Most topographical accounts written after the New Statistical Account rely heavily on it. The Ordnance Gazetteer is an admirable source of general information but it is, generally speaking, inferior to the New Statistical in respect of specific falls. Of the Nineteenth century guides The Scottish Tourist, Anderson (1850), Black (1860) and Baddeley have proved helpful sources, particularly with reference to the better known falls of the Victorian Age. In the case of modern guides The Blue Guides and Ward, Lock and Co's Red Guides are the most comprehensive. Valuable information about falls on salmon rivers is contained in W. L. Calderwood's (1921) book on the subject.

It is from these sources that the Regional Lists of falls have been compiled. All the falls named on the One-Inch and 1:50,000 Ordnance Survey maps have been included. To these have been added falls which are named in the New Statistical Account and, in a few instances, falls named by other sources. Falls unnamed in these places have been included on a subjective basis.

Three further criteria have been significant in this matter. First is the intrinsic interest or impressiveness of the fall itself. The fall in Stank Glen and Easan Coire an Lochain on Braeriach are examples of this type of fall. Secondly there are the associations of a fall. Falls which occur close to monuments or castles, falls associated with particular folk tales, or falls, like those in Eathie Burn where Hugh Miller made his first discoveries, which are connected with famous men are examples of this kind of fall. Thirdly, the question of accessibility is taken into account. Where there are unnamed falls beside a road they are considered for inclusion, whereas remote mountain falls are not given the same consideration. Falls which are beside mountain paths and falls which have been incorporated in Nature Trails are included.

I decided not to exclude falls which had been adversely affected in one way and another. The archeology of waterfalls is an interesting subject in itself. Apart from mills, water supply schemes and hydro electric power schemes falls have been altered in other ways. Some falls in the policies of country houses are artificial. Artificial falls were created by the builders of the Caledonian Canal on the Shangan and Dochfour Burns to prevent these torrential streams from dumping boulders in the canal. Other falls have been consideably altered by fishing interests. Calderwood describes falls in Glen Tilt which were completely removed by blasting.

The regional lists in this book distinguish some seven-hundred and fifty falls. It will be clear from the analysis of the Six-Inch map that there may be a thousand more falls which could be distinguished easily enough. The lists provide a starting point for the visitor.

River Systems

Books treating the river systems of Scotland generally start with the Tweed and conclude with the Border Esk. This system is adopted here; it has the merit of bringing the visitor to Edinburgh near the beginning of the book and taking him to Carlisle at the end of it. The waterfalls of the Borders and Lothian Regions are treated first, then those of Fife and Tayside, followed by the waterfalls of the Grampian Region. Waterfalls are unevenly distributed and they are most logically dealt with within river systems. For this reason sub-divisions have been used. Where a Region or a District makes a coherent sub-division it is used; elsewhere different arrangements are adopted. For example, within the Highland Region the waterfalls of Loch Ness, all of

which are south of Inverness are treated with those of the Findhorn and the Spey; the waterfalls of the Beauly, north of Inverness, are treated as part of the Northern Highlands. Two Highland Districts, Skye and Lochalsh and Lochaber, are combined with a part of Strathclyde to form The West Highlands. The basins of the Forth and the Clyde occupy much of the Central Region and the heart of Strathclyde and, because, for example, they include the waterfalls of Loch Lomond and the Trossachs, they are treated together. Ayrshire and Arran, Galloway and Dumfriesshire form South West Scotland. The divisions used are as follows:

Borders and the Firth of Forth
Sub-divisions: Tweed; Lothians and Fife; Devon

Tay and Earn Basins
Sub-divisions: Earn; Tay (Falls in both basins treated together)

North East Scotland
Sub-divisions: Esk; Dee, Don and Deveron; Buchan; Spey and Findhorn; Ness

Northern Highlands
Sub-divisions: Beauly; Ross and Cromarty; Sutherland and Caithness

West Highlands
Sub-divisions: Skye and Lochalsh; Lochaber; Argyll and Mull

Forth and Clyde Basins
Sub-divisions: Forth; Carron; Firth of Clyde; Loch Lomond; Clyde (Falls treated together)

South West Scotland
Sub-divisions: Ayr and Arran; Solway

A further note on River Systems is given at the beginning of the tables.

Name of Fall
The most commonly used name is given and, except where another form is very well established, Gaelic names, spelt in accordance with the Ordnance Survey Map are used where they exist. If a number of falls occur in a glen the name of the glen is used (e.g. Campsie Glen). If the fall has not got a name, the name of the stream is given. In establishing alphabetical order words like 'waterfall' (eas, steall, sput, linn), 'river' (water, abhainn, burn, allt), 'coire', and 'glen' are ignored unless they form an integral part of the name.

Examples: Den of Fenella: 'F'; Falls of Clyde: 'C'; Eas Mor: 'M'; Steall Coire Lair: 'L'; Buck Loup: 'B'; Alltnacailleach: 'A'; Allt na Cailliche: 'C'; etc.

Grid Reference
The full grid reference, including the two grid letters, is used. Map references are explained on all Ordnance Survey Maps. They provide an index to 1:10,000 and 1:25,000 maps, and to the Ordnance Survey Motoring Atlas. Grid Letters appear on the latest editions of 1:50,000 Ordnance Survey maps.

Examples: Falls of Rogie NH 445 584 1:25,000 map: NH 45 (First figure and fourth figure); Ordnance Survey Motoring Gazetteer reference: NH4458 (First, second, fourth and fifth figures).

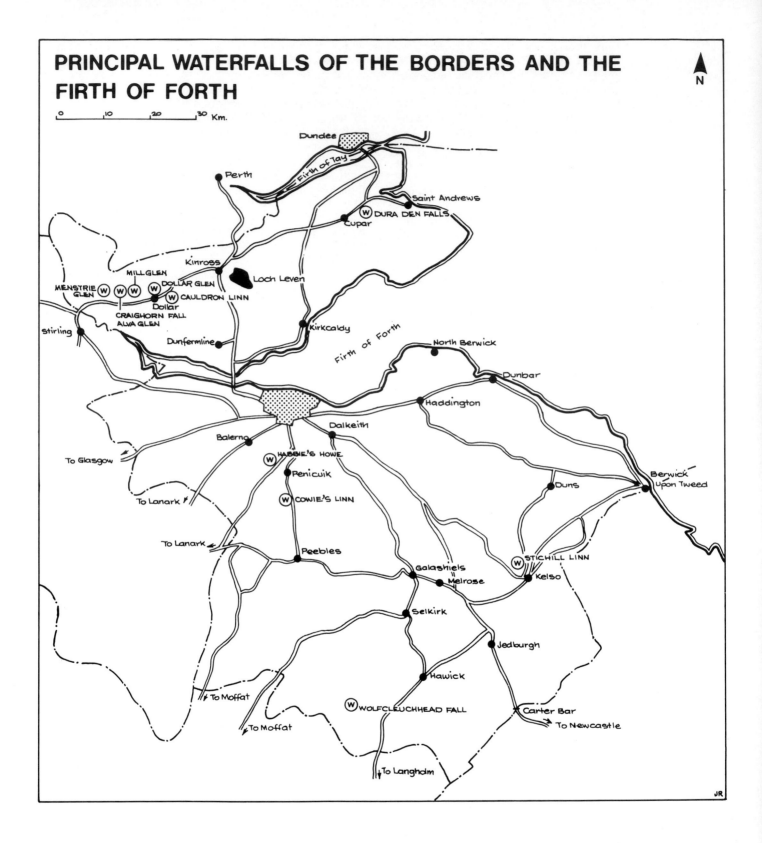

THE BORDERS AND THE FIRTH OF FORTH

Burn of Care, Dollar, below Castle Campbell. PETER DAVENPORT

Principal Falls

Significant Falls	Touring centre
Alva Glen	Alva
Cauldron Linn	Dollar

Interesting Falls	
Cowie's Linn	Eddleston
Dura Den Falls	Ceres
Dollar Glen	Dollar
Habbie's Howe Falls	Penicuik
Stichill Linn	Kelso
Mill Glen, Tillicoultry	Tillicoultry
Wolfcleuchhead Fall	Newick

Also recommended	
Talla Linns	Tweedsmuir

Mill Glen, Tillicoultry. PETER DAVENPORT

Waterfalls of the Borders and the Firth of Forth

The Tweed drains the second largest basin in Scotland, surpassed only by the Tay. Many people hold the Tweed dear for the many exquisite pastoral scenes which it presents throughout its course. Tweed's Well, the source of the main stream, is only 450 metres above sea level: it is not surprising that there are few great falls in its basin. In the rolling moorlands where some of the tributaries of the Tweed rise there are brawling burns which may be classed as waterfalls, but there are only a few places where unsupported falls occur.

Some stretches of broken water make the Tweed and its tributaries attractive salmon rivers—for instance the Ettrick, the Yarrow and the Whitadder, the Jed and the Teviot. J B Selkirk's poem, 'A Border Burn' states the qualities of the many enchanting little burns in the Tweed Basin:

> Ah Tam. Gie me a Border burn
> That canna rin withoot a turn
> And wi' its bonnie babble fills
> The glens amang oor native hills
>
> I see't this moment 's plain as day
> As it comes bickering ower the brae
> Atween the clumps o' purple heather
>
> And cuts such a cantrips in the air
> The picter-paintin' man's despair.

In Berwickshire the only streams on which there are noteworthy falls are the little deans which furrow the rugged coastline.

The Lothians are drained by the Avon, the Almond, the Esk and the Tyne, together with a number of smaller streams, which drain the Pentlands, the Moorfoots and the Lammermuis. There are some cascades in the hills, and the valleys above the windy seaboard are crowded with woods which are highly attractive in parts. Roslin and Habbies Howe are widely-known beauty spots, but it is their associations rather than their waterfalls which attract.

The Devon, in the upper part of its course, used to flow towards Loch Leven: in other words it was a river of Fife. However, it was captured by a tributary of the Forth which flowed in the opposite direction. This geomorphological phenomenon accounts for the famous Devon Gorge. The Vale of Devon is overlooked by the Ochils and in these hills there are numerous little waterfalls caused by dykes, bands of relatively hard volcanic rock.

The peninsula of Fife is drained by only one considerable river, the Eden. Elsewhere there are tiny streams draining picturesque valleys called Dens where there are one or two falls which attract notice. Dura Den is a fascinating place with interesting falls and much to look at besides.

The Borders and the Lothians

Carlow's Linn   NS 097 243

A low fall on the Tweed itself above the old bridge beside Tweedsmuir Church. The pool below the fall, where the infant river slides over broken rocks, is the reputed haunt of a giant trout of legendary size.

Corby Linn   NT 448 295

Cascade on the Long Philip Burn above the battlefield of Philip-Haugh outside Selkirk. The fall can be reached by a pleasant walk down country lanes in the richly wooded countryside outside the town.

Cowie's Linn   NT 234 513

A picturesque fall on the Eddleston Burn in hill country north of Peebles. The quarry through which one passes to see the fall is of considerable geological interest.

> In Eddleston Parish there appears on record a burn called Alden Hisslaner. This I conjectured to represent Allt an Eas Labhair, burn of the loud waterfall, and on inquiry I found that the burn can be readily identified—it formed part of a march—and that it had a noted waterfall, now called 'Cowie's Linn'.   (Watson 1927)

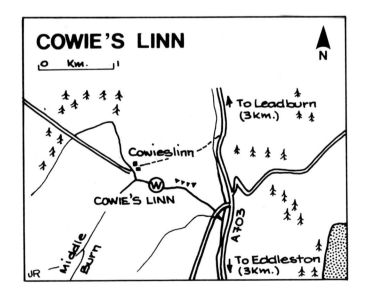

Craigiehall Grotto Waterfall   NT 169 752

The River Almond has a course of some 40 kilometres and drains a basin of some 370 square kilometres. Between Midcalder and Kirkliston it is crossed by a splendid aqueduct on the Union Canal and a viaduct on the Edinburgh and

Glasgow railway. The lower part of its course is through a resplendent wooded ravine. Above Cramond Bridge it skirts the fine estate of Craigiehall, an army headquarters. One of the most charming walks on the outskirts of the capital city is from Cramond Brig along the tree-lined banks of the Almond to the old stone bridge at Craigiehall above and below which the river falls in a series of rapids. Beyond the bridge a stone grotto is set into the river bank beside the most pronounced fall. There are old stepping stones about 500 metres above the Grotto.

Cramond Waterfall   NT 186 765

Old Cramond Brig on the River Almond was built in 1619. At this place James V was rescued from a band of ruffians by Jock Harvieston. Below the bridge a recently established Urban Trail leads to the picturesque village of Cramond. Before it reaches the sea the Almond crosses a fine low fall which has the largest discharge of any in Fife and the Lothians.

Crooked Jock   NT 139 528

Low fall on the tributary burn which joins the Lyne Water above the charming Pentlands village of West Linton.

Dow Linn   NT 229 236

Fall on the Henderland Burn, a tributary of the Meggat Water which joins the Yarrow at St Mary's Loch. Close by is a large flat rock, the Lady's Seat; here, according to legend, the wife of William Cockburn sat so that the fall would drown the noise of James V's troops as they put her husband to death in her husband's own castle, the ruins of which are at the foot of the hill. The tale is the subject of a famous ballad, but Cockburn was, in fact, hanged in Edinburgh. The fall is in a corner, hidden from the road, not far from the old motte covered in pine and oak. It tumbles in two leaps about four metres.

Gameshope Linn   NT 131 141

This burn drains an extensive basin on the north-west side of the White Coomb, the mountain above the Grey Mare's Tail. Above the Talla Reservoir it forms a series of waterfalls. The burn affords an attractive walk in itself.

> The wild, almost savage beauty of the stream and its immediate surroundings, the white water pouring into deep pools, the grey rocks overhung by rowan and birch, the springing heather underfoot, the great gaunt hills closing in on the glen and the feeling of perfect solitude which falls not unpleasantly on the senses, have an appeal of their own.

Near the foot of the burn a tributary forms an attractive cascade, *Witches Linn. (NT 132 202)*

Habbie's Howe   NT 175 565

Designated as a Site of Special Scientific Interest for the abundance of calcicole plants found there, towards the head of the Logan Burn in the Lee of the Pentland Hills. The burn forms a waterfall about six metres in height.

The spot can easily be reached by footpaths from the A702 and from Balerno, but perhaps the finest approach is from Glencorse, as described by Robert Louis Stevenson. 'The dearest burn to me in the world is that which drums and pours, in cunning wimples, in that glen of yours behind Glen Corse Old Kirk.' Glencorse Reservoir has many of the attributes of a natural lake, flaked by rounded green moors. Beyond it is Loganlea Reservoir and at its head the Howe where the burn runs through a gorge of glacial origin.

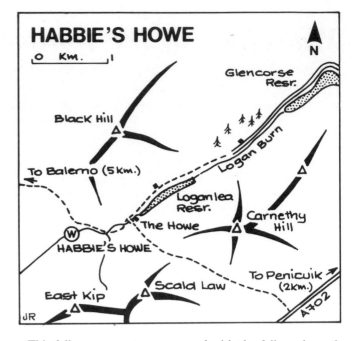

This fall may seem to correspond with the fall so elegantly described in Allan Ramsay's narrative poem 'Gentle Shepherd', published in 1725:

> Between twa' birks, out o'er a little linn
> The water fa's and makes a singan din,
> A pool, breast-deep, beneath as clear as glass
> Kises, with easy whirls, the bordering grass.

However, most writers agree that the Logan Burn site is not the true Habbie's Howe, which can be found at Newhall in the valley of the North Esk near Carlops at the foot of the same Pentland Hills. This site agrees in many more particulars with the pastoral scenes described in the poem. The Ordnance Gazetteer describes the place as follows:

> Still higher up, agreeable to the description in the dialogue of the second scene, the Hollow beyond Mary's Bower, where the Esk divides it in the middle and form a linn or leap is named the Howe Burn; and the hollow below the cascade with its bathing pool and little green, its birches wild shrubs and variety of natural flowers in summer, its rocks and the whole of its romantic and rural scenery coincides exactly with the description of Habbie's Howe.

It matter little which of these two attractive places is the real scene of the poem. Both are worth a visit.

Hownam Salmon Leap   NT 774 188

This fall on the Kale is attractively situated above the village of Hownam.

Kirkhope Linns   NT 383 239

At Ettrickbridge End the Ettrick Water forms a series of rapids in a gorge call Kirkhope Linns considered to be the most attractive natural feature of a wild parish.

In the gorge the most notable fall is *The Loup. (NT 385 241)*

Linn Dean Cascade   NT 465 598

This waterfall on a headstream of the Tyne is under the main road at Soutra Hill on the Woodcot Estate.

Jaw Linn
NT 063 631

The Linhouse water is a headstream of the Almond. Linhouse itself dates partly from 1589 and is set in attractive grounds outside the New Town of Livingston, from which Jaw Linn is relatively easily accessible. At the foot of Linhouse garden is an artificial lake and where the stream tumbles over a weir at the foot of the lake it is joined by a tributary which falls in a cascade. The weir and the fall are both about eight metres high and make a picturesque combination.

Linton Linn
NT 592 771

In East Linton the Tyne tumbles into a narrow gut, *Linn Jaw*, which gives the fall its name. It provides the head for the famous Preston Mill (National Trust for Scotland).

Linmill Fall
NS 912 722

Fall on the Lin Mill burn, A tributary of the Avon, at Avonbridge.

Linmill Fall
NT 113 787

This fall on the borders of Abercorn and Dalmeny Parishes quite close to Hopetoun House is 17.5 metres high. It was caused by the same volcanic sill as the one on which the mansion is situated.

Falls of Monks Burn
NT 181 573

Low falls in the rolling foothills of the Pentlands above the site of the 'genuine' Habbie's Howe. They are the subject of a well known print.

Pease Dean
NT 789 708

A deep wooded ravine near Cockburnspath in Berwickshire which was, for long, an obstacle to communications on the East Coast. There are tiny waterfalls on the little brook which drains into Pease Bay as there are on the burns which tumble down the other deans in the locality. Pease Dean was bridged in 1786. Burns visited the Dean on his tour of the Borders.

Pease Dean is under Cockburnspath Tower, a Border fortalice belonging to the Homes. There is a coastal waterfall on a raised beach on Cockburnspath Burn.

Tower Dean (*NT 789 698*) has two prominent falls.

Logan Burn

Falls of (see Habbie's Howe)

Rhymer's Glen
NT 527 328

The Huntly Burn on the Abbotsford Estate drains this famous glen where, it is said, Thomas the Rhymer met the Queen of the Fairies and made her his mistress. Higher up, on the same burn, is Cauldshiels Loch. The whole area is rich in associations with Sir Walter Scott.

Roaring Linn
NT 678 134

In the environs of Jedburgh the A68 Trunk Road crosses and recrosses the fine river Jed. Roaring Linn is the appropriate name of the most prominent rapid on the winding river. Native elm, ash, birch, oak, rowan and alder clothe the steep banks of the salmon stream and remind one of the much more extensive Jed Forest in which the monks of Jedburgh Abbey once pastured their pigs and sheep and cattle.

Robert's Linn
NT 538 206

This fall of about ten metres is situated beside the remote moorland road, the B6399, from Riccarton to Hawick near the summit of the now disused Waverley railway line. The Maiden Paps, splendidly named hills, dominate the scene. Robert's Linn appears to be the termination of the tribal boundary wall, the Catrail.

Roslin
NT 274 625

Roslin Glen is noted for its literary and historical associations. Roslin Castle and Roslin Chapel attract many thousands of visitors, and the walk along the left bank of the North Esk from Loanhead affords fine views of Hawthornden. The river flows through a wooded gorge with low falls and rapids under sandstone cliffs. The area gets its name from the fall, the Roslin.

Stichill Linn
NT 706 375

There are few falls in the Borders: the market town of Kelso is fortunate in having Stichill Linn, a very beautiful fall on the Eden, about twelve metres in height and reached from the B6364.

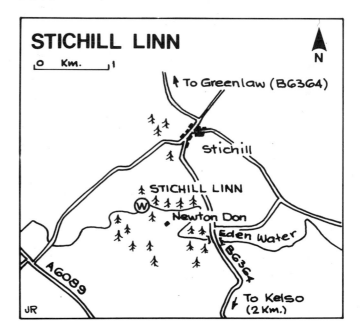

Stichill is close to Ednam, birthplace of the nature poet James Thomson (1700–48). Thomson's 'Seasons' contributed to the increasing interest in the landscape which characterised the eighteenth century. Thomson's first encounter with a waterfall may have been at Stichill Linn. In the poem there is a fine description of a waterfall:

> Smooth to the shelving bank a copious flood
> Rolls fair, and placid, where collected all,
> In one impetuous torrent, down the steep
> It thundering shoots, and shakes the country round.
> At first, an azure sheet, it rushes broad;
> Then whitening by degrees, as prone it falls,
> And from the loud-resounding rocks below
> Dash'd in a cloud of foam, it sends aloft
> A hoary mist, and forms a ceaseless shower.
> Nor can the tortured wave here find repose;
> But, raging still amid the shaggy rocks,

Talla Linns, at the head of the Megget Pass, in an area where there are few unsupported falls. Associated with Sir Walter Scott. BRYDON COLLECTION

Now flashes o'er the scatter'd fragment, now
Aslant the hollowed channel rapid darts;
And falling fast from gradual slope to slope,
With wild infracted course, and lessened roar,
It gains a safer bed; and steals, and last,
Along the mazes of the quiet vale.

Talla Linns   NT 137 202

Talla Water forms a series of striking cascades above the Talla Reservoir at Tallalinnfoot, the scene of the Conventicle in 1682 described by Scott in *Heart of Midlothian*. In *From the Border Hills* M Clavering writes:

Talla comes 'loupin' owre the linns' not quite perpendicular but steeply enough to drop in a succession of lower falls which foam from one pool to the next below in ever gathering volume and force. A tiny path, used mostly by the sure-footed black-faced sheep and their shepherd, follows the left side of the Linn so closely that it is possible to look from it down into the deep chasm which the water has worn in the rock and see the silver white fall pouring over the dark stone. Dizzying and deafening though it is to lie there on the very brink it is well worth it to anyone who admires the sight of a hill burn's unbridled strength in spate.

Wolfcleuchhead Waterfall   NT 330 088

Near Hawick, in the Forestry Commission's Craik Forest, reached by a forest trail from the forest village. The trail leads from a car park beside the Althouse Burn which is a modest stream almost hidden in the woods. There is a great variety of bird life and at least one pair of herons nest there. The fall is on a tributary where the valley narrows and it is hidden in the trees until the last moment. An eight-metre fall of the apron type, impressive in winter.

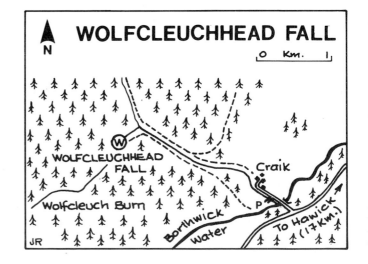

The Devon Basin

Alva Glen

NS 835 977

Alva Glen is the finest of the four main Ochil Glens, the others being Menstrie, Tillicoultry, and Dollar. At Alva there is a vertical displacement of 3000 metres in the rocks along the Ochils Fault where coal measures are brought into contact with volcanic rocks of Old Red Sandstone Age. The latter rocks give the Ochils Escarpment its distinctive appearance and give rise to the numerous waterfalls found in each of the glens.

A fine public park at the foot of the glen leads to a steep section beside the burn where there are a number of weirs. The first major fall occurs where the path comes to the foot of a steep slope surmounted by a zig-zag path. It is necessary to advance a little way and then retrace your steps in order to see the fall properly. It rejoices in the somewhat unprepossessing name of the *Big Fall*.

The next fall occurs beyond the zig-zags. It is a charming hidden fall and it is necessary to descend sharply from the main path to see it, or rather to listen to it. This is *The Smuggler's Cave*.

The Glenwinnel Burn is the principal tributary to the Devon and it joins Alva Glen by the *Craighorn Fall* (NS 885 988), 22 metre high. The whole of this finely proportioned fall is seen from a pleasant belvedere just below the glen track. The water cascades through a narrow gap beyond which a mountain path leads us to Ben Cleugh, the highest of these hills. There are falls further up Alva Burn and Glenwinnel Burn which can be explored. It is possible to return to Alva by an attractive path overlooking the Devon Valley which crosses the Carnaughten Glen. The falls on this burn are well seen from the A91.

From the Glenwinnel Burn beyond the Craighorn Fall a well-marked miners' track leads down Silver Glen with its famous old mines which were once assayed by Sir Isaac Newton when he was Master of the Mint. The mines were discovered in 1712 by Sir John Erskine and worked with considerable success for many years.

There are four noteworthy falls in *Silver Burn*. Other falls in the neighbourhood of Alva include those in Balquharn Glen, the most difficult and awkward of access in the Ochil Glens.

Cauldron Linn

NT 005 988

Cauldron Linn is the last fall on the Devon before it reaches the more sequestered part of its course. It is now disfigured by giant cast-iron pipes. It used to be on everyone's itinerary, but nowadays few visitors venture to see it. In contrast to the falls on the Devon at Rumbling Bridge, where the river makes a number of short leaps in a spectacular gorge, Cauldron Linn presents the awe-inspiring sight of a substantial stream hurling itself in a double fall over a considerable drop. The fall is of the same type as Reekie Linn, and, if it had not been the victim of early industrial development, it would have the same reputation. The fall was also substantially altered by a rock-fall in 1881.

Pennant, visiting the fall in 1769, described it:

Here the river, after a short fall, drops on rocks hollowed in a strange manner into large and deep cylindrical cavities, open on one side, or formed into great circular cavities like cauldrons . . . one in particular has the appearance of a vast brewing vessel; and the water, by its great agitation, has acquired a yellow scum exactly resembling the yeasty working of malt liquor.

In a letter written in 1787, Robert Burns described a visit:

After breakfast we made a party to go and see Cauldron Linn, a remarkable cascade in the Devon about fives miles from Harviestoun; and after spending one of the most pleasant days I ever had in my life, I returned to Stirling in the evening.

The falls are not marked on maps, and they are awkward to reach because paths are overgrown. The best approach is from Muckhart Mill, but they can also be tackled from the footpaths along the spectacular Devon Valley Railway.

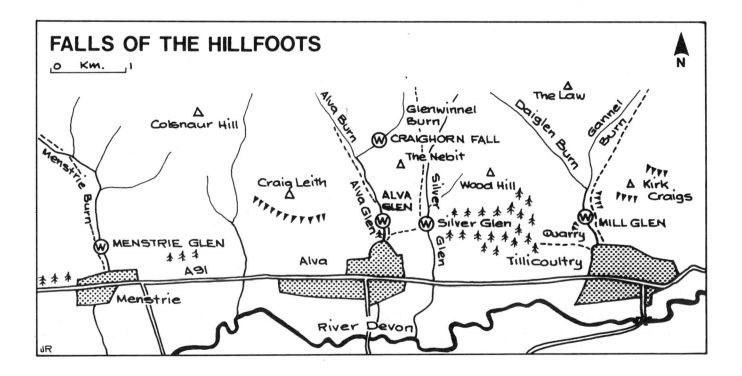

Craighorn Fall see Alva Glen
Craiginnan Fall see Dollar Glen

Deil's Mill
N7 016 997

Where it leaves the hills, the Devon, which used to flow towards Loch Leven, changes course abruptly at the Crook of Devon. It has been captured by an old river which used to follow the course of the lower Devon. Where this river cut back its course in order to effect the capture the present river flows through an impressive gorge which, at its narrowest part, is crossed by the Rumbling Bridge. The river has carved deep potholes in its bed and the rattling of the stones which carved the potholes has given the bridge its name. The whole area is a classic example of river erosion and for this reason is something of a mecca for geologists.

Only when visitors make their way through the grounds of the Rumbling Bridge Hotel, a privilege reserved for patrons, do they appreciate that the present bridge is built on top of an earlier bridge dating from 1773. Rumbling Bridge used to be on every Victorian itinerary, but it is a good example of the way in which grand scenery can be neglected. The elaborate paths, bridges and other structures erected to enable the Victorians to appreciate the curiosities of the gorge are now derelict and in a dangerous state. It is no longer possible to make the exciting railway journey through the gorge. The place was popularised by the Hon. Mrs Sarah Murray, an indefatigable waterfall enthusiast.

There is a series of low falls the chief of which is the Deil's Mill, so called because it continues to grind on Sundays. It can still be safely visited from the hotel.

Falls of Devon
NN 993 032

The upper part of the river Devon provides a winding route through the Ochils from the splendidly named village of Yetts o' Muchart to Gleneagles. At a place called St Serf's there is a prominent little fall just below the A823.

Higher up, at the village of Glendevon, is the *Black Linn*. (*NN 993 042*) This is a fine fall situated just below the road bridge.

The term, the Falls of Devon, is sometimes used collectively to include Cauldron Linn(qv) and the De'il's Mill(qv)

Dollar Glen
NS 960 993

When the Argyll family took possession of it in the fifteenth century, Castle Campbell was called Castle Gloom. Colin Campbell had the name altered by Act of Parliament, presumably on the grounds that he required something more cheerful. Castle Gloom is situated on a steep promontory between the Burn of Sorrow and the Burn of Care in the Parish of Dollar, a name held by some to be derived from Dolour. These names belie what is generally a cheerful enough place on a south-facing slope. In fact Gloom, or Gloum, means chasm and it almost certainly refers to the narrow gorge of the Burn of Sorrow called the Windy Pass. The same root gives the name Glomach, grandest of Scottish waterfalls, although there are disputes about that as well. Gloom Hill still appears on the map above Dollar, a more reliable etymology for which is steep glen.

The glen was improved by the Dollar Amenity Society in conjunction with the National Trust for Scotland. Castle Campbell, surely the most impressively situated fortalice in Central Scotland, was presented to the Trust in 1950 by Mr Kerr of Harviestoun and is now in the care of the Department of the Environment. It is usual to follow the steep road in a car from Dollar to Brewlands where there is a car park not very far from the Castle by level path, but to do this is to miss the charm of the glen; unless there are very old or very young members in the party, it is better to go on foot from the village, following the path which climbs beside the burn. Little time is saved in a car since there is nearly always heavy traffic on the road.

The first fall on the burn is called the *Silver Linn*. Where the glen forks the righthand burn leads directly to the Castle. This is the Burn of Care. On it, above the Castle, are *Hempy's Falls* (NS 962 992) and *Craiginnan Falls* (NS 961 994).

A splendid round is completed by descending the Burn of Sorrow where there are *Sochie Falls* (NS 960 993), also above the Castle and, below it, Windy Pass which is traversed by a system of bridges.

Falls of Knaik
NN 831 111

Above the Roman Camp of Ardoch at Braco, the Knaik is attractive; a woodland path leads beside the river to St

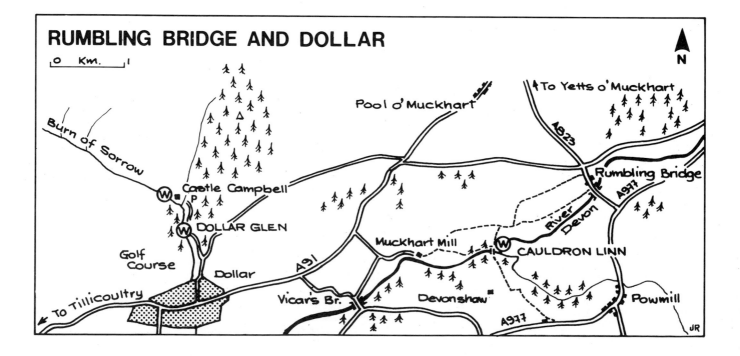

Ringain's Loup and towards Braco Castle. At the loup are two rock platforms at either side of the river; above this there is a substantial river fall of about four metres at the Mill of Ardoch from where it is possible to see two further falls upstream.

Linn Mill Fall (Clackmannan)   *NS 926 929*

The fall is situated where the Black Devon tumbles over a rock sill on the road from Clackmannan to Kinross. Such was the popularity of the Falls in the basin of the Devon that Linn Mill Fall is the subject of an attractive turn-of-the-century post-card. Today it would hardly be considered worthy of such treatment.

Logie Burn Falls

Tiny waterfall above Logie Kirk in the delightful corner of what was Stirlingshire under Dumyat, the western bastion of the Ochils.

The Loup   *NS 801 997*

Above the Spa town of Bridge of Allan there are superb deciduous woodlands reached by steep side roads which lead eventually to the battlefield of Sheriffmuir. This end of the Ochils is drained by the Wherry Burn which, in its lower reaches, flows through the densely-wooded Kippenrait Glen. The principal fall is called the Loup, but it is the luxuriant trees rather than this fall which will leave a lasting impression of the place. Oak, wychelm, ash and birch predominate and, in the golden autumn the glen is fine indeed, one of those places much more frequented in Victorian times than nowadays.

Menstrie Glen   *NS 848 974*

> O, Alva's hills is bonny
>   Tillicoultry's hills is fair
> But to think on the braes o'
>   Menstrie
>   It makes my heart fu' sair.

No hill in Scotland, not even Ben Nevis above Fort William, looks so impressively steep as Dumyat above Menstrie. This fine little hill also affords what is probably the most magnificent view to be had in Scotland from anywhere of comparable height. The way to it is by Menstrie Glen which is thus much frequented on this account. There are ten falls, sufficiently noteworthy to be marked on the six-inch OS map, on the burn and its tributaries. The glen is very steep in its lower part and the principal fall is hidden from the path to the hills. A bed of coarse tuff and agglomerate is crossed by a dyke to form the fall.

Mill Glen   *NS 912 977*

Like Alva, Tillicoultry has made the most of its glen, which lies at the foot of Ben Cleuch. In order to mark the demise of the former system of local government the citizens established a modern nature trail in their glen in 1975. The splendidly produced guide is one of the finest of its kind obtainable. The guide leads the visitor to the junction of the Daiglen and Gannel Burns and back a different way. The lower part of the glen is spoiled by a great quarry, but this in no way detracts from the grandeur of the upper part where there are eight falls altogether.

There are also several falls in the neighbouring Kirk Glen above Tillicoultry's handsome church.

Waterfalls in Fife

Arraty Den   *NO 220 075*

A spectacular den under West Lomond, reached from Falkland by the track leaving the A912 at the Pillars of Hercules—flat stones for resting coffins on, now disappeared, wich gave their name to this spot. Above the fall is Maiden Castle, an Iron Age Fort which can be reached from the road at the head of Maspie Den on the way to Leslie. The den is described by T C Snoddy in his footpath guide *Twixt Forth and Tay* (1966):

> Standing here by the small burn we look up and discover that Arraty Den is a great chasm with broken sides that gradually rise up out of the steep timbered banks and assert themselves as naked cliffs, showing grey and firm against the green background of the hill. They are so high that one looks only a little higher to see the clear sky above the moor. The water falling for ages from the uplands has carved the sandstone sill into four roughly separated blocks, but it is usually only at two of these intersections that the water falls nowadays, and it is only during the rains of winter that you can enjoy the sight of shining cascades.
>   Those who know the moor in this part know that it is not prolific in streams, but on the right occasion you will see, 200 feet or more above you, the slender torrents break somewhat lingeringly into view and fall in shallow silver bands into the depths of the great hollow. In the greenness and gloom they are lost to sight but reappear in the stony channel above the bridge and flow freshly beneath it as you stand and watch. Despite the decay of aged timber this is a beauty spot of great attraction, a bosky hollow which could only have been carved in its present height and depth out of the high sandstone rock by ages of attrition.

Craighall Den   *NO 400 107*

This natural ravine is one a tributary of the Ceres Burn above the village. There is a marked sandstone gorge with oak, beech and hazel. An SWT Trail follows the ravine to the site of Craighall, the magnificent renaissance house, now taken down, which stood at the head of the glen. There is an interesting lime kiln nearby and the leaflet points out a number of other features. The waterfall is reached by diverging from the path. It is in a pleasantly shaded nook at the foot of a steep bank. The burn falls about five metres over a basaltic sill.

Dura Den   *NO 414 4155*

The Ceres Burn joins the Eden just above Dairsie Bridge. It drains an area of sixty-five square kilometres, and, in the last part of its course, flows through a highly picturesque Upper Old Red Sandstone gorge called Dura Den which lies between Dairsie Bridge and Pitscottie. The basin of the Ceres Burn is a fascinating district in a region associated with a charming coast. It is very well worth while leaving the 'Golden Fringe' to visit it.

The principal industry in these parts was for long connected with the manufacture of brown lines. Flax and jute mills were crowded into the narrow den. It is said that the workers who lived in the little cottages, which can still be seen between the road and the burn, tired of eating the salmon they took from the chattering stream. The enterprise of these Fifers is still remembered on the map for the name of the village of Dairsie was changed to Osnaburgh because American buyers favoured German Cloths which were so-called. Dairsie Bridge has been subject of innumerable pictures by water-colourists. Above it stand the Church and the Castle and to the east is open pastoral country. Along the road to Pitscottie, however, the bleached cliffs of Old Red Sandstone are soon in evidence. A fine fall of about 7.5 metres is seen beside the road (*NO 416 150*) where a tributary tumbles into the Ceres Burn.

The tributary drains a hidden valley where the secluded village of Kemback with its charming church, its coaching inn and its tiny pantiled cottages occupies a tiny plateau. The burn falls through beechmast and bluebell carpeted woods from a dam higher up. Beside it a path climbs to the village.

There were five mills—Yoolfield, Dairsie Mill, Blebo Mill, Kemback Mill and Pitscottie Mill—and they afford ample evidence for the industrial archaeologist of today of the productivity of these places in the nineteenth century. The cottages built in the 1830's are passed and at the Mill Owner's House (Grove House) are the Dura Den Falls. There is a substantial weir at their head which is crossed by a bridge. Below, the burn cascades over natural rock and, turning to spread out at its foot, it falls over an apron of the yellow sandstones and forms a fall of about 7.5 metres.

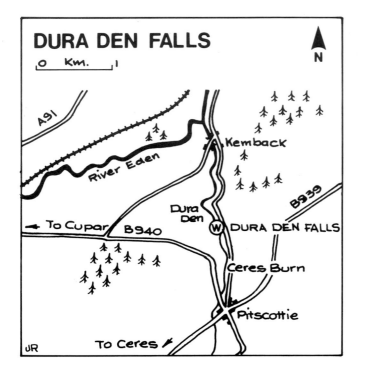

The whole scene, beech, oak and ash woods, half-derelict, half-restored industrial buildings, has great appeal. The den became celebrated by geologists when fossil fish—brown impressions on the pale yellow sandstone—were found in abundance. Such fossils are fairly widespread, but rarely occur in these quantities. The fish had a primitive skeleton and were protected by an armour of bony plates. They probably lived in lakes like the Great Lakes in North America. In addition to its industrial archeology and its geology, Dura Den is also of interest to historians. A Covenanter's Cave provided a refuge in the den.

Visitors will almost certainly continue to Ceres to visit the Folk Museum and other attractions of this tiny burgh. South of the village, higher up the burn is Craighall Den(qv).

Fordel Waterfall   *NT 148 851*

Fordel Castle is of interest because of its unusual plan. It now stands in the policies of Fordel House which were for long considered the finest gardens in Fife. The whole estate stands on the edge of a plateau commanding extensive views of the Firth of Forth from Queensferry and the Bridges to the Isle of May. The principal fall occurs on a winding burn which drains this upland, flowing through a well-wooded glen: it is 15 metres in height. The proprietors of the estate owned the rich colliery of Fordel where, the author of the *New Statistical Account* reported, coal had been mined continuously for 240 years in 1836. The fall is formed from the combined waters of the burn and a drainage level of the mine. The policies are now the site of a Caravan Park the entrance to which is from Gordon Lodge on the by-road from Hillend.

Glen Burn Falls   *NO 189 059*

The heart of Fife is drained by the gentle Eden which rises in the Lomond Hills. The Glen Burn, its true headwater, falls 150 metres in a spectacular ravine above the Sanatorium at Kinnesswood. From the ravine there are highly sensational views of the Howe of Fife and the Southern Highlands. The ravine provides a way to Bishop Hill, the most westerly of the Lomond Hills situated above Loch Leven. At Bishop Hill the best-established Gliding Club in Scotland has its headquarters. The largest of the white sandstone outcrops above Glenvale is a climbing ground. A cave, at the foot of the cliff a short distance below the waterfall, is called John Knox's Pulpit.

Groupie Craigs Fall   *NT 250 912*

Low fall set in the now somewhat impenetrable policies on the edge of Kirkcaldy.

Keil Den   *NO 412 029*

This characteristic Fife Den is above Lundin Links. At the head of it is an attractive ruin, Pitcruvie Castle, and the walk to it is a pleasant excursion. The name of the little resort celebrates its connection with golf, but the place used to be called Lundin Mill. Above the site of the mill is a nice little fall in red sandstone.

Maspie Den   *NO 235 068*

In the ground of the House of Falkland which are open to the public from time to time. A steep road leads over the Falkland Hills to Leslie. The glen forms by far the most attractive approach to these hills. The principal fall, at the head of the glen, is of the curtain type and it is generally possible to pass behind it.

Starley Burn Waterfall   *NT 227 858*

This coastal fall is between Burntisland and Aberdour. It is formed by a burn which crosses the carboniferous limestone, and the water has petrifying qualities. The tiny harbour at the foot of the burn is called Carron Harbour. It was built by the great iron company to carry limestone to their works at the head of the Forth. Across the bay in Burntisland is the magnificently restored Ross End Castle.

THE TAY
AND
EARN BASINS

Principal Falls

Outstanding Falls	Touring centre
Falls of Bruar	Blair Atholl
Reekie Linn	Alyth

Significant Falls	
Falls of Acharn	Kenmore
Black Spout	Pitlochry
Falls of Beich Burn	Lochearnhead
Falls of Braan	Dunkeld
Hermitage Falls	Dunkeld
Falls of Moness	Aberfeldy
Falls of Tarf	Blair Atholl
Fall of Urrard	Pitlochry

Interesting Falls	
Cargill's Leap (Falls of Keith)	Blairgowrie
De'il's Cauldron	Comrie
Falls of Dochart	Killin
Falls of Dovecraig	Killin
Falls of Edinample	Lochearnhead
Falls of Lochay	Killin
Falls of Allt Ollach	Comrie
Linn of Tummel	Pitlochry
Falls of Turret (Sput Hoick)	Crieff

Also recommended	
Slug of Achrannie	Alyth
Buchanty Spout	Crieff
Sput a' Chleibh	Comrie
Falls of Allt Da-ghob	Aberfeldy
Falls of Keltneyburn	Aberfeldy
Falls of Monzie	Crieff
Sput Rolla	Comrie

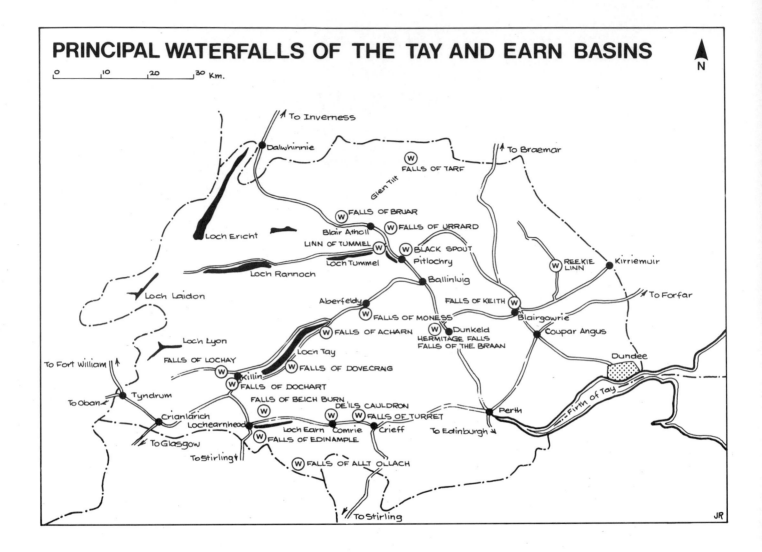

PRINCIPAL WATERFALLS OF THE TAY AND EARN BASINS

N

0   10   20   30 Km.

To Inverness

Dalwhinnie

To Braemar

W FALLS OF TARF

Glen Tilt

Loch Ericht

W FALLS OF BRUAR

Blair Atholl   W FALLS OF URRARD

LINN OF TUMMEL

W   W BLACK SPOUT

Loch Tummel   Pitlochry

Loch Rannoch   REEKIE
W   LINN   Kirriemuir

Loch Laidon   Ballinluig

To Forfar

Aberfeldy   FALLS OF KEITH

W FALLS OF MONESS   W   Blairgowrie

Loch Lyon   W FALLS OF ACHARN   W Dunkeld   Coupar Angus

FALLS OF LOCHAY   Loch Tay   HERMITAGE FALLS
FALLS OF THE BRAAN   Dundee

To Fort William   W FALLS OF DOVECRAIG

W Killin

Tyndrum   FALLS OF DOCHART

To Oban   FALLS OF BEICH BURN   Perth

Crianlarich   DE'ILS CAULDRON   Firth of Tay

Lochearnhead   W   W FALLS OF TURRET

Loch Earn   Comrie   Crieff   To Edinburgh

To Glasgow   W FALLS OF EDINAMPLE

To Stirling

W FALLS OF ALLT OLLACH

To Stirling

JR

Waterfalls in the South East Highlands: the Tay and Earn Basins

Readers of books on mountaineering may have conceptual difficulties in dealing with the mighty river Tay. Corrie Ba, where the Tummel rises, is in the Central Highlands within easy reach of the West Coast; Ben Lui near which the headwaters of the Tay itself gather is close enough to Loch Awe; the roaring Tarf tumbles out of the hidden recesses of the Cairngorms; and Perth seems miles away from any of them. Perthshire and Tayside are useful divisions to remember, but there are bits of the Tay in Argyll and Strathclyde.

The Tay is the greatest river of Scotland; its tributaries, the Earn, the Isla and the Tummel, are bigger than many other rivers which find their own way to the sea. Tayside embraces almost the entire basin of the great river together with that of the North and South Esks which are not considered here to be part of South East Scotland. In its publicity for itself the Regional Council calls Tayside 'the Region of the Rivers', and the region is pre-eminent in its waterfalls. John MacCulloch (1824), who reckoned that he had seen more waterfalls in Scotland than anyone else, asserted that, of the four finest cascades in Scotland, three were in his native Perthshire. It is probable that he never saw the great falls of the North West, but his verdict, at a time when such matters were carefully considered, is intriguing. Two of the falls, so highly-rated by MacCulloch, are now adversely affected by hydro-electric power schemes and few will know the third by name. His four were Foyers and, in Perthshire, the Falls of Tummel, the Falls of Urrard and the Falls of the Bruar.

Apart from these three the Tay Basin has many other well-known waterfalls: the roaring falls of the Braan at Rumbling Bridge; the salmon leap at Buchanty Spout; the firmly picturesque falls of Acharn; and the two best known falls in Scotland nowadays, the Falls of Moness in the Birks of Aberfeldy and the delightful falls of Dochart. All of these falls are well-known to tourists and make an impressive list, but many would prefer those falls found in less-frequented places. The Tay Basin also accommodates the waterfalls of Glen Lyon, of Glen Tilt and of Rannoch Moor which are just as fine as the better known falls aforementioned.

There is no doubt that some of the falls of the Tay have been adversely affected by hydro-electric power schemes. The most serious losses are the Falls of Tummel and the Falls of Lochay. The Falls of Turret have also been almost equally badly done by, in this case by a Water Board scheme. Spates are arranged from time to time in the interests of amenity and of fishing, but the rock-strewn channels of some rivers close to frequented places have inflicted lasting damage to Scotland's greatest asset, her incomparable scenery. It is true that many of the works—dams and power stations—are wonders of modern engineering and the little power station below the Falls of Lochay is a masterpiece of modern architecture. Indeed some would argue that, because of the combined efforts of the Hydro Board, the Forestry Commission and the National Trust for Scotland, the Fa Lin of Tummel is as attractive a place as ever it was.

The falls of the Tay Basin are set in richly wooded straths and in intricately varied glens backed by mountains of character. They are attractive in themselves, but, because they are so often easy of access and have long been known, they have associations which lend even more interest to them. The Wordsworths visited the Falls of Acharn. Burns wrote the best poem ever written about a waterfall: it is about the Falls of the Bruar. Queen Victoria, whose image is so staid, visited many of the Waterfalls of Central Scotland, and her expedition crossing the Tarf below the Falls must rank as one of the most adventurous she undertook. That unlikely waterfall enthusiast, Charles Dickens, praised the Falls of Lochay.

Much more would be said about the basin of the Tay but two further superlatives must suffice. Where the river falls over Campsie Linn it forms the greatest waterfall in Britain although it is only a metre or two in height. However, no other fall approaches it in volume. The Falls of the Bruar are some 60 metres in height all told and, in flood, they too rank among the great falls of Scotland.

The Earn is sometimes considered a completely separate river from the Tay because it enters the estuary of its sister river rather than the river itself. For most purposes, however, including calculations as to the size of the basin of the Tay, it is regarded as a tributary. The gentle, but grand basin of the Earn has a dozen falls of quality.

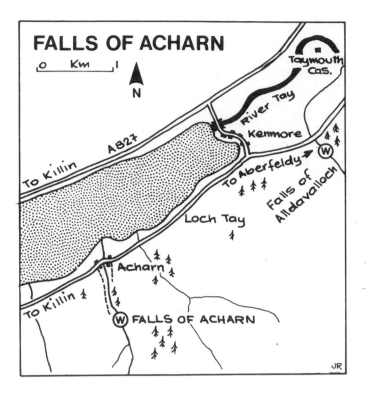

Falls of Acharn   *NN 758 430*

These Loch Tayside falls are visited from the unclassified road which runs from Kenmore to Killin along the south bank of the loch. The views of Ben Lawyers from this road are an ample justification for choosing it in preference to the more usual route by the A827. Burns and other visitors have been unanimous in asserting that the country around Taymouth combines much that is best in Scotland. 'The scenery at and around Kenmore is of the finest and most pleasing description and embraces all the elements of the picturesque' says Black's *Guide* of 1861. Anderson's *Guide to the Highlands* describes the Falls of Acharn:

> The burn precipitating its waters over the side of a deep and wooded dell, first performs a perpendicular descent of fully 50 feet separating towards the bottom into two vertical streams which are caught by a small basin, whence the water escapes by successive inclined leaps, the whole forming a cascade apparently about 80 or 90 feet high.

The Wordsworths visited these falls in 1803 and Dorothy gives a graphic description of the Grotto which sounds as if it were in execrable taste:

> We entered a dungeon-like passage and, after walking some yards in total darkness found ourselves in a quaint apartment stuck over with moss, hung about with stuffed foxes and ornamented with a library of wooden books covered with old leather backs, the mock furniture of a hermit's cell. At the end of the room, through a large bow window, we saw the waterfall, and at the same time looking down to the left, the village of Kenmore and part of the lake—a very beautiful prospect.

Joseph Farington who visited the Falls in 1801 gives a more complete account of them than most visitors:

> Having ordered our dinner and beds we went by the South side of the lake two miles to see the falls of water in the Bourn of Acharan. Here again we had a steep ascent to climb, which we were told was an eighth part of a mile to the falls, but we found it a full threequarters of a mile before we reached the top. There are three falls. The uppermost fall which is the smallest passes under a bridge. It is not large but the rocks are shaped in a picturesque manner and the trees are loose and well-shaped. From this fall there is a path through a wood which covers the whole bank of the bourn and by it we descended to the second fall which is larger and more varied. The lowest, great fall is approached through a subterraneous and narrow passage in some parts quite dark, at the end of which is a door which opens into a circular room called the Hermitage, and through a window opposite to the door the fall is seen. The appearance of it is very pleasing and singular, and its height considerable. The stream breaks out from a dark hollow near the top of the rock and falls in two lines splitting in its descent in various directions, and again collecting till it shoots into a bottomless depth, as it seems from this point. The trees which fringed the fall contrasted by their lively and various tints with the dark brown and black colour of the rock over which the white foam dashed. The face of this scene is high and widespread and has a remarkably dressed appearance for a work of nature in which no art can have been used. Were it on a smaller scale it would be called elegant or pretty, its size gives it a higher claim, yet it is not grand, wanting in boldness and rudeness of form to give it that character.

This passage is typical of Farington who describes many waterfalls in Perthshire. A great searcher after the picturesque, he was ready to condemn nature if it did not come up to his expectations. In this respect he was a follower of William Gilpin, the high priest of the picturesque who had visited the Falls of Acharn some years earlier:

> One inducement to this voyage was a cascade on the banks of the lake which had been represented to us as an uncommon piece of scenery. A pompous preface so often produces disappointment, that, expecting disappointment here, we were agreeably surprised. We found a very beautiful scene. It is not indeed of so sublime a kind as that of the Hermitage at Dunkeld. It is of a tamer nature, gliding down an excavated rock; but meeting with enough interruption to give it variety. Its accompaniments are very beautiful. The rock it falls from is lofty and well-broken: it graces the centre of a little woody theatre; which nature seems to have made on purpose for it, and where it is shown to much advantage. Lord Breadalbin, to whom it belongs, introduces the stranger to it through a sort of subterranean passage, the necessity for which did not appear. It is an exhibition which wants no aid to give it consequence.

The Burn of Acharn drains a basin of about 16 square kilometres which is less than that of the Falls of Moness. The falls are in a hanging valley above Loch Tay and occur on flaggy Dalradian rocks. The water-mill at the entrance to the glen is now a craft shop.

The Slug of Achrannie   *NO 278 528*

There are few rivers with three such fine falls as the Falls of Canness, Reekie Linn and the Slug of Achrannie on the Isla. The Slug is reached by crossing the Meglam below Airlie Castle and following the left bank of the Isla for about three kilometres. The path affords dramatic views of the sandstone gorge cut by the river. At the Slug, where the path ends, is a fall of 15 metres: this curious word refers to a narrowing in the river bed through which the boiling Isla pours. There is a lower fall, the Wee Slug, downstream. Visitors to Reekie Linn should retrace their steps to the farm track which joins the Lintrathen road.

Eas nan Aighean   NN 425 430

Remote fall in a ravine above Loch Lyon.

Falls of Aldarvalloch   NN 784 452

Falls in woodland above the road from Aberfeldy to Kenmore at the point where there is a splendid view of Taymouth Castle. As the falls lie between Moness and Acharn they have been completely overshadowed. In the heyday of waterfall enthusiasts when Murray compiled his guidebook, they earned a passing mention. A succession of linked cascades in a fine wood, they are now rather difficult to approach.

Eas Anie   NN 289 284

This is a fine hanging waterfall on Ben Chuirn where the infant Tay first falls to the level of Strathfillan. It can be seen from the A82 at the Cononish Bridge at Dalry. The fall is the site of one of the most celebrated lead deposits of the Central Highlands. A fault brings Dalradian Schists into contact with Moinian rocks, and mineralised veins up to 20 feet thick occur. The Earl of Breadalbane developed the mines there which led to the growth of the village of Tyndrum and which established him as one of the richest landowners in Britain. A track leads from Cononish Farm to the mines and provides an obvious route up the mountain. It gives a grand view of the falls.

Eas an Aoin   NN 736 247

When he improved Dunira in the late eighteenth century Viscount Melville provided an object lesson for his neighbours. The house itself is now taken down but it was part of a scheme which combined artifice with wild nature in a landscaped garden of much distinction. Eas an Aoin, a fall in a ravine above the house, was used in this scheme. Lady Sarah Murray was suitably impressed by it:

A shallow burn bounds the lawn to the west, issuing from a very steep, thick-wooded narrow glen; and this burn, at about a mile above the house, rushes through branches of trees over boken rocks of considerable height, forming a very picturesque fall. The rustic bridge, and the walks to and from this fall, are very judiciously executed.

Falls of Auchessan   NN 446 282

Glen Dochart, between Killin and Crianlarich, was described by William Gilpin;

From the pleasing environs of Killin we launched out into a wild country which nature had barely produced; but had done little to adorn. In general we had few forms of picturesque beauty, at least in the larger part. In the smaller we often found them in the winding of rivulets, in their rocky beds and in their bustling cascades of which we had great variety.

Of these tributary burns Allt Essan, leading from Loch Essan (the loch of the waterfalls) perched on a shelf above Loch Iubhair and commanding splendid views, stumbles into the Dochart by a series of pretty falls above Auchessan.

Falls of Balnaguard   NN 940 510

At Balnaguard there is a wooded ravine drained by the eponymous burn. A fine juniper wood and some notable landslips have encouraged the Scottish Wildlife Trust to establish a reserve there. The falls consist of three cascades on flaggy rocks. At the foot of the burn is an old lime kiln of some interest to industrial archeologists.

Sput Ban   NN 728 476

Glen Lyon, which some assert is the finest glen in all Scotland, affords a fine combination of mountain, river, woods and wild-flower banks. Its entrance, above Fortingall, is the Pass of Lyon where the outliers of Ben Lawers and Cairn Mairg crowd in on the river which tumbles through a wooded gorge with splendid beech trees. Sput Ban is a fall of a few metres in the throat of the gorge, the first obstacle encountered by salmon ascending the Lyon. In spite of hydro electric power schemes higher up, the impetuous river is generally well supplied with water, and the fall and the rocky gorge are well worth seeing. Above Sput Ban is MacGregor's Leap where Gregor MacGregor leaped eight yards from an uncertain footing to an insecure landing when pursued by Sir Colin Campbell's bloodhounds in 1565.

Sput Ban see Falls of Keltie

Falls of Barvick   NN 850 245

The Barvick Burn drains a basin of seven and a half square kilometres below the Blue Craigs above Crieff. At the Brae of Monzievaird it tumbles 150 metres in a succession of highly attractive falls to the boulder-strewn bed of the Turret. The falls are reached by a wicket gate on the left at the entrance to Glen Turret. A footpath follows the true left bank of the burn. Because the basin drained by the little stream is quite inconsiderable the falls can only be seen to advantage after rain. In *The Road to Rannoch and the Summer Isles* Ratcliffe Barnett (1924) wrote with affection about this area:

To me April comes never more sweetly than in the glades and glens of Perthshire. The face of the countryside is like the face of a friend—plain or beautiful, it takes a lifetime to know it, and even then the true lover is lost for language. So have I, many times, taken the road round the Knock at Crieff and, dreaming in the sun, over the rail of the wooden bridge that crosses the limpid Shaggie Burn, on my way to the old, familiar glen. And yet—these green haughs, these deep gladed woods, the smell of the pines and the thunder of the waterfall on a sunny April day seem like a miracle of God than ever.

On this road the towny traveller usually sits down to rest himself beside his beloved on an iron seat below the Barvick Falls, before returning to the midday meal at home, that intolerable tyranny which no true tramp can abide. But, for the wandering man, the day's adventure is just beginning so he climbs up the right bank of the waterfall, finding his way through the sludgy loam of the woods, clambering over fallen trees, and peering down into the gorge where the river tumbles headlong in many a white waterfall. It is a steep path till you reach the highest fall and come to a little greystone bridge that crosses this moorland stream where it enters the wood. Here you will find an idyllic seat on the parapet as you look towards the brown hills and listen to the whaups.

Falls of Barvick, *Perthshire, especially impressive after rain.* PETER DAVENPORT

FALLS OF BEICH BURN

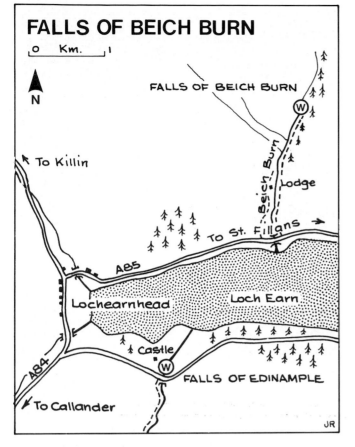

Falls of Beich Burn
NN 694 145

Glenbeich is not frequented by tourists. It is a quiet pastoral glen stretching into the low hills between Loch Earn and Loch Tay. The burn, like the Burn of Ample opposite it at the head of the loch, follows the line of the Loch Tay Fault and, where it crosses the fault there is an impressive fall which deserves to be much more widely known than it is. It compares favourably with many other falls in the Tay Basin and, unlike some of them, it is unaffected by the depredations of the Hydro Board. In his book, *Striking and Picturesque Delineations of the Grand, Beautiful and Interesting Scenery around Loch Earn*, Angus McDiarmid (1816) describes the 'cataract of Glen Beigh'. After the fashion of the day it is a complex description, but it leaves one in no doubt that he regarded it as one of the principal wonders of the district. It is surprising that few other writers have referred to it at all.

A track leads up the glen from Ardveich and provides a grandstand view of the impressive cascades on the *Allt Iaruinn* (*NN 616 254*) beneath Glenbeich Lodge. In spate these falls are imposing enough At the head of the gorge the burn enters it from the right and falls sheer into the steep-sided basin which holds the plunge pool. 'The burn is precipitated in considerable volume over a sheer precipice of 50 feet into a well-like cavity from which it issues through a narrow cleft into a deep black pool.' The falls are highly attractive, delightfully situated in a quiet deciduous wood, perfectly proportioned and full of interest for the visitor to Lochearnhead.

Birnam Falls
NO 016 416

A pretty walk of two kilometres from Birnam leads by the road up the right bank of the Inchewan Burn to the semi-circle of stone seats called the Seven Sisters. Beyond, a narrow path by the stream leads to the falls which are small but picturesque.

Black Linn see The Hermitage

Black Spout
NN 954 578

Situated in attractive woods south-east of Pitlochry, Black Spout is at the centre of a web of footpaths leading to and from the town. The Edradour Burn forms a series of falls, 36 metres high. The centrepiece is a fine twin ribbon of white water against pitch-black rocks about 20 metres high. The fall is set in an amphitheatre and a belvedere provides a particularly fine front view of it.

Black Spout, Pitlochry. Engraving by W B Scott (1811–90) from drawing by Andrew Donaldson (1790–1846)

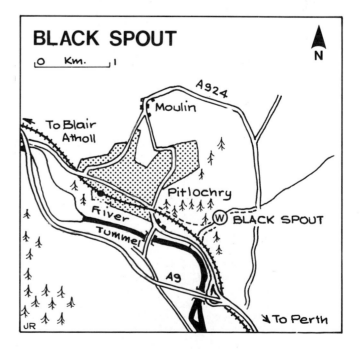

Falls of Braan
NN 997 412

Before it joins its sister river, the Tay, the River Braan, a roaring, tumbling mountain stream, falls for five kilometres over a spectacular series of waterfalls. This series is initiated in a most dramatic way by a 25 metre fall at Rumbling Bridge, so-called from the way in which the river seems to shake it. The bridge is at the foot of a hill in an open wood on a by-road off the A822. The gorge narrows to a few feet and the little bridge requires very little superstructure. From it you can see the fall and the gorge. From an insecure rock platform, you can look down into the fearful chasm below the bridge. The Braan drains a substantial basin: its discharge at the falls exceeds that of Reekie Linn. The Falls of the Braan combine a considerable discharge with a remarkable height: in this respect, they are exceeded in Scotland only by the Falls of Kirkaig and the Falls of Clyde.

Brig o' Balgie Falls
NN 577 467

Above and below the Brig o' Balgie on the Lyon there are charming low falls linking (at the right time of the year) salmon-filled pools of clear water. The bridge gets its name from the bag-shaped pool below it. Just above the bridge is an architectural gem, the little gatehouse to Meggernie Castle, built by Colin Gorach, Mad Colin Campbell, in about 1830. The gatehouse is a perfect miniature of much more modern date.

The Falls of the Bruar
NN 818 663

The Bruar rises beyond Ben Dearg and flows at first over miles of bare gneiss. However, parts of the upper basin of the burn are peat-covered—it is up to 15 feet thick in places—so the flow of water in this considerable tributary of the Garry is regulated to some extent, and the famous falls usually repay a visit. They occur where the Bruar tumbles to the level of its much attenuated sister stream above Struan. There are three distinct sets of falls with an aggregate height of 60 metres set in the woods planted by the fourth Duke of Atholl in response to Burns' Humble Petition of the Bruar Water.

This is Burns' finest poem associated with the Highlands. The poet wrote to the Duke after his stay of three days in September 1787:

> I have just time to write the foregoing and to tell you that it was—at least the most part of it—the effusion of half an hour spent at Bruar. I do not mean it was extempore, for I have endeavoured to brush it up as well as Mr Nichol's chat and the jogging of the chaise would allow it. It eases my heart a good deal as rhyme is the coin with which a poet pays his debt of honour or of gratitude.

These two or three days were the happiest of his life, Burns afterwards declared. His poem with its jaunty characterisation of a highland stream provides a splendid memorial of his visit.

THE HUMBLE PETITION OF
BRUAR WATER

to the Noble Duke of Athole

My lord, I know, your noble ear
  Woe ne'er assails in vain;
Emboldened thus, I beg you'll hear
  Your humble slave complain
How saucy Phoebus' scorching beams,
  In flaming summer-pride,
Dry withering, waste my foamy streams
  And drink my crystal tide.

Falls of the Bruar, 19th century engraving

The lightly-jumping, glowrin trouts
  That thro' my waters play,
If in their random, wanton spouts
  They near the margin stray;
If, hapless chance! they linger lang
  I'm scorching up so shallow,
They're left the whitening stanes amang
  In gasping death to wallow.

Last day I grat wi' spite and teen
  As Poet Burns came by,
That, to a Bard, I should be seen
  Wi' half my channel dry;
A panegyric rhyme, I ween,
  Even as I was, he shored me;
But had I in my glory been,
  He, kneeling, wad ador'd me.
Here, foaming down the skelvy rocks,
  In twisting strength I rin;
There high my boiling torrent smokes,
  Wild-roaring o'er a linn;
Enjoying large each spring and well,
  As Nature gave them me,
I am, altho' I say't mysel,
  Worth gaun a mile to see.

Would then, my noble master please
  To grant my highest wishes,
He'll shade my banks wi' tow'ring trees
  And bonie spreading bushes.
Delighted doubly then, my lord
  You'll wander on my banks,
And listen monie a grateful bird
  Return you tuneful thanks.

Buchanty Spout, *Glen Almond. Salmon attempt the almost insuperable barrier.* PETER DAVENPORT

The sober laverock, warbling wild,
　Shall to the skies aspire;
The gowdspink, Music's gayest child,
　Shall sweetly join the choir;
The blackbird strong, the lintwhite clear,
　The mavis mild and mellow,
The robin, pensive Autumn cheer
　In all her locks of yellow.

This, too, covert shall ensure
　To shield them from the storm;
And coward maukin sleep secure,
　Low in her grassy form:
Here shall the shepherd make his seat
　To weave his crown of flow'rs
Or find a shelt'ring, safe retreat
　From prone-descending show'rs.

And here, by sweet, endearing stealth,
　Shall meet the loving pair,
Despising worlds with all their wealth
　As empty idle care;
The flow'rs shall vie, in all their charms
　The hour of heav'n to grace
And birks extend their fragrant arms
　To screen the dear embrace.

Here haply too, at vernal dawn,
　Some musing Bard may stray,
And eye the smoking, dewy lawn
　And misty mountain grey;
Or, by the reaper's nightly beam
　Mild-chequering thro' the trees,
Rave to my darkly dashing stream,
　Hoarse-swelling on the breeze

Let lofty firs and ashes cool
　My lowly banks o'erspread,
And view, deep-bending in the pool,
　Their shadows' wat'ry bed
Let fragrant birks, in woodbines drest
　My craggy cliffs adorn,
For the little songster's nest,
　The close embow'ring thorn.

So may, old Scotia's darling hope,
　Your little angel band
Spring, like their fathers, up to prop
　Their honour'd native land!
So may, thro' Albion's farthest ken,
　To social-flowing glasses
The grace be: 'Athole's honest men
　And Athole's bonnie lasses'

It is probable that the planting of trees at the Falls of the Bruar was a topic of conversation at Blair Atholl when William Gilpin visited there in 1776: he was the authority on such matters. It has certainly been a topic for many writers since then. Dorothy Wordsworth visited the Falls in 1803:

The Hermitage, Dunkeld. The National Trust for Scotland has restored the old Summer House, now centrepiece of a nature trail which leads through magnificent woodland – of sycamore, oak, beech, alder and Douglas firs. A place of pilgrimage for notable visitors to Scotland in the eighteenth and early nineteenth centuries. PETER DAVENPORT

After having gone for some time under a bare hill, we were told to leave the car at some cottages and pass through a little gate near a brook which crossed the road. We walked upwards of at least three-quarters of a mile in the hot sun, with the stream on our right, both sides of which were planted with firs and larches intermingled—children of poor Burns' song; for his sake we wished that they had been the natural trees of Scotland, birches, ashes, mountain ashes, etc; however 60 or 70 years hence they will be no unworthy monument to his memory.

Two other redoubtable lady travellers visited the falls at about the same time as Dorothy Wordsworth. Lady Sarah Murray visited them in 1799:

I only saw a very small part of Glen Bruar, namely its fall of water out of the glen, which is reckoned very fine; and though the sides are very bare, it certainly is so. The great number and variety of smaller falls, extending all the way down from the high fall to the houses in the town of Bruar (in the Highlands every thing is a town, if it consists only of a cluster of houses), are very pretty; and one in particular is extremely curious, the water having perforated the rock and made itself an arch, through which it tumbles in a very picturesque style. I first went on the east side of the water, in a small carriage to see the high fall; but the lesser falls are to be seen on the west side; and a fine scrambling walk it is, over fragments of rocks, stone dykes (walls), and ground full of springs, but the beauty of the scene repays the fatigue of following it up to the summit of the high fall. Since I saw the Falls of Bruar, the Duke of Atholl has had an arch thrown over the high fall from rock to rock, and the banks planted; these plantations, when grown up, will render the falls completely beautiful.

Elizabeth Grant of Rothiemurchus is more critical:

We did not spend our time at the Castle, we walked to the falls of the Bruar, first brought into notice by Burns and then made too much of; as besides planting the banks and conducting a path up the stream, so many summer-houses and hermitages and peep-bo places of one sort and another had been perched on favourite situations, that the complete character of the wild torrent was completely lost. Nature was much disturbed, but no ill-taste could destroy so grand a scene. We were fortunate in finding plenty of water leaping in wide cascades over rocks of every size and shape, for there had been rain a few days before.

The larch woods for which his estates became famous were created by the 'planting Duke' between 1774 and 1830. However, they were planted as much for commercial as for aesthetic purposes. The woods at Bruar were destroyed by the storms of 1879 which led to the Tay Bridge disaster; they were re-planted thereafter.

Other famous visitors to the falls included William Gilpin in 1787, Joseph Farington in 1801 and Queen Victoria in 1844. Farington left a similar account to those quoted above. However, the chief significance of his visit was that he persuaded Turner to visit the falls in 1803. It is suggested that Turner's most famous picture of a waterfall, the watercolour called 'A Mountain Torrent', was inspired in this area. The mountain torrent which forms the subject of the picture is clearly a tributary waterfall typical of the district. There is a drawing of the bridge over the Lower Fall in the Scottish Lakes sketchbook compiled by Turner in the course of his visit.

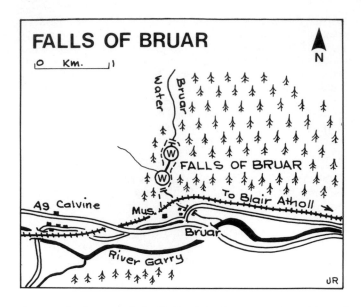

Appropriately enough the Falls of the Bruar are the subject of a poem in Lallans by John McDonald, published in 1981:

> The reek o' pine-wuids
> Muckel bowders tasht
> Tae abstract airt
> And doon ablow us
> Kirstal wi' a troot set in't.

(English readers who may have had sufficient difficulty in coping with some of Burns' dialect words may find it helpful to have it pointed out that all of the words used are variations of similar English words.)

Nowadays there is a signposted walk leading to the falls from the A9 at Bruar, by-passed by the new road. The entrance to the glen is deside the Bruar Falls Hotel and the Clan Donnachaidh Museum which now occupies the cottages referred to by Sarah Murray and Dorothy Wordsworth. The clan includes the Robertsons, the Duncans, the Reids, the MacConnachies and others. The Highland Railway is crossed by a subway, and the line of the Wade Road is crossed further up. There are two low falls which will be considered substantial enough on the way up, but which will be seen to be mere interruptions after the falls themselves have been reached. There is no mistaking the Lower Fall which pitches five metres under a stone bridge before rushing underneath a natural arch in the rock. Beside the bridge is a viewpoint from which the visitor can see the Middle Falls. You pass through an arch to stand on a rock platform above the river. In the background there is an apron fall of about five metres and in the foreground a double fall of about ten metres. From the Lower Bridge one can proceed by either bank of the stream to the Upper Falls, but only the path on the left bank of the stream affords a view of the falls.

The principal fall is not encountered closely, but it appears to be not more than 20 metres in height although it is sometimes stated that it is higher than this. Above it, beneath the Upper Bridge, is a series of lesser falls with a height of three or four metres each. The woods around the falls are very fine, but one cannot help feeling curious about how the place looked when Burns saw it without its accompaniments: Elizabeth Grant may have been right in asserting that it was a better place then.

However, with its associations with Burns, Turner and others, its brawling burn with its magnificent rock architecture, its fine views of Ben Vrackie, Farragon and Schiehallion, Glen Bruar should be visited by all who can arrange it. These are the greatest falls of Perthshire.

Buchanty Spout   *NN 932 283*

This low fall at Buchanty Bridge in Glen Almond is an almost insuperable barrier for salmon which nevertheless try to leap it. The Almond drains a basin of more than 100 square kilometres above the fall which is about four metres in height. The intrepid Sarah Murray states:

> On a sudden the eye is unexpectedly caught by the sight of a mill and the river running in a very narrow channel to the bridge, with the trees hanging over it, and wood feathering down to the water over huge rocks on which the bridge rests; also the roaring water, bursting through its dark and close passage, to fall with a loud noise under the arch, altogether rendering this spot beautifully picturesque.

Campsie Linn   *NO 124 340*

This fall has the distinction of carrying the greatest volume of water of any in Britain. It is the only cataract on the Tay proper. The fall lies north of the early factory village of Stanley and is the scene of Eachan MacIan's death in Scott's *Fair Maid of Perth*. Above it is the site of a priory belonging to the Abbey at Coupar Angus situated on a rocky bluff above the river. Just to the North is the mansionhouse of Stobhall built by the Earl of Perth on a courtyard plan. The Linn is caused by two doleritic dykes which intersect and have the appearance of a single dyke as they cross the river.

The Falls of Camserney   *NN 814 497*

These falls near Weem in the Appin of Dull occur on a burn parallel to the Keltneyburn which precipitates itself with even greater steepness down the hillside. The burn is less substantial than the Keltney, but the falls are higher. 'A picturesque fall on it, about midway between Coshieville and Weem, makes a broken and tortuous descent; and struggles and dashes milky foam over a precipitous and rugged channel' (*Ordnance Gazetteer*).

The Falls of Canness   *NO 206 770*

In the remote upper reaches of Glen Isla beneath the cliffs of Caderg, the Canness Burn tumbles from the plateau in a dramatic waterfall. It is at the heart of the Caenlochan National Nature Reserve where lime-rich rocks support a diverse alpine flora. The name Canness is derived from the Gaelic Cadha an Eas, the pass of the waterfall. Queen Victoria visited Caenlochan in October 1861:

> Another half hour's riding again over such singular flat tableland brought us to the edge of the valley of Cairn Lochan, which is indeed 'a bonnie place'. It reminded me of Clova; only there one did not see the immense extent of mountains behind. Cairn Lochan is a narrow valley, the River Isla winding through it like a silver ribbon, with trees at the bottom. The hills are green and steep, but towards the head of the valley there are fine precipices.

Eas Chiabhlain   *NN 731 592*

The road between Kinloch Rannoch and Pitlochry passes above the Tummel at Dunalastair. In the narrow gorge the river has been dammed and water from the loch is led by a 15 metre aqueduct to the Tummel Power station, the heart of the first—between-the-wars—hydro-electric power scheme in Perthshire. At this point the Tummel passed over two fine falls of which only Eas Chiabhlain is now visible. In most conditions it is a rocky channel with little water in it, but it is an atmospheric place and the character of the fall can be imagined.

Sput a' Chleibh
NN 734 178

At the Spout of Dalness, which is the alternative name for this fall, the Water of Ruchill (which drains Glen Artney) is a considerable highland river and it tumbles over flaggy rocks in a narrow gorge making a fall of no great height, but one of some attractiveness. A footpath leads to a bridge over the river at a narrow gut.

Falls of Conait
NN 520 458

At Kenknock the Lyon is joined by the Conait which tumbles in a hanging valley from a wild upland in which there were formerly two lochs, now dammed and joined into one. The water is led away in a pipeline, so, unfortunately, there is generally little water in the charming river Conait which forms a series of beautiful cascades. The river is situated in an old wood consisting of Scots Pines.

Fall of Coilig see Falls of Lochay

Allt Coire an Easain
NN 257 489

There is no mistaking the way in which this splendid corrie under Clachlet got its name, the Corrie of the Waterfalls. It lies in Corrie Ba, the largest mountain hollow in Scotland, where the headwaters of the Tummel are gathered before following their indefinite course across Rannoch Moor. From Ba Bridge on the old military road across the moor you follow the river into the corrie and the first left bank tributary tumbles out of Coire an Easain to these boggy flats. This fall is a succession of cascades and water chutes on granite, reminiscent of the Cairngorm falls, about 60 metres in height. It was here that the Earl of Mar spied a white hind in 1621 which King James sent a Royal Forester to take alive. This story is admirably reconstructed by Sir James Ferguson in his book *The White Hind* (1963).

> The prospect ahead was menacing. To their right rose a round-topped hill, its rock-strewn slopes sweeping upwards into a rampart of short cliffs against the sky. To their left, a huge spur ran down towards them, knife-edged, covered with snow except where perpendicular rock-faces projected through it. Between a laborious climb led up into the mouth of another narrowing valley, streaming with little burns, which curved steeply leftward out of sight against a snow-streaked ridge that overtopped both the round hill and the sharp spur. Up there, Robert Campbell explained, shouting against the wind, up that hillside strewn with rocks and pouring with water, lay their route. That was Corriessan––Coire an Easain, the hollow of the waterfalls.

Above the first fall, at the true lip of the corrie, is a further fall, a cascade of 24 metres, not very far below the delightful corrie lochan at the heart of the place. One might suppose that Coire an Easain had earned its name, but the ultimate fall in the corrie is a stunning vertical corrie-headwall fall beyond the lochan. If this fall had a greater catchment it would be of the same quality as the Garbh Uisge at Loch A'an.

Linne Cumhan
NN 670 568

A little visited fall above Rannoch on the slopes of Schiehallion.

Falls of Allt Da-ghob ('the forked burn'), Glen Lyon. The tributary burn leaps down spectacular falls to tumble under an old packhorse bridge. The falls drop at least 50 metres before joining the salmon river. DAVID I HARVIE

Falls of Allt Da-ghob
NN 696 471

Glen Lyon is so variously splendid that it would be wrong to pick one favourite place, but among the most memorable spots is the confluence of the Allt Da-ghob, the forked burn, and the Lyon opposite Chesthill. The sparkling waters of the tributary burn pitch down a steep bank to join the river under a stone arched bridge. This bridge is of uncertain date, but is not earlier than the seventeenth century, an old pack-horse bridge. However, like many another in Scotland, it is called the Roman Bridge. Another name is the Black Bridge, a reference perhaps to the fact that lying north of the huge massif af Ben Lawers the bridge is often in shade. The falls are higher than they at first appear, falling at least 50 metres into the salmon stream. A footbridge across the Lyon provides access from the motor road.

Spout of Dalness see Sput a' Chleibh
Dei'l's Cauldron see Falls of Lednock

Devil's Cauldron
NO 387 459

This is the interesting fall seen from the road from Glamis to Dundee (A928) at the entrance to Glamis Den in Glen Ogilvy at the foot of the Sidlaw Hills. The burn tumbles out of an old mill dam to form a white apron of water in a rich old wood. The poet, Thomas Gray, noticed it on his visit in 1765. He was one of the first intellectuals to visit Scotland and he had a high regard for the countryside which he saw. His enthusiasm can be said to have led to the beginning of the tourist trade in the Lake District about which he wrote more extensively than he did about Scotland. However, he was an advocate of Celtic culture, and there is little doubt that Gray, pre-eminent amongst those who made the Grand Tour on the Continent in the early part of the eighteenth century, was among the first to remind the English that they should not forget to visit their own islands thoroughly and in particular that they should visit Scotland.

Falls of Dochart   NN 571 323

Some might quarrel with the inclusion of a series of rapids like the Falls of Dochart in a gazetteer of the waterfalls of Scotland, yet it is probable that there are more visitors to this place than to any other falls in Scotland and that those who see them certainly consider them to be waterfalls. It may be that more tourists pass the Falls of Falloch or the Falls of Leny, but neither of these falls, although they are beside the road, can be seen from it. The Falls of Dochart can not only be seen, but they constitute such a temptation that, if they can stop, few passers-by will miss the opportunity of so doing. Farington is quite definite about the matter:

> We could not have seen them to more advantage, for the flood of waters, rushing in every direction not only filled the spaces formed by frequent inundations, but presented all the varieties which different interruptions could give it. The whole scene appeared from different situations singularly curious and interesting. On moving to different points on the rocks which divided the waters I was still more delighted whle contemplating particular points of these extensive falls where I found the stream associated with mills and other objects on its margin, and a noble background of hills rising above them producing together most beautiful compositions.

Lady Sarah Murray is also very enthusiastic:

> The linn at Killin is very striking, and uncommon. The Tay advances to it from Glen Dochart, and widens to a very considerable breadth as it approaches Killin; which is a row of small houses facing the linn; the road only between it and the houses. The broad bed of the river is there choked up by large masses of rock lying on one another, in every kind of form and direction. These fragments of rock have been, most of them at least, washed thither by floods, and in the course of years have collected sufficient soil to unite many of them together, so as to form rough islands, covered with beautiful bushes, and trees of no great size; but sprouting from every crevice, branching and weeping over the rocks, in a style that delights the eye. Two small bridges, from rock to rock (but not in a line), lead from the south to the north side of the river. Just at the bridges the river is divided by the head of a small rocky high-banked island. This nook is the terra firma between the bridges; against which, and the rocks before it, the water dashes, foams, and roars to such a degree, at the time of flood, that it is scarcely possible to hear the sound of a human voice, even close to the ear. I wonder that the inhabitants of Killin are not all deaf (like those who are employed in iron or copper works), from the thundering noise of the rushing waters. Standing on either of the romantic bridges, the scene around is prodigiously grand, awful and striking.

Today the falls are much as those two travellers described them. It would not be surprising to find that they were the single most popular subject for the camera in Scotland for they are pre-eminently 'picture postcard' falls. The crowds looking

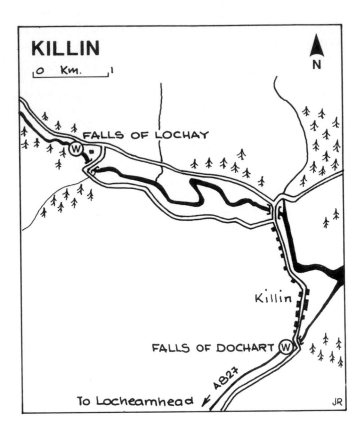

at the falls when the salmon are running are usually very numerous. However, there is one place at Killin which is always quiet, the ancestral burial ground of the MacNabs. Seton Gordon (1948) describes it:

> Through the heart of Killin the Dochart thunders, and in heavy water its spray bathes the MacNabs' ancestral burial ground of Inchbuie. Inch Buie, the Yellow Island, which may have been an ancient stronghold, is densely shaded by veteran beeches and pines and golden moss covers the ground.

The MacNabs emigrated to Canada in the early nineteenth century, and they have a curious connection with the Falls of Niagara. It is said that when the United States invaded Canada it was a MacNab who was responsible for sending a blazing American gunboat over the falls.

Dornock Mill Fall   NN 884 185

Low fall on the trunk stream of the Earn.

Falls of Dovecraig   NN 682 368

Above Ardeonaig there is a very fine view across Loch Tay to Ben Lawers. The Allt a Mheim, the Manse Burn, referred to in old guide books as the Kidd Burn, tumbles down the hillside to the old church beside the loch, forming attractive cascades above the road and, below it, falling 15 metres sheer in dense woods. John Leyden, a follower of Sir Walter Scott, mentions the fall in his *Tour* and places it second only to Foyers.

Fall of Dron   NO 136 151

Picturesque fall in a den above Balmanno Castle called Ram's Heugh. Above it is a spot called the Wicks of Balgie from

FALLS OF DOVECRAIG

0 KM. 1

N

To Kenmore
(11 KM.)

FALLS OF
DOVECRAIG

Loch Tay

Allt a' Mheinn

Ardeonaig

which Sir Walter Scott considered there was one of the finest views in Britain. The fall is mentioned in old guide books as the nesting place of water ouzels.

Dubh Eas
NN 676 408

The Lawers Burn was at one time the only way by which the ascent of Ben Lawers was made. It tumbles in an interesting series of linked cascades called Dubh Eas in an old pine wood.

Sput Dubh
NN 584 261

This is the wet-weather fall high up on the mountainside above Glen Ogle which used to lend interest to the long climb out of Lochearnhead on the railway if it was a wet day. It can now be seen from the nature trail which follows the line.

Dunalastair Falls
NN 712 585

Mount Alexander was once one of the finest mansion houses in the Highlands. Its wooded grounds occupy a rocky knoll and were the work of Robertson of Struan (1688–1749), the chief of the Clan Donnachaidh, who was outlawed three times for his adherence to the Jacobite cause. The falls are situated at the end of the rock basin occupied by Loch Rannoch. They thus occupied a situation analogous to that of the Falls of Leny at the foot of Loch Lubnaig. However, the basin became silted up; so the falls were, at one time, separated from the loch by alluvial flats, which are now inundated to form the Dunalastair Reservoir. The dam is situated where the falls were. The redoubtable Lady Sarah Murray gives some account of them:

> Not half a mile below Alexander is the famous fall of the Tummel River; its noise is heard at a great distance; and it is a stop to the salmon, it being far too high for them to leap. It must be full 40 feet high . . . few equal it in majestic grandeur, at the time of a great flood, not only on account of the rise of river and the prodigious body of water in it, but chiefly for the wild appearance it exhibits, when dashing furiously, in all the different forms which can be imagined, over the huge and irregular rocks at the cataract.

It must have been a considerable fall, which makes the feat of the clansmen who jumped the Tummel at this fall all the more remarkable, for this is another MacGregor's Leap.

Falls of Allt Eachain
NN 918 625

These falls tumble into the Garry at the Pass of Killiecrankie opposite the car park for the National Trust for Scotland Visitor Centre. When it has been raining they are very fine, but the paths beside the burn are dangerously steep and the falls are difficult to approach. They are bridged by a viaduct on the Highland line in the pass.

Falls of Edinample
NN 602 225

The Burn of Ample and the Beich Burn are aligned with one another on either side of Loch Earn. They occupy long narrow valleys which owe their existance to the Loch Tay Fault which has shattered the adjacent rocks to make a belt of easily eroded countryside. The Falls of Edinample are where the Burn of Ample falls steeply to the level of Loch Earn.

There are three cascades which, although they are close to the road, cannot be seen from it. A rather awkward little path leads down the east side of the burn into a tree-filled den. The upper fall of about six metres is still obscured by a corner. The two lower falls are very picturesque and since the little burn drains a basin of 16 square kilometres there is nearly always sufficient water in it to make a visit to the falls worthwhile. They are situated in the grounds of the charming Edinample Castle, a white-washed seventeenth-century tower house, associated with the MacGregors. The house itself is not open to the public, but it is seen to great advantage across Loch Earn from the other side. In all the Falls are 20 metres in height.

Falls of Fender
NN 880 667

The vigorous Fender burn descends to the Old Bridge of Tilt from Beinn a' Ghlo. It forms three marked waterfalls between Fender Bridge and the Tilt. The uppermost fall is the highest and most attractive. The lowest fall occurs at the confluence between the two streams where the Fender makes a spectacular leap to join its sister burn, here in a gloomy gorge, in a staircase of five falls ten metres high.

Eas Eoghannan
NN 424 422

Fall above Loch Lyon.

Eas Fhiuren
NN 398 445

The fall of the stripling is situated in a remote Perthshire ravine where the headwaters of the Lyon gather. This is Duncan Ban MacIntyre country.

Garbh Dun see Falls of Gaur

Falls of Garry
NN 793 657

The Garry keeps company with the Great North Road. Wordsworth's famous line sums up the Garry of old:

> And Garry, thundering down his mountain road.

Nowadays it is one of the saddest sights in the Highlands to see the Garry, much attenuated in the summer months. Its stony bed beside the road is ugly. The river has been sacrificed in the interests of hydro-electricity, its headwaters being led from Loch Garry into the basin of the Tummel. In the winter months it is sometimes possible to see the Garry in its old form. Salmon are now prevented from ascending the river which was once one of the most notable for its salmon leaps. The principal falls are in a gorge below Struan where road and railway bridge the river together. They can be seen from what appears to be a natural rock platform at the foot of the gorge. In fact it is the foundation of a 'view house' built to enable visitors to watch the fish leaping at the falls. They were blasted in the interests of the fishery in 1907. Queen Victoria was enchanted by the Garry, noting in her diary that it was 'very fine, rolling over large stones and forming perpetual falls with birch and mountain ash growing down to the water's edge'.

Falls of Gaur   NN 465 568

These falls on the River Gaur receive notice in old guide books because they could be heard such a long way off across Rannoch Moor when the river was in spate. They are formed at the place where much of the water from that vast wasteland tumbles down into the Tummel valley. The principal fall is now marked by a weir, but some idea of the natural character of this fall, the Garbh Dun, can still be obtained. Perhaps because it is so far from other kinds of development, the loss of these falls at the point where the Road to the Isles sweeps away towards Corrour, seems to be a particularly sacrilegious act.

Sput Hoick see Falls of Turret

Hermitage Falls   NO 005 416

The principal feature of interest beside the falls on the Braan below Rumbling Bridge is the Summer House called Ossian's Hall. It was first built in 1758 for the third Duke of Atholl. Its name was changed to Ossian's Hall in 1783 and it had a chequered history. 'It was blown up and destroyed by some malicious person, much to the loss of visitors, in 1869. The miscreant was never found out, but the summer house has been re-built' (*Murray's Guide* 1894). Like many another such folly it fell into decay in the twentieth century but it was restored by the National Trust for Scotland in 1952. It is now the centrepiece of the Trust's Nature Trail beside the Dunkeld by-pass on the A9.

The classical stone summerhouse was built on a rocky bluff above an inclined fall of about six metres. It was so placed that the fall was entirely hidden by its walls. *Black's Guide* (1861) describes it in its heyday:

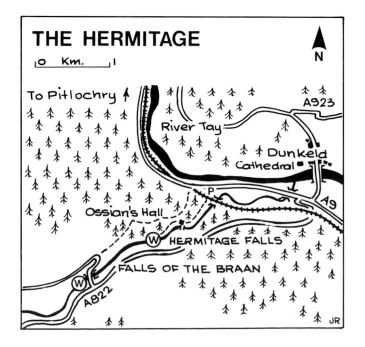

Opposite the entrance is a picture of Ossian playing upon his harp and singing songs of other times; but the panel upon which the picture is painted being suddenly drawn aside by the guide the cataract, foaming over its rocky barriers, and roaring with a voice like thunder, is revealed. The sides and ceiling of this inner apartment are lined with mirrors which reflect the waterfall under a variety of aspects, sometimes as if precipitating its torrents upon the spectator, sometimes inverted, as if rushing upwards into the air.

Wordsworth regarded such tricks with distaste and condemned the Hermitage as 'devised out of a sick man's dream'.

Gilpin considered the Hermitage Fall to be very fine—one of the grandest and most beautiful he had ever seen. Ossian's Hall was not decorated in those days, but there was a 'suitable' inscription at Ossian's Cave, further upstream, when Gilpin visited it. He went on to describe another inscription that he found:

As we passed along the higher banks, we saw another inscription engraved upon a rock within the bed of the river; and as we descended to it, we expected to see an account of some life preserved, or some natural curiosity found upon that spot; but when we arrived at it, we were informed, in fair and handsome Roman characters that a hole in the rock, near the inscription (scooped as there were many, by the vortices of the river) was on such a day, some years ago drunk full of punch by a set of gentlemen, whose names are inscribed at length. The achievement appears to have been great in its way; but one should have been sorry to see the name of a friend recorded on such an occasion.

The Nature Trail starts from the car park and passes under the Highland line. In a short distance the path is in the midst of magnificent woodland in which sycamore, oak, beech and alder are well represented, but the chief glory of this wood is its Douglas Firs. The habitat is rich in woodland plants and birds and the boisterous River Braan tumbles pleasingly beside the path. It is as fine a piece of estate woodland as there is in Central Scotland, a testimony to the Dukes of Atholl.

There are two falls of some consequence. Immediately above the bridge there is the fall at Ossian's Hall. Higher up there is a similar fall below Ossian's Cave.

The Hermitage was a place of pilgrimage for almost all of the distinguished visitors to Scotland in the eighteenth and early nineteenth centuries. They were firmly divided into two camps, those who approved of the embellishments made and those who did not. Lady Sarah Murray approved:

Every step from the house (the Duke of Atholl's House in Dunkeld) to the Hermitage is beautiful. After crossing the Tay ferry, where the banks of that smooth river are charming, winding and finely wooded. I entered a shrubbery that soon led to the river Brand, dashing through a rough bed of large stones. Opposite the shrubbery are high rocks, covered with wood, and picturesque to a great degree. As I advanced I came to lofty projecting rocks on each side of the river, striving, as it were, to kiss each other; they are united by a simple bridge of one arch through which, deep below, by a very confined rocky channel, the water forces itself; scarcely recovered from its foaming rage at the falls just above, which is partially seen through the high arch. On entering the Hermitage I was astonished. The contrast between the room, the beautiful cataract, and its scenery, is beyond description striking! The mirrors in the room so far from being absurd (as some Tourists say) multiply every object they reflect, and thereby increase the delight. A large bow window, down to the floor of the room, faces the fall, and indeed hangs over part of it; so that the reeking spray dashes in with violence, if the sashes be open. The noise of the cascade is excessive, and the view of the river above it is charming; rendered so by the great variety of small falls, wood, and projecting rocks.

Farington was more critical. He stated that Ossian's Hall was 'a mere modern summer house ill-adapted to the style of the landscape'. One of the most critical was Robert Heron:

The mirrors afford various reflections of the whitened volume of water, as it pours down the cataract; like smoke, like flame, like boiling oil. This is a conceit of which the contriver was probably very proud, but, I must confess, that I could not help considering it with sentiments other than those of admiration.

The Hermitage is the scene of a central episode in William Combe's *Doctor Prosody*. This is the sequel to the author's *Doctor Syntax*, describing a tour of Scotland, in which he mocks the kind of travels undertaken by Lady Sarah Murray and Farington. The Doctor's party arrive at the Hermitage:

It seemed to the bewitched eye
Reflected from the roof on high
To take the varied forms of flame
Which all the torrent could not tame
Of boiling oil, or reeking smoke
Pour'd o'er the precipice of the rock
Charmed with the view our Doctor fell
To sketching . . .
When Doctor's dog drew on his master
A most unheard of, dire disaster

The dog, on entering the room, sees the images of a dozen other dogs and begins crashing about the room chasing them. Doctor Prosody determined to put a stop to the tumult:

Seizing a staff he aimed a blow
Full at the dog, but, to his woe
He missed his aim, to pulverise
A glass of wondrous form and size
After much serious damage done
The cur at length is seized upon

The Doctor and his friends are obliged to offer to pay for the damage.

The falls are associated with artists as well as writers. Charles Steuart was engaged by the Duke of Atholl to paint local scenes for Blair Castle, and George Steuart, his brother, provided pictures for Ossian's Hall. Charles' picture of the Black Lynn Fall on the Braan (1766) can still be seen at Blair. The Photographer Royal, George Washington Wilson, made the Hermitage the subject of various picture postcards and stereoscopic cards in Victoria's reign.

Humble Bumble
NO 063 161

Series of murmuring little linns on the Water of May, splendidly named.

Jenny's Gush
NO 028 124

Gentle falls on open rocks in a fine wood above Dunning.

Linn of Keith
NO 178 457

The ireful Ericht crosses the Old Red Sandstone as do its sister rivers the Isla and the Esk and, like them, it has carved an

Linn of Keith. Salmon used to be so plentiful here that masters were required not to give salmon to apprentices more than three times a week. PETER DAVENPORT

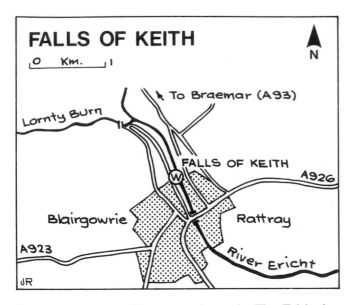

FALLS OF KEITH

0 Km. 1

N

To Braemar (A93)

Lornty Burn

FALLS OF KEITH

W

A926

Blairgowrie

Rattray

A923

River Ericht

JR

impressive gorge in this spectacular rock. The Ericht has, indeed, worked to such good effect that the falls are, perhaps, much less impressive than the gorge itself which, below Craighall, constitutes one of the most magnificent box-canyons in Scotland. The rapids in the gorge above Blairgowrie have long been impounded to provide water-power and twelve flax mills were crowded beside the river in the nineteenth century. The area is still of interest to industrial archeologists: there is a

fine disused breast-shot water-wheel at Keithbank Mill, for example.

The Falls of Keith are the principal falls in the series. The river tumbles five metres through a narrow cleft in the sandstone, reached by a fine riverside walk from the town. The falls are not so prominent as they once were as they were blasted in the interests of salmon fishing, and to render them safer. In spate the rocks are submerged, but in ordinary conditions it used to be possible to leap across the river. The alternative name for the falls is *Cargill's Leap*. They are so called because the Covenanter Donald Cargill leaped the falls after his banishment from the Barony Church in Glasgow. The leap is more difficult than it looks: numerous accidents have taken place at the falls. Higher upstream are the *Falls of Lornty* on a tributary burn.

In the seventeenth century salmon were so abundant that there was a statute, of some antiquity then, that commanded masters not to force apprentices to feed on salmon more than three times a week. The Spanish Ambassador was astonished to find that, on the Ericht, the inhabitants used neither rod nor spear to catch salmon. The obliging fish jumped into pots set on the rocks, presumably at the Falls of Keith.

Falls of Keltie   NN 862 253

Of the four sets of falls near Crieff the Falls of Keltie are the least accessible and the least spoiled. They are situated in steep woods on a tributary of the Shaggie Burn. Overgrown paths lead to the centrepiece, *Sput Ban*, an unsupported fall of about 20 metres.

Falls of Kenknock, on the upper Lochay, seen here against the Forest of Mamlorn.
HAMISH BROWN

Falls of Keltneyburn   *NN 773 497*

The Keltney, a tributary of the Lyon, drains a considerable basin under Schiehallion. It descends from the mountain pass followed by the old Military Road from Aberfeldy to Dalnacardoch by Tummel Bridge, and runs through a richly wooded dell which is a Scottish Wildlife Trust Reserve. There are three falls, all striking in spate, and the view from the confined channel of the burn is picturesque. The highest fall is 20 metres.

Above the ravine is Garth Castle built by the Wolf of Badenoch and fairly recently restored. One of his descendants caused his followers to murder his wife in the den of Keltneyburn. At the entrance to the glen is a good example of rural industrialisation in the early nineteenth century with former corn and cotton mills, a dyeworks, a smithy, and workers' cottages.

Fall of Kenknock Alternative name, used in old guides, for the Falls of Conait in Glen Lyon.

Falls of Kenknock   *NN 468 363*

These low river falls on the upper Lochay are much photographed. They are charming in themselves, but it is the backdrop provided by the peaks of the Forest of Mamlorn which completes the picture. The most prominent peak is Ben Challum.

Loups of Kenny   *NO 305 532*

These low falls on the Meglum are below the Loch of Lintrathen and correspond to the Slug of Achrannie and Reekie Linn on the Isla which joins the Meglum above Airlie Castle. The castle—the remains of an enceinte wall, gateway and tower—is attached to a classical mansion house. There is a walled garden with fine topiary and a laburnum walk in the grounds of the castle. The wild garden connected to the Den of Airlie with its superb riverside walks beside the falls in the old Red Sandstone Gorge. The garden is open under the Scottish Gardens Scheme.

Falls of Kidd Burn see Falls of Dovecraig

Falls of Killichonan   *NN 548 583*

Falls on a wild burn above Loch Rannoch.

Falls of Lawers see Dubh Eas

Falls of Lednock

The Lednock rises between Loch Earn and Loch Tay. Its headwaters and those of several other streams are impounded in Loch Lednock under Ben Chonzie and then diverted through a tunnel from the reservoir to the underground power station at St Fillans. The river follows the boundary of a mass of granite and plunges into a gloomy and precipitous gorge which marks the place where it crosses the Highland boundary Fault. The falls are situated in the broadleaved woodlands which make Strathearn so attractive. The most spectacular feature in the forge is the *De'il's Caldron* which can be seen from the Nature Trail which leads up the river to join the Hydro Board road near a tiny car park. The roaring stream cannot be seen in full, and no visitor of a timid disposition will care to dispute that this abyss may, indeed, be one of the gateways to the underworld. The fall can be impressive in spate, but there is sometimes very little water in it. Further downstream is a lower fall called the *Wee Cauldron*.

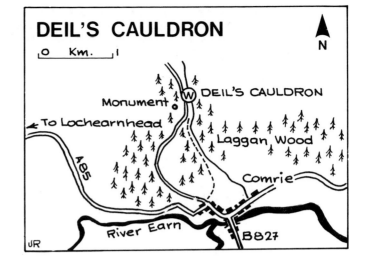

Falls of Lochay   *NN 543 351*

Of all the falls affected by the hydro electric power schemes of the Tay basin the Falls of Lochay are the sorriest sight. This is not because they have been more adversely affected, but because the essential ingredient of the glen was its quiet pastoral charm, an attractive glen delicately wooded in its lower reaches. The gorge where the falls occur marks an abrupt change in the character of the place; it resembles Chisholm's Pass in Glen Affric—above it is a much wilder kind of countryside. A general view of the falls can be had from a little hill above the lowest of them. They consist of fine cascades of white water against black rocks in a closely wooded narrowing of the glen. There are six cataracts in all in two groups of three with a considerable pool between them.

Joseph Farington is lyrical about the falls:

> The ride to it is beautiful. A little before I got to the fall I stopped at a cottage and took with me as a guide an elderly man who had all the civility which is so common in the highlands. He told me he had been a soldier and had served abroad.

> Lord Breadalbane, to whom the estate of Coilig belongs, had made good pathways to three points from which the fall may be viewed. The first point is the finest and I was equally surprised and gratified on seeing so noble a fall accompanied as it is by rocks simple in their forms, in their height and breadth proportioned to the vast body of water which fell between them. Before I saw the fall I expected to find it a pleasing garden stream not having heard it spoken of by persons who have visited this country, and was the more surprised to find it of a size and character resembling the falls of Clyde, though not equal to the two principal of those falls (Cora Linn and Stonebyres), the accompaniments above the rocks being inferior in grandeur, but superior to Bonnington Linn the third and uppermost of those falls.

> It is only a few years since this fall was noticed sufficiently to make those who tavelled through this Country acquainted with it, but it is now recommended to all who go to Killin in search of picturesque scenery *Journal* (October 1801).

Farington, and other writers, refer to these falls as the Falls of Coilig. Lady Sarah Murray was, for once, defeated by the Falls of Lochay, underestimating—as many another visitor must have done—the distance from Killin.

The most celebrated visitor to the falls was Charles Dickens who wrote enthusiastically to John Forster about them after his visit in July 1841. Dickens must be thought of by most people as essentially urban, but he was an appreciative traveller who enjoyed both Scotland and the Lakes:

> We left Lochearnhead last night and went to a place called Killin, eight miles from it, where we slept. I walked six miles with Fletcher after we got there to see a waterfall; and it was a magnificent sight, foaming and crashing down three great steeps of riven rock, leaping over the first as far as you could carry your eye, and rumbling and foaming down into a dizzy pool below you, with a deafening roar.

There is some compensaion for the attenuation of the falls, except in spate, in the stylishness of the power station. It is a fine example of the way in which modern architecture, which can be so disagreeable, can be used with finesse. Although they are modern in style the buildings, set in the middle of a finely landscaped site, have links with the traditional architecture of the district. The walls of the machine room and offices are of local stone, the roof of copper sheeting which has weathered agreeably and the facings of spruce. It is an asset to the district.

Falls of Lornty see Falls of Keith

Eas nan Luib   NN 679 171

The fall at the bend in the river, Eas nan Luib, occurs in upper Glen Artney.

MagGregor's Leap see Dunalastair Falls and Sput Ban

Falls of Milton Burn   NN 963 308

Falls on a tributary burn in Glen Almond.

Falls of Milton Eonan   NN 572 462

The splendid mountain pass between Loch Tay and Glen Lyon descends beside a roaring mountain burn which joins the Lyon at the Brig' o' Balgy. There is a succession of splendid mountain falls on the burn above the little township.

Falls of Milton Roro   NN 623 466

Roaring falls above the Lyon on the Allt a Chobhair, the foaming burn.

Falls of Moness   NN 852 474

These very famous falls were considered by MacCulloch to be among the four finest in Scotland, and they are justly celebrated. A succession of famous visitors to the Highlands all comment favourably on them. Burns' description is the most distinguished:

> The braes ascend like lofty wa's
> The foaming stream deep roaring fa's
> O'er hung wi' fragrant spreading shaws
>   The Birks of Aberfeldy

> The hoary cliffs are crowned wi' flowers
> While o'er the linn the burnie pours
> And rising weets, wi' misty showers
>   The Birks of Aberfeldy.

It is generally considered that Burns confused Aberfeldy with Abergeldie on Deeside, for his poem is based on an old folk tune from those parts, and there is a singular absence of

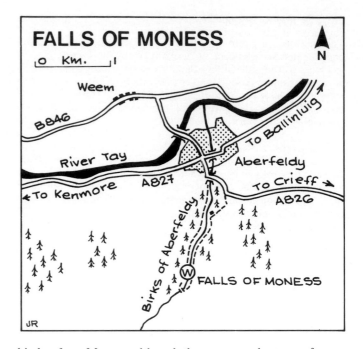

birches from Moness, although there seem to be trees of every other variety in abundance. These things do not matter in the least because the poem has brought lasting fame to Aberfeldy. In contrast to the rather pretentious heroic couplets which Burns chose for his poem about the Fall of Foyers, the metre seems to be exactly right for this delightful den which is the setting of the Falls of Moness.

Lady Sarah Murray, too, reserves her warmest praises for the uppermost fall:

> The water then spreads and forms one of the most beautiful cataracts in nature.

Aberfeldy takes its name from the uruisg, or water sprite, Pheallaidh who was supposed locally to have his domain near the upper fall. From the village this fall is reached by a walk of about three kilometres from the car park at the foot of the glen. The lower part of the glen consists of fairly open woodland beside the clear rocky bed of the Urlar Burn, but the glen soon narrows and trees and shrubs crowd in on one another, clinging to the steep banks down which tributary streams tumble to form the first falls seen. There are three falls in all, the lower and middle falls being quite commonplace. The upper fall which cascades splendidly into a natural amphitheatre is 15 metres high.

There is an excellent little guide to the falls prepared by the Scottish Wildlife Trust in conjunction with the District Council.

Falls of Monzie   NN 885 253

The Shaggie Burn, apart from its atmospheric name, is noteworthy for the private hydro-electric scheme which provides power for the estate. There are three falls, the highest of which is 16.5 metres. They occur in the deep wooded gorge above the Castle. The most open and attractive of the falls occurs at the bridge reached from the Wade Road close to the Foulford Inn.

Falls of Allt Mor   NN 662 588

These are the very striking falls in Kinloch Rannoch. The Allt Mor slides in a most undisciplined way over huge rocks right into the middle of the village. The steep part of the burn's course is about 100 metres in height and, in spate, the falls present a formidable sight. Lady Sarah Murray's comment was: "I never beheld so singular a cataract."

Eas Mor   *NN 536 453*

This is the fall on the Lyon at the great bend in the river between Gallin and Moar. The falls sometimes go under the names of these two places. Eas Mor is often the name given to the first fall on a river to stop fish.

Linn of Muckersie   *NO 075 155*

The water of May rises above the remote Ochil village of Path of Condie. It is famous for its agates which are found in the vesicular lavas of these hills and these orange-red stones can be found in the stream which, at the linn, forms a characteristic fall in an Old Red Sandstone gorge.

Falls of Ness   *NN 885 157*

Fall in Old Red Sandstone on the Machany Water near Muthill.

Falls of Ochtertyre see Falls of Turret

Fall of Allt Ollach   *NN 584 261*

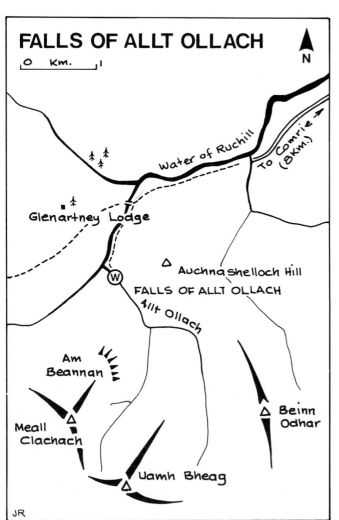

By far the most attractive falls in Glen Artney are close to Glenartney Lodge. At the end of the public road there is a car park and picnic place. From it there is a pleasant little walk to be had to the Falls of the Allt Ollach. These charming falls remain hidden until the last moment. The burn tumbles 18 metres over a series of four cascades, the greater part of the fall occurring where the burn descends over two rock walls at the foot of the series. This unexpected little dell is finely situated under Am Beannean, an outlier of Uamh Bheag. The falls are not well known and the visitor will probably be undisturbed.

Eas Pheallaidh   *NN 653 475*

The mischievous water sprite that gave its name to Aberfeldy left its footprint, so they say, at Craig Dianaidh in Glen Lyon. Another lair which it occupied was the wooded ravine of the Inverinain Burn where these falls occur.

Reekie Linn   *NO 255 537*

Reekie Linn is the finest fall of its kind in the East of Scotland. It is close to the Bridge of Craig on the Glen Isla road at Kilry. In ordinary conditions there is a fall of six metres followed by a fall of 18 metres which, in spate, unite to form a single fall of great beauty. The Isla is one of the most considerable rivers unaffected by abstraction on which such a notable fall of this kind occurs. It is comparable with the Falls of Kirkaig and the Falls of the Braan. The apron of white water is precipitated into a plunge pool 36 metres deep. At the bottom of the fall is a cave called the Black Dub where, it is said, the local laird, having killed a man, hid from the law. However, in the middle of the night, he saw the devil in the form of a black dog and gave himself up the following day.

The fall is reached by a short walk from the bridge and footpaths lead to it on both sides of the river. That on the south side leads through a wooded estate. That on the north side is probably the more popular of the two and it leads across a charming meadow before reaching the fine open pine wood at the head of the fall. There are a variety of viewpoints including a splendid promontory full in the face of the fall. The amphitheatre in which the fall is situated is embowered by oak, birch and various conifers. It is a truly imposing place.

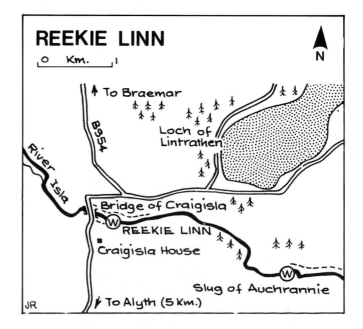

Sput Rolla   *NN 729 284*

Eight kilometres from Comrie by the Hydro Board road to Loch Lednock is Sput Rolla, now much attenuated except when the river is in spate. It is a spectacular and unusual fall of the apron type situated in a cleft in prominent rocks immediately below the dam. This is an impressive structure, rendered awe-inspiring by the knowledge that it is specially reinforced to make allowance for the earthquakes known to occur on the Highland Boundary Fault. In spite of the reassurance, one would prefer not to be present if a 'quake occurred. Sput Rolla is a high fall and it is well worth visiting after rain.

Sput Rollo see Sput Rolla

Rumbling Bridge Falls see Falls of Braan (Dunkeld)

Falls of Tarf   *NN 982 796*

Few falls so remotely situated have been the subject of so notable a painting as the oil by R P Leitch depicting Queen Victoria crossing the falls. This crossing, made by Victoria in October 1861—not such a great achievement, perhaps, as some of her mountain expeditions, but a remarkable journey none-the-less—was also the subject of a drawing by Carl Haag. It is recorded by Victoria in her diaries:

> After luncheon we set off again. I walked a few paces; but as it was very wet and the road very rough by Albert's desire I got on again. A very few minutes brought us to the celebrated ford of Taff (Poll Tarff as it is called), which is very deep— and after heavy rain almost impassable. The Duke offered to lead the pony on one side and talked of Sandy for the other side, but I asked for Brown (whom I have far more confidence in) on the other side. Sandy MacAra, the guide, and two pipers went first, playing all the time. To all appearances the ford of the Tarf is not deeper than other fords, but, once in it, the men were above their knees— and suddenly in the middle, where the current from the fine, high, full falls is very strong, it was nearly up to the men's waists.

The expedition through Glen Tilt is still a very fine one. The Falls of Tarf are 19 kilometres from the Old Bridge of Tilt and it is a further 16 kilometres to the Linn of Dee. The mountain

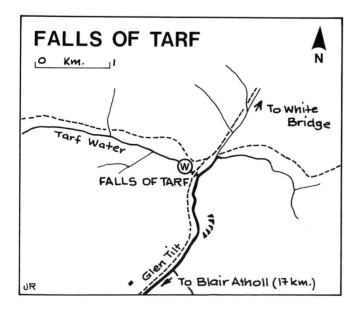

trench occupied by Glen Tilt is walled on its southern side by Beinn a' Ghlo, reckoned to be as extensive as some English counties. But one must not underestimate the extent of the mountains to the north in which the Tarf, a more considerable stream than the Tilt, rises. More than three kilometres from its junction with the Tilt, the Tarf flows over bare rock slides and forms a series of falls in a steadily deepening gorge which, like that of the Tilt, is eroded along a shatter belt of less resistant rock. The finest of the falls cannot be seen from the crossing in Glen Tilt, but it can be viewed by climbing the slope on the north bank.

The Tarf is now bridged by the Bedford Memorial Bridge erected in memory of an Englishman who was swept to his death trying to cross the Tilt in 1879. Visitors should take note of the evidence provided by this statement—the month was August, and he was trying to cross the Tilt because the Tarf was impassable. An expedition to these falls should only be undertaken after due consideration and their further exploration should only be undertaken with extreme care. However, the main staircase of three falls is very fine and an expedition to see them will be amply rewarded.

Falls of Glen Tarken   *NN 668 252*

These falls were at one time a highlight of the railway journey from Crieff to Lochearnhead. They are now somewhat difficult of access, but the river tumbles in a succession of falls of the same type as the Falls of Cruachan.

Falls of Tilt   *NN 876 654*

Falls on the Tilt above the Old Bridge of Tilt. The falls three kilometres above Blair Castle have been removed by blasting in the interests of salmon-fishing. The falls on the Tilt are low, but it is a fine mountain river, full of interest.

Eas Torra Mhoir   *NN 462 558*

This fall occupies the same position on the Blackwater, a tributary of the Gaur, as the Garbh Dun. Like it, it is subject to major abstraction, which is a great pity in such a remote place.

Linn of Tummel   *NN 907 600*

The height of the Fall of Tummel, where the river narrowed and leaped five metres into a swirling pool, has been reduced by the establishment of Loch Faskally. The National Trust for Scotland had the happy idea of renaming the place the Linn of Tummel.

The Linn is now no more than a rapid, but it is very finely set, and just as much of an attraction as ever it was. This kind of loss, where the fall is eliminated by the raising of the level of the water below it, is the opposite of the kind where the fall is lost by the abstraction of water above it. Since, in the latter case, the fall is generally restored in spate, this kind of loss must be counted the more serious. At the Linn of Tummel there is more of a fall of water, of course, in dry conditions. Since the Fall of Tummel was counted one of the finest in Scotland, and it is the only one of the premier tourist attractions to have been submerged, this must be counted the greatest depredation by the Hydro Board, but the greatest possible care has been taken in the matter and, artificial though the environment is, it is not without its interest to the discriminating visitor.

However, the loss of this site should not be minimised. John MacCulloch's description (1824) suggests what it was like:

> It is a peculiar and rare merit of the cascade of Tummel, that

it is beautiful in itself, almost without the aid of its accompaniments. Though the water breaks white, almost throughout, the forms are so graceful, so varied, and so well-marked, that we can look at it long, without being wearied at the monotony and without attending to the surrounding landscape. Whether low or full, whether the river glides transparent over the rocks, to burst in foam below, or whether it descends like a torrent of snow from the very edge, this fall is always various and always graceful. The immediate accompaniments are, however, no less beautiful and appropriate; and the general landscape is, at the same time, rich and romantic; nothing being left to desire, to render this one of the most brilliant scenes which our country produces.

A granite obelisk near the old falls marks the visit of Queen Victoria in 1841 and there are various other memorials. Swinburne used to bathe here and, in his letters, he attacks the memorial in his most roguish vein:

The Tummil is here very pretty, but much defiled by memories and memorials of the Royal Family. At the waterfalls—significant of who shall say what other effusions?—Her Majesty has set up—I should say erected—a phallic emblem in stone; a genuine Priapic erection like a small obelisk, engraved with her name and the date of the event commemorated, whatever that may have been. It is an object which would surely have caused 'our orphan' to blush and shed a few tears. As I presume, it stands there forever, in honourable reward of the late Prince Consort's virility, it should have borne (instead of the hackneyed 'Sic Sedebat') the inscription: 'Sic Arrigebat Albertus Bonus.'

The falls deserve to be known for this rich joke if for nothing else. However, they were the subject of a notable painting by Lionel Constable in 1851, one always attributed to him, and of watercolours by various other artists including William Beattie Brown, John Blake MacDonald and Waller H Paton. Many writers refer to the falls. James Hogg visited them in 1802:

Visited the fall of Tummel, a fine cataract—was surprised to hear that salmon sometimes ascended it; but this was not the only instance I had as proof of the courage and agility of the Highland salmon, having seen sundry other great falls some of them higher than this, which they ascended annually in great numbers and which it would never have entered the heads of our salmon to have attempted.

There is now a delightful National Trust for Scotland Nature Trail leading to the Linn of Tummel, established in 1970. The old fall, set in its fine woods and backed by Creag Toor Fionn, was reached by the Old Bridge of Garry, now gone as well, but replaced by a good-looking modern bridge. A path led to the road further on and eventually to the Queen's View. It was generally agreed that the best view of the fall was to be had from the south bank where it is backed by the hill of the waterfall, Tor an Eas. This is reached by going upstream to the Coronation Bridge erected to celebrate the Coronation of King George V.

Falls of Turret
NN 839 243

Just above Crieff the Earn is joined by the Turret. The name means the little dry one, no doubt because the river often disappeared in its own boulder-strewn course, even before the building of the Turret Reservoir, one of the largest public water supply undertakings in Scotland. Sadly, the renowned Falls of Turret, of which the principal fall is *Sput Hoick*, have been considerably affected by this scheme. The falls are about three kilometres north of the mansion house of Ochtertyre which is surrounded by one of the grandest private woodlands in Scotland, noted for its tall trees. The alternative name for the falls is the *Falls of Ochtertyre*. They occur where the Turret crosses the Highland Boundary Fault, and they are reached either from the house or from Crieff by the hamlet of Hosh. Sput Hoick is ten metres high, a fine unsupported fall. Ratcliffe Barnett writes lyrically about Ochtertyre:

These woods at dawn are full of bird music. Later on the cuckoo haunts the hills with its wandering voice. The little brown squirrels run wild. Flowers star the pathways— primroses, anemones, hyacynthe—and always the found of falling water fills the glade Turret with a delicious sheen.
 On a flat bluff rock overlooking the deep linn of the falls there is a seat. You look right down the little valley to the distant hills of Ochill. To me, in the early spring, it is the

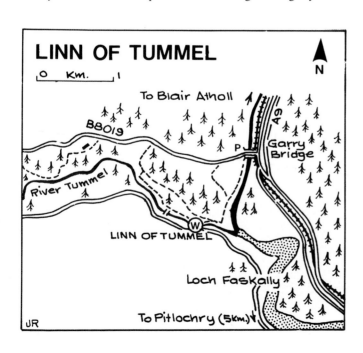

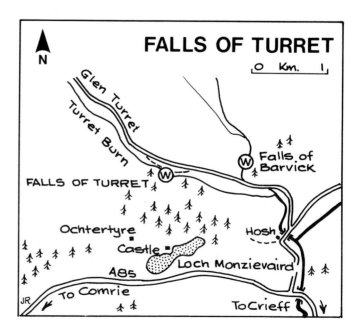

Valley of the Purple Mist. For just before the trees break into greenery, the tangle of a million twigs in this wooded gorge of the river makes a transparent mist of purple-grey, delicate, elusive and far more beautiful than all the later leafage of summer. Behind the seat a mass of red osiers fills the lush hollow by the path, making a crimson glow beneath the trees. Such are the early beauties of these glades and glens—purple mist in the valley and crimson fire in a dingle of the wood.

Falls of Tyndrum   NN 345 287

These falls occur on the trunk stream of the Tay at the bridge near Tyndrum on the A82. The river Cononish tumbles very attractively over a band of flaggy schists.

Fall of Urrard   NN 925 650

A rude stone in the grounds of Urrard House marks, if local tradition is to be believed, the spot where Dundee received his mortal wound at the Battle of Killiecrankie. It is for this reason that the name Urrard is known, if it is known at all. Claverhouse's Stone is marked on the map, and the tale is well told in the National Trust for Scotland Visitor centre which clings to the side of the road above the Soldier's Leap on the Garry. Near Urrard House is the beautiful cascade of An t-Eas, the waterfall, formed by the Allt Girnaig. MacCulloch asserted that he considered it one of the four most beautiful cascades in Scotland: a Perthshire man must be allowed a little prejudice in favour of his native county. It is certainly surprising that the fall has received very little notice in guide books since *Black's Guide* of 1861; nor is the fall marked on the old six-inch County Map, or the new 1:50,000 map. It is a very good example of the way in which scenes which delighted the Victorians have been neglected in modern times.

The fall is reached either from Druid or from the by-road from Aldclune which climbs into a splendid open birchwood above the Pass of Killiecrankie. The prospect of Ben Vrackie and across the pass is very fine indeed. Just before the fall is reached there is a grand view over the moors to Beinn a' Ghlo.

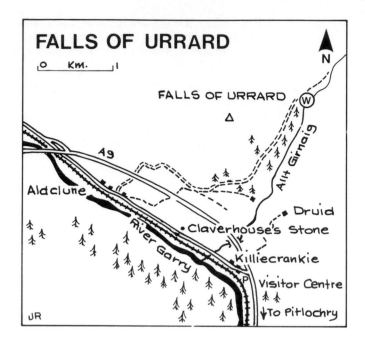

The fall itself is best reached from the left bank of the burn. The Allt Girnaig pitches from a wooded gorge into a lovely pool. The fall is about ten metres high, somewhat diminished by abstraction, but not rendered unattractive by it. It is a straight fall against an impressive rock face in singularly beautiful surroundings.

York Cascade   NN 874 662

This is the attractive fall on a tributary of the Tilt in the grounds of Blair Castle. It is so named to mark the appointment of one of the family as Archbishop of York. It is the subject of an etching in Pennant's *Tour*, although few would recognise it as a likeness.

NORTH EAST SCOTLAND

Principal Falls

Outstanding Falls	Touring Centre
Falls of Badan Mosach	Kingussie
Falls of Foyers	Fort Augustus

Significant Falls

Altnarie	Forres
Falls of Bachnagairn	Glen Cova
Feith Buidhe	Cairngorms
Black Falls	Fort Augustus
Allt na Cailliche	Invergarry
Falls of Dee	Cairngorms
Falls of Divach	Drumnadrochit
Falls of Eidart	Kingussie
Falls of Coire Garbhlach	Kingussie
Garbh Uisge	Cairngorms
Landseer's Falls	Kingussie
Linn of Muick	Ballater
Falls of Coire Odhar	Cairngorms
Falls of Unich	Glen Esk

Interesting Falls

Linn of Avon	Tomintoul
Corrimony Falls	Drumnadrochit
Cullachy Falls	Fort Augustus
Falls of Drumly Harry	Brechin
Loups of Esk	Glen Esk
Den Fenella	St Cyrus
Falls of Feugh	Banchory
Falls of the Glasallt	Ballater
Falls of Knockie	Fort Augustus
Falls of Lui	Braemar
Falls of Moriston	Invermoriston
Linn of Quoich	Braemar
Linn of Ruthrie	Charlestown of Aberlour
Allt Saigh	Invermoriston
The Stulan	Ballater
Falls of Tarff	Fort Augustus
Falls of Torgarrow	Forres
Falls of Truim	Newtonmore
Falls o' the Derry Lochan Uaine	Cairngorms

Also recommended:

Loup of Edzell	Edzell
Linn of Dee	Braemar
Falls of Allt Ladaidh	Invergarry
Vat Falls	Ballater

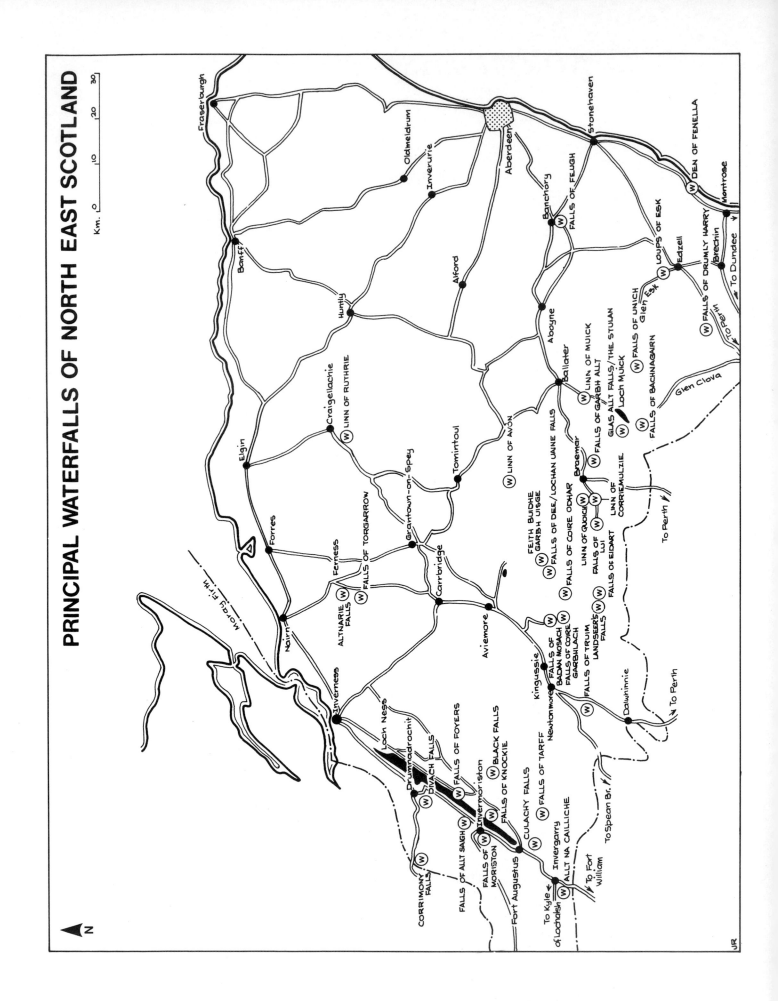

PRINCIPAL WATERFALLS OF NORTH EAST SCOTLAND

N

Km. 0   10   20   30

Fraserburgh
Oldmeldrum
Inverurie
Aberdeen
Banchory
W FALLS OF FEUGH
Stonehaven
DEN OF FENELLA W
Banff
Alford
Aboyne
Ballater
W LINN OF MUICK
FALLS OF UNICH
Loups of Esk
Glen Esk W
Edzell
W FALLS OF DRUMLY HARRY
Montrose
To Dundee
Brechin
To Perth
W FALLS OF BACHNAGAIRN
W FALLS OF GARBH ALLT
GLAS ALLT FALLS/THE STULAN W
Loch Muick W
Glen Clova
Huntly
Craigellachie
W LINN OF RUTHRIE
Elgin
Grantown-on-Spey
Tomintoul
W LINN OF AVON
Braemar
LINN OF QUOICH W
W FALLS OF COIRE ODHAR
FALLS OF DEE/LOCHAN UAINE FALLS W
FEITH BUIDHE
GARBH UISGE W
LINN OF LUI W
FALLS OF LUI
LINN OF CORRIEMULZIE
W FALLS OF EIDART
To Perth
Forres
Ferness
W FALLS OF TORGARROW
Carrbridge
Moray Firth
Nairn
ALTNARIE FALLS W
W
Aviemore
Kingussie
FALLS OF BADAN MOSACH W
FALLS OF COIRE GARBHILACH W
LANDSEER'S FALLS W
W FALLS OF TRUIM
Dalwhinnie
To Perth
Inverness
Loch Ness
Drumnadrochit
DIVACH FALLS W
W FALLS OF FOYERS
Invermoriston
BLACK FALLS W
FALLS OF KNOCKIE
CULACHY FALLS W
W FALLS OF TARFF
Newtonmore
To Spean Br.
CORRIMONY FALLS W
FALLS OF ALLT SAIGH W
FALLS OF MORISTON W
Fort Augustus
Invergarry
ALLT NA CAILLICHE W
To Kyle of Lochalsh
To Fort William

JR

Waterfalls of North East Scotland

Many a burn in unknown corries
Down dark linns the white foam flings
Fringed with ruddy-berried rowans
Fed from everlasting springs

Linn of Dee. *A good example of a waterfall that has almost worn itself out. A small dyke downstream probably marks the site of the original fall.*

Queen Victoria opened the granite bridge in 1857. PETER DAVENPORT

North East Scotland is here taken to comprehend the Grampian Region; those parts of the Highland region drained by the Spey and the Ness, and the Angus Glens. It thus includes almost all of the Cairngorms and the mountains between Strath Spey and Loch Ness. The Beauly and its tributaries are excluded as is the Isla in Perthshire. The rivers of the region reach the sea between Inverness and Montrose. One hundred and twenty-five waterfalls are identified.

The range of hills south of the Dee, the North and South Esks have fine valleys. These Angus Glens with wild corries at their heads and delightful river scenery where their streams cross the sandstone at their foot have a number of grand waterfalls which bear comparison with other Cairngorm glens.

John Hill Burton's description of the Cairngorms still applies although it was written in 1864:

> The depth and remoteness of the solitude, the huge mural precipices, the deep chasms between the rocks, waterfalls of unknown height, the hoary remains of the primaeval forest, the fields of eternal snow, and the deep black lakes at the foot of the precipices are full of such associations of awe and grandeur and mystery, as no other scenery in Britain is capable of arousing.

Two great rivers, the Spey and the Dee, drain much of the Cairngorms and provide a focus of interest, but the region between the Cairngorm Hills and the sea is complex so far as drainage is concerned, and the Findhorn, the Lossie, the Deveron, the Ythan and the Don all occupy considerable valleys. There is, too, a host of other, smaller streams which require consideration.

The Dee rises at a greater elevation than any other river in the British Isles and, although it is more than 125km long, the declivity of its course is considerable. No river has a more spectacular start. The Dee falls 150 metres over the lip of the Great Corrie of Braeriach and there is no more awe-inspiring sight in the Cairngorms than the Dee Waterfall seen from the Angel's Peak. The rushing river drains the mountain corridor through

Falls of Garbh Allt, *in the forest of Ballochbuie which was purchased by Queen Victoria in 1878.* PETER DAVENPORT

which the famous hill pass, the Lairig Ghru, makes for Mar Lodge. The long track marches with the river, its fords, its bridges and its waterfalls marking the long miles to Royal Deeside.

At the Linn of Dee, a rocky gorge 150 metres long, the river falls 15 metres. In reality it is an old waterfall, once much more precipitate than it now is, but over the course of geological time the river has worked its way back to virtually eliminate the fall. This illustrates the principal of 'grading', the tendency of rivers to even out the profile of their beds and, below the Linn, the Dee is much more evenly graded. However, although the Dee has a reasonably well-graded course, almost all of its tributaries tumble over falls to reach it. At the Slog of Dess, for example, there is a prominent fall at the edge of an outcrop of granite and the acid waters of the burn have cut a gorge below this in limestone. The waterfalls of the middle Dee attracted the interest of Queen Victoria and stories about the Royal Family add interest to many of them. The Dee, with its superb woods and its royal associations, is one of the most attractive rivers in Scotland.

Much of the Grampian Region consists of a relatively low lying tableland, the Buchan Plateau. The main rivers occupy broad straths and are relatively evenly graded. The Ythan, for example, only falls 240 metres in a course of 42 kilometres from its source to the sea. There are low falls at Auchterless, but otherwise the Ythan is a gentle stream. The Deveron, which flows into the North Sea at Banff, offers fine sport for salmon and trout fishermen, but there are few waterfalls in its basin. Where smaller streams fall into the sea from the edge of the plateau there are attractive dens with charming falls which add interest to a stay in such pleasant places as Buckie or Cullen. Like the Ythan and the Deveron, the Don is a fine salmon river but that part of its course where one might expect to find most falls has been 'beheaded' and is now occupied by the Avon, the main tributary of the Spey and there are, in fact, many fine falls there. The chief interest, so far as waterfalls are concerned, is thus concentrated on the Dee.

Speyside now enjoys an international reputation for tourism. Rivers are one of the keys to this. The Spey is a swift river, unusual in that it falls further in the lower part of its course than it does in the middle, but it is a river of rapids rather than waterfalls. There is no spectacular fall easily accessible to all and, apart from the wet-weather fall near Cluny's Cage, the falls of the Spey play a small part in the landscape which the average tourist sees. The river and its tributaries are more significant for canoeing and fishing, and for providing sweet water for whisky. This makes those falls which there are – and there are many fine cataracts in the Spey Basin – relatively private places worth seeking out.

For all the traffic which passes up the Great North Road from Perth to Inverness, few folk visit the Falls of Truim, beside the road, and fewer still may visit this charming gorge now that the road has been improved. There are several other falls on the headwaters of the Spey which can be visited from Newtonmore. There are also fine falls in Glen Feshie and Glen Avon. Above Achlean, in Glen Feshie, are the Falls of Badan Mosach,

in fine Caledonian pine-woods, as exquisite a combination of wood and falling water as there is in Scotland. The Cairngorms are scarred by gigantic corrie cliffs, and deep glens drain these level moorlands. Where the little burns which have gathered water on the plateau tumble to the floor of the glens there are fine corrie waterfalls like the Falls of Coire Odhar in Gleann Einich. In the valley of the lower Spey where the river flows through a deep trench, there are attractive falls on tributary burns.

The River Findhorn is perhaps the most exciting in Scotland. The upper part of its course is through wild moorlands, but below Drynachan it becomes wooded, and below Dulsie Bridge richly so. Throughout its course there is a succession of incised meanders and rock gorges in crystalline schists, granite and Old Red Sandstone. The river and its tributaries are subject to sudden heavy floods, due to the constricted nature of its course. The most spectacular floods occurred in 1829, the river rising forty feet at Dulsie Bridge and fifty feet at Randolph's Leap.

The little river Lossie rises in the bleak moorlands south of Dallas and follows a winding course to Elgin. At Kellas there is a marked series of river terraces and, further downstream, a series of rocky gorges through which the river flows in a succession of rapids. The grandest fall is, however, on a tributary burn, the Leonach at the Ess of Glenlatterach.

The basin of the Spey and the basins of the adjacent rivers have few falls that are well-known, but the river scenery of these basins is probably unsurpassed in Scotland.

The hinterland of Inverness is extensive. The Ness itself has a number of considerable tributaries which are really separate rivers. They drain the heart of the Highlands and their basins embrace much renowned loch scenery. Their tributaries stretch far into the interior where the low moors of the east culminate in extensive peaks close to the west coast. Distances are great and, sometimes, the scenery is, frankly, dull, but there is a distinctive quality about these blue-brown deer forests which epitomises the Central Highlands. It is generally agreed that the view of the mountains at the head of Loch Quoich from the Pass of Glengarry is the finest to be had from a public road in Scotland.

The principal geological feature is the Great Glen. This huge, glacially-deepened, rift gives rise to what is probably the best-known fall in Scotland, the Fall of Foyers. The Farigaig, its companion stream, probably once formed an equally impressive fall, now eliminated over the course of geological time. There are other falls, similar to Foyers although situated on smaller streams, which occupy the steep slope between the 'lake district' which stands on a shelf above the great glen and Loch Ness. Opposite, there are torrential falls on the steep slopes on the western side of the Loch, but in several places the wall is breached by larger rivers which issue from the remote watershed above the west coast and have much more evenly graded courses. These mountains have the heaviest rainfall in the North, Loch Quoich averaging 2880mm. The Moriston makes the most imposing river falls in the Highlands where it joins the Great Glen.

The Basins of the North and South Esks

Arbirlot Falls
NO 608 402

Arbirlot – the ford of Elliot – gets its name from the Elliot Water which falls to the coast through the splendid Den of Kellie where there is an attractive fall, above which is the parish church in an ancient graveyard. Kelly Castle is further downstream. Arbirlot Bridge is a favourite subject for post cards.

Bachnagairn Fall
NO 242 747

This is the principal fall in Glen Clova. Bachnagairn belongs to Balmoral and the shooting lodge, from which a fine path crosses to Loch Muick, is beside the brawling South Esk amid pines and larches. The lodge is now ruined, but its site is highly attractive. The fall, where the river leaps eighteen metres, is almost hidden in the trees.

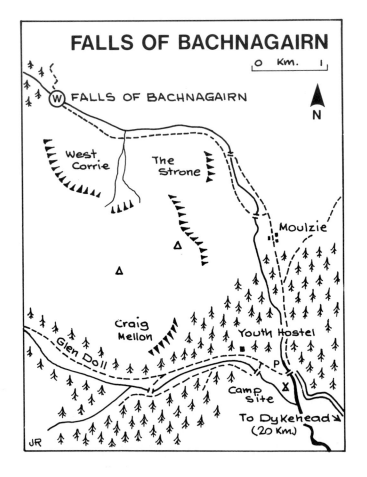

Buckie Den
NO 694 524

This is a ravine with waterfalls from six to nine metres high situated near Lunan Bay.

The Falls of Damff
NO 385 792

Stag Falls are hidden in the upper part of the spectacular gorge of the Unich. The Falls of Unich can be easily reached without leaving the valley floor, but to reach the Falls of Damff it is necessary to follow the mountain path which crosses the mica-schist terraces at the foot of Hunt Hill and climbs to the plateau above. There is a fine wet weather fall hanging on the crags of Hunt Hill above the path. Mountain hares and deer haunt this gorge. There is only one easy way to reach the heather covered tableland and it is essential to follow the path. At the head of the staircase of white water which falls below the path are the falls, two sensational leaps of the curtain type. The Unich falls over a smooth rock wall in a mass of turbulent water of singular impressiveness. The falls drop away from the spectator on the path and have a total height of about twenty four metres. Between the Falls of Damff and the Falls of Unich, the Water of Unich tumbles 230 metres. The only fit comparison is with Glomach, and, of remote mountain falls, these may be equalled, but they are not surpassed. It is possible to return to Loch Lee by going on towards Unich Stables, crossing the Unich and following the path which descends by the Shank of Inchgrundle. The Falls of Damff are 7.5 kilometres from Loch Lee Kirk.

The Falls of Drumly Harry
NO 452 624

These extraordinarily named falls occur on the Noran, a tributary of the South Esk which drains Glen Ogil. This little valley lies between Glen Lethnot and Glen Clova and contains a reservoir. The falls are above Easter Ogil and are reached by a farm road which leads from the house to the hills beyond above the left bank of the stream. A faint path goes through thickety woods to the brink of a deep ravine in which the falls are situated. There is some evidence of old paths, but today the falls are quite inaccessible from above. The only way to see them properly and inspect them at close quarters is to walk up the burn. They can, however, be seen from above where rhododendron bushes cling to the steep loose soil of a near vertical slope. The Noran turns a corner and there are two closely spaced falls of about four metres before the little river plunges into a cauldron called Dout Hole and through a narrow

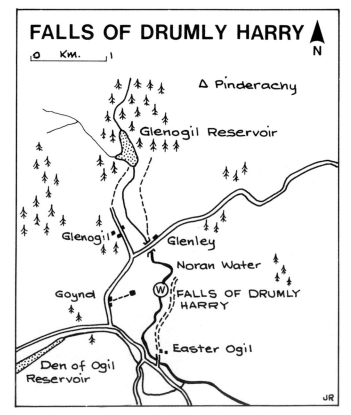

water chute to precipitate its water to the floor of the ravine. This fall, a mass of white spray, is about ten metres in height. On the opposite bank, from which no better view can be obtained, is the site of a former castle which guarded the entrance to the glen.

There is no accounting for the strange name. It does not seem to be a corruption of the Gaelic. Drumly means turbulent and that is appropriate enough, but there is no explanation for Harry.

The Loup of Edzell   *NO 573 689*

Edzell Castle and Garden are at the entrance to Glen Lethnot, the valley of the West Water. Unusually, the Castle is situated a good distance from the river but the map indicates an older site called Castle Hillock further on. Just beyond this is a car park from which access can be gained to the river in its wooded gorge. The river is crossed by a footbridge and a path follows the West Water for less than a kilometre to the Loup, a fine fall of about three metres where the river crosses massive blocks of sandstone tilted against the current. There is a variety of trees with birch and hazel prominent. On the other bank is a grand holly tree. The place is plagued with rabbits.

The Loups of Esk   *NO 593 717*

At the Rocks of Solitude the North Esk enters a stretch of eight kilometres of unsurpassed loveliness. Its red sandstone gorge is flanked by the superb riverside estate of the Burn. The river has cut a series of deep pots in the rock and the Loups are a series of little falls by way of which it descends sweetly to well below the noted old bridge at Gannochy. The gorge is

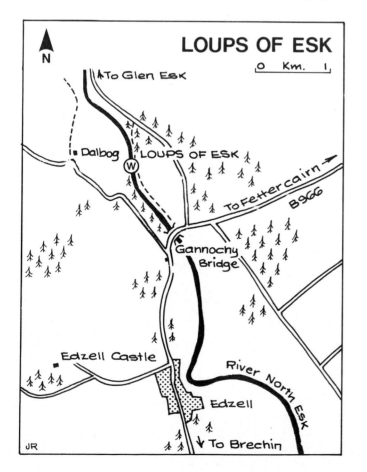

magnificently wooded – a cultivated woodland with many deciduous trees. The house was built in 1891 and the grounds were carefully laid out with fine paths to show off the exquisite river scenery. A suspension bridge, the Loups Bridge, built near the principal fall, is now disused.

Access to the river at the Rocks of Solitude can be obtained from the Loch Lee road near a folly. There is a further marked fall here.

Den Fenella   *NO 771 665*

Den Fenella is half way between Inverbervie and Montrose on the A92. Fenella's Castle is some miles away close to the Cairn o'Mounth road and it is there that Fenella is said to have murdered King Kenneth III by means of a fiendish device: a bronze image of the king holding an apple which, when he took it, released a hail of arrows from behind an arras. After the murder Fenella fled and allegedly fell to her death in the Den near St Cyrus. The dramatic fall, twenty metres high, is certainly a place where one could kill oneself and whether the legend is true or not it lends atmosphere to the place. The fall is immediately under the road bridge and is reached by a path which begins at the road. From the viaduct on the now disused Bervie Railway there is a grand view of the cascade.

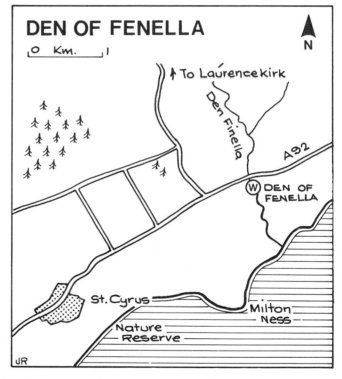

Falls of Corrie Fee   *NO 242 747*

Corrie Fee is generally considered to be the finest mountain corrie in Angus.

Gracie's Linn   *NO 488 807*

In his fine book on the Cairngorms, Adam Watson (1975) rates Glen Esk the loveliest of the Angus Glens.

> Its long twisting course surpasses most Highland glens in variety, with fine old birch woods, bright green bracken, bare heathery hills, river shingles and linns, and prosperous

hill farms. Higher up stretch·vast plateaux of peaty moors, wild glens with rugged cliffs, and high stony hills.

The mixed character of the glen is nowhere better revealed than in the valley of its principal tributary, the Tarf which has its gathering grounds in the bowl of hills crossed by the Fir Mounth and Fungle tracks. Gracie's Linn is situated beside the road to the Baillies, a remote hill farm and is reached in 2km from Tarfside after crossing a bridge over a tributary burn. The little river runs in a low gorge at the foot of which is an appealing bathing pool where the water runs still and deep for some metres. The linn is a little way upstream from the pool where a great boulder is jammed across the gorge forming a twin fall some three metres high. From the bank above the stream you can see, in one direction, broad heather-clad hills – the Hill of Cat and the Hill of St Colm included – and in the other are the green farmlands and rich woods of the Lower Esk. Dominating the scene, on the top of the Hill of Rowan, is the monument erected by Fox Maule, the arrogant Earl of Dalhousie, who erected it to himself (and some others) while he was still alive.

The Falls of Mark   NO 394 833

Queen Victoria crossed from Balmoral to Glen Mark by the Ladder in September 1861. Below the cottage there is the Queen's Well, a Victorian edifice with a massive canopy erected by Fox Maule, Earl of Dalhousie, who rode to the march to meet her. The Queen refers to the very pure White Well in her account of the visit. Above the cottage there is a series of falls on the Water of Mark. They can be reached by paths on either side of the river. The path on the right bank passes a Jacobite refuge among the rocks.

The Loups of Noran Water   NO 471 602

These are low falls below Noranside. The North Esk is a fine spring salmon river and the removal of weirs lower downstream mean that pools like those at the Loups of Noran are sometimes overcrowded.

The Trollochy   NO 880 798

The splendid cliffed coast south of Stonehaven has many attractions for the sight-seer. At Crawton a fine waterfall, the Trollochy, goes headlong over the cliffs.

Falls of Unich   NO 385 800

At the head of Glen Esk the principal affluent of Loch Lee is joined by a major tributary, the Water of Unich, which forms most spectacular falls underneath the frowning cliffs of Craig Maskeldie and Hunt Hill. The falls are reached from the new Loch Lee Kirk where there is a car park by following the Glen Clova path past the Old Kirk and Invermark Castle. Above Invermark Lodge is a rough mountain torrent which falls well down the hillside. At the head of the loch, beside which you are sure to have lingered to watch the water birds, the Glen Clova path by the Shank of Inchgrundle is seen climbing the hillside. To the left and to the right is Craig Maskeldie with its prominent East Ridge rising sharply to the sky line. This prominent crag becomes increasingly prominent until opposite it you cross the Lee by a bridge, from which point the view across the wet green floor of the head of this glen opens up. The falls come into view and they can be reached by traversing round underneath the lumpy Hunt Hill. These wild mountain falls consist of three cascades (of four metres, four metres and 12 metres) the lowest fall being the most impressive. The appeal of the falls is their openness – there are no dark chasms here – and the sheer force with which the Unich hurls itself to the valley floor at most seasons of the year is a compelling sight. Finally it is clear that this is simply the last grand statement of a mountain explorer who threads his way up the path beside them to the Falls of Damff.

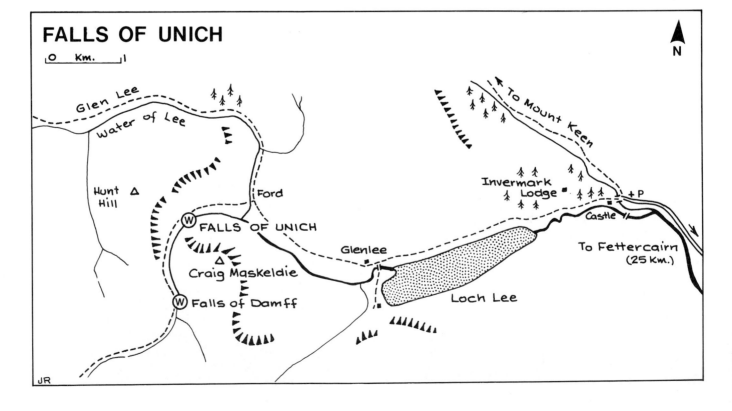

The Dee Basin

The Piss o' the Coire Boidheach   NO 231 835

This is the spectacular waterfall, 60 metres high, on the face of the long broken cliff which lies south of Lochnagar and north of the Dubh Loch, Eagle's Rock. The cliff is made of granite and the fall is the principal feature of it. The burn, called the burn of the beautiful corrie, falls 175 metres into the Dubh Loch. This is sometimes considered to be an oppressive place, but the Eagle's Rock can often have a sunny aspect. On a fine day the fall makes an excellent objective for an excursion from the Spittal of Glenmuick and it was a favourite with Queen Victoria who mentions the place a number of times in her Journal.

Breakneck Falls   NO 197 812

This is the colloquial name given to the corrie headwall falls seen in the upper part of Glen Callater, just east of Loch Kander. Eas Allt Briste Amhaich is a grand mountain fall, formed where the stream comes down over the cliffs of Loch Kander. There are a number of other falls on the precipices at the head of Glen Callater, but this is by far the most impressive.

Linn o' Callater   NO 159 880

A fall situated above the bridge over the Callater Burn on the A93 close to the point where it joins the Clunie Water.

Linn o' Clunie   NO 151 914

A focal point in Braemar is the bridge over the Clunie Water which 'dashes in leaps and falls through the midst of the village to join the Dee' (Murray's Guide). Its most prestigious leap is called the Linn o' Clunie.

Falls of Connie   NO 085 882

These somewhat unprepossessing falls on a lively little tributary of the Ey seem to be mentioned in many guide books which ignore far finer falls. They can be easily reached from Inverey in the course of an exploration of that other favourite with the writers of guide books, the Colonel's Bed. The Ey is an attractive stream with numerous small Falls and pools in the gorge by the Colonel's Bed.

Corbie Linn   NO 860 882

Corbie Pot or Corbie Linn is situated in the Den of Kincausie at Maryculter where the big house stands on a shelf above the Dee. The Crynoch Burn tumbles over the shelf to join the main stream at Milton Bridge, for long a traditional halting place when coaches plied between Aberdeen and Banchory. Fragments of a chapel built by the Knights Templar can be seen beside the river. The linn is thus associated with the crusaders, in particular with Sir Godfrey Wedderburn, accused of trifling with the affections of a Saracen lady. The linn is a very beautiful fall, noted for the wealth of plants which are usually found at higher altitudes.

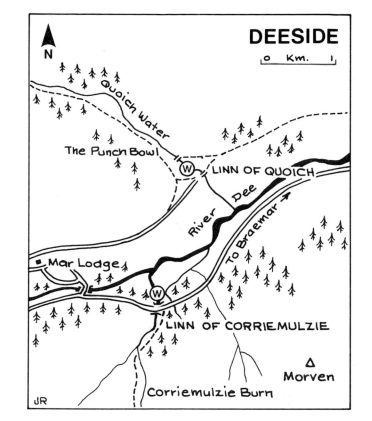

Linn of Corriemulzie   NO 112 892

This fall, between Braemar and the Linn of Dee, is one of the most frequently visited on Deeside. The road crosses the burn by a graceful, high-arched bridge which is seen to good effect from the foot of the fall. The prospect of the valley from hereabouts is fine. There are notable spruce and larch woods and the green banks of the Dee are diversified by gravel and shingle at this point. The fall is a grand silvery cascade falling for fifteen metres in twin ribbons of water set in a profusion of beautiful birch trees. A I McConnochie (1900) describes the early hydro-electric power installation there:

> The heating and lighting of Mar Lodge are both effected by means of electricity. To supply the motive power the stream of Corriemulzie has been harnessed. Some distance above the falls a large dam has been formed for the accumulation of the necessary water. At the falls there is a headlong rush which develops fifty horsepower in the turbine, and at the adjoining power-house the dynamo develops power to the amount of 240 volts, and at the lodge, about a mile distant, 170 volts, the power being transmitted by overhead copper cables. The supply of water is utilised during the night, so that the beauty of the falls is not interfered with.

The name Corriemulzie suggests that the burn was used to provide power for a mill.

Falls of Alltan Dearg   NO 286 837

Falls abound on Deeside. Queen Victoria was very enthusiastic about them all. The Falls of Alltan Dearg are on the steep slopes above Loch Muick and she gives an account of her visit to them on the day she heard of the death of the Duke of Wellington when the Royal party climbed up the zig-zag path to the crest above the falls and made their way to the Glas Allt before descending to the head of the Loch. The falls derive their name from the red granite which they expose. The walk described remains very attractive indeed.

Chest of Dee   NO 013 886

At the Chest of Dee the river flows over a series of rapids crossing a succession of square rock shelves. There are three distinct steps in the course of about 100 metres beneath which are deep, beautifully clear pools. The Chest, so-called because of the square shape of the rocks, is some distance below the Lairig Ghru path at a place marked by a clump of birches.

Falls of Dee   NO 944 991

This cascade is higher than Glomach and its setting is highly spectacular. Yet it is generally neglected in any consideration of the principal waterfalls of Scotland. There are higher mountain torrents and, of course, a series of little falls of this kind cannot be said to outrank a fall consisting of one or two resplendent leaps. Nevertheless, this is the only example of a trunk stream of a major river in Great Britain having its origin at so great an elevation and forming such a splendid fall. The fall is admirably described by Alexander in his classic guide to the Cairngorms:

> The river runs underground among great stones and then comes a tiny meadow of crisp mountain herbiage watered by the spray of the cataract falling like a ribbon of lace from the rim of the corrie, 500 feet above. The stream does not descend in one leap, but down innumerable steps of red granite, polished smooth; and the cascade in its height, in the crystal purity of its setting devoid of all trees and rank foliage of the ordinary waterfall is unique in these islands.

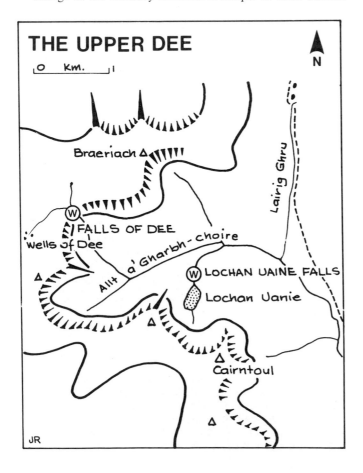

The famous poet James Hogg visited the upper Dee and celebrated it in these famous lines:

> the grisly cliffs which guard
> The infant rills of Highland Dee,
> Where hunter's horn is never heard
> Nor the bugle of the forest bee:
> Mid wastes that dern and dreary lie
> One mountain rears its might form
> Disturbs the moon in passing by
> And smiles above the thunderstorm.

The Dee Waterfall provides a route to the plateau from the Lairig Ghru. It is a straightforward climb in good weather, but it should only be undertaken by the experienced.

Linn of Dee   NO 062 895

At the Linn of Dee the river narrows to a little over a metre in width. The channel is cut in schistose rocks and, below the present falls, there is a series of round pools. The Linn of Dee is a good example of a waterfall which has almost worn itself out. Downstream is a small dyke which probably marks the site of the original fall. It is possible, when the water is low, to step across the stream in safety, but it was here that young Byron caught his lame foot and was saved from a fatal fall by a companion. The ornamental granite bridge at the Linn of Dee was opened by Queen Victoria in 1857.

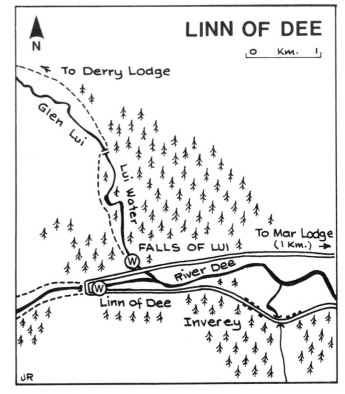

Derry Falls   NO 043 952

These falls are seen on the way from Derry Lodge to Loch Etchachan and the Lairig an Laoigh. The old path follows the left bank of the burn and rises through the Caledonian Pine Woods of the Cairngorms Nature Reserve. Just beyond the point where the track leaves the river, about 2km from the Lodge, are the falls. The Derry Burn flows over a rocky bed which can be clearly seen through the bright water.

Slog of Dess

NJ 567 004

The Slog of Dess is the very pretty fall beside the road to Lumphanan from the Deeside Road, the A93. The name is almost certainly a variant of Slug, a narrowing. The fall is about four metres high.

Easan Eidh

NO 088 863

Falls on the Ey Burn above the Colonel's Bed. This picturesque gorge gets its name from the tradition that one, Colonel Farquharson who was on the side of Viscount Claverhouse at the battle of Killiecrankie in 1869, took refuge on a ledge a few feet above the water. The falls can be visited in conjunction with an excursion to the Falls of Connie.

Coire Etchachan Fall

NJ 002 002

A corrie headwall fall above Loch Etchachan well seen from the foot of this magnificent corrie loch.

Falls of Feugh

NO 701 950

The scenery at the Bridge of Feugh is recognised as some of the finest on lower Deeside. The old bridge is a bottleneck and it is regrettable that a second bridge – an unpleasant wire cage – has been erected beside it to accommodate pedestrians. The river falls in a rocky channel and in spate it is a most attractive sight. As many as fifty salmon have been caught in a day in the large pool below the falls. Salmon and trout leap these falls in the summer and autumn.

Falls of Garbh Allt (Garrawalt)

NO 198 898

These are truly royal falls. They are situated in the Forest of Ballochbuie which is generally regarded as the most attractive woodland estate on Deeside. The superb pine forest of Ballochbuie was purchased by Queen Victoria in 1878. The Garbh Allt, the rough burn, rolls over several banks in a series of beautiful cascades:

> Here, oft by wild and wimpling stream
> From alpine summits bald,
> The bard has sung his doric theme –
> 'The Bowers of Invercauld'

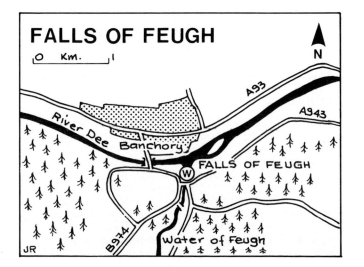

Because the falls are the property of the Queen access to them is sometimes restricted. The old road on the south bank of the Dee was closed when Balmoral was built. The river is crossed by a romantic looking old bridge, erected by General Wade as part of his military road from Blairgowrie to Inverness and at most times the public are permitted to cross it to reach the falls. This is also a route to Lochnagar still followed by mountain parties. It crosses to Glen Clova and Glen Doll by the 'Smuggler's Shank' along which whisky was conveyed to the south.

Queen Victoria descended from Lochnagar by this route.

> The view as one descends, overlooking Invercauld and the wood which is called Ballochbuie, is most lovely. We saw some deer in the wood below. We rode on till after we passed the burn and had nearly got to the wood. We came another way down by a much rougher path; and then from the road in the wood we walked up to the Falls of Garbhalt. The rocks are very grand, and the view from the little bridge, and also from the seat a little lower down, is extremely pretty.

The view referred to is of Beinn a' Bhuird which is seen to very great advantage. There are three falls and although there is not a great volume of water the scene has always attracted tourists. It is true that the author of *Black's Guide* (1861) complains that the scene is deficient in interest because it does not have the mysterious, frightful character derived from falling into a black cauldron. However, it is the very openness of the falls which has commended them to most people. The burn at the foot of the falls is crossed by an ornate footbridge which is the best point of vantage. Below the falls is the Danzig or Garbh Allt Shiel which is still a favourite with the Royal Family. The shiel was originally the farm steading of a Danzigger.

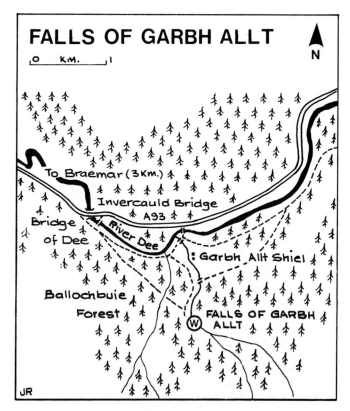

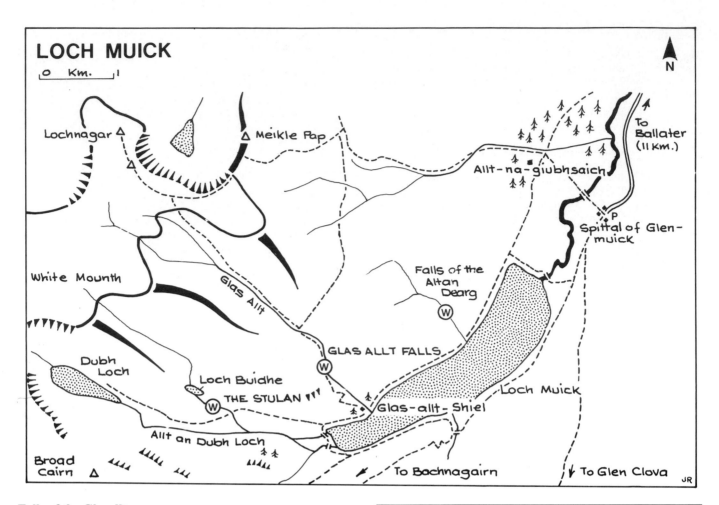

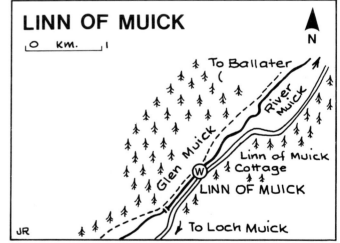

Falls of the Glasallt   NO 271 830

This fine fall at the head of Loch Muick was a favourite with
Prince Albert and after his death Queen Victoria, who felt that
the lodge at the foot of the Loch, Allt-na-Guibhsaich, had too
many painful associations for her, ordered that a royal holiday
cottage, the Glas-allt Shiel, should be built at the foot of the
falls. The mountain torrent falls 50 metres and the cottage is
built on the deltaic fan at its foot. The Loch and Lochnagar are
both magnificent and, if Byron's poem is hackneyed, even
banal, its epic form is appropriate.

Yet Caledonia, beloved are thy mountains
Round their white summits, though elements war
Though cataracts foam, stead of smooth flowing fountains
I sigh for the valley of dark Lochnagar.

Falls of Lui   NO 067 900

Of the several falls in the basin of the upper Dee the Falls of
the Lui are seldom visited. The Lairig Ghru path by Derry
Lodge leaves the public road at the foot of Glen Lui where
there is a locked gate 5km south of the Lodge. The cascades of
the Lui are hidden from the road in a stretch of pine forest and
the two pretty falls are often missed. Like the Quoich, the Lui
flows over blue grey schists which give the water a memorable
quality. An elaborate scheme to build a salmon pass was
initiated after the Second World War, but it was unsuccessful.

Eas nam Meirlach   NO 132 785

Fall, near Cairn Aosda, on the Cairnwell Burn, the thieves'
fall, no doubt a hiding place.

Linn of Muick   NO 332 895

This is perhaps the most frequently visited and best known of
all Deeside falls, apart, of course, from the Linn of Dee itself.
Since the Muick itself is a very considerable tributary of the
Dee and it is fed by waters regulated by both the Dubh Loch
and Loch Muick, the fall is nearly always in good condition. It
is formed where a band of epidiorite crosses the river. The
lower part of Glen Muick is well-wooded, but as the narrow
road begins to climb the valley closes in and rock outcrops
begin to appear. The Linn is an open fall where a substantial
body of white water is hurled with considerable force by means
of two leaps into a deep pool. A steep fish pass has been hewn

Glen Quoich. Charles Cordiner (1746–1794) illustrated his own accounts of journeys to the North of Scotland, penetrating remote glens which were not then tourist attractions. Engraving by Peter Mazell, first published 1788.

into the rocks on the west bank to enable salmon to climb what must be one of the most abrupt obstacles to be surmounted by this means. The Linn of Muick is ten metres high. It was famous even in Pennant's time since he comments that the pool beneath the falls 'is supposed by the vulgar to be bottomless'. The road climbs beyond the falls out of Linn Wood towards the Loch. There is no convenient stopping place for cars on the east bank. On the opposite bank, the Princess Drive runs close to the river leading to Allt-na-guibhsaich.

Falls o' Piper   *NO 253 965*

Fall on the Crathes Burn close to the A939.

Linn of Quoich   *NO 111 912*

The Quoich is a powerful mountain stream which flows over schists forming a series of deep potholes from which the name of the river is derived. Tradition has it that, in 1715, at the Earl of Mar's Punchbowl above the falls, the Jacobite leader treated his supporters to a punch made up in the enormous pothole in the river, the side of which is now broken. The river falls over a succession of rocky ledges where the micaceous schists render the water sparklingly clear. Above the falls is the hill called Creag whose crags are clad with larches, but the woods beside the river are pine. The narrow linn, beneath the footbridge, is reminiscent of the Linn of Dee although the fall is steeper. The pools above it are entrancing and lead to the very fine fall at the Punchbowl. The Linn of Quoich is at the end of the by-road from the Linn of Dee.

Sheeoch Linn   *NO 742 908*

The Sheeoch is a tributary of the lower Dee and the Linn is above the Slug Road from Banchory to Stonehaven (A957) which affords such fine views of Deeside and the North Sea. The Burn of Sheeoch joins the Dee at Kirkton of Durris where there is a charming den. 'There is no prettier spot more heedlessly passed by than Durris at the Bridge of Sheeoch where the road is carried over the stream. The bridge has an elegant arch, and the dell has quite a romantic appearance.' The linn is reached from the farm of Blairydryne, visited incognito in 1530 by James V. The Sheeoch (the Fairy Burn) falls over a linn underneath a hill called the Ord.

The Stulan   *NO 256 824*

This is the attractive mountain fall on the little burn which drains Loch Buidhe in the White Mounth. It is encountered on the path from Loch Muick to the Dubh Loch. The name is correctly spelled Steallan, the little spout.

Linn of Tanar   *NO 385 890*

Glen Tanar is 20km long and there are 2,000 hectares of woodland, much of it indigenous pine forest. The Linn of Tanar may be visited by diverging from the Mounth path at the Shiel of Glentanar. Here there are pretty falls on the main stream in the deserted upper reaches of the glen. At the Bridge of Ess, at the mouth of the glen, there is an imposing tower carried across the public road beside the bridge over the rocky gorge of the river.

Allt an Lochain Uaine Waterfall (Cairn Toul)   *NN 960 983*

The sharp peak of Sgor an Lochain Uaine, the peak of the green tarn, was named The Angel's Peak by early visitors to the district to distinguish this fine hill from the Devil's Point. The Green Tarn lies at about 910 metres on a rocky perch below the summit, situated in a tiny corrie which forms part of the magnificent rock amphitheatre, the most impressive in Britain, between Braeriach and Cairn Toul. The burn which drains the lochan tumbles in a torrential mountain waterfall – a series of cascades like the Falls of Dee. The most continuous of the falls is perhaps 50 metres high. It is particularly well seen from Braeriach and the burn forms a line of ascent to the plateau. The fall, the tarn and the peak are scenic assets of the very first quality.

Falls o' the Derry Lochain Uaine   *NO 024 987*

There are four little green lochs in the Cairngorms. Each one has great character and each has its advocates as the finest of the four. This tarn has a fine fall on the headwall of the corrie which must always be remembered because beside it William Smith, an Abernethy poet and poacher, had a turf hut for shelter. He wrote the very beautiful folk song 'At the burn of the little green tarn' which praises the place. The fall can be visited on the way to the Derry Cairngorm.

The Burn o' Vat Falls   *NO 425 995*

This is one of Scotland's famous natural curiosities. It is situated on the Allt na Dabhaich which rises on Culblean Hill close to Ballater. Beside the A97 there is a tea room and a path leads up the burn to the Vat, an extraordinary rocky gorge in which the principal feature is a smooth hollow in the granite like a collapsed cave, the Vat itself. At its head is a fine little waterfall where the burn enters this huge pothole. The gorge above the fall also repays exploration.

Buchan

The region North and East of the Grampians is not noted for any grand waterfalls, but there are half a dozen, at least, which deserve mention.

Rootie Linn   *NJ 756 372*

In the basin of the Ythan, near Fyvie.

The Loup   *NJ 833 621*

Near Troup Head on the North Coast is the Tore of Troup, a den of much interest. The Loup is the principal waterfall.

Den of Craig   *NJ 471 248*

At the head of Strathbogie on the A941 from Dufftown to Alford is the Den of Craig. Craig Castle is finely situated above this deep glen and the policies embrace footbridges and pathways which enable the visitor to see the waterfalls.

Falls of Tarnash   *NJ 443 490*

Near Keith are the Falls of Tarnash which have always been a favourite with local people. An old mill, situated at the foot of the falls, is a favourite subject for artists.

Linn of Keith   *NJ 428 511*

Keith has a fine Roman Catholic Church and was the birthplace of Scotland's only post Reformation Saint, St John Ogilvie. The Castle where he was born is now ruined, but part of a castle built on the same site remains. It is finely situated above the Linn of Keith once a very impressive fall which was blown up in 1830 after floods.

Linn of Deskford   *NJ 511 628*

There are fine waterfalls in Cullen where the burn tumbles into the sea *(NJ 504 667)*. However, the most notable fall is the Linn of Deskford ten metres high. Under the Bin of Cullen on a neighbouring stream is the *Linn of Rannas (NJ 464 644)*.

The Spey and Findhorn Basins

Falls of Achlean see Falls of Badan Mosach

Falls of Achneim   *NH 857 482*

These falls are less remarkable than the gorge in which they are situated. Above Cawdor Castle the Riereach Burn drains a dull moorland between the Findhorn and the Nairn and at Riereach Bridge it begins to fall sharply in a series of cascades in a precipitous ravine etched in conglomerates which is crossed at Achneim by a footbridge 32 metres above the water. This gorge and the *Cawdor Waterfall (NN 839 483)* on a tributary, the Allt Dearg, are linked in the Tumbling Waters Nature Trail which starts at the Castle.

Glen Altnarie   *NH 931 435*

This outstanding fall is sadly neglected nowadays. It is a short distance from Dulsie Bridge, a beauty spot on the Findhorn of which Charles St John wrote

> What spot on earth can exceed in beauty the landscape comprising the Old Bridge of Dulsie, spanning with its lofty arch the deep dark pool, shut in by grey and fantastic rocks, surmounted with the greatest of greenswards, with clumps of ancient weeping birches, backed by the dark pine-trees.

At Dulsie Bridge the Findhorn flows through a granite gorge and all the little burns which join it form attractive cascades. The most considerable of these on the north bank is the Allt na Airidh. The fall on this burn was highly thought of by the Victorians because the glen was the subject of a popular romantic painting by John Thomson of Uddingston in 1832. Thomson was a close friend and admirer of Scott and the picture made a substantial impact on the movement, led by Scott, which transformed attitudes to the Highlands. It has become fashionable to dismiss this over-romantic view, but few visitors to the Glen today will fail to be impressed by this fall. In the words of the Ordnance Gazetteer the burn 'makes a profound and very romantic fall within a deep, wooded, sequestered glen'. Birch and pine predominate in this wood,

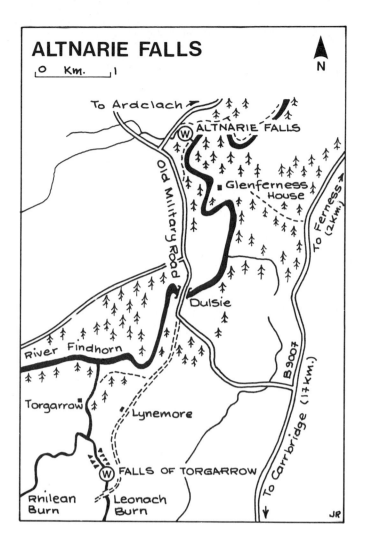

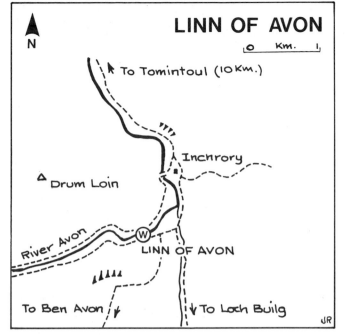

Linn of Avon

NJ 175 073

The translucent quality of the water in the Avon, the principal tributary of the Spey, is renowned. At the Linn of Avon close to the remote shooting lodge of Inchrory, it falls over a series of broken rocks with deep, clear pools between them. A path leads up Glen Avon to the Fords of Avon and Loch Avon through some of the loneliest mountain country in the Grampians.

Falls of Badan Mosach

NN 858 971

This is one of the most charming places in the Cairngorms, accessible to the ordinary tourist, but frequented by mountaineers. Above the road-end at Achlean the Nature Conservancy at one time established a nature trail, now discontinued, above the flats of the Feshie. It climbed to the Allt Fearnagan by the easily graded stalkers' path which climbs to Carn Ban Mor above Loch Einich. You reach the burn soon enough. It slides, imperceptibly at first, among the Caledonian pine-wood of Badan Mosach. It is not until you have followed it downstream for some way that you begin to realise that its succession of little cascades forms part of a major fall, fifty metres in height. The burn turns this way and that and seems to gain momentum. Its branching channels form a pattern of whitewater amid red and green trees and from the foot of the burn you look up to see an exquisite scene, characteristic of the Cairngorms.

Linn of Brown

NJ 125 205

The Burn of Brown is the main feeder of the Avon and the Linn is just above the picturesque bridge on the old military road from Grantown to Tomintoul which is the boundary between the Grampian and Highland Regions. The glen, correctly the Bruan, is a favourite stopping place on the road from Speyside to Deeside. The linn is beside the road on the Grampian Region side. The burn flows through a very restricted passage in the rocks forming a series of cascades. It almost seems to be roofed over and, for this reason, it may be found disappointing.

but just in front of the view-house, now neglected and firmly locked, is a very fine silver fir. What is so charming about the fall is the way in which the burn changes direction at its head so that the whole fall of 27.5 metres is seen from the side. The Altnarie is reached from the by-road which leaves the old military road from Grantown to Fort George and goes to Ardclach. The footpath leads down to the Findhorn below Glenferness. From the foot of the burn a superb fisherman's path leads back to Dulsie Bridge now high above the river, now beside it as it rushes as brown as brown ale through the wooded, wild-flower banked gorge. It provides a magnificent view of Glenferness House built in 1837 in the Greek style. The house, its grounds and the furious river are unrivalled in Scotland.

Allt Arder

There are low falls on this burn which tumbles down into the Spey near Knockando. It was severely affected by the floods of 1829 and there is a graphic account of what took place in the Ordnance Gazetteer, based on that of Sir Thomas Dick Lauder (1830). The respect in which the little burn is held is illustrated by the considerable viaduct built 15 metres above the stream on the Speyside Line, now disused.

Ess of Auchness

NJ 114 490

Fall, South of Dallas, on a tributary of the Lossie.

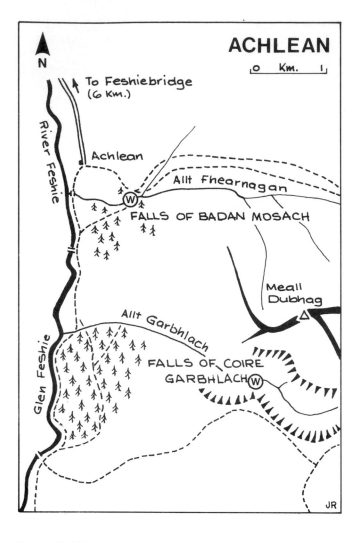

Easan Buidhe   *NN 548 942*

These are the only falls on the Spey proper and they will disappoint those who visit them hoping to see that fine river, already a notable stream, plunging over a considerable cataract for they are really no more than a series of rapids formed where the river crosses a rock barrier at Shirramore in the strath at the foot of the Corrieyarrick Pass beyond Laggan Bridge. It is nonetheless a very charming scene worth seeking out, particularly where, at the foot of the rapids, the Spey divides to flow round a pine-clad island.

Cadha an Fheidh see Cluny's Cage Waterfall

Falls of Calder   *NN 701 994*

The Falls of Calder are low, restricted falls on the river above Newtonmore. They can be reached by a footpath from the elegant arched bridge over the river built in 1820 and designed by Telford, or from the Glen Road which leads to Glen Banchor. Near the falls is the old mill of Banchor. Above is the birch-clad slope of Creag Dubh and beyond are the hills of the Monadhliath of which the most striking is The Chailleach. Beyond the falls is the Luib, a horse-shoe-shaped bend in the river, and the Glen Road crosses the Allt a'Chaoruinn. The broad, low falls on the Calder above this point are called *Little Falls*. Glen Banchor is an attractive, secluded enclave characteristic of the hidden delights of Speyside.

Cawdor Waterfall see Falls of Achneim

Chriochaidh Falls   *NH 851 105*

These hidden falls are close to the A9, within sight and sound of that overcrowded road, yet seldom visited. They make a fine short excursion from Lynwilg, the curiously Welsh sounding place beside Loch Alvie. The name means the field of the bag. The path leaves the busy main road and goes by Loch Alvie, with its wild ducks and oyster-catchers, across from the picturesque, whitewashed church restored by Sir Basil Spence. A track leads to the farm of Ballinluig and then traverses the moorland edge under Creag na-h-Uamha, the Crag of the Caves. The second burn which is encountered is the Allt Chriochaidh and a path climbs the hill above the stream to a large, flat stone from which the double fall of about thirty metres is well seen. There are very fine retrospective views of Tor Alvie and the Cairngorms.

Cluny's Cage Waterfall   *NN 669 957*

High up on Creag Dubh above the Laggan road from Newtonmore is a spectacular wet-weather fall. The cliff, a magnificent wall of mica-schist, 150 metres high, is a fine rock-climbing ground. It afforded a hiding place for Cluny MacPherson when he was a fugitive after the Forty Five. His castle stood close to the foot of the crag. These impressive falls, the only falls in Scotland close to a public road, remind one of the 'Bridal Veil' falls of the Alps where the water atomises.

Eas A'Choin Duibh   *NN 734 845*

The Falls of the Black Dog are situated in the wild gorge of Coire Bhrodain above Gaick Lodge. This remote and little visited part of the Grampians has an atmosphere all its own. No one would suppose that such unpromising moors could give rise to the spectacular scenery in the environs of the lodge. The moors end in steep bluffs, of which the most notable is Sgor Dearg, above a wide glen occupied by two broad lochs. Above Loch Bhrodain is a rugged corrie, one of several in these parts where birds of prey build their eyries. In his book *The Central Highlands* Seton Gordon gives the best account of the naming of the corrie, of the loch and of the falls:

> There is an attractive legend on the naming of this loch to be found in MacBain's Place Names. A hunter in some way became the owner of a litter of fairy pups, but before they grew up a fairy or demon took from him all except one. The hunter was left with a single jet-black cuilean which the demon, for some reason, first handicapped by breaking its leg. The name of the pup was Brodan. At this time a white fairy deer lived on Ben Alder, and, with his black, supernatural hound Brodan, the hunter determined to hunt it. Together they went to Ben Alder and found the deer above Loch Ericht. A long and stern chase began, and when they reached Loch Vrodin of Gaik the dog was close to the fairy deer. Almost together the two plunged into the loch, and half-way across Brodan overtook the elfin deer and seized it in his strong jaws. On the instant deer and dog disappeared for ever, and the loch was named Loch a'Bhodain Bhrodain (the genitive of Brodin, anglicised into Vrodin) after the hound.

The corrie is reached by the path to Sgor Dearg behind the lodge. There are pretty falls at the entrance to the corrie and, on the left, the Allt Dearg tumbles in a dizzy fashion into the main burn forming a wet-weather fall of about forty metres.

Ahead is the gorge, best seen from the true right bank of the stream. In this wild cleft are the principal falls where the burn turns a corner and the water tumbles into the side of the gorge, narrow at first but spreading into a white apron of water against black rock. The falls are perhaps twenty metres in height. From only one point is it possible to get a view of the falls in their entirety. It is the very heart of the forest of Gaick.

Falls of Divie see Falls of Feakirk

Ess of Dorback   *NJ 008 460*

The Dorback falls fifteen metres in a series of falls above and below Ess Bridge on a by-road near the A940 at Glenernie. A wicket-gate at the bridge admits the visitor to a path which leads to the foot of the falls. In common with the Findhorn and the Divie, the Dorback runs black as stout in spate. This rumbustious burn drains the remote Lochindorb and the total area of its basin above the falls is 80 sq km. It is thus a considerable stream, although its existence might not be suspected from the tableland over which the main road runs. In 1829, during the Moray floods, the floodwaters of the Findhorn backed up so far that the Dorback flowed in the reverse direction.

Dreggie Falls   *NJ 024 283*

Impressive local falls, situated on the outskirts of Grantown-on-Spey, which form an admirable objective in themselves, or offer interest en route to Castle Grant or Loch-in-Dorb.

Dulnain Bridge Falls   *NH 992 250*

These charming falls, about three metres high, are at the head of the gorge on the Dulnain above the point where it joins the Spey. Your author, always an avid seeker after information concerning waterfalls, once encountered a fisherman there and engaged him in conversation. 'Do these falls have a name?' After giving the matter some thought, as fishermen are wont to do, the fellow replied, in a measured way, 'Aye, we call them The Falls'. The Falls are just below a Grant stronghold, Muckrach Castle, presently being restored.

Dun Cow's Loup   *NH 197 554*

In its gorge below Dallas the Lossie flows in a succession of rapids. The furthest downstream of these is the Dun Cow's Loup.

Ess of Duthill   *NH 929 278*

This is the isolated fall beside the mountain road which climbs steeply from the humped-backed bridge over the Duthill Burn to the prominent col, Beum a'Chlaidheimh, between the Spey and Findhorn basins. The road between Carrbridge and Forres, the B9007, commands exceptionally fine views of the Cairngorms. The ruined farm of Ess is seen on the left and a little way beyond it a path crosses a heathery bank to the fall. It provides a pleasant surprise because the Duthill looks to be a very insubstantial stream at this point. However, it spreads out over a rock apron in a birch-filled hollow to form a twin fall of some eight metres. It is a friendly place amid inhospitable moors. The 1:25,000 map refers to the falls as the Falls of Ess.

Falls of Slochd Beag (Glen Feshie)   *NN 845 896*

The Slochd Beag, the little trough, is at the head of the lower part of Glen Feshie. It forms a 'false pass' appearing to provide a way ahead when the glen turns a corner. The Slochd Beag is a steep-sided glen and the stalker's track keeps well above the burn, but it is possible to keep to the valley bottom. This way leads to a very fine double fall about 20 metres in height. Sparkling white water tumbles down in a wild setting. The falls can be seen in full only from the right bank of the stream which also provides a route to the top of the falls. Above them is a splendid waterslide where the Allt Coire Bhruic joins the Allt Lorgaidh.

Eidart Falls   *NN 914 886*

The little river Eidart joins the Feshie close to the watershed between the Spey and the Dee. It is a substantial mountain stream, notoriously difficult to cross in spate, which drains a wild stony basin of some 33 square kilometres. Above the confluence with the Feshie it flows through a highly attractive gorge about 500 metres long. Beneath the bridge over the Eidart built by the army is the most considerable of a succession of falls. It is a magnificent leap of about twelve metres. The clear mountain water falls into a fine pool, easily accessible. It is an oasis beneath remote hills. Above the falls are the outliers of the Monadh Mor which can be reached by following the track beside the Eidart. If this objective is too remote the gorge itself should be explored as far as an upper fall of about six metres where the river rushes through a narrow cleft to make the leap.

Glean Einich

Glean Einich is the heart of the Rothiemurchus Estate. It is drained by the wild, rumbustious Beanaidh. At its head is Loch Einich, set in a magnificent, U-shaped trough between the corries of Braeriach and the buttresses of Sgoran Dubh Mor. It is, perhaps, the most perfect mountain lake in Britain. If it is overshadowed by Loch Avon in savage grandeur, it remains a place of singular impressiveness. The wild river was formerly subject to artificial spates by means of a weir at Loch Einich, the remains of which can still be seen. These spates were used to float logs to the Spey. The lower part of the glen is still forested. It is reached from either Coylumbridge or Loch an Eilein and it must be approached on foot or by bicycle through the forest of Rothiemurchus.

The tributaries of the Bennaidh form exceptionally fine waterfalls all of which are of the 'hanging valley' type. The first tributary to be encountered is the Beanaidh Bheag, the Little Bennie, difficult to cross in spate. It drains the northern face of Braeriach. Its principal feeder originates in Coire an Lochan. It forms the fall which stands out so distinctively in the view from Aviemore. The next stream up the valley is *Easan na Bruaich (NH 924 018)*, the little waterfall of the height, beside which a path leads to Braeriach. Before Loch Einich is reached a prominent stalkers' path climbs to the left and crosses the tumbling burn which falls out of Coire Bogha Cloiche, the corrie of the stone bothy. There is a very fine double fall on this stream above the foot of the loch. The outlook towards Sgoran Dubh Mor, Sgoran Beag and Sgor Goath is very fine indeed, and there is no pleasanter vantage point from which to contemplate these magnificent precipices than the *Falls of Coire Bogha Cloiche (NN 923 998)*.

The path continues to climb into *Coire Dhondail* at the head of which it crosses a fine twin fall *(NN 925 979)* where the burn

which has crossed the plateau from Einich Carn descends precipitately into the corrie over angled slabs. Pretty in late summer, this place can be highly dangerous at other times of the year because of the steep snow.

At the head of Gleann Einich are the Falls of Coire Odhar, described elsewhere. These falls dominate the head of Loch Einich and were sometimes considered to be the highest falls in Scotland. They are always a singularly impressive feature of this wild place.

Falls of Ess see Ess of Duthill

Falls of Feakirk   NJ 036 447

These falls occur on the Divie, the principal tributary of the Findhorn. They are situated in the parish of Edenkillie which is traversed by the A940 and the original main line of the Highland Railway. The falls are reached from the parish church, a low whitewashed building dating from 1741. There is a fine seven-arched masonry viaduct on the old Highland Railway, now disused. It was constructed across the Divie in 1863 and it is 145 metres long and 32 metres high. The country under the Knock of Braemoray affords many fine cross-country walks and, like many districts on the edge of well-known tourist resorts, it tends to be neglected by visitors. A farm road leads over the heather-covered, curlew-haunted plateau with its gnarled birches and, beside the falls, fine pines. The falls themselves which lie below the bridge which leads to the farm of Feakirk are pretty, but, in most conditions, poorly illuminated. There is a series of low falls, each three or four metres in height.

Feith Buidhe Cataract   NH 995 015

This is the highest cataract in the Cairngorms. Like the Falls of Dee it cannot be compared with the Falls of Glomach, or with other unsupported falls, for it is broken. If, however, it is considered to be a waterfall, and the Allt Coire Eoghainn in Glen Nevis is not, it is the highest inland fall. It is certainly the highest body of falling water which can be conveniently seen – all of a piece – from its foot and it has incomparably the grandest setting. What is astonishing in the light of these facts is that it is almost overshadowed by the Garbh Uisge Cataract, its companion at the head of Loch Avon.

The Feith Buidhe drains the tiny Lochan Buidhe, the highest sheet of standing water in Britain, which sits on the high stony plateau between Cairn Gorm and Ben MacDui. For most of the year the declivity which it occupies is a considerable snowfield, the edge of which is marked by the precipitous crags over which the burn tumbles in a highly spectacular cascade. From the topographical point of view the Feith Buidhe is the true headwater of the Avon, but a more considerable body of water drains into the Garbh Uisge which joins it before the Delta at the head of Loch Avon. The waterslide is 250 metres in height and its slabs provide, for experienced mountaineers, a very fine late summer route from the Loch to the Plateau. In spate the Feith Buidhe is a savage stream unsurpassed in the rock architecture of the stream itself and of the mighty crags which dominate it. There is, it is generally agreed no

Falls of Eidart, Glen Feshie. Mountain falls at the head of a glen unsurpassed for the grandeur and variety of its waterfalls. HAMISH BROWN

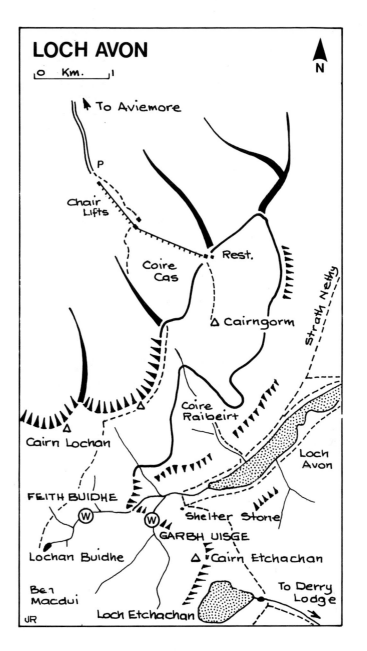

Feith Buidhe, the highest cataract in the Cairngorms; can be conveniently seen, all of a piece, from its foot. For much of the year seen in snow. LOUIS STOTT

savage a scene on the mainland of Great Britain than the head of Loch Avon unmatched for sheer wildness. The grandeur of the setting is due to the magnificent cirque of cliffs, Carn Etchachan, Shelter Stone Crag and Hell's Lum Crag which rings the head of the loch. The Feith Buidhe occupies the centre of the breach in these cliffs descending between Shelter Stone Crag and Hell's Lum Crag, the Garbh Uisge joining it from the corner of Shelter Stone Crag. It is a truly magnificent situation for a truly magnificent stream.

Glen Feshie

Glen Feshie, held in great affection by those who know it well, provides the easiest of the three crossings between the Spey and the Dee which traverse the Cairngorms but it is the longest route. The main stream and its tributaries drain a vast empty quarter given over to deer. The forests of Glen Feshie are more varied than the pine forests of Rothiemurchus and Abernethy. There are many very fine pine trees, but alder, birch, rowan and willow also occur together with juniper scrub. The wild life of the glen is the richer for this.

Queen Victoria visited Glen Feshie twice and gave a good description of the wild, upper part of the glen in her *Journal*:

> The rapid river, overhung by rocks with trees, birch and fir; the hills as you advance rise very steeply on both sides with rich rocks and corries, and occasional streamlets falling from very high – while the path winds higher and higher. It is quite magnificent.

On one occasion the Royal party stopped for lunch at what she called the 'Falls of Sron a Barin'. It is not clear which of several falls in the upper part of the glen these are. The term can be applied to the fine ribbon fall which occurs on the Feith na Craoibh Chaoruinn which, after an indeterminate course in boggy uplands, plunges in a fall, 36 metres high, into the Feshie under Sron na Ban Righ, the Queen's Nose. The hill is like a nose, true enough, but it would be a very unflattering nose for a Queen to have. One cannot resist the speculation that it got its name from a ghillie in the company of Queen Victoria, but the name is said to be older than that and to be connected with

Bridge Falls, Glen Moriston. Telford threw a fine stone arched bridge over the tempestuous Moriston at the head of these falls. PETER DAVENPORT

Mary Queen of Scots. At this point the Feshie flows over a number of attractive rock terraces which make an entrancing foreground to the falls *(NN 871 888)*.

Sron na Ban Righ stands at the head of the fine glacial breach through which the Feshie, once a headwater of the Dee, breaks through into Strath Spey. The lower end of this breach is guarded by Creag na Gaibhre and Creag na Caillich. At the upper end are the Falls of Feshie *(NN 876 888)* a series of highly attractive, low, river falls, several of them, because of the configuration of the rock in the river bed, of the type that fall in on themselves from three sides making a spellbinding pattern. The best of falls, a succession of linked cascades, occur in the rock gorge below the point where the Allt na Leuma joins the river.

No visit to Glen Feshie should omit Feshie Bridge itself where, as at Tromie Bridge, the river falls over a succession of cascades into a wonderful river pool.

In addition to the falls described in Glen Feshie there are the *Falls of Badan Mosach*, the *Falls of Coire Garbhlach*, *Landseer's* and *Eidart Falls*.

The Flume   *NJ 110 012*

This is an apt name for the very remote fall in the Garbh Choire of Ben a'Bhuird, the highest summit of the eastern Cairngorms and one of the finest of the Grampian Mountains in respect of its corrie scenery. The Allt an t'Sluichd is already a vigorous stream when it reaches the edge of the plateau to make this fall which, in windy conditions, is swept away from the cliff face. In winter it forms a spectacular ice-wall which constitutes the finish to a difficult climb. The corrie can be visited during the high level walk between Ben a'Bhuird and Ben Avon, 14.5km from Invercauld. A descent is made into

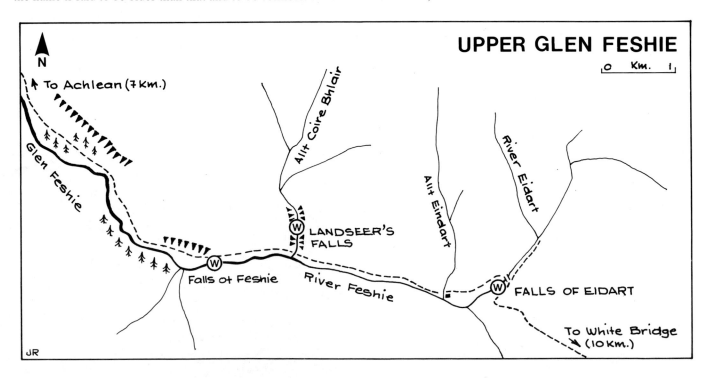

Falls of Feugh, Banchory. Salmon and trout leap these falls in the summer and autumn. As many as 50 salmon have been caught in a day in the large pool below the falls. PETER DAVENPORT

the Corrie by the Sneck. The Slochd Mor, the great pit, which provides an approach to the Garbh Choire can be reached by a long march from Inchrory in Glen Avon by following the river, but this is an exceptionally isolated route, 22.5km from the public road at Delnabo.

Garbh Allt (Nethy)   NJ 014 035

At the Saddle, the pass leading from Strath Nethy to Loch Avon, the infant Nethy tumbles in a mountain waterfall on the side of Cairn Gorm. This remote, but impressive, place offers the safest route to and from Loch Avon from Strathspey and it affords the finest view of this wildest of Scottish lochs.

Falls of Coire Garbhlach   NN 875 947

This fine corrie in Glen Feshie is reasonably easily reached from Achlean. It is opposite Glen Feshie Lodge. The place is noted for its lime-loving plants and is part of the heart of the Cairngorms National Nature Reserve. Its 300-metre walls consist of broken rock and scree, which give it its name, the Rough Corrie and make it a singularly impressive place to visit.

At the entrance to the twisting corrie there is a fifteen-metre unsupported fall on the Allt Garbhlach which seems to bar further progress although, in reality, it can be easily surmounted. At the corrie headwall, and hidden until you are at the very foot of it, is a superb hundred-metre cascade. It may not be so high as other corrie waterfalls in the Cairngorms but it is quite the most graceful of them.

Garbh Uisge Cataract   *NH 997 014*

The Garbh Uisge is the monarch of all the falls in the Spey Basin. It may be exceeded in height by some other mountain torrents and there are many falls which might be considered prettier but the Garbh Uisge is a fall in a setting on the grand scale. It is situated on the main feeder of Loch Avon under the Sticil, the Shelter Stone Crag. This awesome precipice takes its name from the gigantic boulder at its foot which through the centuries has provided a refuge for fugitives and for benighted travellers. It is now a bivouac for climbers and a place for visitors to Loch Avon to take lunch. The Garbh Uisge occupies the first break in the ring of crags at the head of the Loch. The burn and its tributaries have fairly extensive gathering grounds on the plateau and, in spate, the series of falls by which it descends to the loch forms a single cataract of great impressiveness, 110 metres in height. Its final leap, of about thirty metres above the Shelter Stone is one of the most spectacular unsupported falls in Scotland. The whole cataract is about the same height as the Falls of Glomach and since the building of the chairlift to the summit of Cairn Gorm it is almost equally accessible, although it is essential that the excursion to it should only be undertaken by properly equipped parties in suitable weather conditions. The fall can be seen from the plateau by descending to the head of the precipitous granite cliff, Stac an Fharaidh *(NJ 011 029)* 1km south-east of the summit and 2km from the Ptarmigan restaurant. To reach the head of Loch Avon from the chairlift the best way in fine weather is by Coire Raibeirt, south of the summit and west of these cliffs. The Garbh Uisge itself provides the most interesting route to the summit of Ben MacDui, safer than the Feith Buihe, but still a route for experienced mountaineers only. From Deeside Loch Avon is reached by Glen Derry and Loch Etchachan. In adverse weather conditions the escape routes from Loch Avon, by the Nethy or the Fords of Avon, involve long walks of 15km and visitors to the Shelter Stone should always be prepared to undertake them.

Den of Garbity   *NJ 308 522*

A linn in a wooded dell beside the lower Spey.

Ess of Glenlatterach   *NJ 194 534*

Above the Ess of Glenlatterach a great reservoir has been built which has affected this fall which, none the less, remains the most considerable in the basin of the Lossie. The Lenach, or Angry Burn, falls 15 metres at the Ess. Below it is another feature called the Kettle where there is another fall. The falls are reached by by-roads from the A941 which lead to the farm of Glenlatterach.

Laggan Falls   *NJ 234 417*

These are perhaps the finest of the falls which occur on the left bank tributaries of the lower Spey where a host of little streams tumble into the river.

Landseer's Falls   *NN 886 894*

The Allt na Leuma, the burn of the leap, is aptly named. It is so-called, no doubt, because of the charming cascade which it makes where it joins the Feshie. However, it may well be that it gets its name from the high fall which occurs higher up its gorge. The burn is known, in its upper reaches, as the Allt Coire Bhlair and there is a fine description of it in the first volume of the *Cairngorm Club Journal* by R Anderson:

> This burn crosses the Glen Feshie path at an interesting spot, flowing out of a steep, narrow gorge, at the further end of which is discerned a high waterfall. The spot is otherwise interesting as in the immediate vicinity are the remains of some walls which at one time formed part of a hut frequently resorted to by Sir Edwin Landseer. We wormed our way up the gorge by the burnside, as far as possible, climbing over the projecting ledges clambering along the sides of ugly looking gullies and deafening linns, and securing a foothold not always the most trustworthy, owing to the wet and rotten condition of the rock. But all was to no purpose. Very soon a gap faced us that there was no getting round – the burn flowing fast and deep between two sheer walls of rock; and the gap, too, was placed obliquely, so that we had no proper view up the gorge. We had simply a partial view of a huge cleft in the mountain; precipitous rock faces on each side of us, with ferns sprouting from their interstices and a dwarf birch, or aspen, or fir occasionally showing on some of the higher ledges; and at the upper end a tantalising glimpse of a bit of waterfall. Reluctantly we had to retrace our steps – the descent at one point proving not quite so easy as the ascent; but with due caution the difficulty was surmounted. There was now no other course open to us but to attempt to find the waterfall from the ridge above the gorge. Ascending the ridge accordingly – the ridge on the left bank of the burn – we, in a short time, came in view of a magnificent waterfall; a fairly large body of water making the descent by three separate leaps so to speak – first a transverse fall from right to left, then a straight descent for a considerable distance, and then a transverse fall again, but this time from left to right. Each of us made an estimate of the total height of the fall (including all three branches); the average of five separate estimates was 166 feet. It was unanimously resolved to name them Landseer Falls.

Linen Apron   *NJ 324 382*

This picturesquely named waterfall occurs on a tributary, an insignificant tributary, of the Dullan in Glen Rinnes outside Dufftown. The gorge is of considerable geological and botanical interest and a guided walk is described in a booklet compiled by the Deeside Field Club.

Easan Coire an Lochain   *NH 943 003*

Coire an Lochain is the westernmost of the three fine corries on the north face of Braeriach. Although little Lochan Buidhe on the plateau between Cairngorm and Ben MacDui is at a greater elevation Coire an Lochain has the distinction of being the highest 'proper' corrie loch in Britain. It is perfectly described by Seton Gordon (1925).

> Coire an Lochain of Brae Riach is perhaps the most arctic corrie of the Cairngorms. The loch is the highest sheet of water of any size in the British Isles being 3,260 feet (994 metres) above the level of the distant ocean, and yet above

the loch towers a precipice almost 1,000 feet (300 metres) high. From the plateau above this precipice a burn flows. After heavy rain it is a milky torrent but more often it is a small stream although I have never known it dry up. It is named Easan Coire an Lochain or the Waterfall of the Corrie of the Tarn. In winter when there is little snow on the hills but when at that elevation the frost is intense Easan Coire an Lochain becomes a continuous sheet of smooth ice.

The corrie can be reached either from Gleann Einich or the Lairig Ghru, but it is a mountaineering expedition.

Falls of the Mashie   NN 578 908

These falls occur near the low col which divides the basin of the Spey from that of the Spean. The Mashie rises in the Ben Alder Forest and flows parallel to the Pattack. However, the two sister rivers turn away from one another and flow towards opposite seaboards. They are now linked by a conduit which leads the waters of the Mashie from below the falls into the Lochaber Hydro Electric Power Scheme. Strathmashie is the site of many of the adventures of Cluny Macpherson after the Forty-Five. Much of the area is now forested and in the hands of the Forestry Commission. Wade used the south bank of the Spey to cross the Strath, the road from the South coming from Dalwhinnie and that from the north and east coming from the Ruthven Barracks. There is a fine old military bridge over the Mashie *(NN 600 936)* before the road climbs to the Corrieyairack Pass. The falls are just above the bridge on the present A86.

Nethy Rapids   NJ 020 107

These falls add interest to the vicinity of Bynack Stables (Nethy Bothy) which is frequently the objective of a short excursion from Glenmore through the Ryvoan Pass, yet they are frequently missed. On the river below the bothy a few isolated pines can be seen at the head of a marked little gorge. The impetuous Nethy tumbles over several low falls two and three metres high. The place has both isolation and charm and makes a perfect climax to the walk.

Falls of Coire Odhar   NN 913 974

The Falls of Coire Odhar at the head of Loch Einich have more considerable gathering grounds than others in the same glen. In consequence they are generally more prominent. Both the Falls of Dee and the Feith Buidhe Cataract are more continuously precipitate than the Falls of Coire Odhar, but it can safely be said that, on close acquaintance, they yield nothing to the other two in the attractiveness of their individual cascades. The falls form a staircase of icicles in the winter. In the late summer they form a series of sparkling cascades, eight in number, one of which is about forty metres in height. The whole staircase of falls is about 298 metres high. The combined height of these falls thus exceeds that of the Feith Buidhe, about 250 metres, and Eas Coul Aulin, about 200 metres. It could be argued that they are the highest falls in Scotland and some early travellers asserted that this was the case. The falls make a delightful route to the indefinite upland, occupied by dotterel and ptarmigan, between the Braeriach and Carn Ban Mor mountain ranges in the late summer. The view of Loch Einich from the head of the falls is incomparable. The best way to the falls is the long march up Glen Einich, but the shortest route is by the Foxhunters' Path from Achlean in Glen Feshie.

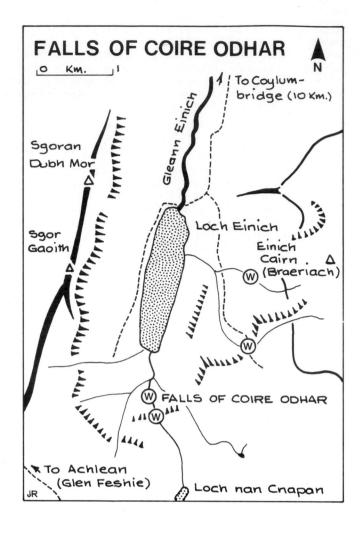

Poolflasgan Bridge Fall   NJ 183 428

This pleasant little fall in a wooded den is formed at the junction of two burns above the bridge in Upper Knockando. It is difficult to believe that friendly little stream wrought tremendous havoc in the great floods of 1829. It carried away a carding mill, a meal mill and several houses all situated below the church.

Portcullis Fall see Falls of Mashie

Randolph's Leap

Randolph's Leap is not a waterfall, although there are considerable rapids between the Leap and the Artist's Pool where the Findhorn plunges through a narrow, highly pictures-que gorge above its confluence with the Divie. However no connoisseur of river scenery should omit this place from his or her itinerary. At the Leap, near Logie Bridge on the B9007, notice-boards explain the legend of the fleeing clansman who leaped the river at this point. It is a complicated and disputed tale and the place would be frequented without it. It is the rock sculpture and the rapid river which give Randolph's Leap its character. Downstream the Findhorn continues to flow through its fine gorge and there is a grand walk from Sluie. On the opposite bank Dunearn Burn Walks give access to a magnificent terraced path above the Findhorn.

Linn of Rothes
NJ 258 484

Fall on the burn of Rothes, a tributary of the Lower Spey.

Linn of Ruthrie
NJ 266 418

This fall, close to Charlestown of Aberlour, is a favourite resort for picnics. It can be reached from the by-road which leads over the shoulder of Ben Rinnes to Dufftown, but the principal route is from the little Speyside town, made good by local scouts. The way leads to a charming double fall of about ten metres in all. Beyond this are further falls about eight metres in height.

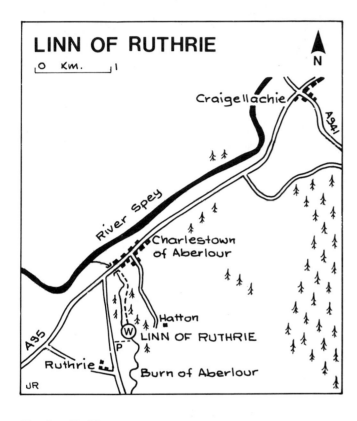

Shepherd's Linn
NJ 208 428

This fall is one of two which occur on the Burn of Balintomb close to Knockando. The valley is tributary to the Spey and the burn falls steeply to the river from the shelf of land on which Archiestown is situated.

Falls of Stron a Barin see Glen Feshie

Falls of Torgarrow
NH 921 391

These spectacular falls occur on the Leonach Burn, the Angry Burn, a tributary of the rushing Findhorn above Dulsie Bridge. They are reached by the track which leaves Dulsie Cottage and goes to the farm of Lynemore. Some distance along it a track drops down to the Findhorn itself and reaches the burn. It used to go to the farm of Torgarrow, now abandoned. There are some attractive woods and pleasant haugh lands before you reach the falls at the foot of which you are confronted by a table mountain of fluvioglacial deposits through which the Leonach and its tributary the Rhiloan have cut steep sided

gorges. The first fall on the Leonach consists of three or four linked cascades which make a graceful sweep twenty metres high. The burn has cut through the sandy deposits to reach bedrock and the heavily contorted schists make attractive patterns in the rock at the head of the fall. Above this there is a steep-sided gorge from which the path escapes on the left to rejoin the track beyond Lynemore and it soon reaches the truly impressive upper falls where there are three distinct leaps the lowest of which is twenty metres high – a big open twin fall on a substantial stream. The upper falls can be more closely inspected by fording the stream above them and descending to a promontory above the main fall. There is a fall of about eight metres on Rhiloan which can be visited from this point. These falls are infrequently visited and appear to be unknown to a wider public. This is quite undeserved. Their wild, moorland setting contrasts admirably with the rich, wooded Findhorn and they are relatively close to the beauty spot at Dulsie Bridge.

Tromie Bridge Falls
NN 788 995

There are friendly low falls where the B970 crosses the Tromie. Further up the same stream the falls below Loch an t-Seilich (NN 757 909) have been adversely affected by the hydro-electric power scheme, but the flow of this fine river through its very charming wooded valley is virtually unimpaired.

Falls of Truim
NN 680 922

The Truim joins the Spey about 5km south of Newtonmore under Creag Dubh. The lower part of its course is through a richly wooded gorge above which the A9 descends into Strathspey. The old main line of the Highland Railway runs beside the road from Dalwhinnie and where it first crosses the old road are the Falls of Truim. There is a succession of cascades, three or four metres high amid pleasant woods beside the rocky banks of the river.

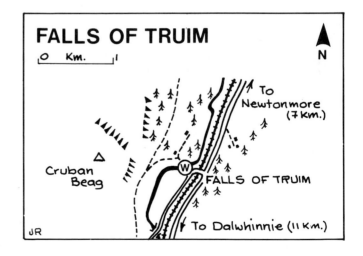

The Ness Basin

Aberiachan Falls
NH 563 349

The Aberiachan Burn forms a series of cascades and waterfalls between three and ten metres high in its helter skelter descent to Loch Ness. The village, which is off the main road (A82), is a charming place with its own museum.

Falls of Truim, between Dalwhinnie and Newtonmore, near the Great North Road and the highland railway. The Truim river is crossed by a Wade bridge. ROBERT M ADAM

Easan Ban   NH 251 106

Falls on the Allt an Eoin in upper Glen Moriston.

Steall Ban   NH 054 127

The White Spout is the prominent corrie waterfall above the 'Road to the Isles' beyond Loch Cluanie. It enlivens an austere landscape of rock and water.

Bird Fall   NH 355 091

Fall above Fort Augustus situated in the Inchnacardoch Forest and reached by the forest road above Whitebridge Cottage beyond the forest office. The burn plunges some thirty metres in dense plantations. The district is interesting because Wade's Road crossed to Glen Moriston here and it was at Fort Augustus that the first hydro-electric power scheme in Scotland was established by the monks at the abbey.

Black Falls   NH 545 140

Even in a district well known for its waterfalls Black Falls bear comparison with many other falls which are better known, doubtless because they are more accessible. The River E, said to be so-called from its shape on the map, is now the principal feeder of Loch Mhor. It is diverted into it at Garthbeg and from there an estate track leads into the hills above the river and away from it. After about six kilometres the track reaches a prominent gap where the falls are situated. The principal fall is a thundering leap of about twenty metres with an apron of four metres below and a six-metre fall immediately above it. The E descends to these falls in their birch-filled glen by a series of rapids and cascades with two distinctive falls in open moorland. The place is remote and atmospheric with excellent views towards the Great Glen.

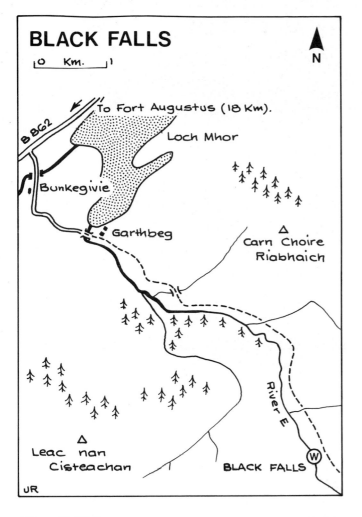

BLACK FALLS

Allt na Cailliche   *NH 273 002*

The spectacular falls, 40 metres high, on the Allt na Cailliche were little known until the Forestry Commission established two fine forest walks there. The car park is reached from the

ALLT NA CAILLICHE

foot of the Pass of Glengarry by the iron bridge which crosses the river below the Falls of Garry. The walk leads through mature plantations which restrict the view until the falls are reached. There is a fine belvedere opposite the breast of the falls which tumble down a tree-girt hillside in two principal stages into a narrow ravine, quite inaccessible, at their foot. An extension to the walk leads further into the hills. Although they are situated on a tributary burn there is usually a good deal of water in them and they are quite as impressive as the better known Falls of Divach.

Calder Falls (Strath Errick)   *NH 571 183*

These falls are well seen across Loch Mhor at the point where a causeway goes to Aberchalder. The Aberchalder Burn descends from a gap in the hills into a birch-filled hollow. An indefinite path leads up to them from Easter Aberchalder. The main fall is a very steep, but not vertical, cascade about twenty-five metres high. Above this there is another fall at the point where the burn tumbles over the edge of the escarpment. There are fine views towards Loch Ness and an intriguing view of the narrow trench of Conagleann.

Eas Coire nan Cnamh   *NG 977 045*

This is the remote fall often visited by those intrepid motorists who cross the pass from Loch Quoich to Kinlochhourn. It is situated at the head of this fine mountain pass and a well-trodden path leads to it.

Corrimony Falls   *NH 373 291*

Corrimony is best known for its Neolithic Chambered Cairn. There is an attractive fall on the upper Enrick about one kilometre south of Corrimony House. Above the fall on the

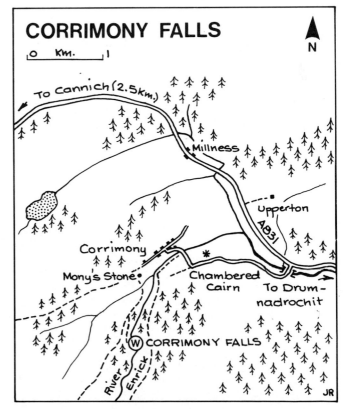

CORRIMONY FALLS

right bank is Mony's Cave where the principal supporters of Prince Charlie hid after the Forty-Five. There is a footbridge near the House and footpaths on both banks of the river.

Culachy Falls   *NH 376 058*

The Culachy Estate at the foot of the Corrieyarrick Pass is close to Fort Augustus on Loch Ness. The Wade road has been diverted and there is a labyrinth of tracks. The falls, on a tributary of the Tarff, are off the Wade road, but can be visited easily enough from it.

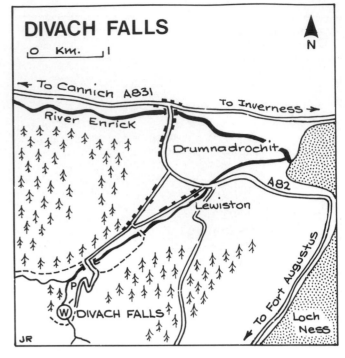

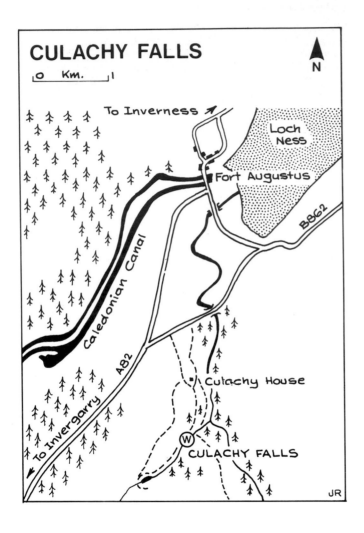

Falls of Divach   *NH 494 273*

These Loch Ness-side falls are frequently referred to in guide books because they are 'higher than Foyers', although the Coiltie and its tributaries are much less substantial streams than the Foyers and its feeders. These falls are well worth visiting on their own account. The approach road from Lewiston is steep and the outlook from the alp that the road leads to is very fine, embracing the most attractive section of Loch Ness. The Forestry Commission have constructed a tiny car park and a delightful path leads into the ravine of the Divach Burn. Divach Lodge, associated with J M Barrie and John Phillips RA, is perched above the falls. The dramatic situation of the house, the fine embowering woods and the falls, some thirty metres high, combine to make a memorable scene.

Dochfour Glen   *NH 603 385*

Artificial falls created by the engineers of the Caledonian Canal in fine woods.

Doe Falls, Glen Moriston   *NH 224 121*

Near the confluence of the Doe, its most considerable left bank tributary, and the Moriston is a simple monument to Roderick MacKenzie who gave his life for the Young Pretender whom he closely resembled. Cumberland's men took him for the Prince, and when he was killed it was thought that the royal fugitive had at last been caught, but the Prince escaped. Prince Charlie's Cave, where he was looked after by the Seven Men of Glenmoriston, is under Tigh Mor na Seilge in Coire Mheadhoin drained by a headwater of the Doe. The falls are close to the entrance to the glen.

Doe Falls, Loch Ness   *NH 411 084*

Like the River Foyers the Doe falls steeply into Loch Ness and there are falls immediately above the lake *(NH 403 098)*. Where the road crosses the Doe there is a fine ruined Wade bridge and a highly spectacular cascade some 30 metres high.

Eas Mac Eoichd   *NH 414 111*

Fall, below Loch Tarff, which, in common with a number of others, tumbles down from the shelf above Loch Ness into the Loch itself.

Falls of Farigaig   *NH 541 244*

The little River Farigaig is the counterpart of the Fechlin. It drains the northern part of Stratherrick, draining Loch Conagleann and the highly attractive Loch Ruthven before tumbling over the shelf above Loch Ness. The view of the Loch close to the Farigaig Gorge, with Dun Deardil in the foreground, is one of the finest. The falls on the Farigaig are not so dramatic as Foyers but the river runs in a fine wooded defile and falls more than twenty metres in two principal leaps. The falls themselves are virtually inaccessible owing to the impenetrable nature of the woodland.

Falls of Fechlin   *NH 495 143*

The Fechlin drains the splendid Loch Killin and then tumbles over the Falls of Foyers. It is now diverted into the River E and Loch Mhor by a barrage on the site of the Falls of Fechlin at the head of a pleasant little gorge above Whitebridge.

The Falls of Foyers   *NH 497 204*

Foyers was, without doubt, the premier waterfall of Scotland. It was known not to be the highest fall, although those who discounted Glomach as a mere mountain torrent for long acclaimed Foyers as such. It was not considered so picturesque as the Fall of Tummel, and it could not be claimed to be a fall on a great river like the Falls of Clyde, but it combined a savage beauty with height of fall and, in spate, a great force of water. Its Gaelic name, *Eas na Smuid*, the waterfall of the smoke, was apt and descriptive. Foyers could, in the eighteenth and early nineteenth centuries, before access was made comparatively safe, be a dangerous and frightening place. The fall was not, as the Scottish Tourist of 1832 proclaimed, 'one of the highest cataracts in the world', but this statement gives some idea of the awe in which it was held.

One of the earliest descriptions of Foyers is given in MacFarlane's Geographical Collections (1720). It gives an account of the river below Loch Killin:

> The river runs very rapid about two miles, then falls down a precipice and makes a great Linn, then it runs six miles and a half and then falls down a greater precipice and Linn and a quarter of a mile downward falls down a third precipice, the most terrible and greatest of all, and for anything we know, in the highlands, and then with great noise and rapidity falls a quarter of a mile downward into the Lake of Ness.

When Dr E D Clarke, the early nineteenth century traveller, saw Foyers he asserted that he considered it to be superior to the famous Italian falls of Tivoli and inferior only to those of Terni. Clarke was only one of many distinguished visitors – Johnson, Pennant, Burns, the Wordsworths, Southey and Wilson, the 'Christopher North' of Blackwood's Magazine, all wrote about the place. It is probably Wilson's apostrophe which has been quoted most often:

> The Fall of Foyers is the most magnificent cataract out of all sight and hearing in Britain. The din is quite loud enough in ordinary weather – and it is only in ordinary weather that you can approach the place from which you have a full view of all its grandeur. When the fall is in flood – to say nothing of being drenched to the skin – you are so blinded by the sharp spray smoke and so deafened by the dashing and clashing and tumbling and rumbling that your condition is far from enviable as you cling 'lonely lover of nature' to a shelf by no means eminent for safety above the horrid gulf. In ordinary highland weather – meaning thereby neither very wet nor very dry – it is worth walking a thousand miles to behold for one hour the Falls of Foyers.

Dr Johnson's comments are also still remembered:

> We desired our guide to show us the fall, and dismounting, clambered over very rugged crags, till I began to wish that our curiosity might have been gratified with less trouble and

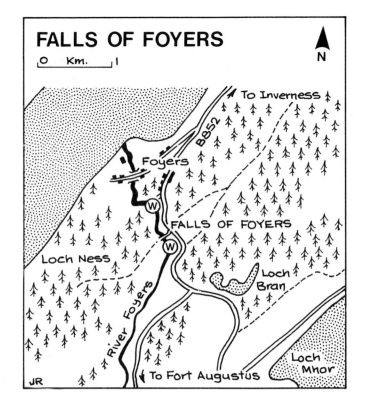

FALLS OF FOYERS

danger. We came at last to a place where we could overlook the river, and saw a channel torn, as it seems, through black piles of stones, by which the stream is obstructed and broken till it comes to a very deep descent, of such dreadful depth, that we were naturally inclined to turn aside our eyes.

Southey was perhaps the most critical visitor and his complaints may have led to the improvement of access to Foyers. He visited the fall with Telford.

> It rained during our halt and continued to rain heavily when the carriage stopt above the Fall of Foyers. The ladies stept down from the coach upon the wall to look down the glen and I went with Mr Telford some way down. It is not creditable to the owner of the property that there should be no means of getting to the bottom of the fall, and no safe means of obtaining a full view from any point except from the high road where it is so foreshortened as to be seen to great disadvantage. The water was so much less than it usually is in this wet country and far too little for the chasm, still it exceeded our waterfalls (the waterfalls in the Lake District in England) when they are in full force and when the river is full it might bear comparison with Reichenbach. The accompaniments cannot be finer anywhere; everything is beautiful and everything – wood rocks, water, the glen, the mountains and the lake below in proportion. There is a higher fall, the river plunging into a deep basin, you see it from a bridge.

Joseph Mitchell relates in his Reminiscences (1883) how Lord Colchester gave him £5 to start a subscription to make a proper path in about 1837 and how he constructed it. Mitchell was a pupil of Telford and continued his work in the Highlands. His appreciation of the quality of Highland scenery is exemplified in his account of Foyers:

> Nature here has done everything. No landscape gardener could lay out plantations amidst cultivated fields with more

graceful effect than Dame Nature has done at this place, in mere sport and playfulness. The river below the Fall sweeps by the house with a quiet and gentle current as if exhausted with its tremendous leap over the adjoining precipice.

The fall is immediately below the road and you approach it by a winding path down a rugged steep to a green point about fifty feet from the bottom of the river. From this station you have a full view of the fall, 150 feet high. It struggles through a narrow chasm of rock not above six or eight feet in width, and then spreads, catching some small projections in the rock, and waving and foaming it descends to the deep, dark gulf below.

The scene is peculiarly wild and grand. You stand in an amphitheatre of rugged and perpendicular rocks fringed at the horizon with waving birch and all is still except the incessant roar of the descending water.

A number of famous engineers have been associated with Foyers. Southey was not above criticising General Wade:

General Wade's road has opened the way to the only view of the Fall of Foyers and perhaps the General did this designedly. But in proceeding to Fort Augustus and indeed in most, or all, of his roads he seems to have, like other road makers, followed the old horse track instead of surveying the country like an engineer.

However, there is no doubt that Wade and his successors did contribute to the popularity of Foyers. The original line from Whitebridge, where the road crosses the Foyers, to Inverfarigaig was away from the loch, but it was abandoned after a few years and the line of the present B852 was adopted. The 'General's Hut' from which the great man was said to have supervised all this work was on the right bank of the river at the site of the Foyers Hotel, opposite Foyers House on the left bank.

The building of Telford's Caledonian Canal also rendered Foyers more accessible. By 1832 R and W Chambers were commenting in their Gazetteer that 'a stone bridge, unfortunately in a poor and unsuitable taste, has been thrown across the ravine'. This is the bridge in front of the upper fall from which the best view of that fall is obtained. It is said that before this a very rudimentary bridge, no more than a tree trunk, spanned the gorge at this point and that a drunkard in his cups rode over it in a storm. On re-visiting the spot he was so appalled at his foolhardiness that he suffered a heart attack and died. However, this is a relatively common folk tale associated with more than one fall and may be regarded as a device to impress visitors.

It is, of course, the *Lower Fall* which is the *pièce de résistance*. Here the river falls into a superb rock amphitheatre. In spate the spray from the fall is enough to obscure it. Because the fall is in an amphitheatre it can be seen to great advantage from Green Point almost opposite. There are innumerable prints of the Fall of Foyers which suggest what a magnificent fall it must have been. Birch, mountain ash and oak clothe the slopes and give the scene a richness of vegetation which is not characteristic of many other falls. At the head of the falls there are banks of rose-root, a fleshy-leaved plant characteristic of damp environments which dry out, the yellow mountain saxifrage, the mossy saxifrage and the golden saxifrage.

Burns is judged not to have been at his best when he wrote his immitative tribute to Foyers, but his couplets do suggest many of its attributes:

Among the heathy hills and mossy rugged woods
The roaring Foyers pours his mossy floods

Till full he dashes on the rocky mounds
Where through a shapeless breach his stream resounds
As high in air the bursting torrents flow
As deep recoiling surges foam below
Prone down the rock the whitening sheet descends
And, viewless, echo's ear, astonished rends
Dim-seen through rising mists and ceaseless showers
The hoary cavern, wide-surrounding, lowers
Still through the gap the struggling river toils
And still below the horrid caldron boils.

Curiously enough the height of Foyers, which one might suppose would have been firmly established at an early date, is a matter of some dispute. It will be recalled that the early description, already quoted, refers to three linns and not two. The *Upper Fall of Foyers (NH 498 199)* consists of three leaps, the first two of which are close together at some distance from the bridge, the third under the bridge itself. This is the second linn of the early description. Chambers (1832) gives the height of this fall as 200 feet (60 metres) which is the height of the bridge above the water below. *The Scottish Tourist* (1832) gives the height of the upper fall as 70 feet (21 metres), the Ordnance Gazetteer gives the height as 45 feet (14 metres) and some notable authorities, including for example the *Shell Guide*, give the height as 30 feet (10 metres). These differences can, no doubt, be explained by the fact that there are three leaps and the figure given in the Ordnance Gazetteer is widely accepted. There are similar differences in respect of the lower fall. Chambers asserted that the fall is 212 feet (65 metres) high, but this is widely optimistic; the Ordnance Gazetteer gives the height as 165 feet (50 metres). Baddeley and a number of other sources give a height of 90 feet (27 metres) and the Ordnance Survey Map supports this view. At the foot of the fall the 200 foot contour crosses the river. At its head the 300 foot contour crosses the gorge between the upper and lower falls. This is a difference of 30 metres.

The Upper Fall is 430 feet (131 metres) above sea level. This would suggest that the combined height of the two falls cannot exceed 200 feet (60 metres) by any great margin. The river falls under 400 feet (115 metres) between the head of the Upper Fall and Loch Ness, a distance of two kilometres. The British Aluminium Company's original hydro-electric power installation which abstracted water from immediately above the Upper Fall had a head of 360 feet (108 metres).

The attraction of Foyers does not rest simply in its height, but in the quantity of water which it discharges. The river drains a complex basin of more than 250 square kilometres on the shelf above Loch Ness which has been considerably altered by the hydro-electric works. The River E is the principal feeder of Loch Mhor. This reservoir was created by impounding Loch Garth and Loch Farraline and acts as a storage basin for the hydro-electric works. The Hydro Board abstract water directly from Loch Mhor and pump water from Loch Ness into it. The aluminium company, who built the reservoir, abstracted water from a point above the Upper Fall allowing water from Loch Mhor to fall into the River Foyers via the River Gourag. The River Fechlin, which is the name given to the Foyers in the upper part of its course, is now diverted into Loch Mhor. It drains an extensive upland basin including the highly picturesque Loch Killin. It is this river which is described in MacFarlane's Geographical Collections. In ordinary conditions nowadays it is the Breinag, the river which flows below the A852 on the right-hand side as you approach Foyers from Fort Augustus, that supplies the fall with water. A turbine which the Hydro Board installed in the BAC factory by-passes the falls and, in dry conditions when there is insufficient water to drive it, the water is passed over the falls.

Before all these works were undertaken it is probable that the Foyers had an average discharge of about 7.5 cubic metres per second, comparable with that of the Kirkaig today or with that of the Falls of Leny. Its discharge was probably about four times as great as that of the Fall of Glomach, for, although it has a much more extensive catchment, it is in an area of comparatively low rainfall – the rain-bearing winds having spent themselves above Loch Quoich.

The situation of Foyers beside the Caledonian Canal made it almost inevitable that it would be the site of an early electro-metallurgical establishment. The Héroult process extracts aluminium from alumina in an electric furnace. Because great heat is required for the extraction of the metal, early factories were concentrated where electric power could be easily developed and Foyers was one of the earliest to be established in Europe. It was opened in 1896 and closed in 1967. The company converted Old Foyers House, then a ruin, into a temporary hostel while houses were built, and the work was carried out. The company had a powerful and wealthy directorate with Lord Kelvin as scientific adviser. The great man was not above supporting one scheme which was established for the conversion of base metals into gold, but in this case he showed himself to be at the forefront of contemporary technology.

However it is interesting to look back on the public debate which took place when the company's proposals were made known. Opponents of the scheme – the first amenity lobby – included the Duke of Westminster, Canon Rawnsley, a founder of the National Trust, Ruskin and Baddeley. They asserted without any foundation that the vegetation for miles around would be destroyed while the company asserted that they did not believe that this would happen, but even if it did this would not outweigh the benefits which the scheme would bring to the locality. Baddeley in a letter to *The Times* said, 'Their scheme is the greatest outrage on Nature perpetrated this century and the excuses made for it are the most inexcusable'. Defenders of the scheme pointed to the possibility of turning on the falls and illuminating them.

Because of the rock architecture at Foyers it always suffered during dry weather. At these times it was evident that it was not at its best. In ordinary weather a dense mist could be seen rising from the broken water and the noise made could usually be heard at a considerable distance. It rendered opponents of the scheme speechless when a spokesman for the company stated – although the statement was hotly denied by the company – that the falls would not be injured, only there would be no water in them.

Nowadays the factory is an industrial monument. The original turbo-generators – one of which has been retained – are of considerable interest. Indeed the whole locality is highly attractive. Modern guide books tend to play it down, but Foyers is a fascinating place. Loch Ness is at its deepest off Foyers and Foyers is the headquarters of an investigation into the Loch Ness Monster. At Boleskin House Aleister Crowley, the mountaineer and sorcerer, lived from 1900-18. Foyers must have been a strange place during this period with its newly established factory. Crowley was a many-sided man and he and his entourage must have had an impact comparable with that of a 'hippy' colony. He is said to have terrorised the locals. Typical of his public-school sense of humour is the story that he wrote to the Society for Vigilance complaining that prostitution was most unpleasantly conspicuous in the neighbourhood of Foyers. The Society sent an observer who discovered nothing. Crowley informed them that he found it conspicuous by its absence.

The new Power Station and the Wade Bridge at White Bridge should also be visited but, above all, a visit should be paid to the Falls. Seton Gordon (1948), the most authoritative writer on the Highlands of his day, commented 'Although Foyers has changed greatly during the past twenty-five years the scene at the great fall itself has lost nothing of its dignity and grandeur'. Access is straightforward enough. The best viewpoint is on the west bank immediately opposite the fall, or from Green Point.

The geology of Foyers is interesting. Above the fall the river crosses the Foyers Granite which is of interest to geologists because the same rock occurs at Strontian on the opposite side of the Great Glen and indicates the immense movement which there has been along the line of the fault. Below the falls the rock is Old Red Sandstone. The tunnel built by the BAC was excavated in metamorphic rocks and the spoil was dumped in the gorge.

Foyers is situated in the Parish of Boleskine and Abertarff. The old church of Boleskin is situated not far from the falls. In the New Statistical Account the minister interprets the name as 'At the summit of the furious cascade'. However, Watson, a much more reliable authority in such matters, gives the derivation as 'the place of the withies', while the Old Statistical Account called Boleskin 'the parish hanging above the lake'. Whatever the truth of the matter is, the first name seems so appropriate that we should not quarrel with it. Foyers must remain the furious cascade.

Falls of Foyers. Engraving by T Allon and E Radcliffe 1836. This uses tiny figures on the rock shelf of Green Point to emphasise the scale of the falls.

Falls of Garry   *NH 276 019*

At the outlet to Loch Garry there were three rises of about three metres and, to reach the lake, salmon had to make two separate springs. The falls are now dominated by the impressive gravity dam at the foot of the loch and the channels which the river occupies are partly artificial. In spate the falls have the greatest volume of water of any falls in the Ness Basin.

Falls of Ghivach see Falls of Divach

Allt Guish   *NH 475 212*

The Fir Tree Burn, like the Allt Saigh, falls into Loch Ness down the steep sides of the Great Glen. The burn is a continuous cascade and falls 30 metres sheer in one place. From Ruskich, at the foot of the burn, traces can still be seen of the little ale house from which there used to be a ferry to Foyers. Today there is just a lay-by on the busy A82. The Ruskich Forest is famous for its great trees, some birches having a girth of 2.5 metres. The Allt Guish is probably the site of a famous incident after the Raid of Kilchrist, the slaughter of a kirkful of MacKenzies by the MacDonnells of Glengarry in 1700. The MacKenzies sought out a party of MacDonnells and put them to flight. Their leader, Alan MacRaonuill, made one of those prodigious leaps across the stream which seem to figure so largely in Highland legend. The MacKenzie who was in pursuit of him tried to emulate this feat, but he stumbled on the far bank and would have fallen straight away into the ravine had he not caught hold of a shrub, but MacRaonuill took out his knife, cut the shrub and sent him to his death.

Falls of Knockie   *NH 442 140*

Loch Knockie is perhaps the most picturesque of the lochs in the 'Inverness-shire Lake District' and there is a well-situated hotel there signposted from the A862. From the hotel, forest roads lead round the nearby Loch nan Lann with a pretty ford at its outlet. Just below this the burn tumbles twenty-five metres in a sweet fall beside the steep track to Loch Ness. This area has considerable charm and deserves to be better known than it is.

Falls of Allt Ladaidh   *NH 228 006*

Forestry and the depredations of the Hydro Board have made Loch Garry less attractive than it used to be, but it is at the heart of much wild country. There are three fine cascades on the Allt Ladaidh which can be reached by the forestry road from the head of the loch. This burn drains an extensive catchment on the northern slopes of Ben Tee.

Eas Allt a'Mheil   *NH 042 023*

Loch Quoich is a huge reservoir and its old boundaries have been swamped in the interests of hydro-electricity. The road to Kinlochhourn runs along the edge of the loch and one of the more interesting places there is where the Allt a'Mheil tumbles into the loch.

Falls of Allt a'Mhuillinn   *NH 405 128*

The new road along Loch Ness, the A82, is today singularly sparsely inhabited except where there are major rivers. However the name of this little burn, Mill Burn, betrays the fact that the country was once a much more lively place. Cascading falls on the burn can be visited from the road.

Falls of Moriston   *NH 422 164*

Glen Moriston was almost certainly named from Loch Ness. Just above the loch the river tumbles over a series of considerable falls which give it its name, Mor Easan. The Moriston drains what is one of the wettest catchments in Britain. The rainfall in the upper part of Glen Moriston is exceeded by its neighbour, Glen Quoich, but the difference is marginal. The basin is floored by impervious grits and schists. Run-off is immediate and the discharge of this river approaches that of the Clyde above Bonnington Linn.

The wild falls below the bridge on the A82 are among the outstanding river falls in Scotland. In spite of the Moriston Hydro Electric Power Scheme, they remain well worth visiting in spate. They stand in the grounds of Invermoriston House, access to which used to be strictly preserved, but now the

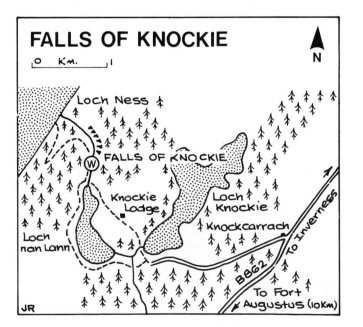

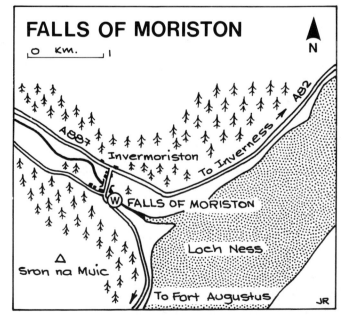

grounds are open to the public beside the river. Nearby are the ruins of St Columba's Chapel. The entrance to 'the long glen of the Grants' is backed by rugged hills. At the falls are two fish passes. The first, built in 1880, climbs the left bank, but it was considered too steep and it was replaced by a longer pass on the right bank. Both passes are worth examination to show what elaborate works were undertaken by proprietors in the interests of salmon fishing. The falls were further eased by the Hydro Board, but the fishing on the Moriston has never been the same since the power scheme. There is a splendid account of the atmosphere in the Invermoriston Hotel in pre-war days in H V Morton's *In Scotland Again* (1933).

The *Falls of Invermoriston* begin at the old bridge of two arches built by Telford, above the modern bridge. On an old postcard on display at the inn they are called *Bridge Falls*. Footpaths lead beside the river through mature woodland, in which beech and pine predominate, to a splendid little stone view house above the main falls which are about eight metres high; from the house there is an unforgettable prospect of the old bridge seen through the single arch of the new. The roaring white water tumbles over the falls at your feet. These falls are the subject of a notable engraving by Mazell in Charles Cordiner's *Antiquities and Scenery of the North of Scotland* (1780).

It is possible to walk to the lochside to see the outfall of the power station which now deprives the falls of some of their former grandeur. In spate, however, the Falls of Invermoriston, which crash about twenty metres between the bridge and the loch, lose nothing. They are an outstanding attraction.

From the Invermoriston Hotel the Road to the Isles leads to Loch Cluanie and Glen Shiel. It is, perhaps, the prospect of reaching such places which causes visitors to overlook the attractions of Glenmoriston. It should not be rushed. In his *Circuit Journeys* Henry Cockburn, the judge who travelled the length of the land between 1837 and 1854, is enthusiastic about the place which he visited in September, 1841:

> I cannot pay these four wooded miles – where the softness of the birch contrasts so naturally with the savage rocky stream – a higher compliment than by saying that they reminded me of some parts of the unrivalled Findhorn, by far the finest of our British torrents. All the rivers are swollen at present, and Moriston was at its fiercest strength.

H V Morton is eloquent, too, about Glenmoriston, which he approached from Cluanie, in *In Scotland Again* (1933):

> I went in bright sunlight through the deepening beauty of Glen Moriston. What a perfect glen it is. If you wish to see a sudden switch from the wild Highland to soft Highland scenery, go through this glen. The deer forests end suddenly. You are in dark fir and birchwoods and the River Moriston tumbles over falls which put Killiecrankie in the shade.

The falls referred to are just below the Dundreggan Dam. Dundreggan, the dun of the wild beast (of the dragon), is the haunt of the Glenmoriston fairies, prone, it is said, to kidnap mothers in milk. Below the dam, of which Cockburn would certainly not have approved, but which is an impressive structure which fits in with the place reasonably well, the river roars as it races over a succession of rocky falls. They take their name from a tributary burn which joins the river at the dam. On old maps they are called the *Falls of Allt Eiric*, but modern cartographers render this corruption *Eas Iarairidh (NH 359 156)*. The falls are extended and not as steep as the Falls of Invermoriston, but the river has a drop of fifteen metres, and as the water crashes between steep rock walls it is very impressive indeed when there is any quantity of water there.

These falls are reached from a lay by, made out of the old road, just below the dam.

Glen Moriston becomes less well-wooded above Dundreggan and there are minor falls on lesser burns in the more open country there. The Allt an Eoin, not far from the track of the Wade Road from Fort Augustus, has *Easan Ban (NH 251 106)*, white falls. On the Balintombuie Burn, above the settlement of that name on the north bank of the Moriston, is *Eas an Tairbh (NH 287 141)*, the fall of the (water) bull.

Falls of Moral see Corrimony Falls

Reelig Glen   *NH 558 419*

An attractive forest trail has been established by the Forestry Commission in these old policy woodlands on the bank of the Moniak Burn. The entrance is off the old A9 (NH 558 432). There are magnificent cedars behind the classical house and the policies are rich in exotic trees with numerous interesting ground plants. Its ferns, mosses, liverworts and fungi are of great botanical interest. There are particularly fine Douglas firs in the woods. Bridges, grottoes and follies add interest to the walk. The falls are on a tributary of the main burn.

Allt Saigh Falls   *NH 454 192*

Allt nan Saighead, possibly the burn of the arrows, but probably Birch Burn, was until recently considered to be the site of the conflict between the MacDonnells and the MacKenzies but the new edition of the Ordnance Survey map locates the skirmish much further from the burn than the old County Map. The burn falls over 450 metres in a continuous torrent. There are two fine falls, one half way up the hillside and one near the mouth of the burn. This can be reached readily enough from the Youth Hostel past a bridge on the old road.

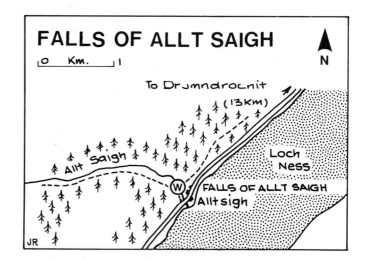

Falls of Tarff   *NH 450 027*

The Falls of Tarff are in the heart of what might be called Lea MacNally country. Readers of his magnificent books about the Cullachy Estate and the deer and eagles found there will have a real sense of this remote country. His photographs and his intimate descriptions of the creatures that live there virtually undisturbed are the finest of their kind. The Tarff drains a considerable basin and its course is precipitate. The infant

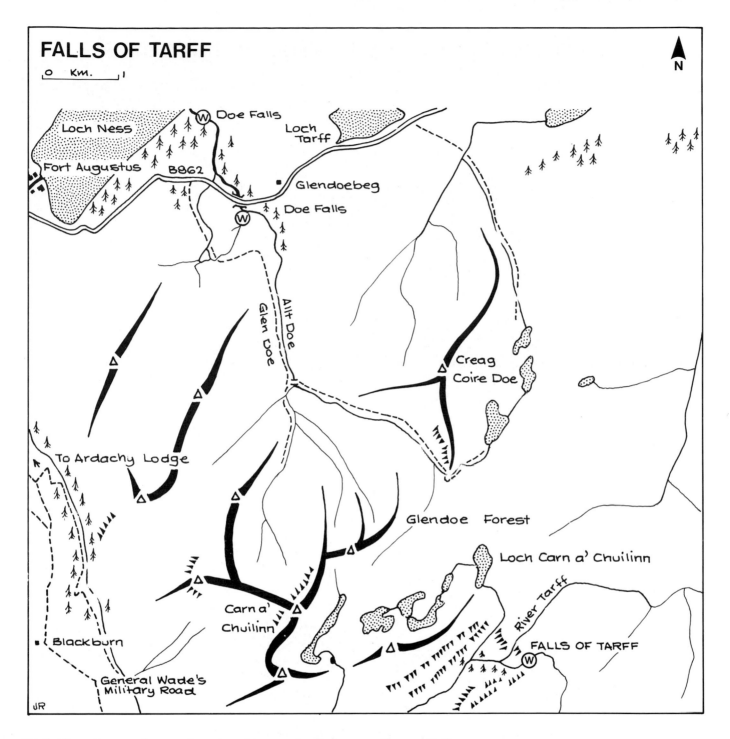

FALLS OF TARFF

0 KM. 1

Loch Ness

Doe Falls

Loch Tarff

Fort Augustus

B862

Glendoebeg

Doe Falls

Glen Doe

Allt Doe

To Ardachy Lodge

Creag Coire Doe

Glendoe   Forest

Loch Carn a' Chuilinn

River Tarff

FALLS OF TARFF

Carn a' Chuilinn

Blackburn

General Wade's Military Road

JR

Tarff 'slips down a short series of rocky cascades before suddenly leaping into space in the Falls of Tarff, descending in one dizzy swoop about a hundred sheer feet' (MacNally). The falls can only be seen in their entirety from a remote hillside because they are concealed in a steep sided rocky bowl. The Tarff flows through a series of gorges below the Corrieyaraik Pass before reaching Loch Ness. The head of the Tarff is best reached by the charming Allt Vingie and the head of Glen Doe, starting from Loch Tarff on the A862.

Falls of Allt Saigh. *This early nineteenth century engraving shows a famous incident in a conflict between the MacDonnells and the MacKenzies.*

Torness Falls   *NH 579 270*

These are pleasing river falls on the Farigaig where it tumbles over two or three sparkling cascades under a modern bridge on the main road between Loch Mhor and Loch Duntelchaig in Stratherrick.

Whitebridge Falls   *NH 485 149*

These pretty falls, perhaps five metres high, are situated on the Breinag, the handsome little river which keeps company with the road from Fort Augustus to Foyers. They are not far upstream from the confluence of the stream with the Fechlin at Whitebridge, the old Wade Bridge which can still be seen today.

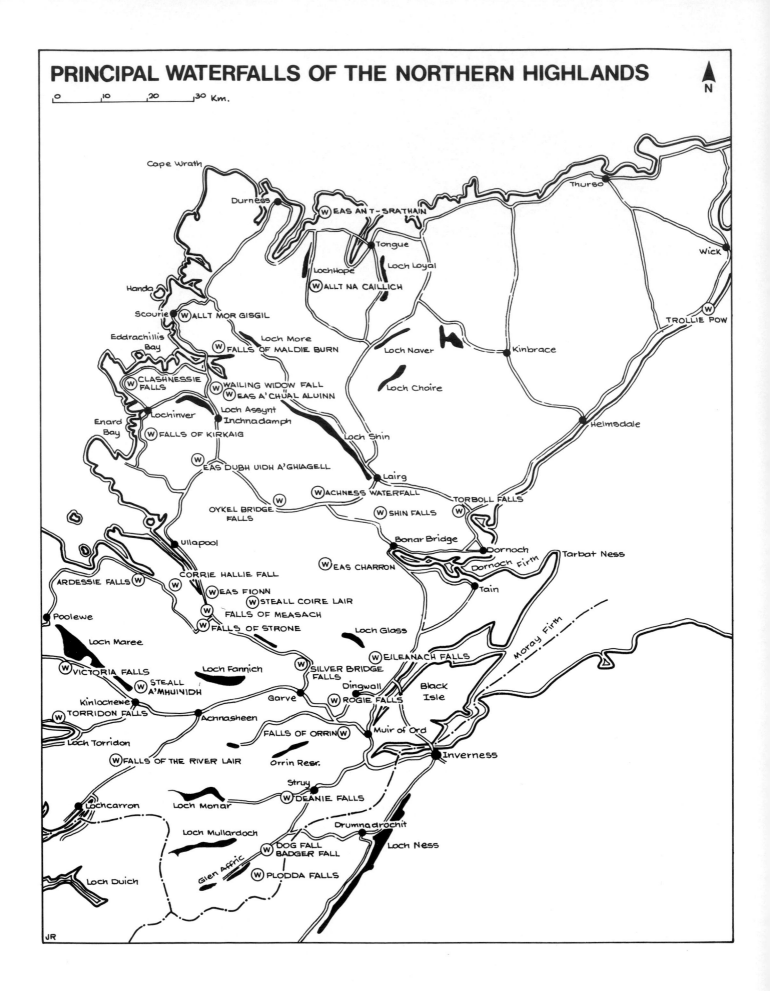

PRINCIPAL WATERFALLS OF THE NORTHERN HIGHLANDS

0   10   20   30 Km.

THE NORTHERN HIGHLANDS

Principal Falls

Outstanding Falls	Touring Centre
Eas a' Chual Aluinn (Eas Coul Aulin)	Kylesku
Dog Fall	Beauly
Falls of Kirkaig	Lochinver
Falls of Measach	Ullapool

Significant Falls	
Allt na Caillich	Durness
Falls of Ardessie	Dundonnell
Badger Fall	Beauly
Deanie Falls	Beauly
Steall Coir Lair	Ullapool
Falls of River Lair	Loch Carron
Pladda Falls	Beauly
Falls of Rogie	Contin
Falls of Shin	Lairg
Torridon Falls	Loch Torridon
Victoria Falls	Loch Maree
Wailing Widow Fall	Kylesku

Interesting Falls	
Eas Clais an Easaidh	Assynt
Falls of Cassley (Achness)	Lairg
Eas Charron (Glencalvie Falls)	Bonar Bridge
Eas Dubh Uidh a Chiagell	Assynt
Eileanach Falls (Black Rock of Movar)	Evanton
Eas Fionn	Ullapool
Steall a Mhuinidh	Loch Maree
Eas Mor Gisgil	Scourie
Falls of Orrin	Contin
Silver Bridge Falls	Contin
Eas an-t-Srathain	Durness
Falls of Strone	Ullapool
Torboll Fall	Dornoch
Trollie Pow	Wick

Also recommended	
Falls of Conon	Contin
Culligran Falls	Beauly
Dunrobin Falls	Golspie
Eathie Den	Rosemarkie
Falls of Kilcalmkill	Brora
Falls of Maldie Burn	Kylesku
Smoo Waterfall	Durness

Waterfalls of the Northern Highlands

For the purposes of this survey the Northern Highlands is held to include all those river basins which drain into the sea north of the Great Glen. This includes the basin of the Beauly in the Inverness District and the rivers of Ross and Cromarty, Sutherland and Caithness. The basin of the Beauly is considered by many visitors to be the most beautiful part of Scotland and many writers judge Glen Affric to be unsurpassed. There are several notable falls in the extensive forests of birch and Caledonian pine including the well-known Dog Fall and the less well-known, but in its way as attractive, Pladda Fall. The area has been widely developed for hydro-electric power and these developments were rightly resisted at the time by those who believed that the scenery of the district was a priceless heritage which would be destroyed by them. Radical changes have taken place, but some of the character of what has been lost can still be appreciated, and there is evidence of a concern for amenity which is more marked than else-where.

Whatever the attractions of the Beauly, for many people Ross and Cromarty District is the epitomy of Scottish scenery. There is no loch superior to Loch Maree, there are no mountains more spectacular than those of Torridon, there is no deer forest wilder than Fisherfield, and, of Scotland's great waterfalls, none is more splendid than that situated in the Corrieshalloch Gorge. Both Glomach and Eas Coul Aulin are hidden falls, remote and relatively difficult of access, even the Grey Mare's Tail cannot be properly appreciated without an awkward little walk. The Falls of Measach are easily reached from either of two main roads. The tree-lined Corrieshalloch Gorge is, however, hidden from passing traffic and the falls retain their wild dignity. Without doubt they are a major tourist attraction.

The principal river basin entirely within Ross and Cromarty is that of the Conon. Baddeley commented that there is a resemblance between the Falls of Rogie and the renowned Falls of Tivoli in Italy. These falls are characteristic of the more subdued landscapes of Easter Ross, and are easily accessible in an area delightfully treated by the Forestry Commission. Much of the rest of the basin of the Conon is, however, more noticeably affected by hydro-electric works and both the Falls of Conon and the Falls of Orrin are attenuated because of this. One of the Board's first small schemes devastated the Falls of Kerry in the West, too. However, Ross is large enough to accommodate these schemes, and many interesting falls are quite unspoiled. There are half a dozen falls in the vicinity of Ullapool, much less well-known than the Falls of Measach, but almost equally picturesque.

In a sense Ross is a region of transition and, as such, it falls short of the Southern Highlands in the delights of wooded glens, and of Sutherland and Caithness in savage desolation, but it is the very combination of the two which gives Ross its charm. Its waterfalls have much interest and offer infinite scope for exploration.

Sutherland and Caithness are composed of paleozoic and archean sediments, old hard rocks. The climate is sub-arctic and, while there are warm, sunny bays and oases of greenery on limestone, most visitors will find the dreary plains of Caithness and the isolated mountains of Sutherland to be desolate places. In particular, although there is a great deal to interest the botanist, it is the general absence of trees which is most striking. However, once acquired, a taste for the North is difficult to satisfy. Conditions are ideal for the formation of waterfalls. The myriad lochs and lochans which occupy rock basins and the extensive peat cover regulate the flow of water. Rocks are angular and the falls are distinctive.

The rockbound coast of the North of Scotland is its supreme glory, a magnificent culmination to the infinitely varied landscapes of mainland Scotland. There are stunning beaches, gaunt cliffs, sensational headlands, cave systems, stacks and a variety of other attractions from colonies of sea-birds to intriguing castles and fishing ports.

Coastal waterfalls occupy a relatively minor place in this galaxy of attractions, but where they occur they greatly enhance the interest of the scene. The outstanding falls are those at Smoo, the *Falls of Geodha an-t-Strathain* (the waterfall cave), *Coldbackie Falls*, and the *Falls of the Clyth Burn*.

There are two or three falls which must rank with the finest in the country. Eas Coul Aulin—the splendid waterfall of Coul—is generally reckoned to be the highest in Great Britain and one of the dozen or so waterfalls which are tourist attractions in Western Europe. The Falls of Shin are grand river falls forming one of the most impressive salmon leaps in Scotland. However, the virtues of these two falls are combined in a third, the Falls of Kirkaig which are regarded as having the most notable combination of volume of water, height of fall and distinctiveness of setting in Britain.

Few of the first tourists to Scotland visited the North, and, in general, few guide books sing the praises of the falls there. Some falls are very remote and difficult of access and hold dangers for visitors who are unprepared or inexperienced in the business of route-finding, but other falls are easily sought out and well worth visiting.

Corrieshalloch Gorge, Falls of Measach. Probably the best known falls in the Northern Highlands, and the most accessible of Scotland's great falls. Some 80 metres high, the falls are dwarfed by the mighty walls of the gorge. A suspension bridge and a viewpoint let the visitor appreciate the awesome majesty of the falls. PETER DAVENPORT

Eas Coul Aulin, above Loch Beag, Sutherland (see p. 110). At 200 metres high, the highest waterfall in Britain. HAMISH BROWN

The Beauly Basin

Badger Fall
NH 308 285

The Eas nam Broc, Badger Fall, is in a forest of birches at the entrance to Chisholm's Pass(q.v.) close to the Fanaskyle Power Station. The fall is reached by a path, a walk of some twenty minutes from the road. It is about ten metres high, a delicate fall, superbly set. Some assert that it is superior to its fellow fall, Dog Fall. The name is derived from the number of badgers which used to frequent the locality where there are notably sandy soils.

Sputan Ban
NH 135 225

The white spouts are remote hillside fall occurring on the Allt Coulavie, prominent at the head of Loch Affric.

Eas nam Broc see Badger Fall

Chisholm's Pass

One reason why the Affric-Beauly system was so admirably suited to water power development was the abrupt falls which occur in the levels of the glens. These 'steps' are characteristic of glaciated river valleys. The Affric itself falls in this way, and the narrow road which climbs from the valley of the Glass to Loch Benevean beside the river falls 150 metres in 5 kilometers. This road is called Chisholm's Pass. Baddeley's account of the glen at this point has not been surpassed:

> The entrance to the Chisholm's Pass, as the most beautiful part of Glen Affric is called, is upwards of two miles beyond Invercannich. Here the road leaves Strathglass and climbs to the right displaying more effectively at every step the grandeur of the glen. As we begin to look over the trees instead of through them we catch glimpses of a rapid stream far below rushing over a rocky bed and fringed to the water's edge by trees of every description. The woods at first rise to the summits of the hills on both sides, but are afterwards overtopped by the long ridges which climb through them from the level of Strathglass to the culminating peaks of Mam Soul and Scour Ouran.

> The best viewpoint for Glen Affric is four miles from Invercannich where the road comes near the Dog Fall. The tourist should not quit Glen Affric without descending through the wood to the stream. The vista up the river from about this point is exquisite in richness of colour and variety of rock contour. In places the stream seems scarcely to stir as it passes over some deep black pool overarched by threatening crag and drooping foliage. Then it emerges into a bright sunlit scene edged by narrow belts of emerald verdure and luxuriant tufts of fern amongst which the beautiful polypody species is specially notable, a very paradise on a fine summer's day.

Chisholm's Pass is as lovely today as it was in Victorian times and the road is much improved. It is true that the river is by-passed by a tunnel, but it continues to fall in a series of cascades, including the Dog Fall and the Badger Fall, which, except in the driest weather, are as handsome as ever.

Eas Chraisg
NH 382 342

River falls on the Glass.

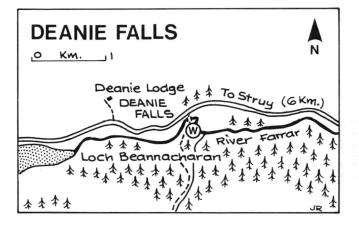

Culligram Falls
NH 377 401

These are the principal falls at the entrance to Glen Strathfarrar where the river drops to the level of Strathglass. There is an underground power station above the falls and they have been skilfully modified so that salmon can ascend them more readily, but the Hydro Board have managed to be quite unobtrusive. The falls are set in a quite magnificent birchwood in a delightfully secluded spot. The river tumbles about five metres below dramatically folded rocks.

Deanie Falls
NH 330 395

Low falls, only two metres high, on the Farrar below Loch Beannacharan. Deanie Power Station is above the falls so they are generally well supplied with water and the Board's works are not in evidence. The falls are at the very heart of the Glenstrathfarrar Pinewood, a National Nature Reserve, which is at its very best at this point. The setting of the falls is exquisite, the prospect of the gorge with its mixed pine and birch woods is excellent in every direction.

Dog Fall
NH 288 283

This is the principal fall on the Affric and, arguably, the finest set fall in all Scotland on that account. W H Murray writes about the fall as it was in **Undiscovered Scotland** (1951):

> Thus our good fortune brought us to a sloping rock at the edge of the famous Dog Fall. Its fame, we concluded, must

lie either in the power and volume of congested water which hurtles down the throat of a small gorge into a cauldron gauged out of solid rock, or else in its beauty. The power of the fall is indeed extraordinary, but not so great as to bring fame itself. What of its beauty, then? So simple that it can scarce be made intelligible. And therein is the Dog Fall's secret and abounding fascination in the eyes of men.

Except at times of spate, the force of the water at Dog Fall is now diminished, but it is still a spellbinding place. It is fascinating because it can never be completely seen. From the footbridge below it roars in a corner at the far end of the gorge; from the shelving rock above it plunges into the gorge at your feet, to be hidden about halfway down.

The ten metre fall is reached from the fine Forestry Commission car park in Chisholm's Pass from which an incomparable Forest Walk, beside the river and across it above and below the fall, leads to a picnic place. Many will regret this degree of formality and regret they do not reach the fall at the head of the pass through undisturbed woods. However, the concern of both the Forestry Commission and the Hydro Board for amenity is well displayed here. Dog Fall remains a must.

The Dhruim   NH 469 422

This is the wooded sandstone gorge where the Beauly used to rush with great force from Eileanaigas to the Falls of Kilmorack over a series of rapids. The Falls of Dhruim is the name applied on some old maps to *Eileanaigas Falls*. Eileanaigas is a large island which divides the Beauly which is still the property of the Lovats. It was the refuge of Lord Lovat when he was exiled in 1697, and it was used by Sir Robert Peel as a summer retreat. There used to be a sawmill below the falls at Tynessie, the place beside the falls. Timber was floated down river from the Chisholm estates. It must have been the scene of some spectacular activity, but today Aigas is the site of a remotely controlled power-station which impounds the waters.

Birch, pine and alder woods clothe the sides of the gorge where, at one point, a group of rocks stand up like needles. 'The whole pass we went along,' wrote Southey, 'is called the Dream.' He had a good ear, and, perhaps, the right instinct, but he went on to admit, 'What the interpretation of this name is I cannot learn.' In fact, Dhruim means hump or back. The water is now considerably affected by the hydro-electric power scheme, being ponded by the two dams at Kilmorack and Aigas. These are interesting enough in themselves and the woods still afford an attractive walk from Kiltarlity Church to Eilanaigas.

Easan Fhithich   NH 328 321

Raven Falls are below Eas Maol Mhairi on the Cannich, further from the road deep in the heart of the wooded gorge where the river drops to Strathglass. The branching falls are about ten metres high.

Eileanaigas Falls see The Dhruim

Falls of Fiadh   NH 206 242

The Abhain Glen nam Fiadh drains the basin beneath the highest mountains north of the Great Glen, Mam Sodhail and Carn Eige. The valley provides a route to their summits and there is an access road through the Forestry Commission plantations which follows an old right-of-way from Glen Affric

to Glen Cannich. The river flows into Loch Benavean close to its head and the falls are about one kilometre upstream. There are three marked cascades in remnant woodland beside the river bank. The falls make an excellent short excursion from the car park which marks the end of the public road. However, no one who visits Glen Affric should omit a visit to Loch Affric itself. From Affric Lodge, at the foot of this exquisite loch, a mountain path climbs due north to cross a col at about 450 metres beneath Sgurr na Lapaich and reach Glean nam Fiadh opposite the Allt Toll Easan, whence it is possible to return to Glen Affric by the Falls of Fiadh.

Falls of Glassburn   NH 368 345

Hillside falls in Strathglass.

Guisachan Fall   NH 290 249

A fall on a tributary of the Abhaim Deabhag on the Guisachan Estate above Tomich. The stream drains the finest part of the Caledonian Pine Forest, enriched with oak and larch, which gives the estate its name. The fall is beneath a road bridge on the principal estate road in an amphitheatre filled with rhododendrons.

Falls of Kilmorack   NH 493 443

These very famous falls were drastically altered by the power scheme which came into operation in 1962. The mighty Kilmorack Dam, below which the lower falls can still be seen, is 25 metres high and it contains a Boreland Fish Lift to enable salmon to reach the Glass. High above the gorge is the kirk which remains the best vantage point. The Upper, or Red, Fall was four metres high and the Lower Fall two metres high. They were for long a very well-known beauty spot and the principal excursion from Beauly. Southey and Telford visited them and Southey wrote:

> The shores are high, the stream is wide and rapid (for it is a considerable river) and the weirs and falls form a scene singularly wild and complicated. On the one side a lad was angling knee-deep in water, on the other a woman was beating linen in the river. Sometimes a dozen salmon have been caught in a single night merely by laying branches along the shelves of rock to catch them if they fail in the leap, and prevent them from falling in the water. Lord Lovat once disposed some boiling kettles about these falls in such a manner that he served his guests with fish which leapt from the river into the pot.

This last story is apocryphal, originating in an occasion when Lord Lovat was showing a visitor, who was unimpressed by the falls, round the grounds. To impress him, he finally pointed out that there were even kettles of boiling water to catch the salmon in, and showed his guest a pot-hole in which the water was so agitated that it looked as if it was boiling. The visitor and countless writers since were taken in.

Eas Maol Mhairi   NH 318 323

These are pretty falls not far from the road at the entrance to Glen Cannich, the glen of the cotton grass. They are easily reached from the by-road.

Eas a' Mhuillidh   NH 280 389

Many say that Glenstrathfarrar is at least equal to Glen Affric.

Loch a' Mhuillidh is the jewel of the glen and, above it, on a tumbling mountain stream is Eas a' Mhuillidh.

Falls of Monar   *NH 218 391*

The Monar Gorge was once the culminating point of Glen Strathfarrar in the old days, but the falls are now generally dry and quite dwarfed by the Monar Dam. It was possible to build this impressive structure, a double curvature arch dam, because of the configuration of the gorge. It is a magnificent piece of engineering.

Plodda Falls   *NH 277 248*

Plodda Falls are situated on a tributary of the Deabhag in the very fine Guisachan Estate about four kilometres from the House. The principal estate road is followed until a track leading to the right is encountered. This leads to the top of the falls. In the New Statistical Account the falls are described thus:

> The proprietor has been at considerable expense in forming a pleasure walk along the banks of this river which possesses all the attractions which the most fanciful disposition of rock and wood can contribute.

Sadly these fine works are now in a state of decay and a visit to the falls is something of an adventure. The path referred to above leads to the top of the falls. The burn, Eas Socach, seems unpromising at first, but soon a pleasant cascade of about eight metres is seen. Shortly after this it becomes apparent that the Deabhag is far below in a deep gorge and that the Socach will have to make a sensational descent if it is to join it. This it does, quite vertically, under a cast-iron ornamental bridge from which there is a vertiginous view of the river thirty metres below.

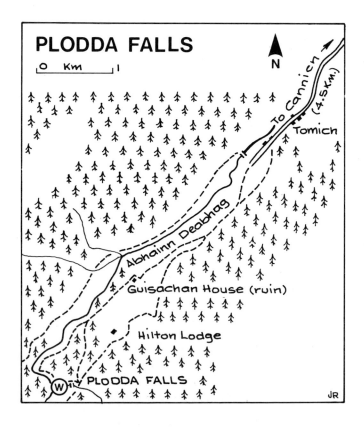

From the bridge a winding path leads to the foot of the gorge at a ford. This point can also be reached by following an estate road past the stables of Guisachan House (a fine place once, but now roofless). It is necessary to cross the river and turn a corner before the falls are seen. A fall of about ten metres is situated on the Deabhag immediately below the fall on the Socach so that the two make a very fine double fall. Indeed it looks as if the Deabhag itself, which is a very considerable stream, makes the leap. Further progress is impossible in ordinary conditions because the paths which clung to the sides of the gorge have collapsed. However, the estate has been acquired by the Forestry Commission and improvements may be made. But this superbly set fall can be well appreciated at present.

It seems probable, although the heights given do not agree with those given here, that the further description in the New Statistical Account of the Guisachan Fall is, in fact, of Plodda. It certainly resembles the latter rather than Guisachan, a much humbler fall:

> The stream is precipitated over a ledge of rock about seventy feet high into a circular basin of considerable dimensions, forming a deep dark linn which, together with the romantic ravine through which the water escapes, is overhung with many species of wood, exhibiting the most luxuriant foliage and, in some cases, very fantastic vegetation—the productions of an uncommonly fertile soil watered by the spray which is continually falling around them. Indeed none but those who have visited this romantic spot can form any idea of the varied scenery which is presented for their observation.

The hyperbole is justified.

Eas Sgaile   *NH 256 397*

Mountain fall in Glenstrathfarrar, the fall of the veil.

Eas Socach   *NH 285 230*

Ravine above Plodda Falls on the Guisachan Estate.

Ealls of Tomich   *NH 320 294*

River falls on the Affric at Fananskyle, subject of a notable study by Poucher.

Ross and Cromarty

Achanalt Falls   *NH 309 619*

The highly attractive falls of Achanalt are now in the heart of the Conon Hydro Electric Power Scheme. An interesting salmon pass, illustrating the sense of amenity which the Hydro Board has, enables fish to climb the drop where the falls were. It is constructed partly in country rock and partly artificially.

Ardessie Falls   *NH 053 859*

Ardessie is a favourite staging post on the long haul between Gairloch and Ullapool. Its falls are a prominent sea-mark which gives the place its name, the point of the waterfalls. The Allt Airdessaidh rises in the Great Corrie of the Forge underneath the Forge, An Teallach, the splendid mountain which dominates the district.

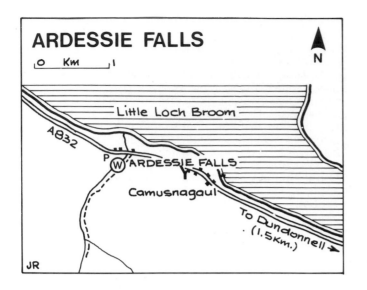

There are three sets of falls, the lowest of which are at the bridge over the main road. Above them the burn tumbles over a succession of falls in a rocky gorge. A footpath leads into the hills on the right bank of the burn and, at a little distance from the road, is a twin fall amid the heather on the open moor which is the subject of the most familiar view of the falls.

Baddely gives the names of the three falls as, respectively, *Bridge Falls*, *Dirrochan Falls*, the perpendicular falls, and *Wide Falls*.

Badachro Falls   NG 782 737

The little village of Badachro is situated where the Badachro River drains into a delightful little west coast harbour. Eas Bad a' Chrotha, the fall of the crofting place, is beneath waterfall point, east of the village. The burn is a noted salmon stream and fish ascend to seven hill-lochs in the hinterland. The greatest obstacle to salmon is Eas Braigh Horrisdale (**NG 817 684**) reached by a wild path which leads to Loch Gaineamhach and thence to Loch Torridon.

Eas na Baintighearna   NH 238 929

The fall of the Proprietor's Lady occurs on a tributary of the Rhiddoroch River above the Old Lodge.

Falls of Balgy   NG 849 538

These river falls, a noted salmon leap, are just above the new road bridge between Torridon and Shieldaig. The river used to interrupt communications along the coast until the early 1960s, forming what was called the 'Balgy Gap'. The falls can be reached by following either bank of the river and there are stepping stones above the old ford. The Balgy drains a considerable basin of some 45 sq km, including Loch Daimh.

Eas Ban (Attadale)   FNG 963 383

Fall on the headwaters of the Attadale River above Loch Carron.

Eas Ban (Loch Garbhaig)   NG 990 709

Remote fall between Slioch and Ben Lair below the footpath from Letterewe to Lochan Fada at the head of Loch Garbhaig.

Eas Ban (Loch Kishorn)   NG 815 410

Fall on the Russel Burn below the famous Bealach na Ba pass. In wet weather there are fine falls on the burns which drain the amphitheatre into which the road climbs.

Eas Ban (Strathnasheallag)   NH 097 773

Remote mountain fall on the headwaters of the Shellag under Creag Rainich.

Black Falls   NH 380 561

These spectacular falls are situated below the Meig Dam in a steep-sided ravine which is virtually inaccessible. They occupy the same position on the river as do the Falls of Conon on the Conon. The roaring falls are some twelve metres in height.

Easan Buidhe   NH 358 702

The Glasgarnoch River drains the remote valley leading to the Diridh Mor, the great divide. The valley, dominated by the mass of Ben Wyvis, has now been flooded to form a somewhat unprepossessing reservoir which is, however, generally considered to have added some interest to the bleak moor. Water is led from the Loch to the Mossford Power Station and in consequence there is little water in the river in the summer months. Easan Buidhe is about a kilometre below the Altguish Inn, noted for its trout fishing, and can easily be inspected from the main road (A835).

Falls of Carnan   NG 897 412

This is the pleasing stream, the burn of the cairns—the Allt nan Carnan, beside which the road from Lochcarron to Kishorn climbs out of Strathcarron. Higher up it forms a dramatic gorge more than a kilometre in length and 24 metres deep where oak and birch trees predominate, but where there is a bewildering variety of trees—hazel, aspen, rowan, ash, wych elm, bird cherry and wild rose. It is for this profusion of trees that the gorge is designated as a National Nature Reserve. At the head of it there is a splendid waterfall.

Falls of Glen Chaorachain   NH 109 844

There is a fine series of falls in Gleann Chaorachain, the glen of the rapid boiling torrent. A land-rover track leads through this splendidly-named glen with its fine woods to a low pass south-east of An Teallach.

Eas Chonaisg see Novar

Eas a Chroasain   NH 198 956

A torrential mountain burn above Loch Achall which falls seventy metres into the loch.

Coneasan

W J Watson (1926) explains in his book about place names that Coneasan is the generic term for a series of waterfalls and rapids so characteristic of many highland rivers. The name is given to the fine series on the Gruinard River (q.v.) and it occurs again in Easter Ross where it is sometimes applied to the remarkable double fall above Eileanach Bridge on the Glass above the Black Rock of Novar (q.v.).

Falls of Conon   *NH 386 578*

The Falls of Conon were, before the advent of the hydro electric power scheme, among the most attractive in Scotland. The falls are a series of cascades below Loch Luichart. They are cut back in the same rock barrier which gives rise to the Falls of Rogie and the dramatic Black Falls on the Meig. The barrier is formed of igneous rocks where the principal falls form a twin staircase situated in a birchwood. A salmon ladder is cut into the rocks.

In spate the Conon carries a very considerable quantity of water and, in this condition, the falls are a fine sight.

Corrieshalloch Gorge see Falls of Measach

Eas nan Cuinneag   *NG 755 498*

This fall is situated near the wild track which climbs from Applecross village beside the Applecross River to traverse under Croicbheinn and leads eventually to Sheldaig. The name, the fall of the buckets, is derived from the prominent potholes in the river bed.

Cul Mor Fall   *NC 153 104*

Cul Mor is one of the less well-known of the residual sandstone mountains which stand on a platform of Lewisian Gneiss in Coigach. It is in the Inverpolly National Nature Reserve above Loch Sionascaig. The best way to it is by Glen Laoigh. From a hidden corrie a burn descends from a tiny mountain tarn, Lochan Dearg a Chuil Mor, and then drops by a prominent waterfall into the glen. The burn provides an interesting route to the summit of the hill.

Ben Damph Falls   *NG 886 538*

There is a grand series of cascades, with one particularly impressive fall, on the Allt Coire Roill above the Loch Torridon Hotel. A path which leads through a pine wood climbs to Ben Damph beside the steep-sided gorge.

Easan Dorcha   *NH 013 525*

This fall is one of the highlights of the exceptionally fine walk through the Coulin Forest from Loch Clair to Achnashellach, with superb views through the trees across the lochs to the Torridon Mountains. The main track over the Coulin Pass does not follow the Easan Dorcha, which joins the Coulin River on its west bank; a subsidiary track, to be preferred, leads beside the falls to cross into the valley of the River Lair.

The Allt nan Dearcag, the burn of the berries, tumbles 90 metres from its junction with the Allt Coire Beinne Leirhe to the footbridge build by Lord Leeds at the bottom of the Coulin Pass.

Eas Dubh a' Ghlinne Garbh   *NG 957 888*

The black fall of the rough glen is on the Inverinavie River in the Fisherfield Forest. In its upper reaches the river is known as Uisge Toll a' Mhadaidh, the river of the foxes' hollow. It is a fine mountain stream flowing across the rough gneiss platform of Wester Ross, regulated by the irregularly-shaped lochans characteristic of the place. Eas Dubh occurs where the burn tumbles to Gruinard Bay. It can be reached by a short walk from the main road. Further inland, at the outlet from Loch Mhadaidh Mor, is *Eas Uisge Toll a Mhadaith (NG 965 873)*.

Falls of Conon, a series of striking cascades below Loch Luichart. These were among the first to be harnessed for water power with the Grampian Power Company's 1920s scheme. ROBERT M ADAM

Eas Dubh (Ullapool)   *NH 151 954*

Fall at the head of the series of rapids and falls in the gorge of the Ullapool River below Loch Achall. It was formerly reached by a steep path from the left bank where there is now a quarry which prevents access. The falls are difficult to see from the right bank of the river.

Dundonnell Upper Falls   *NH 120 818*

Falls above Corrie Hallie (q.v.) on the rumbustous Dundonnel River. They occur where the main road—the Destitution Road built to relieve unemployment during the famine of 1851 at the expense of the MacKenzies of Dundonnell—climbs steeply to the wild pass under An Teallach which leads to Braemore. The growing desolation of the scene is relieved by an impressive series of cascades which seem to appear then disappear as the road twists and turns. The highest fall, of about 20 metres, is situated below Fain Bridge.

Eathie Falls   *NH 773 641*

A deeply secluded dell of exquisite though savage beauty; one of those hidden recesses of nature in which she gratefully reserves the choicest of her sweets for the more zealous of her admirers.

This description is by Hugh Miller who made his first discoveries in the old red sandstone of the Eathie Burn in the Black Isle. There is a very good cascade of about eight metres at the head of this den.

Everyone who visits the Black Isle should visit Hugh Miller's Cottage in Cromarty which is in the care of the National Trust for Scotland. It is an excellent memorial to the self-taught Scotsman who made many notable contributions to the science of geology.

Otta Swire (1963) relates the following story about Eathie Den:

Just beyond the village lies the unusual and beautiful glen,

Dell of Eathie. What caused such extraordinary red rock scenery I do not know, perhaps earthquake or landslide or mere erosion, but it is certainly quite unlike anything else in the North and well worth a visit. Needless to say, local superstition blamed it on the fairies. Some of them had sinned against their own laws, it was believed, so this strange glen was made for their imprisonment. They are held prisoner in the cliff sides and only allowed out in the dark of the moon, when they cannot dance. This freedom is given to them so that they may visit an old mill nearby to grind their meal. Naturally the imprisoned fairies are very angry and bitter about the whole affair and it is dangerous indeed to meet them trudging to the mill, sacks on backs, for they are almost certain to ill-wish you. Indeed they might carry you off altogether as they once did a piper who was so ill-advised as to play dance music in the glen one dark night for a wager. He was never seen again, but some have heard a sound of pipes playing both piteous laments and gay reels, coming, it would seem, from the heart of the red cliff.

Eileanach Falls see Black Rock of Novar

Flowerdale Falls   *NG 828 750*

These falls make a pleasant excursion from the Old Inn, Gairloch to the head of the glen. There are falls on both branches of the burn which can be reached by a clearly marked track.

Eas Fionn   *NH 232 835*

A forest road leads to Glensguaib which can be reached by car and forms the usual starting point for the ascent of Beinn Dearg. From the edge of the forest a well-marked hill-track leads beside the River Lael, a mountain burn which forms a notable series of cascades, the uppermost of which is Eas Fionn. The water pitches over a rock barrier in a little cove which can be adequately explored only by descending from the track.

Eas na Gaibhre see Falls of Kerry

Eas na Gaibhre   *NG 784 640*

The fall of the goat, on the Craig River above the remotely situated Youth Hostel at Craig in Torridon.

Falls of Garbh Allt   *NH 109 857*

A descent from Coire Toll an Lochain can be made by Coire Guibhsachain which is floored by an extensive pavement of Torridonian Sandstone the edge of which is marked by steep quartzite cliffs. It is drained by the Garbh Allt which forms steep cascades as it tumbles into Strath Beg. The falls can easily be reached by the footpath through a birchwood close to Dundonnell House.

Falls of Grudie   *NH 292 632*

These falls were probably more frequently visited when the main route from the east coast to Loch Broom was by the Grudie burn, ten kilometres long, which drains Loch Fannich. The Falls of Grudie are situated two kilometres above Grudie Bridge. The burn is now adversely affected by the Conon Hydro Electric Power Scheme because water from Loch Fannich is led directly to the Grudie Bridge Power Station. Leum Ruairidh, Rory's Leap, is the name given to a narrowing of the Grudie at the falls. This is where Rory Mor MacKenzie tested his natural son with the challenge: 'If you are a son of mine follow me,' and leapt across the river. The son picked up two deer-hounds and jumped after him.

Glen Grudie (Loch Maree)

The Grudie is the principal affluent of Loch Maree, draining the Kinlochewe Deer Forest. The scenery of this most scenic of all lochs is generally held to be at its finest at Grudie Bridge. Most impressive is the 'peculiarly original and grand' view that there is of Slioch across the loch, but there is also a notable view of Ben Eighe up Glen Grudie.

A track leads eight kilometres up the glen to this dominating peak, at the foot of which is Loch Coire Mhic Fhearchair, one of the half-dozen most impressive corries in Britain, comprising a splendid amphitheatre with the overwhelming 'Triple Buttress' of red sandstone topped by white quartzite. This corrie

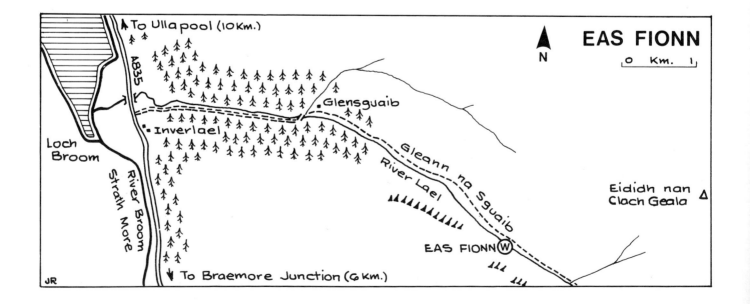

can also be reached, more easily, but less satisfyingly, from the Coire Dubh track in Torridon.

Colin Gibson describes one of his favourite mountain falls, in another of Ben Eighe's corries, in this way:

> On the precipitous north face of the peak called Sgurr Ban, which sends a long quartzite scree down into Glen Torridon, a rivulet issues from some secret crevice of the rocks, and falls as a silver thread sheer down to a rock shelf. On this shelf lies a tiny lochan—a dark pool which overspills into the wild Corrie nan Clach, the corrie of the stones (*NG 978 609*). Further down other streams come to join it. Like a mesh of silver cords they draw the mountain into shape and form a glen. And, as the River Grudie, these waters hurry on their way to Loch Maree. I should add that this cataract of Ben Eighe fades away almost as soon as the rain stops falling. In any case, it is not likely to be seen by many visitors, as Corrie nan Clach is one of our most inaccessible.

There are corrie headwall falls in each of the three main corries of Ben Eighe, but at the foot of Lochan Coire Mhic Fhearchair the burn which drains the tarn cascades in an all-weather fall to the floor of Glen Grudie to perfect the attractiveness of the scene. *The Falls of Glen Grudie (NG 938 612)* command a view of the corrie across the lochan which is outstanding. Visitors who have seen both this corrie and Coire Toll an Lochain on An Teallach find it difficult to decide which of the two is the more attractive, some considering the one too austere, others finding Coire Toll an Lochain too broken for their tastes. There is no disputing that the Torridonian Rocks which epitomise both of them are splendid.

Gruinard River

The Meikle Gruinard drains a very extensive catchment between the magnificent sandstone peaks of An Teallach and Beinn Dearg Mor, the principal feature of which is the splendid Loch na Shellag. The river, situated partly on rough, pock-marked gneiss, is a well-known trout stream. A road, which is an established right of way, leads along the south bank to Shenavall, the bothy at the foot of An Teallach. A short distance from the main road (A832) is a low fall *Linne na Cloiche (NG 961 911)* which can be visited by means of a short excursion. *Eas nan Sonn (NG 975 890)*, the fall of the heroes or the fall of the stakes, and *Coneasan (NG 987 868)* are much more remote.

Corrie Hallie

NH 123 847

The Dundonnell River drains Strath Beag at the head of Little Loch Broom. This truly splendid place is dominated by the notable sandstone peak of An Teallach, the Forge. The climate is mild, although the rainfall, 1829 mm per annum, is heavy. The strath is strikingly wooded with Scots pine, birch, oak, alder, rowan and hazel in contrast to the empty moorlands of much of Wester Ross. These native trees are mixed with limes, sycamores, beeches chestnuts and geans introduced by the MacKenzies. Dundonnell House, built by them in 1769, is sometimes open to the public who are permitted to visit the gardens where there is an aviary of exotic birds.

The Dundonnell is a spate river and salmon encounter an insuperable obstacle at Corrie Hallie. It is important not to confuse Corrie Hallie in Strathbeg with Corrieshalloch in Strathmore although, of course, the two names are the same. In Gaelic the name means 'filthy hollow' and, in Strath Beag it refers to a steep sided gorge at the head of which are the falls.

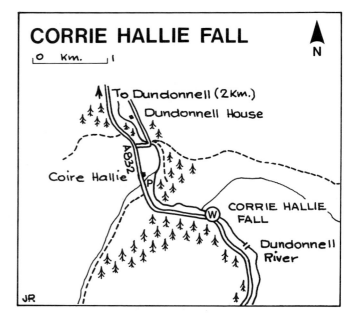

In his book *The Highlands with Rope and Rucksack* E A Baker (1923) described the place:

> The ravine at Corrie Hallie is only 80 or 100 feet deep; but the narrowness is such that stones only two feet long are wedged across. Standing on the railless wooden bridge one looks down between crooked waterworn walls to the spinning pools and shrieking headlong current of the infuriated river visible by glimpses in the blackness. Deer sometimes fall into this terrible place, so we were told, but never reach the loch, their bones are ground up in the tremendous watermill.

The gorge is sometimes called The Gully. The falls are perhaps twenty metres in height, and occur where the river crosses the quartzite which marks the thrust zone between the old hard rocks of the west coast and the Moine of Mid Ross.

Falls of Kerry

NG 838 720

These falls, once highly regarded, now constitute one of the worst examples of the adverse effects of a hydro-electric power scheme in Scotland. The scheme, one of the first small schemes which came into full operation in 1951, was ill-considered and the ugly piping and the empty burn are blots on the landscape. Murray's Guide (1896) described the falls as follows:

> The road descends a narrow and romantic glen traversed by the River Kerrie passing Loch Badnaskalloch. A little further on the river falls in a series of grand and picturesque cascades. It is a charming glen, its lower course completely grown up with firs and pines.

The uppermost fall, near a car park, is *Eas na Gaibhre*.

Steall Coir Lair

NH 288 815

This high fall above Coire Lair in the Ben Dearg Massif falls as steeply as Eas Coul Aulin for 150 metres. The burn tumbles over the lip of a precipice into Loch na Still in a white curve formed by a series of linked cascades. It can be reached by indefinite paths from the Diridh Mor.

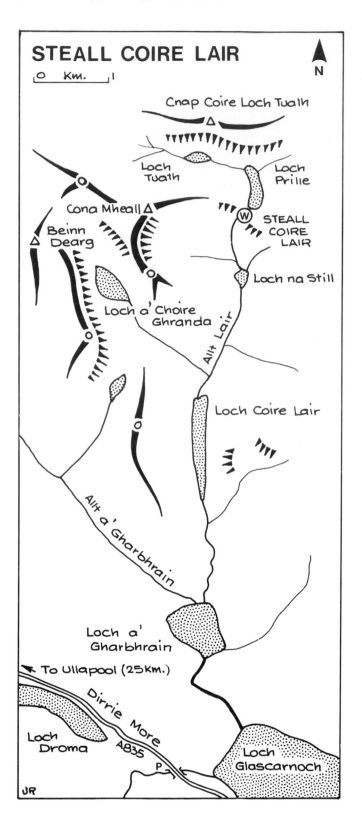

STEALL COIRE LAIR

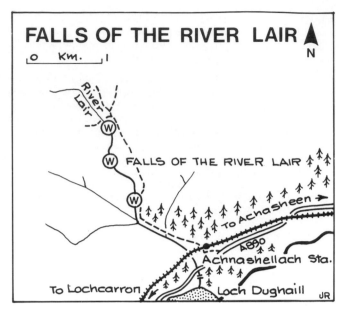

FALLS OF THE RIVER LAIR

kilometres to Achnashellach Lodge, 40 metres above sea level. The uppermost falls are situated beside the track which leads to Loch Coulin, roaring moorland falls in a rocky gorge. The middle falls are seen in the distance consisting of rapids and waterchutes, but the lower falls are reached by sidetracks. These two falls bordered by gnarled pine trees are very fine indeed. Immediately above them is the shapely and impressively steep peak of Fuar Tholl streaked after rain with mountain torrents of its own.

Letterewe Falls
NG 951 716

Falls above Loch Maree which old guide books stated 'look well from the steamer'.

Falls of Measach
NH 204 779

Probably the most renowned in the Northern Highlands, and perhaps the best-known single natural feature in the care of the National Trust for Scotland. They occur in the magnificent wooded gorge at Braemore Junction at the head of Loch Broom called Corrieshalloch, the filthy hollow. The main road from Garve has climbed across the Diridh Mor, the dreary pass between the east and the west coasts. At Braemore the scenery suddenly and dramatically changes. After the moor there are rich woodlands and the soft breezes of the west coast are evident.

Braemore Lodge, now razed to the ground, was for thirty years the highland home of the celebrated civil engineer Sir John Fowler (1817–98), the joint builder of the Forth Railway Bridge. The grounds of the estate were extensively developed by their famous owner who planted 485 hectares of larch and Scotch fir along the river as well as undertaking extensive drainage, fencing and bridgebuilding. He was fascinated by the Highlands and never wearied of speculating about the primeval Caledonian Forest. In the neighbourhood of the house he collected every variety of native tree and shrub. In order to improve the salmon fishing he extended Loch Droma by means of an embankment. 'As the congenial amusement of an engineer's holiday' he constructed the light iron bridges which now provide access to the Falls of Measach and the Falls of Strone.

Like Balmoral, Braemore attracted many distinguished visitors including leading artists, like Landseer and Millais, and

Falls of the River Lair
NG 992 490

It is to be doubted whether there is a more distinctive succession of falls than these grand cascades above Achnashellach. The River Lair takes its source in the ring of steep mountains above Strathcarron and drains first into an upland hollow occupied by Loch Coire Lair. It then escapes over a moorland edge 375 metres above sea level to descend in two

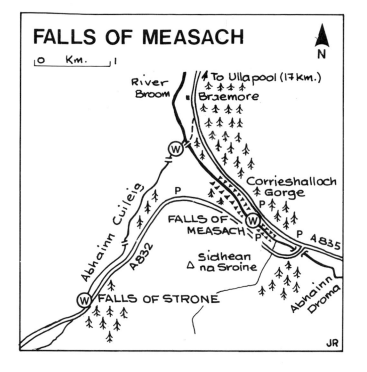

FALLS OF MEASACH

0   Km.   1

N

River Broom

To Ullapool (17 km.)
Braemore

W

Corrieshalloch Gorge

Abhainn Cuileig

P

FALLS OF MEASACH

W

P   A835

A832

Sidhean na Sroine

W FALLS OF STRONE

Abhainn Droma

JR

for species that might have vanished from the region because of moor-burning or grazing by sheep. Sanicle flourishes at the lowest levels alongside ferns and feather mosses, and reappears on rills in company with opposite-leaved saxifrage, mountain sorrel and germander speedwell. The narrow horizontal ledges harbour five species of fern, and greater woodrush, tufted hairgrass and woodmillet, a plant rare in north-west Scotland. The trees which find foothold include wych elm, birch and hazel, and naturalised Norway maple, sycamore and beech. The most numerous shrubs are goat willow, bird cherry and guelder rose. There are trout in the deep pools. Most species of woodland birds are represented and ravens nest on a ledge opposite the view-point.

The Falls of Measach occupy a gorge in psammatic granulites, rocks in the series called the Moine Schists. The gorge is unusual in that it is eroded in crystalline rocks. Almost all of the other notable groups in Scotland are in sandstone. The over-deepening of the gorge took place in glacial times when melt-waters from the ice-cap which occupied the Diridh Mor escaped to the sea. Today water in the river is regulated by Loch Droma, which was further enlarged by the Hydro Board and its waters diverted into the Conon Scheme. There are, however, considerable tributaries from the Fannichs and from the Ben Dearg Massif, and there is generally a reasonable amount of water in the falls.

As seems to be the case with all major falls, there is some difference of opinion about their height. The National Trust for Scotland give the depth of the gorge as 200 feet (60 metres) and the height of the fall as 150 feet (45 metres). The SMC Guide *The Northern Highlands* gives the depth of the gorge as 400 feet (120 metres) and the height of the fall as 270 feet (82.5 metres). Others compromise by giving the height of the falls as 200 feet (60 metres). It is possible that this is the height of the suspension bridge constructed by Fowler above the gorge. However, an examination of the OS Map shows that the head of the gorge is 190 metres above sea-level, and its foot 40 metres above sea-level, giving a total fall of 150 metres for the succession of falls. This would suggest that the SMC figure may well be correct. What is certain is that the Droma forms a succession of falls above the major fall and it tumbles about 120 metres (about 400 feet) between the bridge at Braemore Junction and the Bridge at Braemore. It is unlikely that the falls have been accurately plumbed.

Further exploration of the gorge requires caution, but beyond the viewpoint there is a path which leads into the upper part of the gorge from which a dramatic stack can be seen. An account of an intimate encounter with the falls by a singularly determined angler appears in V Carron Wellington's *Adventures of a Sporting Angler* (1952). It should be sufficiently off-putting to be required reading for anyone tempted to explore the foot of the gorge.

The Falls of Measach are also dealt with by R MacDonald Robertson (1936) in *Angling in Wildest Scotland*. His account of the upper falls, which are frequently neglected, is the best:

famous politicians. In the Visitors Book the following poem associates Gladstone with the Falls of Measach:

> When the dull, dreary session is over the patriots twaddle no more,
> How blithely I breathe the brave breezes which blow round the braes of Braemore.
> Though the Broom like our Gladstone meanders, or foams down with froth in a spate,
> Though the stalker, like Dizzy in ambush, for his prey is aye lying in wait.

The present character of the landscape at Braemore owes much to Fowler's influence. The falls were not much noticed before his day, and it is the nearby Falls of Strone which receive attention in early nineteenth century guide books. The name Easan na Miasaich, the fall of the place of the platters, is a reference to the large smooth rounded stones which occur in the river bed above the fall. The more general name for the locality is the Corrieshalloch Gorge, and this box-like canyon is the most striking feature of the place. Indeed the falls, some 80 metres high, are dwarfed by the mighty walls of the gorge and it takes the visitor some moments to appreciate the truly sensational nature of the site. Of all the great falls in Scotland this is the most accessible.

The gorge is easily reached by short footpaths, a few minutes from either of the two main roads which meet at Braemore Junction—the A832 and the A835. Such is the scale of the Northern Highlands that the place is rarely overrun with visitors and it retains much of the sense of savage nature which such tourist attractions further south have inevitably lost. The other asset which the falls have is that they can readily be seen face on. From either the suspension bridge or the viewpoint the full majesty of the falls can be appreciated; no other great falls can be seen in their entirety with such ease.

The gorge is part of a National Nature Reserve managed by the Nature Conservancy. Robin Prentice's account in the National Trust for Scotland Guide emphasises this:

> The gorge is a very special habitat for plant life. The latter must survive in conditions of high humidity and poor light. Here, though Corrieshalloch is deficient in lime, is a haven

> We followed the narrow and perilous zig-zagging rocky path, which leads along the side of this fearful gulf to the stone bridge, passing on our way the uppermost fall (close to the bend of the road near the main entrance gate to Braemore Lodge), which resembles somewhat the delicate drapery of a Shetland shawl, as its gossamer-like waters which descend into a deep recess, sparkle in glistening spray, over a series of shelving rocks.

> Just below the divergence of the Dundonnell Road, we perceived that the long deep ravine commenced, forming in its course three distinct beautiful waterfalls within a distance of roughly one hundred yards. There are trees and shrubs,

which, as they ascend, ledge above ledge of this awful chasm, take the eye some time to grasp the reality; only gradually do we come to realise the sublimity of the situation.

Robertson also draws attention to two folk tales associated with the Falls. In the first a stag pursued by a hound bolted to the edge of the chasm and tried to leap it but both the stag and the dog plunged into the depths. On moonlight nights the apparition of the stag and the hound can still be seen in the vapour rising from the falls and the cries of the stag and the snarls of its attacker can be heard rising from the ravine below.

The second folk tale tells how the young men of the district were marched along the boundaries and scourged. Those who could not bear the punishment threw themselves into the gorge, where they were believed to be rescued by the water-fairies who transformed them into the spirits of great warriors. The cries of the young men are also heard at the falls on moonlight nights.

The Falls of Measach are the subject of a fine reflective poem by the contemporary Scottish poet, Norman MacCaig:

> The wind was basins slopping over.
> The river plunged into its ravine
> Like coins into a stocking. The day
> Was like the buzzard on the pine.
>
> It looked at us with eyes like resin
> From some shelf of the scaly past
> And could see nothing in between,
> For it knew nothing it had lost.
>
> But we were our continuation
> And saw our graves behind us like
> Waterfalls marking the stages
> To some rich plunge into the dark.
>
> Let the wind spill some other gust
> And the day like the buzzard will
> Sail, and sink invisible
> As a fossil in the distant hill

The Falls of Measach are classic waterfalls. Most visitors to the North of Scotland will have the opportunity to see them. Do not pass them by.

Steall a' Mhuinidh   NH 024 648

Steall a' Mhuinidh is the prominent mountain fall which falls the best part of one-hundred metres over a buttress of Beinn a' Mhuinidh above Kinlochewe. It is well seen across the head of Loch Maree. The mountain is of great geological interest because the sequence of rocks usually encountered in Torridon —gneiss, then sandstone, then quartzite—is capped by gneiss, the same rock as is found at the base of the series, illustrating the effects of the folding which has taken place.

The cliff over which the silver fall drops is quartzite. At the foot of Ben a' Mhuinidh is the Letterewe Forest which was once very much more extensive than it now is. The oakwood had an understory of hazel and holly and, before the depradations of the ironmasters, was one of the richest plant communities in the Highlands, the classical north-west of Osgood MacKenzie.

The fall is held in particular esteem by climbers, because a notable climb was undertaken there by G T Glover and Dr Inglis Clark in 1899. It was remarkable for both its conception and its execution at that time. In their account of the climb the two authors praise the fall as a fine sight. They relate how they had to spend a good deal of time 'gardening' because of the rich vegetation resulting from the proximity of the climb to the fall. According to Dixon's admirable guide (1925) the name of this

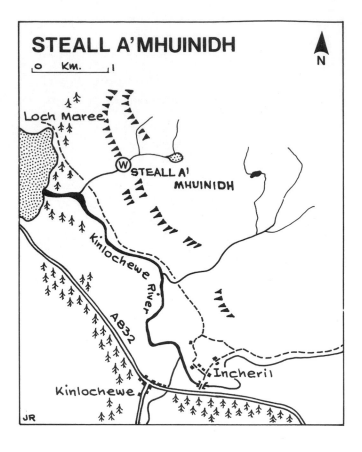

fall, as he very delicately puts it, 'approximates to that of the Swiss "Pisse Vache"'. It is indeed, the spout of piss.

Easan Mor   NG 771 775

Fall marking an old coastline above a raised beach in Wester Ross.

Muirton Falls   NH 446 545

Now the site of the Tor Achilty Power Station, on the Conon, could be compared with the Falls of Kilmorack although a fault means that the gorge is not so impressive.

Novar Gorge (Eileanach Falls)   NH 557 683

This gorge is one of the great natural curiosities of Scotland. Situated on the River Glass it is reached by a footpath from the village of Evanton. The chasm, carved in Old Red Sandstone, is two kilometres long, and displays to an unusual degree the overdeepening which can take place in this formation. It is five times deeper than it is wide. In places the walls of the ravine overhang considerably. It is not easy to see the gorge although there are sensational views of the gorge where 'the river passes through a profound and bosky chasm and makes in the progress a series of romantic cataracts and cascades' (Ordnance Gazetter). The tributary streams which fall into the gorge form silver waterfalls, the full height of the walls.

No one who visits the gorge should be unaware of the story of the Lady of Balconie who was wont to go for walks there. One day she asked her maid to accompany her, and the two women encountered a dark stranger. The maid refused to go into the gorge although her mistress implored her to come. When it was evident that she would not the Lady of Balconie

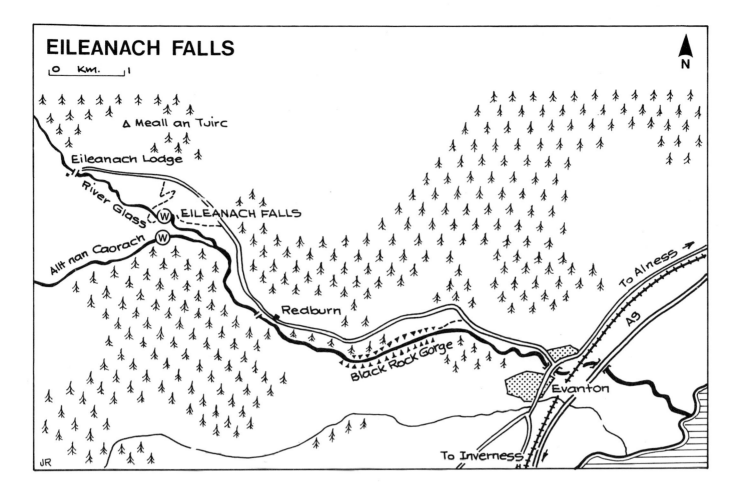

EILEANACH FALLS

threw her keys to the girl. The keys struck a stone, Clach a Cholumain, which can still be seen. The Lady of Balconie did not return. Some years later a local man went fishing in the gorge and left his catch beside the Glass. When he got home his wife suspected that he had caught more fish than he had brought home and questioned him. He said that the Devil had taken the fish, so she sent him back to get them. The fish had gone, and there were tracks leading into the gorge which he followed. They led to a cave where the man found the Lady of Balconie chained to an iron chair next to an iron table. It was, indeed, the Devil who had taken the fish and the man was horrified to find two dogs barring his means of escape. The Lady of Balconie diverted their attention while the man made good his escape, and that was the last that was seen of her.

The River Glass is a considerable stream carrying much of the drainage of the eastern flanks of Ben Wyvis. Above the gorge of the Black Rock it is joined by its principal tributary, the Allt nan Coarach. The road which follows the north bank of the Glass leads eventually to Eileanach Bridge below which are the spectacular *Eileanach Falls*. These can be reached by forest roads. *Eas a' Chonaisg (NH 557 683)* is a very considerable double fall at a corner which crashes forty metres in a rock gorge. There is a parallel fall on the Coarach, *Eas Poll a' Ghreusach (NH 556 681)*, much more difficult of access. Both of the falls are situated near the edge of the Old Red Sandstone.

Falls of Orrin   NH 469 517

When Augustus Grimble published his famous book on the Salmon Rivers of Scotland he carefully measured the Falls of

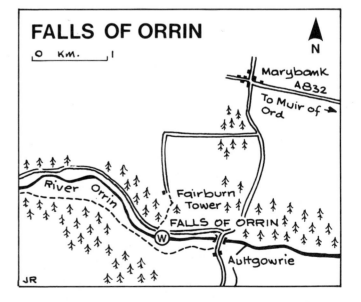

FALLS OF ORRIN

Orrin which have for long, been considered the highest salmon leap in Scotland. Grimble measured the level of the pool at the foot of the falls and the level of the pool at the top in what he considered to be average conditions. Their height is 4.8 metres (16 feet). The sheer leap required was, he decided, greater than elsewhere. There are, of course, falls whose apparent height is greater which are ascended by salmon, but these falls have intermediate pools which enable the fish to climb a natural staircase similar to a salmon ladder.

The falls are due to an outcrop of conglomerate in the Old Red Sandstone which is more resistant than the shales and flagstones below; the same formation which gives rise to the Falls of Kilmorack on the Beauly. The Orrin is a turbulent stream, forty kilometres long, which has now been harnessed in the Conon Hydro Electric Power Scheme. A new loch has been formed eight kilometres above the falls. A grandstand view of the falls is obtained from a bridge.

Above Loch Orrin the *Falls of the Allt Loch a Ghormlaich* (*NH 252 458*) are situated in the remote uplands of the Strathconan Forest.

Core na Poite Waterfall   *NG 828 448*

The corrie of the still under the dramatic cliffs of Bheinn Bhan in Applecross cradles three lochans at two levels. The burn which connects them to the flower of the glen forms a series of fine cascades.

Falls of Polly   *NC 087 137*

The little River Polly drains Loch Sionascaig and tumbles in a succession of falls to the sea at Enard Bay. Above and below Loch na Dail there were substantial falls, but the lower falls have been eliminated in the interests of salmon fishing. The Upper Falls, eight metres high, are surmounted by means of a salmon ladder. A short excursion from the road.

Falls of Rogie   *NH 445 584*

North of Contin the main road (A832) crosses the Blackwater by an imposing three-arched bridge at the Achilty Inn. The road climbs easily through the superbly wooded Blackwater

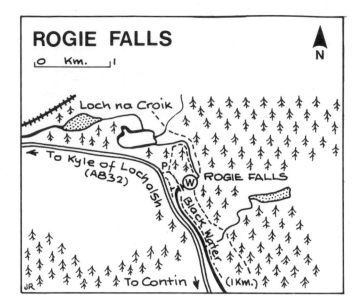

Falls of Rogie. *Among the principal attractions near Strathpeffer.*
HAMISH BROWN

Pass and, on the right going north, there is a well-constructed car park in an old quarry whence a well-designed forest walk leads to the Falls of Rogie. The rushing Blackwater itself is outside the catchment area of the Conon Scheme, but its headwaters are diverted into it. However, in spate these falls are truly impressive and there is generally sufficient water in them to make them worth a visit. In low water conditions the main body of water comes down in two steps and then makes a considerable leap of, perhaps, eight metres. A lesser body of water comes down a water chute. At the falls a suspension bridge crosses the Blackwater leading to the woods on the other side and providing a good view of the falls in spate, if the spectator has the nerve to cross it.

Of all the falls in Easter Ross these are the most worth visiting. Apart from the approach already described they can also be reached by a very attractive footpath by Loch Kinellan from the charming spa town of Strathpeffer. They are also accessible from the forest car park at the main road bridge whence a visit to the falls can be combined with the Torrachilty Forest Trail.

Otta Swire (1963) is not taken by the changes brought about by the Hydro Board and the Forestry Commission at the falls but she writes about them with affection:

Strathpeffer is, one might say, the boundary of Eastern Scotland; within a few miles of the village the scenery and vegetation alike become that of the West. After passing a few fields thicker with stones than seems possible, we reach moor and birch woods and that sign-manual of the West, bog myrtle. A mile or two further on, up a road to the right, are the Falls of Rogie, once a wonderfully beautiful mountain river where one could sit in the heather watching the salmon leaping at the Falls, surrounded by small moor flowers and shaded by wild trees. The little golden bog orchid which grows here first grew when the Virgin Mary, walking over the moor, stopped by some marshy ground to tuck up her robe. As she undid her golden girdle for the purpose, it slipped through her fingers into the peat bog and sank out of sight. Where it had fallen the little golden orchids grew, hoping she might make herself a new girdle from their honey-scented heads. Wherever she stepped through the heather the little white star flower of the moor sprang up, emblem of her purity. Now the Falls are a 'Beauty Spot' with a suitable car park and all the latest improvements.

Rosemarkie Glen

A characteristic east coast glen above the Black Isle village of Rosemarkie. The falls (*NH 725 584*) are situated in Swallow Den.

Silver Bridge Falls   NH 402 639

These fine picture-postcard falls occur where the main road re-crosses the Blackwater above Garve. The river tumbles pleasingly over gritty rocks both above and below the bridge, having a total fall of about ten metres.

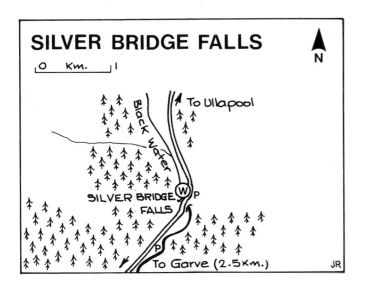

Eas an-t-Sinidh   NH 258 927

Four square falls on the Rhidorroch River some 15 kilometres from Ullapool. The river tumbles about twenty five metres over an angular rock ledge just above the confluence of the Rhidorroch and the Douchary. The spray which rises from the falls gives them their name, Smokey Falls. Permission can generally be obtained to take a car as far as the Old Lodge which gives very fine views along Loch Achall.

Smokey Falls see Eas an-t-Sinidh

Falls of Strone   NH 181 770

Glen Mor, the principal arm of Strath More above Loch Broom, affords an interesting example of the way in which intrinsically attractive places can be quite overshadowed by popular resorts of a similar character close at hand. The gorges of the Cuileig are a short distance from the Corrieshalloch Gorge, and in some ways superior. It is true that the principal fall is not so high as the Falls of Measach, but the Cuileig is not subject to abstraction and its falls are more varied. In Anderson's *Guide* and Black's *Guide,* published in the second half of the nineteenth century it is these falls, the Falls of Strone, which are singled out for attention. It seems likely that before Fowler constructed his suspension bridge the Corrieshalloch Gorge was considered either inaccessible or dangerous.

The falls derive their name from the headland or promontory between the Cuileig and the Droma called the Strone. The gorge can be entered from its foot at Braemore where there is a footbridge over the Droma which leads to the lowest falls. A network of footpaths and footbridges permit exploration. The

footbridges are elegant affairs erected by Fowler, now in a rather sad state of repair, to be crossed at the visitors' risk. The lowest falls occur at the Sanctuary Pool, an idyllic spot. They rejoice in the somewhat unprepossessing name of The Linn (*NH 192 788*). There is a fine high fall in the gorges of which there is an energetic account in V Carron Wellington's *Adventures of a Sporting Angler* (1952). At the head of the gorge is a singularly beautiful twin fall, fifteen metres in height, the right-hand branch of which forms a very attractive staircase of white water, *Bridge Fall.* This fall can be easily visited from the Dundonnell Road.

The Cuileig rises in the Fannichs and drains the lovely Loch a' Bhraoin, the loch of the shower. There are a number of wet weather falls on the mountain streams which feed this loch of which the pillar-like fall on the Allt an Eas Bhig is the most prominent. Under the remote Bealach nah-Imrich, the pass of the flitting (unlikely as that may seem), is Eas an Uillt Grannda (*NH 114 711*).

Eas an Tairbh   NH 684 838

Fall, below Bailecharn on Edderton Burn, the fall of the bull, so-called, according to Watson, because it is associated with the legend of a water-bull which haunted its banks.

Falls of Talladale   NG 918 673

The Loch Maree Hotel at Talladale was visited by Queen Victoria in September 1877. The visit is commemorated by an

Falls of Talladale, in the basin of Loch Maree. By the pioneering scenic photographer George Washington Wilson (1823–93)

inscription in Gaelic on a monument, the translation of which is over the entrance to the hotel. Close by the Talladale River enters the loch by a series of rapids. The falls are about 2.5 kilometres up country and can be reached by a Forestry Commission track on the right bank of the stream. The district is being re-afforested, but Talladale was the site of an old ironworks based on the oakwoods of Loch Maree and the water-power readily available.

Eas Teampuill   NG 953 422

A beautiful fall in the low hills above Strathcarron Station on the Kyle line.

Torridon Falls   NG 869 573

There is a series of very fine falls on the Amhainn Coire Mhic Nobuil above Torridon House. At the stone bridge over the river is a National Trust for Scotland car park whence it is a short distance to the finest of the falls. The series is set in a magnificent ravine which is deeply entrenched in a pine wood.

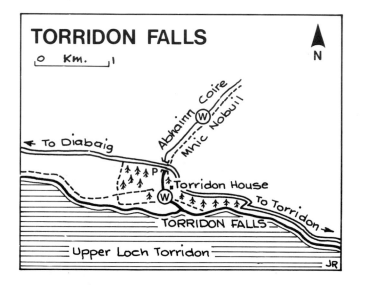

From the bridge a roaring white waterfall is seen at the head of the gorge. The burn tumbles over falls, rushes over rapids, swirls in pot-holes and hurries through narrowings between rock walls. Swinburne holidayed in Torridon with Edwin Harrison in a reading party under the supervision of the renowned Dr Jowitt. In his biography of the poet, Gosse relates that walking over rough country Swinburne became footsore and then deeply depressed and silent. 'Suddenly, however, they came to a waterfall and, in an instant, he was transformed, dancing before it in an ecstasy of delight and adoration.' In his poem 'Loch Torridon', written a quarter of a century later are these lines:

> And through the twilight leftward of the way
> And down the dark, with many a laugh and leap
> The light blithe hill-streams shone from scaw to steep in
> glittering pride of play.

The path leads to Beinn Alligin, Beinn Dearg and Liathach. It is possible to regain the Torridon Road by Coire Dubh. The circuit of Liathach which can be accomplished thus is not to be missed. It leads to a further series of fine cascades higher up the same burn.

Victoria Falls

Queen Victoria was something of a connoisseur of waterfalls and it is somewhat ironical that these falls are the ones that bear her name. In her journal she wrote:

> Here we first took our tea and then got out and scrambled up a steep bank to look at a waterfall, a pretty one, but very inferior to those in our neighbourhood at Balmoral.

The falls have been somewhat off the beaten track until recently when the Forestry Commission established a car park and a short forest trail. The burn tumbles some twelve metres in two steps. The falls were the subject of one of the earliest studies of the highland landscape by the noted Victorian Photographer-Royal, George Washington Wilson.

Sutherland and Caithness

Allt na Caillich   NC 465 455

This splendid mountain waterfall is beside the path to Ben Hope, the most northerly Munro, a singularly imposing mountain of mica-schist and quartzite which rises steeply above Loch Hope. The fall gets its name, Alltnacaillich, from a woman who, according to legend, lost a calf and discovered it on the brink of the precipice over which the burn falls, but, in

Torridon Falls. Thought to be the falls at which the poet Swinburne danced in delight. One of the pleasures in setting out for Ben Alligan or Liathac from Torridon is the succession of falls, rapids and swirling potholes on the Amhainn Mhic Nobvil. HAMISH BROWN

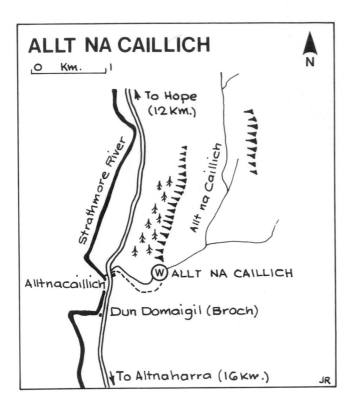

ALLT NA CAILLICH

0   Km.   1

N

To Hope
(12 Km.)

Strathmore River

Allt na Caillich

W ALLT NA CAILLICH

Alltnacaillich

Dun Domaigil (Broch)

To Altnaharra (16 Km.)

JR

the excitement, both she and the beast fell to their deaths when she lost her footing. At the base of the long line of cliffs which lead up to Ben Hope stood a dwelling where the gaelic poet, Robb Donn, was born in 1714. He never learned to read and write and composed his poems in the Sutherland dialect, his verses being handed down by word of mouth until they were published in 1829. He was a herdsman and gamekeeper to Lord Reay who knew and loved this country and its waterfalls.

Ardvreck Falls   NC 241 238

These small scale falls are delightfully set in a birch-filled hollow above the A837 at Ardvreck Castle. From the fall on the Allt a Chalda Beag there is an enchanting view of the ruined keep above Loch Assynt. The burn, which is generally well supplied with water for so small a stream, descends eight metres in three stages.

Achness   NH 468 029

The Cassley rises on Ben Mor Assynt and flows for 32 kilometres through a wild and lonely valley to join the Oykell at Rosehall. Rosehall is at the head of the Kyle of Sutherland and boats used to come upstream as far as the confluence of the two rivers, making it a busy place. The Cassley drains a basin of about 250 square kilometres and generally has a considerable quantity of water in it. At Achness there is a fine gorge with a series of falls. The uppermost fall, about six metres in height, is

Victoria Falls. Now easily approached from a Forestry Commission car park. COLIN ALSTON

Falls on the Douchary River, near Ullapool. HAMISH BROWN

Falls of Rogie, near Strathpeffer. HAMISH BROWN

Fairy Glen, Rosemarkie. HIDB

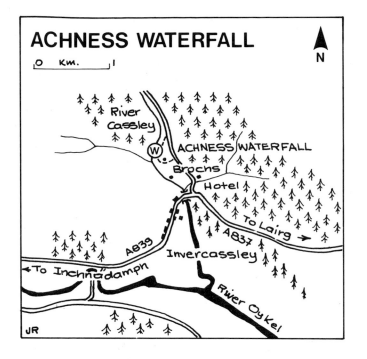

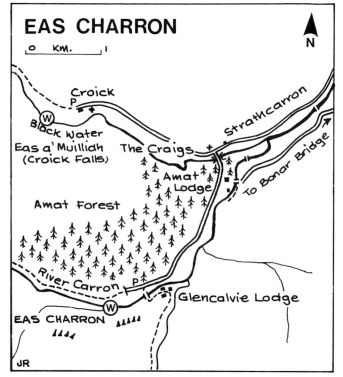

abrupt. The lower fall is a broken apron of rock twelve metres in height which forms a rapid in spate, but which affords a number of intermediate pools enabling salmon to ascend the river. This formidable obstacle rivals the Falls of Shin as a spectacle when the fish are on the run.

There is an old cemetery on the bank of the river. Visitors are warned to use a path way from the river bank to avoid being ensnared by anglers. A pleasing footpath leads beside the falls in charming woods.

Falls of Balnacoil   NC 803 114

The fisheries of the turbulent river Blackwater, the principal tributary of the Brora, are divided by fine double falls at Balnacoil Lodge. The low gorge in which they are situated is bridged and the falls make a pleasant walk from the road at the head of Loch Brora. A little distance above the falls is an imprissively situated broch, Castle Cole, which is worth visiting.

Falls of Borgie   NC 648 545

The River Borgie follows a boisterous course of some sixteen kilometres from the chain of mountain lochs under Ben Loyal which culminates in Loch Loyal itself. The river is regulated by a succession of salmon weirs but there are natural falls, well worth seeing in spate, about five kilometres from the road by a forest track.

Bigburn Falls see Dunrobin Falls

Eas Charron (Glencalvie Falls)   NH 459 888

Hugh Miller described a visit to 'the dark hills and alder-skirted river of Strath Carron' with its bleak gorge 'where the lofty sides approach so near that for the whole winter quarter the sun never falls on the stream below'. This gorge, above Glencalvie Lodge, is the site of the Falls of Carron, *Eas Charron*. The Carron is a much-celebrated salmon river draining a basin of 400 square kilometres. Its tributaries

include another Blackwater and the Calvie which drain the remote Glencalvie and Freevater Deer Forests, from the former of which the falls derive their Sunday name.

The main fall is a serious obstacle for salmon, but, because the rocks dip downstream and form an inclined chute at the top of the fall, the fish can ascend it in low water conditions. In these conditions, too, it is possible to stride across the river at this point. The steep sides of the gloomy gorge described by Miller, clothed in birch, pine and alder, are made accessible to fishermen by a network of paths, ladders and walkways.

Eas Choul   NH 311 832

A remote fall above Glenbeg beyond Deanich Lodge reached by the Hydro Board road from Strath Vaich. The hanging valley fall is in the new Ross and Cromarty District, but it belongs to a river system which is otherwise situated in Sutherland.

Eas Choineas   NC 409 446

This is one of a succession of falls in the rocky gorge of Glen Golly, south of Loch Hope. A track follows the river from Gobernisgach Lodge.

Clashnessie Falls   NC 054 301

Eas Clais an Easaidh is situated above the hamlet of Clashnessie on the Stoer Peninsula to which it gives its name. The fifteen metre fall dominates the place, dropping sheer over a black dyke. The stream is regulated by a network of lochans on the moor above, including Loch an Easain, Loch nan Lub, Garbh Loch Mor and Loch Poll Dubh. There are footpaths along either side of the burn and stepping stones at the foot of the fall.

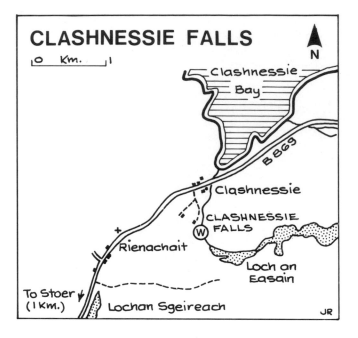

Falls of Clyth Burn see Trollie Pow

Clyne Fall   NC 892 064

Fall of eighteen metres above the mans at Clyne near the A9.

Eas Coul Aulin (Eas a' Chual Aluinn)   NC 280 277

Two hundred metres high, Eas Coul Aulin is the highest
waterfall in Britain. Inevitably it is compared with the Fall of
Glomach which was for long considered the highest fall. Tom
Weir considers this problem:

> How does it compare to the Fall of Glomach? On the scale of
> beauty I would hand the prize to the Eas Coul Aulin because
> of its open situation and variety of outlook to the head of
> Loch Glencoul and the green strath running inland beneath
> the grey rampart of Ben More Assynt. But it has nothing of

the overpowering weight of compressed waters hurtling into
the Glomach ravine. You can stand back at the Eas Coul
Aulin. You are not perched among the waters as on that
giddy pinnacle at Glomach.

Most writers would concur with this and perhaps conclude
that comparisons are odious. Undoubtedly Eas Coul Aulin is a
fall which everyone should try and visit. It is not more difficult
of access than Glomach. There are three ways to get there from
the road to the north (A894): by boat from the Kylesku Ferry,
on foot along the shore of Loch Glencoul, and the usual
route—from above Loch Ganvich by the Bealach a' Bhuirich
—the pass of the roaring. It is five kilometres from the road,
259 metres above sea level, and the pass rises to 487 metres.
The track leads beside the loch and crosses its principal feeder
which it follows on the further bank to Lochan Bealach a'
Bhuirich before climbing relatively steeply to the pass. Less
than a kilometre beyond the summit of the pass the track
crosses a stream beside a lochan. This stream is followed to the
edge of the cliff where the fall occurs. It is quite practicable to
descend beside the fall for a short distance in order to
appreciate its full majesty. Visitors can descend the terraced
face of the cliff to the foot of the fall. It is the foot of the fall
which is reached by boat or by the route beside Loch Glencoul.
The disadvantage of this route is that there are steep cliffs
above Loch Beag and above Eilean an Tuim which must be
avoided by traversing the steep slopes 60 metres above Loch
Glencoul. The full face of the cliff, Leitir Dubh, which is
dominated by the fall, can be seen only from the glen but,
however daunting the prospect, it is better to climb back to the
top of it in order to return quickly to the road.

The whole of the Ben Mor Assynt massif is of great interest
to geologists and naturalists. This applies to the Glas Bheinn
district where Eas Coul Aulin is situated. It is at the head of
Loch Glencoul that the Moine Thrust is most clearly under-
stood. This is the line along which, 400 million years ago, the
sediments which form the Caledonian Mountains collapsed
against the old land mass made up of the old hard rocks of the
west in the Caledonian Orogenesis. The rocks to the south-east
were thrust over the rocks on the other side for a distance of
about ten miles (16 km). The folds were so intense that older
rocks were pushed over younger rocks so that in places it is
possible to drill a hole and meet the same younger rock twice

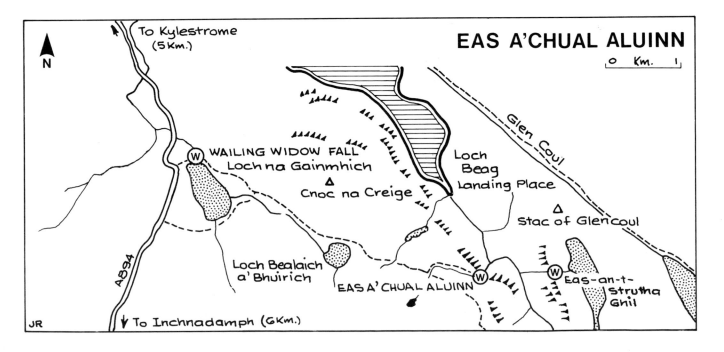

with an older rock in between. Quinag consists of Torridonian Sandstone; Glas Bheinn consists of Lewisian Gneiss, the older rock; between the two at the outlet to Loch na Gainmhich are Cambrian Rocks, younger than either of them. It was the discovery of this thrust plane in 1883 that led geologists to establish what had really happened for the first time. One thrust plane occurs at Loch Gainmhich and the Moine Thrust Plane at the Stack of Glencoul.

The ordinary visitor may find all this beyond him for there is little to see on the ground except with a tutored eye. The visitor will nevertheless be impressed with the atmospheric quality of these remote mountains. Glas Bheinn itself looks a very dull mountain from the main road; Quinag steals the show. However, no sooner is the main road left behind than Glas Bheinn begins to reveal the quality of its rock architecture. Coire Dubh is occupied by the first lochan which is encountered above Gainmhich and above it—its lochan hidden from view—is Coire Dearg. The absence of vegetation and the greyness of the rocks is striking. Indeed no mountain is more appropriately named. These corries and those above the fall are favourite gathering grounds for stags. The Bealach is aptly named too.

It is, of course, glacial action which has produced these corries and after the bealach is crossed the visitor obtains his first view of the glacially deepened trench into which Eas Coul Aulin tumbles. The great fall itself cannot be seen yet and as the visitor picks his way down the first burn—not the burn on which the giant lies—what takes the eye is Loch nan Caorach (Sheep Loch) occupying almost all of a basin on the hummocky tableland on the other side of the trench. Out of it Eas ant-Srutha Ghil precipitates itself to give a foretaste of things to come. The Stack of Glencoul is prominent too, an isolated monarch of the country between the two sea lochs of Glencoul and Glendhu.

The burn on which Eas Coul Aulin lies drains a more indefinite upland, but it is easily enough recognised because, above the path, there are two prominent little falls on the burn. They are little for these parts, anyway. There are paths beside the burn leading down to the edge of the escarpment, but they are much less clear than the track which is left. There are further low falls on the burn but Eas Coul Aulin is not seen until the very edge of the escarpment is reached.

There is one mystery about Eas Coul Aulin which I have not solved. That is to establish when it was first recognised for what it is, the 'highest waterfall'. The discovery of Eas Coul Aulin is comparatively recent. It was referred to in nineteenth century guide books and in the Ordnance Gazetteer. There is a passing reference to 'an impetuous tributary making a waterfall of nearly 700' in leap' in Francis H Groome's Ordnance Gazetteer of 1884. Baddeley, the most reliable of guide book writers, makes no reference to it in his guide of 1882/3, but by 1894 he refers to Es-cuallin, a waterfall 'one of the finest in Britain and accounted about 500' high. The whole burn goes headlong over the cliff.' In another part of the same guide, however, Glomach is still referred to as 'the highest and wildest in Scotland'. The height which Baddeley gives is interesting because it has been established that Eas Coul Aulin falls 511 feet before it begins to sprawl over the fan of rock debris at its foot. However, such questions may be considered academic by the visitor to the fall; at least Baddeley encourages him to go there. What is much more surprising is that it is only on the new edition of the 1:50,000 map that the Ordnance Survey names the fall. The correct name, Eas a' Chual Aluinn, is given. Inexplicably, for there are few limitations as to space in these empty acres, the most recent one-inch map, indicated this important fall simply by the word 'waterfall'. The change was probably brought about by pressure from George McCord of Glasgow and John Feilden whose enthusiasm for waterfalls extends to a prot-

racted correspondence with the survey over a variety of questions connected with a number of falls.

Between the world wars most guide books continued to refer to Glomach as the highest fall and several referred to Eas Coul Aulin in terms which disqualified it from consideration. The most enthusiastic account of the fall occurs in R MacDonald Robertson's *Wade the River, Drift the Loch* (1948). E W Hodge in the SMC Guide Book *The Northern Highlands* (1953) and Campbell Steven in *Enjoying Scotland* (1971) also deal enthusiastically with the fall.

Comparisons between falls are difficult to make, but they are clearly related to the size of the basin which the fall drains. The volume of water in a fall is also related to 'stream order' which can be established by counting the number of tributaries which the stream receives. It is interesting to compare Eas Coul Aulin in this way with the Fall of Glomach. Although the SMC guide says the two streams are comparable in size, this is not, in fact, the case. Eas Coul Aulin drains a basin of about four square kilometres and has a stream order of seven; the Glomach drains a basin of some twenty square kilometres and has a stream order of about twenty. It is clear that Glomach is the more considerable stream and likely to be the more impressive stream under most conditions. It is estimated that the discharge of Glomach is about 1600 litres per second in average conditions while the discharge of Eas Coul Aulin is about 250 litres per second. For comparison the Falls of Kirkaig discharge 7000 litres per second. The natural reservoirs which serve Glomach are much bigger than those lochans which impound the water above Eas Coul Aulin, the largest of which is Loch a' Choire Guirm.

The name of the fall which, as it consists of three parts, most English people will refuse to come to terms with anyway, means 'the splendid waterfall of Glencoul'. It is entirely appropriate, but it would be as well if the local name, The Maiden's Tresses, were used. This originates from a folk tale of a local girl betrothed to a man she did not love, who hid along the cliffs of Leitir Dubh. When she was sought out she threw herself over the cliff and her tresses spread out to form the waterfall. It is a sad tale for what, when most visitors see it, will be a sunny place.

Eas Crom   *NC 230 078*

The Crooked Fall is situated above Loch Urigill on the slopes of the Cromalt Hills

Croik Falls see Eas a' Mhuilinn

Eas Poll an Damarin   *ND 075 183*

Fall on the coast at the Ord of Caithness close to the deserted village of Badbea.

Eas Dubh see Amhainn Mor

Easan Dubh   *NC 236 208*

Wet weather fall above Inchnadamph.

Sput Dubh see Lothbeg Cascade

Duist Falls see Kildonan Falls

Dunrobin Falls   ND 832 016

The Golspie Burn issues from Loch Horn and flows eight kilometres through a fine glen. Dunrobin, a fine mock gothic castle, stands at its entrance. Dunrobin Glen affords an attractive walk from the bridge in the metropolitan little village of Golspie. A signpost directs the visitor to the curiously English-sounding 'Bigburn Waterfall'. The name is a corruption of 'beag' meaning 'little'. The path crosses and re-crosses the little burn until the impressive 12-metre fall is reached.

Einig Fall   NH 381 999

Some five kilometres from the point where the Einig joins the Oykell, it enters a four-kilometre long gorge which forms a succession of waterfalls. At the bottom end of the gorge there is a singularly beautiful fall about five metres high above a superb pool for anglers.

Easan Feidh   NC 586 252

This is a remote fall under Ben Kilbreck above Loch Choire reached over the Bealach Easach, the pass of the waterfalls, from the Crask Inn. Enterprising visitors will note that this headstream of the Helmsdale has been 'beheaded' by the Naver and wonder whether they should pan for gold there. There is a low fall much further downstream close to the confluence of the Navar and the Mallart at Achadh an Eas (*NC 673 375*), the field of the waterfalls.

Bridge of Forss Falls   ND 035 685

Rough falls, eight metres high, which give the river its Norse name.

Eas na Gaibhre   NC 395 136

Upland fall on the Cassley.

Gaim Eas   NH 487 915

Fall beside the bridge to East Amat Lodge near the scene of the eviction of the crofters from Glencalvie graphically described by John Prebble in *The Highland Clearances*.

Easan Garbh Mor   NC 269 528

Two falls on the Achriesgill Burn between Riconich and Gualainn which relieve the somewhat dreary moorland between Laxford Bridge and Durness.

Gledfield Falls

River falls on the Carron.

Eas Mor Gisgil   NC 181 417

The patchwork of hummocky little hills, wild lochans and devious burns of the gneiss country is nowhere better exemplified than in the neighbourhood of Scourie. From these low hills there are stunning views across Edrachillis Bay studded with dozens of islands to the Stoer Peninsula and there is no finer vantage point than the little hill above the fall on the Allt Mor Gisgil. Eas Mor Gisgil is fed by Loch nan Uid, the last in a chain of lochs and lochans draining eighteen square kilometres of moorland. It is a fine roaring fall of about twelve metres in

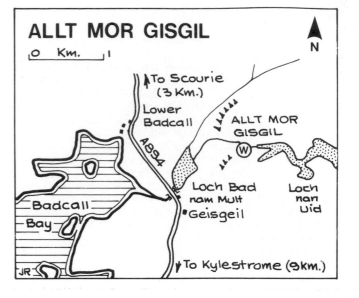

height which can be reached by a track of sorts beside Loch Bad nam Mult.

Eas Glutha   NC 987 341

Remote fall on the Glutt Water.

Inchnadamph

At Inchnadamph in the heart of Assynt there are significant outcrops of Durness Limestone which give rise to lime-rich soils which support rare flowers and dwarf willows. The limestone pavements and caves which are characteristic of the rock lend unusual interest to the area. The best known caves are those of the Allt nan Uamh, but there are also notable caves in the valley of the Tralligill Burn (q.v.).

Kilcalmkill Falls   NC 844 097

Kilcalmkill refers to an early Christian church, St Columba's Cell established beside Loch Brora. It was taken by a local family and corrupted to Carrol, a name which still survives in Carrol Rock, the magnificent crag which dominates the loch. The Kilcalmkill Estate of old is now called the Gordonbush Estate and the lodge is situated on the northern side of the loch. Beside it the impetuous Allt Smeoral, the burn of the thrush, plunges to the waterside under the loch road. The lowest of the three falls, about 12 metres high, is difficult to see but an estate track leads to a bridge over the uppermost fall of four metres. From the left bank the middle falls, the most attractive of the three with a natural rock bridge, can be seen from a path. There is a famous etching of the falls in Charles Cordiner's *Antiquities and Scenery of the North of Scotland* (1790). It is fanciful, but no less interesting for that. Ossian, with harp, and other figures are seen in the foreground. Cordiner's description is:

> Near to Carrol are some charming fields bounded by a craggy hill; from a cleft in the middle of the hill rushes forth a torrent, which passing under a natural bridge of rock, dashes down a precipice, and forms a wild and beautiful cascade in its fall: the noise of the torrent echoing in a lofty and deep cavern shagged with shrubs and ancient trees, among which the wildfowl make their nests; the rivulet murmuring around insulated piles of rock; and the distant prospect of these halls and monuments of ancient heroes, forcibly recall to mind the

images of the Ossian song. Here, perhaps, has Carril, whose name is preserved in these scenes, mused his wild and desultory strains: here 'amidst the voices of rocks, and bright tumbling waters he might pour the sound of his trembling harp'. Whether the memory of the lapsed ages was preserved by the bards, or if only, like a morning dream, the visions of Ossian came in later days yet 'pleasant are the words of the "song",' well do they paint these wilds, in all the striking forms of their native grandeur and beauty.

Kildonan Falls   *NC 905 212*

The River Ullie (the Helmsdale River) drains a wild and remote moorland country of considerable lochs. Its lower course is relatively low-lying but it is broken by a series of falls and rapids near Kildonan Lodge. The most considerable of these falls, the Kildonan Falls, consists of broken rocks some four metres in height where the river tumbles picturesquely in its bed. Above Kildonan Station are the Duist Falls (*NC 903 220*), twin falls two metres in height, which have formed the subject of numerous pictures by amateur artists. The Kildonan Burn was the site of the gold rush of 1869 which, as is traditional in these matters, gave rise to a rapid influx of prospectors, the staking of claims, to panning for alluvial gold, to makeshift housing and tented villages, and to a wild and lawless period of development in a remote part of the country. Both the Kildonan Burn and the Suisgill Burn are worth exploring for their associations. Where the main road crosses the Kildonan Burn at Baile an Or, the township of gold, is the attractive *Baile An Or Waterfall* (*NC 912 217*), five metres in height.

Falls of Kirkaig   *NC 113 177*

The Falls of Kirkaig are on the boundary between Ross and Cromarty and Sutherland beneath Suilven, the mountain which rises so dramatically from the peneplain of old hard rocks above Lochinver and Inverkirkaig. Examination of the map shows that the geomorphology of the Fionn Loch area is complicated. The loch is aligned with Loch Veyatie and with

Loch Bad na Muirchin and its outlet by the River Kirkaig appears to be unnatural. It seems certain that the Kirkaig occupies a relatively recent channel in geological terms which it is still cutting back very quickly. At one time it followed the more natural line now occupied by the River Muirichinn and, at another, the course of the Allt a Mhuillin. The present course of the Kirkaig has been established since glacial times and the rushing river is now in a long narrow trench at the head of which are the falls. They are 18 metres high and, since the river drains a major system of lochs, there is always a considerable volume of water in them. In this respect the Falls are generally acknowledged to be the finest in Scotland. They combine height, volume of water and distinctiveness of setting.

The birch-filled gorge in which the river flows provides an obvious route to the hills from Inverkirkaig. There is a succession of pools each of which marks a previous site of the falls, but the track climbs away from the river onto the heather-clad moor and only anglers climb down to the stream. Where the path divides the way to the falls is obvious enough and it leads to a magnificent belveder opposite the falls. The white water is etched into a cleft in the rocks and, in low water conditions, it is possible to see that there is an eerie cave behind them. At the very foot of the path is a rope to enable anglers to net their fish. The river teams with salmon which are often confined to the two inaccessible pools at the foot of the falls. The walk to the falls or to the Fionn Loch and Suilven—and no one who visits the falls should omit the short walk beyond to see the view of the mountain across the loch—is quite magnificent.

Lothbeg Cascade

In Charles Cordiner's *Remarkable Ruins and Romantic Prospects of North Britain* (1795) there is a view of what he calls the Lothbeg Cascade at the mouth of the Burn. The fall tumbles dramatically over an old sea-cliff. The fall was eliminated in 1818 when the Earl's Cut was made to drain the alluvial flats at the mouth of the Loth. *Sput Dubh* (*NC 940 093*), south of Lothbeg, is formed where the Allt na Cuile falls into the sea.

Eas Creag an Luchda   *NC 311 330*

Remote fall at the head of Glendhu, the other arm of Loch Cairnbawn besides Loch Glencoul. It occupies a similar position on the valley side to Eas Coul Aulin, but is not so high.

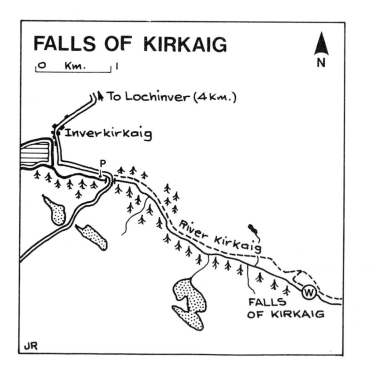

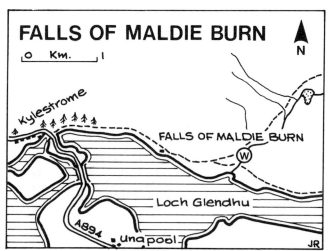

Maiden's Tresses see Eas Coul Aulin

Falls of Maldie Burn
NC 251 342

The Maldie Burn has a short, precipitpous course from Loch Leathaid Bhuain, 180 metres above sea level, to Loch Glendhu. It tumbles 75 metres in three splendid cascades beside the track from Kylestrome to Loch More.

Mare's Tail
ND 220 335

Coastal fall on the Mill Burn, Force which forms a prominent sea-mark. The name confirms the strong Norse influence in Caithness—'force' means 'watefall'—and a Viking Castle clings to nearby cliffs.

Eas a' Mhuilinn
NH 451 913

These falls are above Croik on the Blackwater. The village is the site of the little Telford church where the evicted tenants of Glencalvie gathered to seek the help of their minister. The name 'mill fall' reminds us nowadays of the active community who once lived here. *Croik Falls* were eased in the sixties to enable salmon and sea trout to ascend the Blackwater.

Falls of the Amhainn Mor
NC 211 122

The network of lochs in Sutherland is perhaps the most striking feature of the landscape. They are interconnected by short rivers—'uidhs'—and where there is a difference in level between them there are impressive falls. *Eas Dubh Uidh a' Ghiagell* is a good example. It lies between the Cam Loch, a very beautiful, island-studded loch divided by a peninsula, and Loch Veyatie, ten metres lower. There are six low falls which can be reached easily enough from the main road at Elphin.

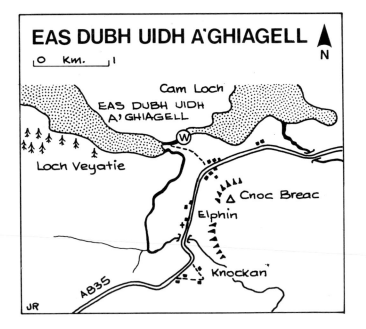

Moral Falls
NH 514 926

River falls above a noted angling pool on the Carron. In Gaelic Eas Morail means 'magnificent waterfall'.

Eas Cnoc na Morar
NH 401 861

Fall on the Glen More River in the Glencalvie Forest beside the road to Deanich Lodge.

Corriemulzie

This is the exceptionally remote glen at the head of the River Einig in the Freevater Deer Forest in Kincardine Parish. The river enters a gorge below Corriemulzie Lodge and tumbles over a succession of river falls. Salmon are prevented from entering the Letters Burn by insurmountable falls at its mouth. The place-name is interesting—coire muillidh—for there were five mills in this empty valley before the clearances.

Glenmuik Falls
NC 372 134

Salmon cannot ascend the Cassley beyond these falls which consist of an upper fall of three metres and a lower fall of seven metres.

Oykell Bridge Falls
NC 382 012

The Ordnance Gazetteer gives a good description of these fine river falls:

> Several hundred yards above the inn at Oykell Bridge, the Oykell tumbling along a rugged and declivitous channel makes a series of wild cataracts terminating in one bold and very formidable fall. The banks which overhang this multiplied linn are quite precipitous and exhibit, at spots where no soil can be detected by the eye, several large fir trees springing up from curiously twisted roots.

The principal fall referred to is four metres high. The Oykell rise in the Dubh Loch Mor Corrie of Ben More Assynt and there is a succession of falls in the upper part of its course (*NC 310 182*).

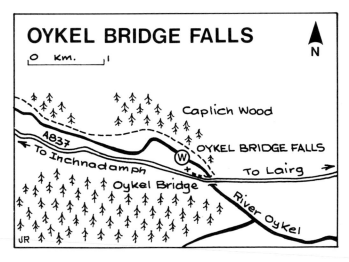

Eas Ruigh ant-Saigart
NC 263 213

Fall, above Inchnadamph, on the Allt Poll an Droighinn, the fall of the Priest's Shieling.

Eas Saigh Caime
NC 264 220

Fall in the Tralligill Valley, possibly the fall of the blind bitch.

SHIN FALLS

0 Km. 1

N

To Lairg

Shin Forest

SHIN FALLS
W
P

A837

To Inchnadamph
Kyle of Sutherland

B864

A836

To Bonar Bridge

JR

Shin Falls

NH 576 993

The Shin has one of the most spectacular salmon leaps in north Scotland. The Ordnance Gazetteer (1884) comments that its appearance has been marred by blasting and that this accounts for its flattened look. It has, of course, been incorporated in the most northerly power scheme, but it is a scheme which has been well carried out—the Hydro Board having learned from earlier mistakes—and, in most conditions, the falls are not adversely affected. The river drains the very extensive basin of Loch Shin and flows through an attractive, well-wooded valley to reach its gorge at the head of the Kyle of Sutherland. There are other falls in the gorge including Little Shin Falls. Shin Falls are best approached from the back road, B864, rather than the main road from Bonar Bridge to Lairg.

Allt Smoo

NC 418 671

The cliffs at Durness are of limestone and contain the most celebrated cave in Scotland, the Cave of Smoo. It is partly eroded by the sea, but it was largely fashioned by the underground river which can be seen entering the cave south of the road (A838) by a waterfall of 24 metres. Sir Walter Scott was very impressed by the cave:

> There is an exterior cavern of great height and breadth, like the vault of a cathedral. Within this huge cave and opening by a sort of portal, closed half way up with a ledge of rock, we got access to a second cavern, an irregular circle in form and completely filled with water. This was supplied by a considerable brook which fell from the height of at least eighty feet, through a small aperture in the rocky roof of the cave. The effect of the twilight, composed of such beams as could find their way through the cascade as it fell, was indescribably grand.

Letter to Robert Southey

The outer cave can be entered on foot at most states of the tide, but the floor of the two inner chambers is always under water. The cave can be visited by boat at high tide, but the vessel has to be lifted over the ledge described by Scott to reach the second chamber. It is only by boat that the foot of the waterfall can be seen, but its eerie roar can be heard within and a view of the inner chamber, illuminated by the holes in the roof, obtained by scrambling up onto a rocky shelf beside the entrance. Beyond the waterfall is a third chamber, 30 metres long, accessible only to sub-aqua divers. The head of this notable fall can, of course, be seen by crossing the road.

It is not surprising that the Smoo Cave with its gothic entrance was for long regarded as the entrance to the Underworld, inhabited by the Devil himself. There is one splendid legend attached to it. Lord Reay, who fought on the continent with Gustavus Adolphus, was said to have encountered the Devil there on several occasions and bested him. The Devil therefore hid in Smoo Cave in order to take his revenge, but before he could do so the dawn came and rendered the Devil powerless. He therefore blew the holes in the roof of the cave by which the Allt Smoo falls into it. Scott was very impressed with the atmosphere:

> A water-kelpie or evil spirit of any kind of aquatic propensity could not have chosen a fitter abode, and, to say the truth, I believe, at our first entrance when all our feelings were afloat at the novelty of the scene, the unexpected splashing of a seal would have routed the whole dozen of us.

Such feelings of terror were no doubt induced by local people, many of whom made their living by smuggling. The cave was a favourite place to hide excisable liquor when the gaugers were about.

Eas an t-Srathain see Waterfall Cave

Easan t-Strutha Ghil

NC 289 277

A spectacular mountain fall on the opposite side of the same valley as that occupied by Eas Coul Aulin. It provides a mirror image of the great fall and, although its basin is similar, it is just as high—it could be argued that it is even higher. Indeed the contours are even more spaced than those on the opposite side of the glen. Loch nan Coarach, the loch of the sheep, provides an extensive reservoir for the fall. Campbell Steven has dubbed the valley of the Amhainn an Loch Bhig, the Waterfall Glen. With these two giants the name is appropriate.

Eas an Tabhrainn

NC 228 067

Wildcat Fall is situated above Loch Urigill at the foot of the Cromalt Hills.

Eas nan Toll Dubha

NH 446 894

A river fall on the Carron between Glencalvie Lodge and Alladale Lodge.

Torboll Fall

NH 745 985

Torboll Fall is a fine fall on the River Carnaig at the head of Loch Fleet. The name betrays the Norse influence close to the East coast. It is beside the fine mountain road which runs from Bonar Bridge to the Mound by Loch Buidhe. An elaborate salmon ladder, 34 metres long, by-passes the fall. It was one of the very first such devices to be built. From the road the full face of the fall is seen. It is about 20 metres high and begins with a steep waterchute in slanting rocks before plunging abruptly into a pool. A path leads to a bridge above the fall. In Victorian times Princess Alexandra paid a formal visit to the place and the path is still called the Princess's Path. It provides an attractive terraced walk above the river to another bridge downstream. Both the fall and the salmon ladder, with its long steps and elaborate pools, repay a visit.

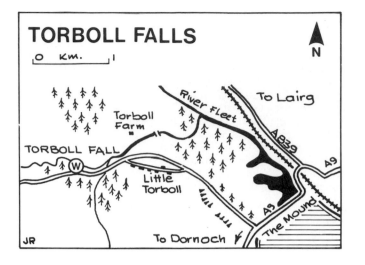

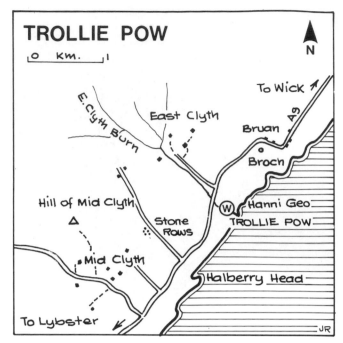

Torgawn Falls

NC 212 320

Fine roadside fall on the burn which tumbles down from Quinag above Kylesku. The falls lie in a birch-filled hollow along the road to Drumbeg and their foot is obscured by the trees.

Tralligil Burn

This burn—the Troll's Gill—drains the limestone moorland above Inchnadamph where there are notable caves. The Cnoc an Uamh Cascade is a 60-metre underground waterfall, a waterslide, in the most extensive cave system. It can be explored safely in dry weather but the expedition is best undertaken with an experienced potholer. From the caves and waterfalls of the Tralligill Burn a stalker's path climbs to Loch Fleodach Coire and leads eventually to Eas Coul Aulin. A shorter route leads to the falls above Calda House on Loch Assynt. The two falls, Easan Chalda Mor (*NC 256 238*), are fine cascades on a superb moor with splendid views.

Trollie Pow

ND 307 386

Trollie Pow is the local name for the falls on the East Clyth Burn which falls into Hanni Geo. Nearby is Gunn's Castle. Geos are spectacular inlets eroded by the sea along lines of weakness, frequently in Old Red Sandstone. They are often associated with waterfalls which contribute to the deepening of the inlet. At Hanni Geo there is a tiny beach. Further South Clyth Harbour was the mouth of the West Clyth Burn, but in glacial times it was blocked by boulder clay, forcing the burn to find another way to the sea. The rivulet now falls into Ceann Hilligeo and it has cut a deep gorge—crossed by the road bridge at Occumster—in which are the Falls of Clyth Burn (*ND 271 354*) by the last of which it tumbles 24 metres into the sea, which is inaccessible at this point in most conditions. The spectacular cliffs, rock shelves and stacks of 'the Grey Coast' are very fine.

Easan Uaine

NC 269 528

The loch of the green waterfalls, Loch an Easain Uaine, is situated north-east of Arkle in a magnificent amphitheatre in the hills, unsuspected when the mountain is seen from the high road to Durness. Arkle, the mountain name which became nationally famous when a string of racehorses was named after these remote northern peaks, is composed of quartzite. It is the

haunt of pine marten, the snow bunting and the eagle. The corrie is best reached from Achfary at the foot of Loch More whence a track leads to the col between Arkle and Foinaven. The falls are corrie waterfalls of the most splendid kind.

Wailing Widow Fall

NC 243 293

The falls below the Sandy Loch, Loch na Gainmich, between Inchnadamph and Kylesku are unjustly neglected. The Allt Cranaidh forms a spectacular gorge, more than thirty metres deep, in Cambrian Quartzite at the outlet to the loch. The fall can be reached by a short walk from the main road (A894) by an indistinct footpath. At the head of the gorge is an angular rock wall over which the burn precipitates itself with tremendous force into an abyss some thirty-two metres below. At the centre of the fall is a prominent rock buttress which has given rise to two legends associated with the place. In the first a ne'er-do-well called Donald the Moss married a local girl, but one day he encountered a local man with a fine plaid. Donald the Moss coveted the plaid and fought with the man to take it off him, in the course of which fight the local man was killed. Donald the Moss took to the hills, but a hue and cry was set up after him and he was eventually captured by the sandy loch and hanged (with a rope which he was forced to make himself) from the buttress in the gorge.

The other tale gives the Wailing Widow Fall its name and is related in V Carron Wellington's book *The Adventures of a Sporting Angler:*

> It appears that some centuries past, a widow with her only son occupied the lone ferryman's cottage which stood where the Kylesku Inn stands today. They survived mainly by their hunting instincts which always assured them of a bird or a fish for the pot. The meagre pittance received for ferrying passengers and cattle across the narrows of Loch a Chairn Bhain to Kylestrome and back was far from sufficient to sustain them.
>
> One day, however, the hapless youth was gored to death by a vicious stag and finally tossed over the precipice into the gorge below. That same evening the distracted mother found

her missing son at the foot of the falls, and, as she knelt by his mangled body her grief knew no bounds. A terrific storm broke loose amongst the surrounding hills as though intent on rendering each one asunder. The rock-faced precipice over which the infuriated waters roared, subsided under the impact burying the unfortunate woman beside her son. The agencies of time and water have carried away the debris but the monumental structure remains to commemorate the tragedy.

The monumental structure referred to is a natural statue formed by the buttress which seems to resemble the figure of the peasant woman. There is a remarkable photograph in the book to illustrate it.

Beside the Wailing Widow Fall a steep path climbs a gully by which it is possible to reach the loch. A visit to the fall can thus be combined with a visit to Eas Coul Aulin. The Allt Cranaidh also forms distinctive falls beside the main road which climbs steeply from Kylesku.

Waterfall Cave (Eas an t-Strathain)   *NC 491 639*

South of Whiten Head, Loch Erribol, there is a conspicuous waterfall which descends fifteen metres into the sea over the mouth of a cave. The cave, Geodha an t-Strathain, does not extend so far inland as the more famous sea cave, Fraisgill Cavern, also on Loch Erribol, but the fall renders it interesting. There is an interesting account of a trip to the cave—which must be made by boat—in *Angling in Wildest Scotland* by Ronald MacDonald Robertson (1936):

> In flood . . . the cascade is transformed into one broad rush of curling, wrestling water out of whose chaotic foaming surface scarcely the outline of the cave dare show itself as the waters throw up wreaths of gauzy spray, forming brilliant rainbows in the sunlight with one fantastic features in one breathless rush of creamy white, lashing the jet-black sea-pool into a fermenting, seething mass of foam.
>
> Everything picturesquely attractive is to be found in the vicinity of these falls. You have mountain and moor, wood

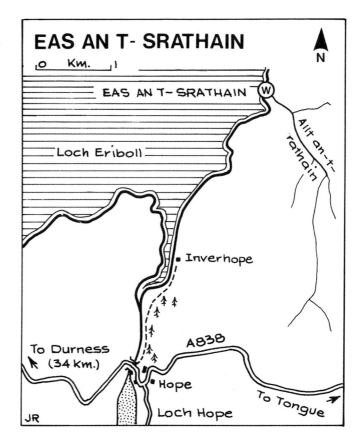

and water, cascade and cliff, rocky ridges and flowery banks, sleeping pools and impetuous currents.

Westerdale Falls   *ND 130 518*

Low falls on flat rocks on the Thurso River. Nearby is an intriguing mill and a broch, Tulach Buaile a Chroic.

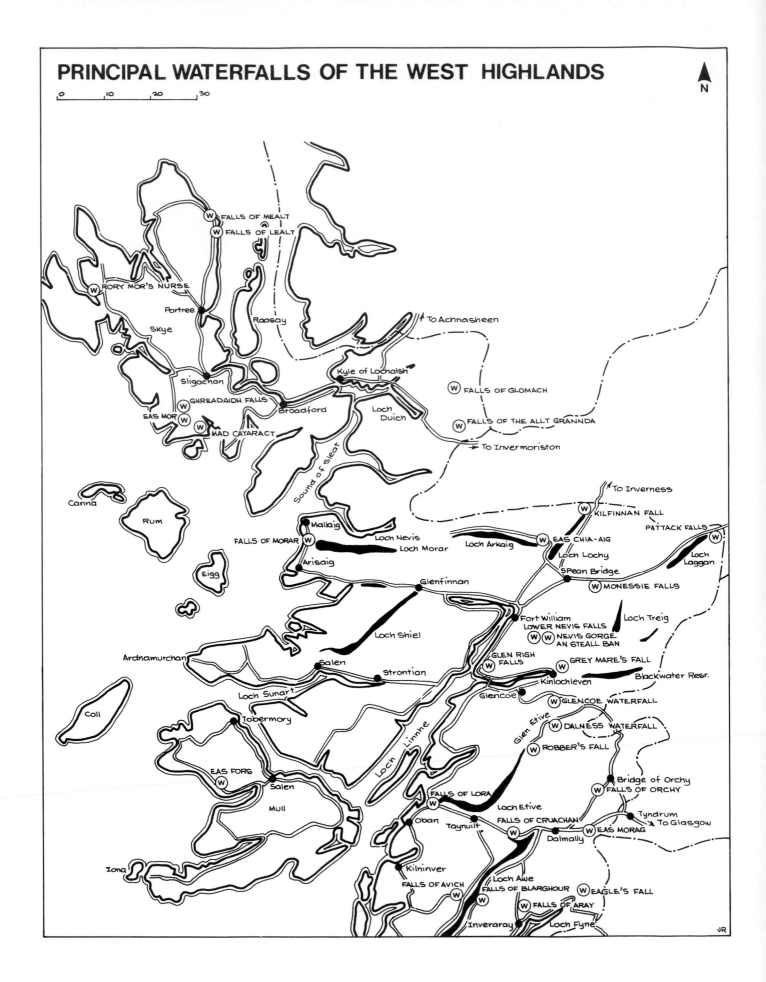

PRINCIPAL WATERFALLS OF THE WEST HIGHLANDS

N

0   10   20   30

Ⓦ FALLS OF MEALT
Ⓦ FALLS OF LEALT

Ⓦ RORY MOR'S NURSE
Portree
Raasay
Skye

To Achnasheen

Kyle of Lochalsh
Sligachan
Ⓦ FALLS OF GLOMACH

Ⓦ GHREADAIDH FALLS
Broadford
Loch Duich
EAS MOR Ⓦ Ⓦ
Ⓦ MAD CATARACT
Ⓦ FALLS OF THE ALLT GRANNDA

To Invermoriston

Sound of Sleat

To Inverness

Canna
Rum
Ⓦ KILFINNAN FALL
PATTACK FALLS

Mallaig
Loch Nevis
FALLS OF MORAR Ⓦ
Loch Morar
Loch Arkaig
Ⓦ EAS CHIA-AIG
Ⓦ
Arisaig
Loch Lochy
Loch Laggan

Eigg
Glenfinnan
SPean Bridge
Ⓦ MONESSIE FALLS

Loch Shiel
Fort William
Loch Treig
LOWER NEVIS FALLS
Ⓦ Ⓦ NEVIS GORGE
AN STEALL BAN

Ardnamurchan
Salen
Strontian
GLEN RIGH
FALLS Ⓦ
Ⓦ GREY MARE'S FALL
Kinlochleven
Blackwater Resr.
Loch Sunart
Glencoe Ⓦ GLENCOE WATERFALL

Coll
Tobermory
Glen Etive
Ⓦ DALNESS WATERFALL

EAS FORS
Ⓦ ROBBER'S FALL

Loch Linnhe
Salen
Bridge of Orchy
Ⓦ FALLS OF ORCHY
Mull
FALLS OF LORA
Ⓦ
Loch Etive
Tyndrum
To Glasgow
Oban
Taynuilt
FALLS OF CRUACHAN
Ⓦ EAS MORAG
Ⓦ
Dalmally

Iona
Kilninver
Loch Awe
FALLS OF AVICH
FALLS OF BLARGHOUR
Ⓦ EAGLE'S FALL
Ⓦ
Ⓦ FALLS OF ARAY
Inveraray
Loch Fyne

JR

WEST HIGHLANDS

Principal Falls

Outstanding Falls	**Touring Centre**
Fall of Glomach	Kintail
Falls of Lealt	Portree
Falls of Kinlochmore (Grey Mare's Fall)	Kinlochleven
An Steall Ban	Fort William

Significant Falls	
Achluachraich Gorge	Spean Bridge
Eas Cia Aig	Spean Bridge
Eas Forss	Mull
Falls of the Allt Grannda	Kintail
Glencoe Waterfall	Glencoe
Lenach Gluthin (Falls of Aray)	Inveraray
Falls of Mealt (Kilt Rock Waterfall)	Portree
Eas Mor	Glen Brittle
Nevis Gorge	Fort William
Lower Falls of Nevis (Polldubh Falls)	Fort William
Pattack Falls	Newtonmore

Interesting Falls	
Falls of Avich	Loch Awe
Falls of Blairgour	Loch Awe
Falls of Cruachan	Loch Awe
Dalness Waterfalls	Glencoe
Eagle's Fall	Inveraray
Greeta Falls	Glen Brittle
Kilfinnan Falls	Spean Bridge
Falls of Lora	Oban
Mad Cataract	Skye
Eas Morag	Loch Awe
Falls of Morar	Arisaig
Rory More's Nurse	Skye
Falls of Orchy	Loch Awe
Falls of Glen Righ	Fort William
Robbers' Waterfall	Glen Etive

Also recommended	
Ease nan Arm	Kintail
Eas Bhradhain	Skye
Eas nan Clag	Loch Awe
Linn of Pattack	Newtonmore
Eas Mor Chuil an Duin	Glenelg
Eas Mor (Talisker)	Sligachan
The Waterfall (Sandaig)	Glenelg
Falls of Shira	Inveraray

The West Highlands

They emerge out of butchers' trays of kidneys, flecked with black, erupt over stones Millais painted Ruskin on, plunge through jet funnels crossing swords with each other as if sharpening fish eaters. The shades of porphyry sew their flowing thread with an undertone of Napoleonic hardness, a hint of thrones, tombs as in old churches. Too catholic for restrictive practices under wooden bridges they blaze back aromatic, fragrant with weed and ling in the dour face of the leaning kelpies human with anoraks. Above them the brook is red with iron

(George MacBeth, *Waterfall in Glen Nevis*).

It is one of the happier accidents of local government re-organisation that Skye and Lochalsh have been brought together in a new district. Two outstanding areas of natural beauty are thus united. In this book the district forms the northern division of the West Highlands. To the south is Lochaber which includes part of the old Argyllshire as well as that part of Inverness-shire centred on Fort Willam. Thus Loch Nevis and Loch Hourn, Ardnamurchan and Morvern are united with Ardgour, the basin of the Spean, and the country beside Loch Linnhe in a single local authority. This is the heart of the West Highlands. Finally the area includes the new district of Argyll which has been somewhat attenuated by the transformation brought about in the reorganisation in comparison with the great county of Argyll, but it still includes the island of Mull and extends from Buchaille Etive Mor to Campbeltown.

Here Glen Garry is excluded and considered with that part of the Great Glen into which it drains—North East Scotland. Cowal is excluded and considered with the Clyde. The headwaters of the Spean which rise on the Ben Alder range and are strictly speaking part of Badenoch and Strathspey are included here.

The West Highlands are highly attractive. The main watershed is close to the coast and the short rivers tumble down steep glens to the sea. There are few inland lochs of any size, but the scenery of the West Coast is incomparably enhanced by many notable sea lochs, and the mountains abound in charming hill lochans. Communications are sometimes difficult, but it is rewarding to overcome problems and seek out hidden places.

Skye and Lochalsh have much in common, although there are contrasts between them. The Torridonian rocks of the Lochalsh Coast are continued in southern Skye. However, the spectacular mountains of Skye are made up of gabbro and granite, those of Kintail of Moine Schists. In northern Skye a basalt plateau gives rise to scenery not found in Kintail. Both are areas of heavy rainfall with more than 250 rain days per year. All of the rivers are short, characteristic of the West Highlands, but they fill rapidly after rain and give rise to spectacular falls.

The 1:50,000 map indicates more than 75 waterfalls in Skye. The word appears with much more than its usual frequency. Larger scale maps increase the number until it may be supposed that they are so commonplace as scarcely to merit description. Yet there are a number of reasonably well-known falls which are well worth seeking out. Lealt and Mealt are unsurpassed among coastal falls and Eas Mor is a distinguished mountain fall. Falls are numerous, too, in Kintail. Glomach is probably the most famous waterfall in Scotland, acknowledged as the most awe-inspiring unsupported fall in the country. However, some people consider that too much fuss is made about it, and that two or three other falls in Kintail are its equal.

The early activities of the British Aluminium Company confirm the vast potential of the Lochaber District for water power. Many once famous falls are, however, much less spectacular than they once were as a consequence of these developments. Fortunately Glen Nevis which has attracted several schemes has been successfully defended from all of them. W H Murray characterised the glen as Himalayan and was the first writer to evaluate the stupendous waterslide of Alt Coire Eoghainn, 375 metres (1,250 feet) in height, which falls into Glen Nevis from Ben Nevis. The falls of Polldubh, of the Nevis Gorge and An Steall Ban in Glen Nevis are all of the first rank.

The 'Waterfall Line', the West Highland Railway, is less exciting than it was because its falls have been attenuated by the Lochaber Power Scheme. Travellers on the line were horrified and delighted to have to put up the carriage windows as the train rushed downhill through the Spean Gorge at Achluachraich. This was to avoid the spray which could be even more wetting on the return journey as the train struggled up the hill towards Loch Treig. The waterfalls of Lochaber are rich in associations. Prince Charlie found shelter in the neighbourhood of several of them and the last fairy in Scotland was seen at Chlinaig. The most intriguing tale is, perhaps, that of the witch of Cia-Aig.

Lochaber is highly glaciated and there are distinctive shorelines of ice-dammed lakes—the parallel roads—in Glen Roy and elsewhere. The country rocks are metamorphic schists with granitic instrusions except in the south where there are basaltic cliffs at Ardtornish—the high cliff of the waterfalls—providing a foretaste of Mull.

Mull is in many ways like Skye and its finest waterfalls are on the coast. The basalt plateaus of this island and its near neighbours terminate abruptly and provide sites for many dramatic falls, of which Eas Fors is the best known. On the mainland of Argyll there are few districts as attractive as Glen Etive. The cattle thieves of Lorn must have given their name to the Robbers' Waterfall for it is certain that several hundred head of cattle could be concealed at low water in the crooked gorge below the fall. At Dalness the Etive itself forms the grandest of its many falls. But these by no means exhaust the falls of Glen Etive, and on a fine day cars pull into every available stopping place on the narrow little road down the glen so that their occupants can dawdle beside the pleasing cascades of the infant river.

There is a fine series of falls on the Orchy and there is a variety of falls in the basin of Loch Awe. The more subdued landscapes of South Lorn, Kintyre and Loch

Fyne might be expected to have fewer great falls but there are picturesque falls on the Aray, and Eagle's Fall is remote, but well worth seeking out, tucked away in the Arrochar Alps.

It is perhaps for their extensive seascapes that the West Highlands are best known. The mountains of the district, too, are known all over the world. The cataracts of the West Highlands deserve to be equally widely appreciated.

Skye and Lochalsh

Eas Aboist
NG 157 518

One of several coastal falls on the west-facing side of Loch Poolteil, Duirinish in Skye.

Eas nan Arm
NG 993 132

Eas nan Arm is so-called because defeated Spanish soldiers abandoned their weapons in the pool here below the fall during the Battle of Glenshiel in 1719. The site of the battle is about halfway down the wild, narrow defile of Gen Sheil which is nowadays the principal route into Kintail from the east. A small government force defeated an army of 2,000 Highlanders under the Earl of Seaforth assisted by 300 Spaniards sent by Cardinal Alberoni to support the Old Pretender. The soldiers fled over the Bealach na Spaiteach, Spaniards' Pass, which crosses the mountains called the Five Sisters of Kintail above Glen Sheil. It was the rebellions of the first half of the century which led to the construction of military roads under Wade and Caulfield during the second half. That through Glen Sheil was under construction when Johnson and Boswell passed through the district. Johnson was clearly very impressed with Glen Sheil, as visitors will be today. The modern road does not quite follow the old and where a modern bridge crosses the burn just above one of the old bridges you will find this very fine little fall.

Bearreraig Waterfall
NC 515 525

This was one of the three great waterfalls of the Trotternish Peninsula, and it was generally thought to be the finest fall on this magnificent coast. However, the Storr Lochs Hydro Electric Power Scheme has harnessed the waters of the Bearreraig River and diminished the fall. Derek Cooper (1970) in his very charming book on Skye quotes this nineteenth century description of it:

A streamlet falls sheer over an extraordinary high precipice, and forms a cascade which, though but a toy in bulk of water, appears as seen from the sea below to be singularly beautiful and grand.

The river descends to sea level in a steep-sided gorge where the falls occur. It is a perfect example of the way in which sills cause waterfalls to be formed and how they recede as the softer rocks underneath are worn away by the relentless power of the stream. A flight of 674 steps leads down the gorge. The Bearreraig River drains a basin of 13 square kilometres. The Storr Lochs scheme, approved in 1948 and opened in 1952, raised Loch Leathan to the level of

Loch Fada by a dam 55 metres long and 11 metres high. The spillway is 140 metres above sea level and a huge pipeline carries the water from the dam to a power station below the cliffs at sea level. Beside the pipeline a cable railway climbs the cliff for the transport of men and materials. The station has a capacity of 2,850 kilowatts and is the second largest of the Board's 'small schemes'. It has brought enormous benefits to the island.

Eas a' Bhradain
NG 533 265

The salmon fall, a waterfall of the Red Cuillin under Marsco and Ben Dearg. The foot of the principal fall is now crossed by the re-aligned A850 at the head of Loch Ainort.

Falls of Glen Brittle Forest

These falls are included in the Ramblers' Association/ Ordnance Survey *Walkers' Britain* (1982), and are somewhat misleadingly named, for while they are in the Forestry Commission's Glen Brittle Forest, the approach is from Glen Eynort to falls above Loch Eynort. A forest walk of 9 kilometres links characteristic falls with views from both the head and the foot of falls. There is a path to *Eas nam Fitheach* (*NG 386 272*). The first falls encountered on the walk are those on the *Allt Daidh* (*NG 387 267*). The walk then leads to the head of some good falls. Off the line of the walk are falls on the *Allt Dabhach* (*NG 376 236*) in Coire Mor. An extension of the walk gives superb views of the Coolins.

Eas na Coille
NG 465 372

A series of cascades not far from the A850 in Glen Varrigall, between Sligachan and Portree.

Carbost Waterfalls
NG 373 310

One of the most distinctive malt whiskies of Scotland, Talisker, is distilled at Carbost on Loch Harport. The little burn which tumbles down the hillside to the distillery is said to cross 14 falls. The uppermost, and most attractive of these is well seen from the by-road to Talisker itself.

Falls of Carnach
NH 032 273

The Falls, above Loch na Leitreach in Glen Elchaig, receive little attention from the writers of guide-books, no doubt because they are overshadowed by the Fall of Glomach. They deserve to be more widely known: they hold their own in distinguished company. Many visitors find the Fall of Glomach disappointing because it is not possible to see the whole cataract; the Falls of Carnach enjoy a similar situation to the Fall of Glomach, but they can be seen in their entirety.

In her affectionate book about Kintail, Brenda G Macrow relates the following story about them:

In 1921, a ghillie to Mr Wills of Killilan was one day wandering alone along the path beside this fall. Suddenly, to his great astonishment, he heard music coming from the stream—fine classical music such as he had heard broadcast from Edinburgh and Glasgow concert halls. Full of wonder, he hastened back to tell his friends—but, though several people visited the fall at different times, the strange music was not heard again. It was suggested by a doctor on holiday that the lodestone in the burn might possibly have picked up wireless waves from the air—but that was the nearest that anyone could come to giving an explanation. Apart, that is, from the inhabitants of the glen, who had many explanations of their own. . . .

The fall is made up of four closely linked cascades, an initial headlong leap of perhaps twn metres, two steep waterslides of about 15 metres each and a final drop of perhaps 20 metres, 60 metres in all. They are hidden from the glen as you climb up towards them, but once into Coire Easach, the corrie of the waterfall, you see them all. The lacy white fall in a green hollow makes this an appealing place in itself, but by following a stalker's track to Loch Lon Mhurchaidh and the Glomach one may combine the two falls in a single excursion.

Falls of Allt Daraich   NG 492 294

The gorge of the Allt Daraich provides an excellent short excursion from the Sligachan Hotel. The ravine can be followed very easily as far as a brawling fall of mountain water about 500 metres from the inn.

Duirinish

The western peninsula of Skye, Duirinish, is made up of somewhat monotonous hills best exemplified by Macleod's Tables, the flat topped hills which are a noted landmark for mariners. Where the tabular lavas which make up these hills reach the sea there are majestic cliffs, the best-known of which is Waterstein Head. There are many singularly beautiful coastal waterfalls along this coast, some permanent, some wet-weather falls and almost all subject in stormy weather to be lifted above the top of the cliffs, 300–350 metres high, so that they resemble so many waterspouts. Between Dunvegan Head and Waterstein Head are the highest cliffs, imposing at all times but, on a fine day with black cliffs streaked with white cataracts falling into green sea water, a never to be forgotten sight. The *Moonen Burn* (*NG 156 458*) which drains Loch Eishort forms a spectacular fall, 105 metres high, south of Waterstein Head. It is a sensational feature amid magnificent coastal scenery and is particularly well seen from Hoe Rape, the high sea cliff. There are further falls between Hoe Rape and Idrigill Point. Inland there are falls on the Lorgill River and other burns.

Falls of Coir Easaich (Glen Elchaig) see Falls of Carnach

Falls of Allt na Feadon   NG 603 158

These wet-weather falls are prominent in the view across Loch

Eishort from Ord in Sleat. The burn falls 150 metres (500 feet) over a cliff.

Falls of Glomach   NH 018 256

The grandest natural wonder in Kintail. The Allt a' Ghlomaich, the Burn of the Chasm, has its source on the high ground north of Beinn Fhada (Ben Attow). If flows in a transverse mountain valley between a' Glas Bheinn (Glasven) and Sgurr nan Ceathreamhnan (Kerrinan) occupied by three upland lochs: Loch A' Bhealaich, Loch Gaorsaic and Loch Thuill Easaich. The mountain river which issues from the lowest of the three lochs is about the size of the Kelvin or the Water of Leith. After about three kilometres it plunges over the Fall of Glomach and tumbles into Glen Elchaig below Loch na Leitreach.

The extent of this mountain basin and the presence of the three lochs which act as natural reservoirs mean that, unlike some other mountain falls, there is generally a sufficient quantity of water in the burn to make the Fall of Glomach interesting. However, it is the height of its unsupported fall which makes Glomach Scotland's premier waterfall. It is sometimes stated that Glomach is Scotland's highest waterfall. This is not the case, but it is certainly the grandest.

The height of the fall is variously given. It is sometimes stated that the chasm into which the river plunges is 225 metres deep and that the water falls 105 metres sheer. Both of these figures are exaggerations. The latter is derived from the first measurement of the fall given in the New Statistical Account. In 1836 the minister, the Rev James Morison, writes:

Its height, lately ascertained (without instruments) as accurately as the nature of the ground admitted of, is 350 feet. At a distance of about 50 feet from the bottom the water meets with a slight interruption from a shelving projection in the rock. This, however, adds to, rather than subtracts from the peculiar interest and grandeur of the scene—forming a kind of resting place for the eye in surveying this stupendous fall and giving occasion to an increased volume of spray which must ever contribute to the imposing appearance of such scenes.

Curiously Mr Morison does not refer to the rock buttress which, in most conditions, divides the fall and is the most distinctive feature of it. Perhaps the Minister intended to say that the 'interruption' occurred 50 feet from the top of the fall. This seems likely because the whole of the fall cannot be seen from the point described, but there is an interruption at the foot of the main fall.

W H Murray (1968) says the river falls 25 metres (80 feet) to the buttress, and then drops 66 metres (220 feet) into a hidden pool. The height of the first slide is sometimes given as 60 feet, but this seems rather low. Clearly the height of the fall does not exceed 105 metres. There are a number of low falls below Glomach and it is probable that these give rise to the figure of 112 metres (370 feet) which is given in a number of reference books. The top of the fall is 327.5 metres above sea level, and from this point to the junction with the Allt na Laoidhre there is a fall of 144 metres (475 feet).

The minister's description of the fall continues:

There is, however, independent of this break, and in any weather a mighty fall of 300 feet. But the interruption alluded to is not at all perceptible when there is any great body of water in the river (Girsac) and on such occasions the fall is unbroken, terrific and sublime. The best view is obtained from a solitary tree about 100 feet down the ravine to the south-west of the fall, in a situation the most

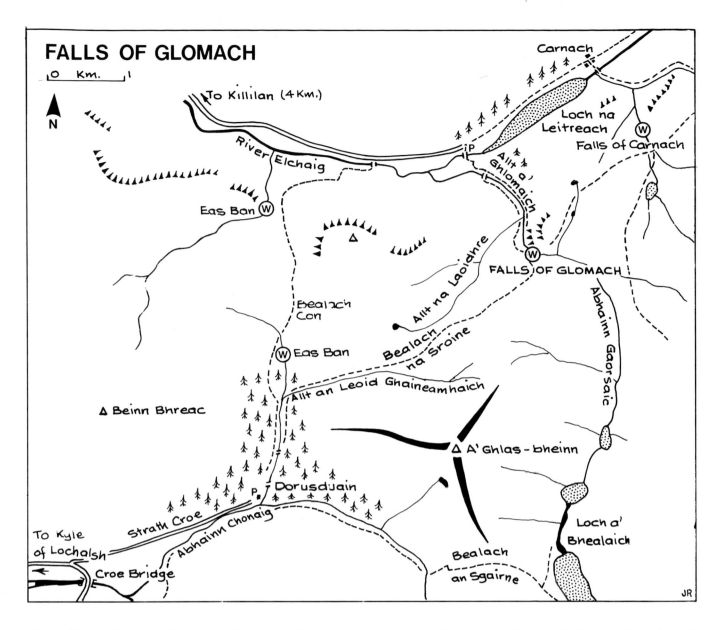

FALLS OF GLOMACH

favourable possible for getting a complete view of the whole scene.

The Hidden Falls, the Gloomy Falls and the Forbidding Falls are all soubriquets which have been applied to Glomach. They are the subject of a splendid poem by Andrew Young:

Rain drifts forever in this place
Tossed from the long white lace
The Falls trail on black rocks below,
And golden-rod and rose-root shake
In wind that they forever make:
So though they wear their own rainbow
It's not in hope, but just for show,
For rain and wind together
Her through the summer make a chill wet weather.

In *The Mountain Vision* Frank Smythe relates a Strange ghost story about the district:

My strangest experience happened in the Highlands. I was walking over the hills from Morvich on Loch Duich to Glen Glomach and the Falls of Glomach. It was a bright sunny day, and there was nothing in the least sinister about the vista of cloud-chequered hills and the distant blue of the sea. In crossing the ridge before dropping down to Glen Glomach I passed for a short distance through a grassy defile. There was nothing outwardly sinister about this pass and the sun shone warmly into it, yet when I entered it I at once encountered—that is the only word to express it—an atmosphere of evil.

Smythe goes on to describe his feeling that something terrible had once happened there and how, after his lunch, he saw a vision:

A score or more of ragged people, men, women and children, were straggling through the defile. They appeared very weary, as though they had come a long way. The pitiful procession was in the midst of the defile when of a sudden from either side concealed men leapt to their feet and, brandishing clubs, spears and axes, rushed down with wild yells on the unfortunates beneath. There was a short fierce struggle, then a horrible massacre. Not one man, woman or child was left alive; the defile was choked with corpses.

Smythe was convinced that he had had a genuine psychical experience and that he had been vouchsafed a backward glimpse into a blood-stained page of Highland history.

The Falls were presented to the National Trust for Scotland in 1941 by the proprietors of the two estates in which they lay. They now constitute a key part of one of the Trust's most extensive mountain properties. They can be reached in several ways, but an expedition to the falls is a considerable undertaking. They are situated in remote mountainous country and are highly dangerous in wet weather conditions. It is sometimes said that the falls should be seen in spate and waterfalls are, in any case, sometimes considered to be suitable excursions for wet days. Neither of these considerations should be allowed to play a part in determining suitable conditions for a visit.

From Ardelve you go by Loch Long and Glen Elchaig. Visitors with cars can obtain access to the private road beyond Killilan by signing the visitors book. There is a little car park below Loch n Leitreach. The A E Robertson Memorial Bridge crosses the Elchaig at this point beside stepping stones. The foot of the loch can be reached by walkers from Dornie by Camas Luinie where there is an attractive waterfall called Eas Ban *(NG 942 279)*. Another way, for walkers from Dorusdain, is by Bealach Con, Dog Pass. This track passes another *Eas Ban (NG 983 261)* above Glen Elchaig.

The top of the fall is 1.5 kilometres from the Memorial Bridge. There is a bridge across the Glomach erected by the National Trust for Scotland. It must be used in spate, but, in other conditions, either bank of the burn may be followed as far as the Allt na Laoidre, the left-bank tributary of the Glomach at the foot of the gorge.

From the Allt na Laoidre the path to the top of the fall sweeps away from the burn climbing the hillside to the right. Another path leads into the chasm itself to provide the most dramatic and interesting views of the fall. However, this path should only be used by experienced scramblers and should not be attempted in wet weather.

From Glen Elchaig, too, there is an alternative route to the right bank of the Glomach by Carnach and the Allt Coir Easaich. The right bank gives a more complete view of the fall, but is it a much more dangerous place, far more difficult of access. In wet weather the Glomach may be impossible to ford.

In wet weather conditions the recommended route is from Dorusduain, above Croe Bridge. There is a forestry car park and the way is signposted as far as the open hillside. At Dorusduain the glen forks under A' Glas Bheinn. The path to the Falls of Glomach climbs north-west through spruce and larch woods to emerge at the foot of the Bealach Con. A burn is crossed and the track climbs steadily towards the Bealach na Sroine, the Pass of the Nose. Above the woods there is a further *Eas Ban (NG 974 238)* on a tributary burn. The Bealach na Sroine is a narrow defile from which the path traverses the side of A' Glas Bheinn to the top of the falls, five kilometres from Dorusduain.

The longest way to the falls is by the Bealach a Sgairne, the Rumbling Pass, or the Pass of the Clattering Stones which leads to Glen Affric. This is the track which goes south east under A' Glas Bheinn. It was for long the principal way into Kintail from the East and for this reason it is called *the* Bealach, or the Pass of Kintail. The watershed is crossed by another narrow defile from which there is a dramatic view of Loch a' Bealach, the uppermost of the three lochs above Glomach. Beyond it Sgurr nan Ceathreamhnan which Hamish Brown has dubbed 'the Kangchenjunga of Scotland'. There is an intermittent path by the three lochs to the lip of the fall. The scene is increasingly dominated by the splendid little peak of Carnan Cruineachd. By this route it is ten long kilometres to Glomach from Dorusduain.

Glomach gets scant attention from the writers of books.

Baddeley is at his most ironic:

Except after heavy rain the celebrated Falls of Glomach, the highest and wildest in Scotland, are apt to disappoint the visitor, the depth of the fall being hardly sufficient compensation for the lack of picturesque surroundings. Glomach can only be seen to advantage when it can hardly be got at. There is but little accessory beauty of fern or other foliage, though the tourist who is weary of his life will find a small mountain-ash overhanging the abyss on which he may strive to carve his initials higher up than any previous tempter of fate (1892).

The most affectionate account of Glomach comes in Brenda G Macrow's *Kintail Scrapbook*. She devotes two chapters to the falls, and relates a number of folk tales about the district. Of these the following is the least alarming for intending visitors to the falls:

Another tale recounts how a man from Duilich visiting the Falls, saw a crowd of strangely-attired people gathered on the grass at the foot of the cataract. When he scrambled down the hillside to greet them, they all disappeared, leaving a woman in childbirth lying under a plaid. On questioning the woman, the man was told that he had arrived in the nick of time, as she was being stolen away by the fairies. Out of sympathy he took her to his own house at Duilich, where she seems to have lived in comfort, with no questions asked, for about a year. Then, one day, the man went to Garve market wearing the plaid which had been covering the woman when he found her by the fall. Here a stranger accosted him, recognised the plaid, and demanded the return of his wife who had disappeared in childbirth a year ago! Unfortunately the legend does not record how this odd triangle was sorted out.

The same writer captures something of the quality of Glomach in an account of one of her visits to the Fall:

Clouds of white vapour flew up out of the black gorge, lashing my face and blinding my eyes. Far, far below,

through a mist of spindrift, I could half-glimpse a green chasm winding away down towards Glen Elchaig with the fierce, foaming burn flowing into peat-black pools. The angry voice of the waters echoed and re-echoed from the walls of the great, rocky horseshoe banking the fall.

Glomach is a fine, wild place. It is a must for lovers of Scottish waterfalls.

Allt Grannda   *NH 022 171*

Gleann Lichd lies between the Five Sisters of Kintail and Beinn Fhada. It is occupied by the little river Croe which, in its upper reaches, is called the Allt Grannda. There is a track up either side of the river leading to a pass into Glen Affric. As it tumbles down from this pass the river has something of the quality of the Tees at Cauldron Snout, forming from its brawling, angry waters a continuous fall. The Falls of the Allt Grannda are quite different from the Fall of Glomach, a series of linked cascades rather than a single unsupported fall, but in wet weather they are equally spectacular and form a worthy rival to the great fall. Opposite the Allt Grannda there are fine falls, 24 metres high, above Glenn Lichd.

Falls of Glomach. The highest unsupported falls in Britain, situated in remote mountainous country, dangerous in wet weather. LOUIS STOTT

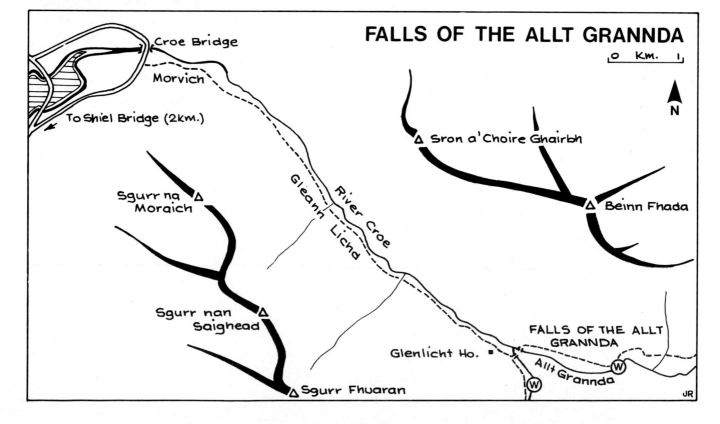

FALLS OF THE ALLT GRANNDA

0 Km. 1

N

Croe Bridge

Morvich

To Shiel Bridge (2km.)

Sgurr na Moraich

Gleann Lichd

River Croe

Sron a'Choire Ghairbh

Beinn Fhada

Sgurr nan Saighead

Glenlicht Ho.

FALLS OF THE ALLT GRANNDA

Allt Grannda

W

W

Sgurr Fhuaran

JR

Eas Mor (A' Chailleach). Boswell and Johnson were much impressed with the variety of falls within reach of Talisker House when they visited there. This is the most noteworthy of the group. JAMES RENNY

Greeta Falls   *NG 410 224*

Particularly after rain—and Skye is one of those places where, if it is not raining, it has just rained—there are very beautiful waterfalls indeed on the Allt o' Choire Ghreadaidh above Glen Brittle. The name is most probably derived from the Old Norse 'Greeta' which means 'gravel' and it occurs as a river name in Lancashire and Yorkshire, as well as in Skye. 'Of all the clear streams in Skye, and they are more than unusually clear,' writes Malcom Slessor in the SMC Guide, 'The Greeta is the clearest and the springs in Choire a' Greadaidh are more numerous than in any of the other corries.' The burn is readily accessible and it descends in a very fine series of cascades, the first of which is encountered a short distance from the road.

Hugh Quigley (1936), who wrote one of the few genuinely critical travel books published about Scotland, is unstinting about the Allt Greadaidh:

Pool after pool lies deep, cut in pale rock, so that the water appears, in quiet weather, like so many pieces of jade—blue, grey and green. In its lower course rowan trees and ferns grow on its banks. Here one must plunge into the cool water to understand the delights of a highland burn.

Hallaig Waterfall   *NG 593 387*

Raasay is a geological curiosity in Scotland, as if the Cotswold Escarpment had been transferred to the Highlands. At the foot of the cliff formed by the escarpment the Hallaig burn forms a coastal waterfall which makes a suitably remote objective for a day trip from the Skye Ferry.

Holm Waterfall   *NG 517 510*

This fall is situated about 3.2 kilometres (two miles) from Prince Charlie's Cave north of Portree, the most spurious of four such caves in Skye. It is opposite Holm Island, one of the possible sites of Tir an Og, the land of eternal youth. These associations of a spectacular coast make it an attractive excursion. It is surely this fall which is described in the New Statistical Account and the Ordnance Gazetteer although both suggest that the fall occurs on the boundaries of Portree and Snizort Parishes, which is where the Bearreraig Waterfall is. However, Murray (1894) puts the fall described at Holm:

On the boundary is a beautiful cascade over a precipice about 90 feet high. Beneath it, and nearly opposite its middle, is an arched hollow path across the rock, so broad that five or six persons may occupy it abreast and so situated that they are secure from the body of water that rolls over them and looks like a thick curved pillar of smoke.

Lealt Fall   *NG 516 603*

This magnificent double waterfall is the grandest in Skye. Close to the main road, it is nevertheless often missed by those in a hurry. It is most imposing from the sea, but beside the burn in the gorge above the fall the tourist can rapidly appreciate the character of the place described as follows by Allan Campbell Maclean (1972):

Few people stop to see what lies below that little bridge, although the glory of Skye is to be found off the road in forays on foot. A short walk through an old quarry and the cliff face is reached, overlooking the gorge; a gigantic cut in the rock starting as a narrow neck where the bridge on the main road spans the river. The Lealt river sweeps under the bridge and plunges into the gorge in a double waterfall. The defile widens into a huge ravine, the towering walls of rock jutting out on either side of a small bay where the river ends its long course to the sea. The salmon fishing station lies at the bottom of the gorge on the south bank of the river.

Seen from above, in the soft light of evening, the fisherman's bothy—low white walls capped with a black roof of tarred felt—appears to have grown naturally out of the ground. Behind the bothy, on higher ground, is the flat square of the drying green a small forest of tall poles draped with nets. The salmon coble, winched ashore, is snug in the lee of the bothy. On a still morning in high summer, as the high prowed coble noses downriver, the scene has a timeless, almost biblical quality. Out in the bay, the sun shimmering on the water, the marker buoys lifting idly on the swell, the patient watcher may be rewarded by a gleam of silver and sun-shot spray; a splash as the leaping salmon goes under.

As is the case with the other falls of the Trotternish coast it is caused by a doleritic sill overlying softer rocks. The Lealt Bridge is 61.5 metres above sea level. The fall thus ranks as one of the major unsupported falls in Scotland.

In addition to its salmon fishing station, reached by the path on the right bank of the river, the Lealt is also interesting for its remains of a diatomite factory which, when the river is low, can be reached by crossing to the north bank of the stream. The zig-zag track which leads back to the road used to be a light railway which brought the diatomite from Loch Cuithir. Diatomite is an earth formed from microscopic organisms which has a variety of uses for insulation and for all kinds of chemical products from explosives to cosmetics.

The works were for drying and grinding the product. From Invertote it was sent to the mainland. It is a good example of a highland industry which, with more government support, could have helped to bring employment to Skye. Instead German competition was allowed to extinguish it between the wars.

Just over a kilometre south of the Fall is Eaglais Bhreugach, the false church, a curious rock where black magic has been carried on. The district deserves to be much better known than it is.

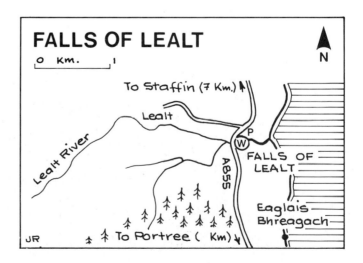

Eas Mor (A' Chailleach)   NG 325 311

When Boswell and Johnson visited Talisker, Boswell said that he was taken to see 15 waterfalls within a quarter of a mile of the house. Of these there is no doubt that the most prominent is Eas Mor which tumbles 45 metres down a big ravine above the farmhouse of A' Chailleach. Subsequent observers have doubted whether there are as many as 15 falls so close to the big house but there are, in wet weather conditions, a number of other torrential streams in the neighbourhood.

Eas Mor (Glen Brittle)   NG 419 215

The grandest mountain fall in Skye is Eas Mor on the Banachdich Burn above Glen Brittle Lodge. It drains the relatively unprepossessing Banachdaich Corrie—unprepossessing, that is, in comparison with the outstanding Coire Lagan next to it. It is this corrie and the magnificent peak of Sgurr Alasdair that beckon from the foot of the Banachdich Burn. However, the Banachdich Corrie provides ready access to the Cuillin Ridge and the Bealach Coire na Banachdich is the easiest crossing. Sgurr na Banachdich is generally regarded as the halfway mark in the traverse of the Cuillin Ridge. Those bound from Glen Brittle for the Bealach, for the peak or for Sgurr Dearg and the Inaccessible Pinnacle will follow the burn by the left bank and be able to visit the fall which relieves the rather dull moor at the foot of the hills. The fall has an open situation at the head of a birch-filled gorge 75 metres deep, the fall itself being about 24 metres high. It is probably this fall that Hugh Quigley (1936) describes so eloquently in his account of the burns of Skye.

One may wake suddenly in the middle of the night and hear the hollow roar of the burns. Rain falling heavily after midnight fills them quickly to the lip, their colour changes from peaty amber to glass green, curdling to foam where the 'force' crashes over an 80-foot drop, corkscrewing savagely before it thunders into the deep pool. The ferns on either side flutter distractedly as the solid wall of water surges past.

Eas Mor (Glen Brittle), the grandest mountain fall in Skye. HAMISH BROWN

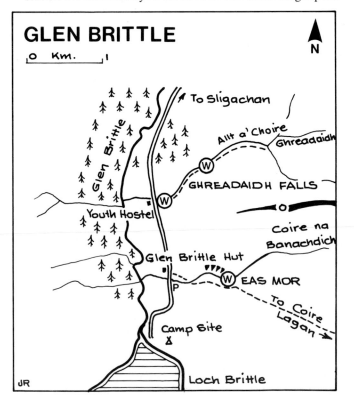

The Mad Cataract   NG 483 196

The Allt a'Chaoich, the Mad Burn, falls straight into Upper Loch Scavaig, strictly Loch na Cuilce, fron An Garbh Choire under Gars Bheinn, the magnificent culmination of the rocky Cuillin Ridge above Coruisk. Its name is an indication of its character and, insignificant as it may appear on the map, this torrential stream is frequently impassable. This torrent cuts prominently across the seemingly impenetrable barrier of rock which rings Upper Loch Scavaig and which is so splendidly captured in Daniell's famous etching of the scene. As is so often the case it is the waterfall that adds the sense of fury to wild places. For a combination of the savage and the picturesque nowhere in Britain surpasses this place. The name given is Victorian. Loch Scavaig is accessible by sea and it became standard practice to sail there and walk beside Loch Coruisk as far as the torrent that descends from Loch a'Choire Riabhaich, the brindled corrie. From here intrepid tourists followed the burn to the ridge where ponies from Sligachan would be waiting to convey them to the Inn, provided of course that they had been ordered in advance. In this sense Victorian tourism was very much better organised than tourism today and one of the penalties of the motor car is that such through trips are seldom arranged because they are no longer economical. There is no doubt that one of the most lasting impressions of the day would be the first sight of the Mad Burn. It falls about 215 metres from a relatively flat part of the corrie. It should be noted that the approach to the burn is for rock climbers only.

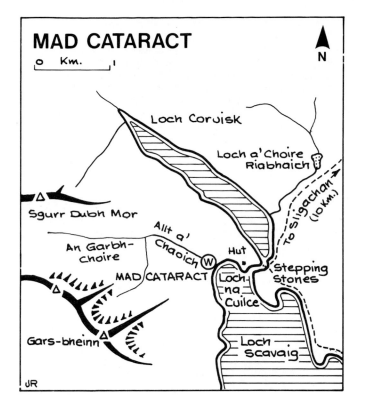

MAD CATARACT

Mealt Waterfall
NG 509 655

The Mealt Waterfall occurs close to the most famous natural curiosity of the Trotternish Peninsula, the Kilt Rock. The rock consists of an upper part of basaltic columns which form the pleated waist of the kilt and a lower part of horizontal sediments in the shape of a fan which because they are inconsistent appear to make a tartan. This same formation gives rise to the fall which is 52 metres high. The main road crosses the burn at the outlet to Loch Mealt, which reaches the very edge of the cliff. There are a number of instances where the outlet from a loch is a waterfall, but this is the only one

where a considerable body of water is perched so close to a sea cliff and falls for such a distance. From quite close to the road there is a magnificent view of the fall backed by the kilt rock. The volume of water in the stream is relatively insubstantial and in stormy weather it is blown back over the road, icing up the road in winter. Like other falls in Trotternish it is best seen from the sea.

Eas Mor (Healaval Beg)
NG 210 413

Mountain fall under one of Macleod's Tables, in Glen Dibidal, Duirinish. The burn which falls over Eas Mor hurls itself into the sea by a coastal fall at Geo Mor (*NG 203 394*). Healaval Beg is the 'table' that one of the Macleods set to impress a nobleman from Edinburgh that Skye was superior to Holyrood Palace.

Eas a Mhuic
NG 795 231

Remote fall north of Kylerhea reached by a coastal footpath north of the ferry.

Peiness Fall
NG 424 462

Peiness, written Benness on some maps, means Pennyland of the Waterfall recalling the Norse custom of using the value of a piece of land—in this case a pennyweight of silver—to describe its area. This smallholding is beside a low fall on the River Snizort, the most considerable stream in Skye which, like one or two others, is entered by salmon.

Portree Waterfall
NG 486 439

This little fall above the harbour in Portree makes an attractive addition to an evening stroll towards Dun Torvaig.

Rory Mor's Nurse
NG 249 489

In the grounds of Dunvegan Castle, mosses, ferns, heaths and embowering forest trees are found in abundance especially where, close to the house itself, a little stream drops in the

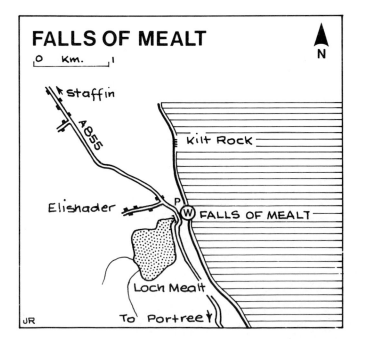

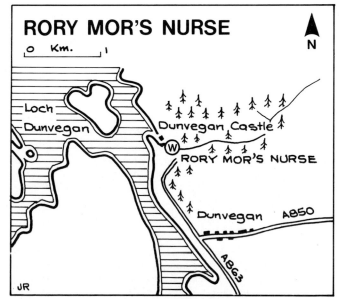

romantic twin cascade known as Rory Mor's Nurse. Scott, the greatest populariser of Sky, referred to it in the lines:

> I would old Torquil were to show
> His maidens with their breasts of snow
> Or that my noble liege were nigh
> To hear his Nurse sing lullaby
> (The Maids—tall cliffs with breakers white
> The Nurse—a torrent's roaring might)

It was said that Rory Mor Macleod, who was knighted by James VI and I, never enjoyed a good night's sleep when he could not hear the murmur of this burn brawling over the fall.

When Dr Johnson visited Dunvegan, Miss Macleod remarked that she found the castle inconvenient and intended to move. Boswell insisted that she should stay put:

> Madam, if once you quit the rock there is no knowing where you may settle. You move five miles at first,—then to St Andrews as the late laird did, then to Edinburgh—and so on till you end at Hampstead or in France. No, no; keep to the rock; it is the very jewel of an estate. It looks as if it has been let down from heaven by the four corners, to be the residence of a chief. Have all the comforts and conveniences of life upon it, but never leave Rorie More's Cascade.

Eas Ruadh   NG 494 310

Fall on the shore of Loch Sligachan, reached by a shore footpath from the Sligachan Inn.

Steall a' Ghreip   NG 462 731

Coastal fall north of Flodigarry in Trotternish.

Camas nan Sithein   NG 140 476

Where the burn from Loch Nor finds its way to the sea between Neist Point and Waterstein Head are some of the most majestic sea cliffs in Skye. The Neist Lighthouse is a favourite with visitors and the bay, Camas nan Sithein, the bay of the fairies, is very attractive. Skye is a great place for fairies and one of their many supposed haunts is the cave at the foot of the waterfall on the burn, the Allt na-h-Uamha.

Eas Tardil   NG 311 570

Remote coastal waterfall by Loch Snizort. It falls 45 metres.

Talisker Waterfall see *Eas Mor* (A' Chailleach) and *Carbost Waterfalls* (above the Talisker Distillery).

Trotternish

This, the north-eastern peninsula of Skye, is made up of basaltic lavas underlain by sedimentary rocks of Jurassic age. The lavas form an impressive escarpment facing east which culminates in the Storr, 720 metres above sea level. Because they are underlaid by softer rocks it is an area of extensive landslips with wonderful rock scenery and it has one of the most impressive coasts in Britain. In *The Hebrid Isles* Robert Buchanan (1873) describes it:

> The whole coast from Aird Point to Portree forms a panorama of cliff-scenery unmatched in Scotland. Layers of limestone dip into the sea, which washes them into horizontal forms, resembling gigantic slabs of white and grey

masonry, rising sometimes stair above stair, waterstained, and hung with many-coloured weed; and on these slabs stand the dark cliffs and spiral columns; towering into the air like the fretwork of some Gothic temple, roofless to the sky; clustered sometimes together in black masses of eternal shadow; torn open here and there to show glimpses of shining rowans sown in the heart of the stone, or flashes of torrents rushing in silver veins through the darkness; crowned in some places by a green patch on which goats feed small as mice and twisting frequently into towers of most fantastic device, that lie dark and spectral against the grey background of the air.

Among the falls of this coast are Lealt and Mealt, both falls of the first rank. On the other side of the peninsula there are no well known falls, but where the little burns which converge on Uig cross the basalt there are dip-slope falls which are not so high but are none the less very pretty.

Falls of Glen Varragill   NG 474 401

The Allt Tota Thaoig falls 120 metres in fine succession of falls above Glenvarragill House south of Portree.

Vaternish

The north-western peninsula of Skye is the most isolated. It is lower than Trotternish but consists of a similar basaltic ridge. Along the shores of Loch Snizort there are a number of coastal falls.

Lochaber

Falls of Achleck   NM 804 601

Falls at the head of Loch Sunart above the village of Achleck.

Gorge of Achluachraich   NN 295 808

The Falls of Monessie are the imposing falls on the Spean in the narrow rocky defile of the Gorge of Achluachraich. There are two main falls: Eas na Smuid (*NN 296 809*) and Easan na Fhearn (*NN 299 810*). Before the establishment of the Lochaber Aluminium Works in 1928 the Spean was a wild rushing torrent here confined to an extremely narrow gorge—a way cut down by melt waters from the glaciers. Now it is much attenuated to provide power for the works and it must be seen in spate to obtain the full effect of a major river thus confined. The falls of Monessie are 7.5 metres in height, an impenetrable barrier for salmon none the less game enough to hurl themselves into the furious waters of this noted salmon river. The confining walls of the gorge make it difficult of access and the topography is such that the West Highland Line is forced to follow the gorge and provides the finest views of it. The account of the falls in *Mountain Moor and Loch* (1895) is a grand piece. The book was produced by the North British Railway Company to publicise its line:

> The gorge is narrow and deep, dark crags, fringed with trees shutting in the rushing torrent which seethes in thunder and foam down the steep and rocky channel, leaping over the obstructing boulders in clouds of spray that beat on the carriage windows when the stream is in spate, for the train runs on the absolute verge of the cataract, separated from the roaring current only by a low parapet. No spectacle on

the line more forcibly impresses the memory than these Monessie Falls the steep black rocks, the dark green foliage at the waters edge, and the white torrent boiling down the rugged bed in a mad, delirious ferment, forming a picture that seems the embodiment of the spirit of the Highlands, proud, turbulent and untameable.

Falls of Achreoch, Achriabhach see *Lower Falls of Nevis.*

Falls of Achnacarry   NN 186 880

These low falls, not so prominent as they once were, are on the rapid river Arkaig within sight of the drawing room windows of the superb Achnacarry House, home of Cameron of Locheil. Augustus Grimble mentions the falls in his account of salmon baskets:

This was once a common way of catching fish all over Scotland and was used in most places where the natural fall of water permitted; and tradition has it that, before the making of the Caledonian Canal changed the level of the Achnacarry waters, near the house here was a basket of this sort into which, when the salmon fell, it also rang a bell to let the cook know.

Ardtornish Falls   NM 699 431

These falls in Morvern give a foretaste of Mull. Ardtornish, the high cliff of the waterfalls, is the promontory opposite Mull which was the site of the castle which, from 1340 to 1500 was the headquarters of the Lords of the Isles, a title taken by the Macdonalds, Earls of Ross. There are only a few fragments of the keep left on the low basaltic headland. Across the bay is Aoineadh Beag where the Allt Mor and the Allt an Liadin fall abruptly into the sea. These are two particularly graceful waterfalls at the base of which are little woods of birch and alder.

Eas Ban (Cour)   NN 239 745

Cour means rapid torrent. This swift stream drains the northern slopes of the Grey Corries, the outliers of Ben Nevis above Glen Spean. Eas Ban occurs in a rocky corrie above the aqueduct of the British Aluminium Company's Hydro Electric Power Scheme and the fall is thus unaffected by it.

Eas Ban (Gulbin)   NN 427 795

This remote fall is on the river which drains Loch Ossian. The Gulbin is a considerable stream with a plentiful supply of water regulated by two lochs (Ossian and Gulbin) and by the vast reservoir provided by Rannoch Moor peat.

Eas Buidhe   NN 098 874

Rapids in Glen Mallie situated in what MacDonald Robertson calls an 'eery ravine'. An Uruisg is said to haunt the spot.

Eas Buidhe see Lower Falls of Nevis.

Easan Buidhe   NG 788 034

The 'yellow falls' occur on the Guseran in Knoydart. They are reached by the low pass north of Inverie which leads to Glen Guseran and provides the obvious route to the distinctive peak of Ladhar Bheinn. Above Easan Buidhe are two further named

falls which occur on the burns which drain the corries north and south of this fine mountain, the most westerly 'Munro'. They are respectively *Eas a Chaoruinn (NG 792 039)* on the Abhainn Beag which drains Coir an Eich and *Eas an Fholaich (NG 803 031)* on the Allt Coire Torr an Asgaill.

Eas Cheanna Mhuir   NN 106 918

Mountain fall towards the head of Loch Arkaig.

Eas a' Choin   NN 010 563

This fall above Duror is on a small burn in a narrow ravine where Stewart of Ardshell hid for three months after Culloden. It is reached by a steep track to an old quarry and is worth visiting.

Eas Chlianaig   NN 276 798

The Falls of Chlianaig have a unique distinction for it was there that it was attested as recently as 1951 that the last fairies in Lochaber had been seen two generations before. The fall is at the head of a steep wooded ravine above Glen Spean just below one of the 'Parallel Roads'. These former shorelines of ice-dammed lakes were at one time known as 'King's Hunting Roads' for it was considered that they were man-made. They even deceived Sir Charles Darwin who considered that they were of marine origin and only changed his mind after a long controversy. The fall is severely affected by the Lochaber Hydro Electric Power Scheme since the burn is dammed above the fall and water is led into the aqueduct which conveys it 24km under the mighty Ben itself to the aluminium works. However these streams often get more water than the system can cope with and it is well worth visiting the fall after a spate.

Falls of Coe   NN 132 565

These are the very beautiful low falls on the Coe, a short distance below the bridge where the old road from Glencoe village joins the A82. They are a favourite stopping place for picnics. The name Linne Buidhe, the golden pool, is given to the Coe at this point.

Eas Cuingid   NG 868 109

Fall in Glen Arnisdale.

Falls of Chia-Aig   NN 175 888

These falls are both interesting and imposing. They are a scenic highlight in what is generally agreed to be one of the least spoiled of relatively accessible valleys in the Highlands, the valley of Loch Arkaig. At its foot is the Dark Mile, once perhaps a dominant avenue of trees, but now a somewhat disappointing line of dead and dying oaks. The tree in which Prince Charlie was said to have hidden, and it never was the right age for him to have done so, has long since fallen and decayed, but high up on the hillside it is still possible to visit Prince Charlie's Cave, better attested than most of his supposed hiding places. A forest walk leads through the rich coniferous woodland of the Clunes Forest which now clothes the slopes above the Dark Mile. Just before the foot of the lake is reached an old bridge crosses the Chia-aig which in fact drains into the lake. A magnificent double waterfall dominates the scene. The roaring little river hurls itself abruptly over a rocky ledge and falls about twelve metres before reaching another rock barrier over which it tumbles a further six metres

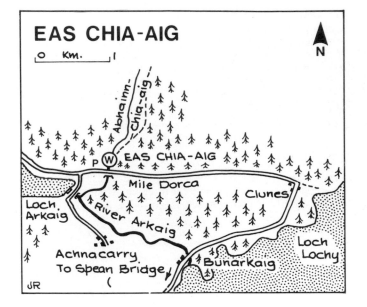

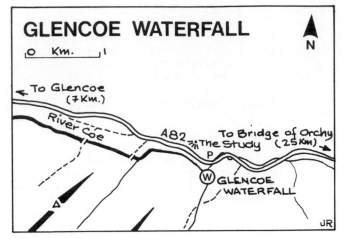

into a dark plunge pool called the Witch's Cauldron. The fall with its densely wooded banks is singularly impressive. Beside the bridge is a good car park and there is a good track up the left bank leading to the forest walk already referred to.

A charming fairy story is attached to the falls. The cattle in the district were suffering from an unexplained malaise and the Camerons consulted a seer about it. The seer attributed the malaise to an old hermit woman who lived beside the lake and said that it would persist until the witch was killed. The Camerons therefore sought her out at her cottage, but when they got there all they found was a cat which they set upon and wounded. However, it escaped and they followed the trail of blood to the Chia-aig Falls where they found the dying cat. They were about to finish the wretched animal's life when it let out a terrifying scream and leapt into the pool. As it leaped, it changed into the witch they were looking for. The Camerons stoned the old hag to death and the malaise did not recur.

Glencoe Waterfall   *NN 184 562*

The Study is one of the classic situations in the Highlands from which a glorious view of Glencoe is obtained. The 'Three Sisters' dominate the scene, three massive spurs of Bidean nam Bian, savage and unfriendly, threatening even, when it is dull, but bold and appealing in fine weather. The Study is a rock platform—its name is derived from the Old Scots word for an anvil and its Gaelic name is 'the anvil of the mists'—at the head of the glen. It is above the gorge made by the river, which is followed by the new road. A singularly beautiful waterfall on the Allt Lairig Eilde is formed where this burn joins the Coe. It is much photographed and contributes to the quality of the landscape, a piece of 'close scenery' to offset the more distant views of the mountains. The busy main road provides few stopping places for the motorist, but the pedestrian can get away from the road soon enough.

The burn falls 20 metres into the Coe, one branch of the twin fall situated in a deep cleft, the other sprawling over the rocks. There is an affectionate account of the fall by R MacDonald Robertson in his collection of fishing tales, *Wade the River, Drift the Loch*

> It is not a very high waterfall but a very lovely one—a towering cascade which spurts out from the humped-back cliff describing a curve before pouring down in a series of low contracted falls from one dark basin to another. The

impending gloomy precipices of this wild glen are of a nature to strike the most unreflective mind with awe; their rugged outlines and bold fronts, scarred with torrents and shattered by storms, form a scene not only wonderful but terrific.

The series of cascades to which Robertson refers may be called *The Upper Falls of Coe*. They are right under the abutments of the road through the gorge and therefore not seen. The wild river tumbles in a succession of falls as far as the Meeting of the Waters.

Eas Dhonnchaidh   *NG 794 119*

Fall, close to the coast, above the entrance to Loch Hourn.

Easan Dudh (Treig)   *NN 308 695*

These are the major falls at the head of Loch Treig on the Allt na Lairige which tumbles down from Lairig Leacach and enters the loch beyond Creagnaineach Lodge.

Eas an Dubhaidh (Eil)   *NM 959 799*

This waterfall is a short distance above the Fort William-Mallaig road at Kinlocheil on the Fionlighe.

Allt Coire Eoghainn   *NN 166 691*

Coire Eoghainn is the corrie under the summit of Ben Nevis above Glen Nevis and the burn which drains it falls down the steepest slope in the kingdom in a continuous torrent. It was W H Murray who first posed the question as to whether if was a waterfall or not. For if it was a fall it was the highest in the land. Murray finally opted for the term 'waterslide'. The burn slides 375 metres.

Finisgaig   *NN 243 805*

In his fine book about the Highlands (1959) Calum MacLean relates the following folk-tale about a waterfall on the Cour. It was told to him by John Macdonald of Roy Bridge after the last war:

> One day a young man on his way to Fort William came to the swollen waters of the Cour and was about to cross the ford. From the depth of the ford came a hollow voice:

> Young man, listen to my word of counsel. When Finisgeig has one calf, a boy may cross the Cour. When Finisgeig has two calves a horse and a boy may cross the Cour, but when

Finisgeig has three calves, neither host nor clan can cross the Cour. I did not heed my mother's warning and here I was drowned.

Needless to say the young wayfarer did not cross the ford, for on that day Finisgeig had three calves—there were three rivulets tumbling over the edge as well as the main stream.

Visitors to waterfalls will be familiar with the way in which streams can be transformed in spate and the canny observation contained in that folk tale is applicable elsewhere.

Eas nam Fitheach   NN 027 813

The fall of the raven is in Glen Suileag above Fassifern, Loch Eil, where Prince Charlie stopped on his march from Glenfinnan. A forestry road leads up the glen and it connects with the Great Glen via Glen Loy. Scott Johnstone (1973) points out the charcoal hearths almost certainly used for iron smelting which occur 2.4 kilometres north of Fassifern. The fall is on the prominent left bank tributary at this point.

The Grey Mare's Fall   NN 187 625

This formidable waterfall was noticed in Anderson and other Victorian guide books, but it seems to have been neglected thereafter, either in the belief that the aluminium works established in 1908 has attenuated the fall to such an extent that it was no longer worth visiting, or in the belief that the works were such a blot on the landscape that it rendered the district unsuitable for tourists. Neither is the case. The author of *Black's Pocket Guide,* published in 1903, pointed out that the fall is pronounced by some to be the finest in the Highlands. The falls, unaltered in any way, disappeared from the map after that. They are, it is true, close to the houses in Kinlochmore, that part of Kinlochleven which was situated in Inverness-shire, but there is a wooded shoulder of a hill between them and the fall. In 1974 the British Aluminium Company in conjunction with the Countryside Commission improved the path which leads over the hill to the fall. About halfway along it the main plunge is seen through the trees. The path then drops down to cross a tributary stream and reaches the foot of the fall gorge. From this point the fall—a wild mass of white water which comes down from an abrupt cliff face—is seen sideways-on and, tantalisingly, neither the top nor the bottom of it can be made out. It must remain thus when the stream is in spate. In dry conditions the narrow gorge can be breached and the very foot of the fall can be attained. The high cliff topped by pines over which the Allt Coire na Ba hurtles 46 metres has the character of a quarry face. At times the fall may be wanting in water for its scale—although Kinlochleven is a notoriously wet place and, if the burn is comparatively short and without a lochan to regulate its flow, this is a rare occurrence. At snow melt the fall is exceptionally fine and on a cold frosty night with a full moon it is indescribably beautiful because of its big scale and the confined nature of the gorge. The impression of great height which the fall gives—and it is the same scale of fall as Foyers, although it is, of course, unaffected by the hydro-electric power scheme—is undoubtedly enhanced by the confined atmosphere of Kinlochleven itself, with the towering peaks of the Mamores seen from base to apex above the trees. Paths lead up both banks of the burn—well away from its steep sides—to Mamore Lodge, the most precipitously situated retreat in Scotland. The Lodge, visited by Edward VIII, now offers luxury rented accommodation for tourists. It overlooks the sensational valley of Loch Leven, the narrow sea loch which has for long so frustrated travellers that they have consistently underrated its scenic

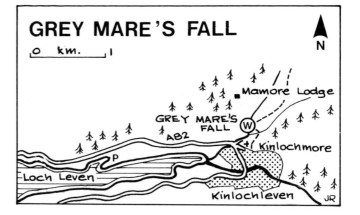

assets. There are a number of smaller falls on the burn above the Grey Mare's Fall. This name appears to be modern: the falls were for long known as the Falls of Kinlochmore——perhaps too prosaic a name for one of the best half dozen great falls in Scotland.

Falls of Kaig see *Falls of Cia-Aig*

Kilfinnan Fall   NN 271 966

Fall above Loch Lochy, reached from the A82 by back tracking from Loch Oich at Laggan Lochs. A path of sorts follows the north bank of the burn well above the stream and leads eventually to Ben Tee. There are fine views.

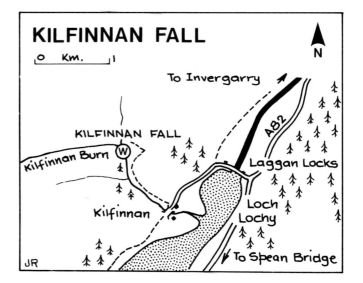

Falls of Kinlochmore see Grey Mare's Fall.

Falls of Kinloch   NM 671 556

There are considerable falls on the Allt Coire an Tuim near Kinloch in the remote western part of Morvern.

Eas nan Long   NN 135 790

Falls on the Lochy close to Tor Castle where tradition has it that Banquo, Macbeth's lieutenant, lived. An avenue in the woods is called Banquo's Walk. The name Eas nan Long means the fall of the ships and is no doubt a reference to the fact that the falls would be the first and final obstacle encountered by ships entering the Lochy.

MacKay's Fall   *NN 195 616*

Above the works at Kinlochleven the river flows through a rocky gorge. Huge slabs of quartzite floor the narrow shelf above the inky stream. About 1 kilometre from the village there is a fine double fall, six metres high, which in spate is well worth seeing. It is the most impressive of a succession of falls between the Blackwater Reservoir and the sea. There are notable falls too on the *Allt na h-Eilde (NN 204 613)* and on the Allt Coire, Mhorair under the old military road by the Devil's Staircase.

MacLean's Towel   *NN 002 652*

This is the glistening, sprawling, tumbling, spilling waterfall seen across Loch Linnhe from the A82 south of Fort William. No name could be more appropriate for a great white fall spread out on the hillside. It is said that the MacLeans will hold Ardgour House as long as the Ardgour Towel remains, but they came into possession of the place by throwing the MacMasters out of it.

Eas Mor (Bernera)   *NG 814 215*

Bernera is the site of barracks built in 1722 to command the narrow crossing to Skye at Glenelg, now decayed. Eas Mor is on the Amhainn Eillg.

Eas Mor Chuil an Dun   *NG 820 171*

This massive apron fall dominates Glen Beg when it is in spate. It is as imposing as any of its kind in the Highlands. An insubstantial enough burn sprawls down a forested hillside about 2 kilometres from Eilanreach. No visitor to the two brochs beside the road can miss it.

Glen Beg is an intriguing place. Eas Mor seems almost to be out-of-scale. The primitive masonry of the brochs is so finely executed that they might have been erected very recently.

Eas Mor (Loch Treig)   *NN 317 715*

This is the big fall under Stob Coire Easain, the principal peak on the west shore of Loch Treig. It can be seen from the West Highland Line as it runs beside the loch.

Falls of Morar   *NM 682 922*

These low falls have the distinction of being situated on what is the shortest river in Scotland. Loch Morar, the deepest trench on the Continent of Europe, is linked to the sea by a river less than a kilometre in length. Where road and railway cross it the sea is close at hand beyond the singing silver beaches beside the road and the lake is in the wooded country beyond the falls, hidden from sight. A few metres difference in sea level would make Loch Morar a sea loch and make the falls another Falls of Lora. The river occupies a broad channel and the low falls in two distinct steps were a magnificent sight because the immense flow of water was consistent, regulated by the deep loch, a perfect natural reservoir. The fall was about two metres in height. They are no longer so impressive as they once were because they were harnessed in 1948 to provide the first small scheme of the North of Scotland Hydro Electric Board. This type of scheme, more than the bigger schemes, serves to remind the tourist of the real significance of the Board's

FALLS OF MORAR

schemes. As recently as our own times they brought light and heat 'on tap' to the Highlands.

Eas na Mucaireachd   *NM 732 499*

Fall in Glen Geal in Morvern at a distinct bend in the river near the A884.

Falls of Mucomir   *NN 182 837*

The falls of Mucomir no longer exist. They have been replaced by a dam and a power station beside the old bridge on the road from the Commando Memorial to Gairlochy. They were for long taken to be natural falls although they were created during the construction of the Caledonian Canal from 1803 to 1822. They thus shared with the famous Italian falls of Terni and Tivoli the distinction of being appreciated as natural phenomena although they were man-made. The level of Loch Lochy was raised by 3.66 metres by closing the natural outlet of the loch by the Lochy and a new course was cut for the river so that it joined its chief tributary at Mucomir. A permanent weir, partly constructed of stone and partly hewn from the natural rock, was erected to form the falls. The overflow from the loch thundered over the falls having a mean discharge nearly as great as that of the Falls of Clyde. They are a sad loss although the power station which has replaced them is as attractively designed as it could be, a fine piece of modern architecture.

Nevis Gorge   *NN 173 691*

Above the car park at the head of Glen Nevis the river flows through a highly dramatic gorge which W H Murray has characterised as being of a Himalayan type, unique in this country. The enclosing walls of the gorge are clothed with a variety of trees. Below, the roaring river thunders through the awful ravine, falling 120 metres. The fall is called *Eas an Tuill*. There are three ways through the gorge, the track which is a continuation of the present road having been constructed after 1900. It is possible with some scrambling to follow a track beside the furious Nevis itself. W H Murray's description of the gorge conveys its character:

Its distinctive character is not Alpine but Himalayan, this despite its relatively small scale. At its top end, on either side of the glen, Ben Nevis and Sgurr a' Mhaim project spurs of

Eas Mor Chuil an Duin. *Dominates Glen Beg when in spate.*
HAMISH BROWN

rock, seeming to pinch off the higher from the lower reaches. Through this rock barrier the river Nevis has carved a deep and tortuous channel. Above that rampart it flows level, but now it bursts through the gut, its white fury gouging pots and cauldrons out of the rock bed, churning past gigantic boulders in a fall of 400 feet. The gorge resounds to its thunder. The walls are wooded in old Scots pines, rowans, birches and oak. Through them a footpath winds up the true

A Steall Ban, *Glen Nevis. One of the truly great falls of Scotland. (Opposite)*
HAMISH BROWN

Kilfinnan Fall, *near Spean Bridge at the head of Loch Lochy. (Below)*
HAMISH BROWN

right bank. It gives clear views of the wild river, of the natural wood on the far side, and in itself is a path of extraordinary interest and beauty. The throat of the gorge is v-shaped. Through its cleft can be seen the wide flash of Steall waterfall.

At the top of the gorge, the path comes close to the huge boulders at the gut. High above are the castellated crags of Meall Cumhann. The scene suddenly alters. Stretching far ahead to the next big bend of the river is a grassy flat and grassy meadow. Following so unexpectedly on the gorge, the bright green flats of this hidden valley through which the river snakes in big slow bends, make a most happy change. The new scene is dominated by the Steall waterfall. Its immense surge of 350 feet down the lower cliffs of Sgurr a'

Allt Dearg Mor. *Beside the mountain pass between Sligachan and Glen Brittle.*
HAMISH BROWN

Mhaim makes it the best waterfall of its kind in the Highlands. (The Falls of Glomach give a bigger single leap but are largely hidden from sight, and the much longer Eoghainn slide is not a true waterfall).

The Nevis gorge, taken alone, has no counterpart in this country and is internationally famous. Its Himalayan character arises from a peculiar combination of crag and woodland and water, which is not repeated elsewhere in Britain. When we add to it the spectacles of the Eoghainn waterslide below and the Steall waterfall above, and the transition to meadow-land on top, the whole becomes one of the principal scenic wonders of Scotland. The Highland Landscape (1962).

Like Glomach and Glen Affric, the Nevis Gorge was the subject of proposals for power generation made by the North of Scotland Hydro Electricity Board. It was suggested that an 80 metre dam should be erected at the gorge, but fortunately the proposals were resisted and the scheme was dropped.

Lower Falls of Nevis   NN 144 683

Where the road crosses Water of Nevis there are very fine falls indeed. The rushing river, terrifyingly powerful in spate, falls twelve metres. A timeworn rock splits the stream in two, but the two branches soon re-unite and a curtain of white water spills into the gorge below. At this point the glen is still fairly open and the birch-clad banks of the river are the central feature of the landscape. The Ben cannot be seen and the principal peak visible is Sgurr a' Mhaim, the quartzite tipped queen of the Mamores. Iain Crichton Smith uses the falls to provide a powerful image in his poem 'Highland Portrait'

The waters of Polldubh, direct and splendid,
will hump unsteady men to a boiling death.

The name given to the falls on large scale maps is Eas Buidhe, the golden falls. They are also known as the Polldubh Falls and the Falls of Achreach or Achriabhach. Polldubh and Achriabhach are the names of the two farms on either side of the river nearest the falls.

Upper Falls of Nevis.

This is the name given to *An Steall Ban* according to Norrie (1898) in *Loyal Lochaber*. In fact, the great fall, which appears to occur on the Nevis itself, is situated on a tributary, although it is, of course, in Upper Glen Nevis. There is a staircase of falls on the Nevis itself under the Grey Corries, Na h-Easain (*NN 223 693*), the waterfalls.

Ossian's Showerbath   NN 140 559

Scotland's all-purpose hero is the warrior-poet, Ossian, a legendary figure who is closely associated generally for no very clear reason, with many of that country's most romantic places. High on the face of Aonach Dudh there appears to be a cave where, because the Coe may be the Cona of MacPherson's 'Ossian', Ossian is said to have dwelt. The approach to Ossians's Cave is called Ossian's ladder and it is not surprising that the waterfall which bounces down from Coire Beith into Glen Coe above Loch Achtriochtan is called Ossian's Showerbath. It was probably christened by climbers. The fall is generally prominent, even when the many wet-weather falls which are such a feature of Glen Coe are dry. The path to

Bidean nam Bian leads between Aonach Dudh and An t-Sron and passes close to the fall.

Linn of Pattack   NN 566 902

The Pattack, the river of potholes, rises on Ben Alder and flows swiftly. From the A86 an estate road, strictly private, provides a long walk in to Ben Alder. The Linn of Pattack is an impressive 12 metre fall below the first bridge. Because the track keeps away from the burn, this bridge can easily be missed. The river falls dramatically at this point into a wooded gorge which is overwhelmed by extensive plantations. The Pattack is a considerable stream and there is a deep plunge pool at the foot of the fall.

On the A86, where the Pattack turns towards Loch Laggan, there are some pretty falls among rocks at a favourite stopping place.

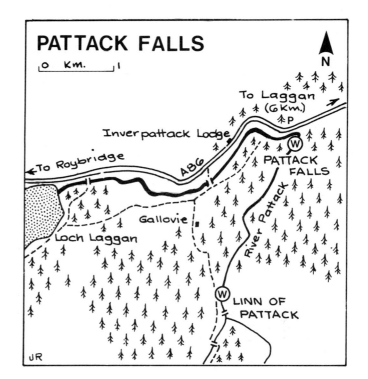

Polldubh Falls see *Lower Falls of Nevis*

Glen Righ Falls   NN 031 629

These falls beside Loch Linnhe are of considerable interest to the geomorphologist because the Amhainn Righ has been diverted by a landslip. A dry valley now occupies its original course, the Dubh Glen above Onich. There is a picturesque staircase of eight falls, 45 metres high, on the little river, the banks of which are densely wooded. The falls are in the Forestry Commission's Glenrigh Forest. An attractive Forest Walk has been established across the scrub moorland between Inchree and Gleann Righ. The moorland is inhabited by friendly goats who may perch obligingly above the falls. These are seen to great advantage, for the river sweeps over the lip of the col and immediately breaks into a low fall. The third in the series, perhaps 15 metres high, is the most imposing.

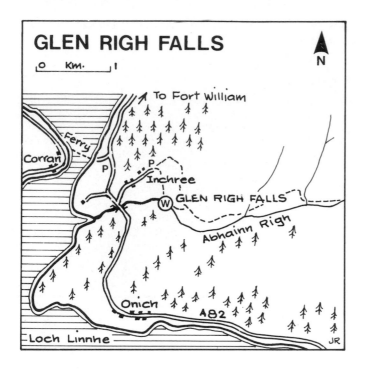

Glen Roy

Glen Roy is visited for its 'parallel roads'. Relatively close to the entrance to what is a very long glen the Nature Conservancy have established a fine viewpoint in its Nature Reserve from which the 'roads' can be seen to great advantage. Above the viewpoint is Coire Mhoannan where, it is said, the Young Pretender spent the night in a cave near a waterfall called *Steall a' Phrionnsa*. This must have been the night before his perilous crossing of the Lochy on his way to Loch nan Uamh and to exile in France. Five kilometres above the viewpoint the Roy tumbles over a low fall, Easan Bhrunachain (*NN 322 900*). The *Falls of Roy (NN 360 920)* are some two kilometres beyond Brae Roy Lodge, sixteen kilometres from the main road (A86). The falls are a noted salmon leap, for the fish are prevented from ascending the Spean by the falls at Monessie. On the Burn of Agie which joins the Roy above the falls there is a natural rock bridge, crossed by one of the 'parallel roads'. Higher up the same stream there is a succession of falls the most prominent of which are Dog Falls (*NN 373 898*).

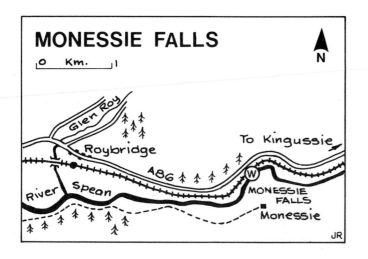

Roaring Mill

NN 121 740

Where the Nevis flows over some broken rocks about a kilometre above the Bridge of Nevis it forms an interesting low fall which, like many another, is considered to be particularly noisy and is given the name Roaring Mill. It is also called *Eas Chiaginn*, the name of a nearby farmhouse. The swift river is quite a substantial stream at this point. The fall has a formal approach with a car park and concreted steps.

Falls of Allt Mor Shantaig

NG 796 140

The description given by Gavin Maxwell of the little waterfall at the mouth of the Allt Mor Shantaig is a masterpiece. It has immortalised a characteristic little fall. Above 'the waterfall' there are more substantial falls on the same stream.

Even the waterfall has changed and goes on changing. When I am away from the place and think of it, it is of the waterfall that I think first. Its voice is in one's ears day and night; one falls asleep to it, dreams with it and wakens to it; the note changes with the season, from the dull menacing roar of winter nights to the low crooning of summer, and if I hold a shell to my ear it is not the sea's murmur that comes to me but the sound of the Camusfearna waterfall. Above the bridge where I used to draw my water the burn rushes over stones and between boulders with alders at its banks, and a wealth of primroses and wild hyacinths among the ferns and mosses. In spring it is loud with bird song from the chaffinches that build their lichen nests in the forks of the alders, and abob with wagtails among the stones. This part of the burn is 'pretty' rather than beautiful, and it seems to come from nowhere, for the waterfall is hidden round a corner and the stream seems to emerge from a thirty foot wall of rock hung with honeysuckle and with young rowan trees jutting from cracks and fissures. But looking up the burn from the foot of the rock the word 'pretty' becomes wholly inapplicable; the waterfall is of a beauty it would be hard to devise. It is not high, for the tall cataracts of 80 feet are some 200 yards higher up its course; it emerges between boulders and sheer rock walls to drop some 15 feet, over about the same breadth from the twilight world of the deep narrow gorge it has carved through the face of the hill over thousands, perhaps millions, of years. It emerges frothing from that unseen darkness to fall like a tumbling cascade of brilliants into a deep rounded cauldron enclosed by rock walls on three sides, black water in a whorled black rock with fleecy white spume ringing the blackness of the pool. Up above the black sides of the pot there are dark green watery mosses growing deep and cushioned wherever there is a fingerhold for soil; and the domed nest that dippers build here every year is distinguishable by nothing but its symmetry. The sun reaches the waterfall for only a short time in the afternoon; it forms a rainbow over the leaping spray, and at the top of the fall, between the boulders it gives to the smooth-flowing, unbroken water the look of spun green glass.

For most of the year the waterfall has volume enough for a man to stand on a ledge between it and the rock and remain almost dry; between oneself and the sky it forms a rushing, deafening curtain of milky brilliance through which nothing but light is discernible. If one steps forward so that the weight of the water batters full on head and shoulders, it is of the massiveness only that one is conscious, and it would be impossible to say whether the water were cold or hot. Only when one steps from it again, and the flying icy drops tingle on the skin, does the sensation become one of snow water.

It would seem that the waterfall could never change, yet

year by year its form differs as a new boulder is swept down by the spates to lodge above its lip; or a tree falls from its precarious grip on the cliff face above and jams the doorway of its emergence; or a massive section of rock breaks away, split by the prising leverage of slow-growing tree roots.

In spring and autumn the natural decoration surrounding the waterfall surpasses anything that artifice could achieve; in spring the green banks above the rock are set so thickly with primroses that blossom almost touches blossom, and the wild blue hyacinths spring from among them seemingly without leaf; in the late summer and autumn the scarlet rowanberries flare from the ferned rock walls, bright against the falling white water and the darkness of the rock.

Eas an t-Slinnean   NN 119 727

This fall on a tributary of the Nevis is on the shoulder of Cow Hill, the famous view point above Fort William. It is reached by the peat road leading from Blarmachfoldach and the Lundavra Road. The views of Loch Linnhe and Ben Nevis are oustanding. Beside the stream is the burial ground of the extinct line of the MacSorlie Camerons of Glen Nevis, Tom-eas-an-t-Slinnean.

An Steall   NN 180 682

This magnificent waterfall in Upper Glen Nevis is the finest in Scotland. It is not so high as Eas Coul Aulin, nor so singularly imposing as the Fall of Glomach, but it belongs to the same league as these two great falls and it is so incomparably well set that it should take pride of place. It is appropriate that the great bulk of Ben Nevis should be offset by Glen Nevis which is judged by many who hold Scotland dear to be the finest of all Scottish glens. It is fine enough at its foot where the public road leads thirteen kilometres under the mighty Ben itself through grand mountain scenery and ends at a fairly recently constructed car park and viewpoint. Beyond the car park the dramatic wall formed by Meall Cumhann, an outlier of Ben Nevis, and the beetling slopes of the Mamores meets the eye and it might be taken to be impenetrable except that a V-shaped notch suggests that the rough track which leaves the car park leads to a pass. An Steall occupies this notch looking as if the roaring water of Nevis itself forms the fall. In fact the Allt Coire a' Mhail, on which the fall occurs, does continue the line of the Nevis but it is a tributary, the main stream turning an abrupt corner. No other fall occupies such an exciting situation. Indeed the scale of the Nevis Gorge which breaches the wall is such that the first sight of the fall—a seemingly tiny ribbon of white water—is one which the traveller must greet with some disbelief. It is difficult to credit that a mighty waterfall occupies such a magnificently appropriate situation and that beyond the sensational Nevis Gorge there is yet another natural wonder to be seen. For such a fall to be seen at all it is clear that its scale must be massive and this fall does not disappoint. An Steall Ban, the White Spout, is 105 metres high. It is situated between Sgura' Mhaim and An Garbhanach. The tributary stream is sufficient to ensure that there is generally enough water for a roaring splashing torrent of a fall, its full height open for all to see. Whatever sense of wonder may have been engendered in

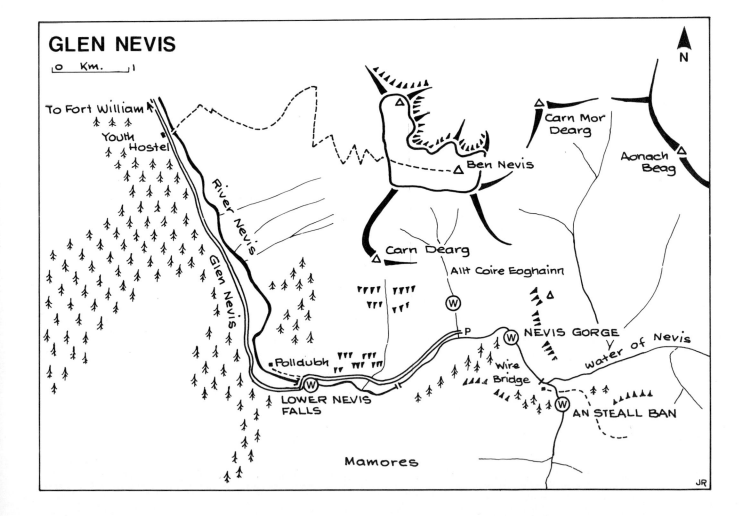

the spectator during the approach through the gorge, it is certain to be heightened by the spectacular change in the character of the Nevis itself, for above the gorge it occupies a flat, relatively open, grassy valley of great pastoral quality. These Elysian Fields, 300 metres above sea level, provide such a contrast with An Steall that its impact is complete. Beneath the fall is the Steall bothy and across the Nevis is a rope bridge appropriate to the Himalayas themselves. An Steall is relatively accessible. It should be visited by everyone who can do so.

Eas Torra Bhain   NM 721 668

These prominent falls are on a little burn which drains into Loch Sheil from the eastern slopes of Ben Resipol.

Eas Tuill see Nevis Gorge

Falls of Tulloch   NN 358 797

These are the first of the series of rapids on the Treig and the Spean which, before the advent of the Lochaber Aluminium Works in 1930, were arguably the wildest rivers under any conditions in the West Highlands. The handbook to the West Highland Railway *Mountain, Moor and Loch* (1894) waxed lyrical about these falls:

> The river is a succession of furious cataracts one of the most striking being seen just after leaving Tulloch. The water thunders down a series of wide steps against a wall of rock so adamantine that the stream swerves at a sharpe angle and rushes in a long race of white spume through a straight chute cut out of the black rock as if with a chisel.

White Falls   NN 396 933

Falls in Glen Roy high up under the relatively low col which leads to the Spey. This is remote country, little frequented.

Argyll

Falls of Allt Airigh nan Chaisteal   NM 408 278

The coastal waterfalls of Ardmeanach in Mull are, perhaps, best seen from a boat bound for Iona. The falls of the Allt Airigh nan Chaisteal are close to MacCulloch's Tree, a fossil cast of a coniferous tree, 12 metres high. The Burg Estate, in which the falls are situated, was acquired by the National Trust for Scotland in 1935.

Aros Fall   NM 520 535

Murray's *Handbook* notes that there are several cascades in the woods around Tobermory and makes particular mention of Aros Fall on the banks of a 'picturesque lake' which after rain is very fine. Aros House, in the grounds of which the fall is situated is now razed to the ground and the park belongs to the Forestry Commission. The fall is on a feeder of Loch Ghurrabain, the crouching loch, on a shelf above the bay.

Falls of Aros

The Aros Burn drains a more extensive basin than might be supposed and it tumbles over two rock shelves above Tobermory Bay in the rhododendron-filled grounds of Aros House in a most attractive way. A forest trail leads from the Tobermory-Salen road to the shore. The lower falls are seen from a bridge on the shore path. The burn falls eight metres in a woody dell. From above the falls there is a charming view of Tobermory. The Upper Falls are broad and in summer are only half-seen through the luxuriant vegetation, like the waterfalls in Chinese paintings. These falls are some 12 metres high and no one who visits them should fail to step onto the rock platform over which they fall, for it commands a superb view across Loch Sunart to Ben Hiant in Ardnamurchan, arguably the best view *from* a waterfall in Scotland.

Falls of Avich   NM 966 140

The long glacial trough occupied by Loch Awe is steep-sided, but above it is a picturesque region of charming low peaks and intimate little lochs, the largest of which is Loch Avich. Much of the area is in the hands of the Forestry Commission, one of whose first estates in Scotland was in this district. A road, which provides access to the plateau and crosses it to Kilmelford, climbs above Loch Awe beside the considerable River Avich giving splendid views. The river drains the loch and cascades down the side of the trough, forming several beautiful waterfalls. A forest walk provides access to roads which are not open to vehicles. The principal group of falls consists of three cascades falling across open rocks which, in most conditions, allow the visitor to have an intimate encounter with the tumbling water.

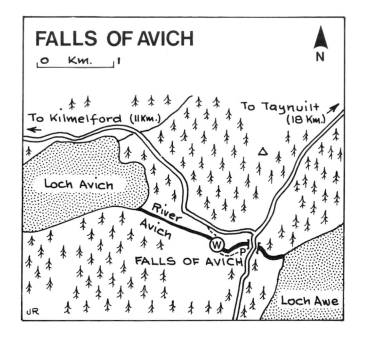

Eas Ban   NR 883 997

Eas Ban, the white fall, occurs in the low hill country at the foot of Loch Awe. It can be reached from the road from Ford to Kilmichael Glen.

Black Linn see Eagle's Fall

Falls of Blarghour   NM 998 131

These Loch Awe-side falls received much more notice in old guide books than they do now. They are the 'big falls' of Argyll. When the *Countess of Breadalbane* plied from Ford to Loch Awe pier, they were one of the principal sights pointed

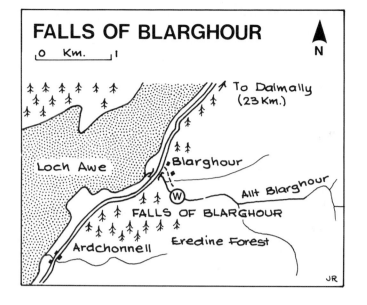

FALLS OF BLARGHOUR

out from the little steamer, 'the spray from which may be seen a long way off in wet weather'. In wet weather this journey must have seemed interminable and, no doubt, travellers would have been only too pleased to fancy that they could see spray rising from the falls through the Scotch mist. In fact, the falls are in dense woods, and it is unlikely that the spray from them can be seen from the loch. Carriages used to run to the falls from Port Sonachan.

Today the falls are accessible only to those who follow the narrow B840, and they are visited by comparatively few of those who do. Just beyond the whitewashed farmhouse of Blairgour a little bridge crosses the burn and a track climbs the hill into Chuil wood. A short distance from the road there is an apron fall of about eight metres. The main falls are in the wood above this and by climbing up the left bank of the stream you reach a belvedere opposite them. Facing you is a singularly impressive sight. The water drops 30 metres sheer in an unsupported fall, narrow at the top, but fanning out at the bottom. The Gaelic name for these falls is Eas Chuil, the fall of the recess. They deserve to be more widely known.

Falls of Brander   NN 053 287

The Allt Brander is the most prominent of several mountain torrents which tumble helter-skelter down the side of Cruachan into the narrow defile through which Loch Awe reaches the sea, the Pass of Brander. The stream drains the principal corrie under the very summit of Cruachan, Coire Bhochail. The principal falls cannot be seen from either the road or the railway, both of which are tucked under the mountain. In wet weather the little stream which flows out of Loch na Cuag forms an attractive fall of white water on the opposite side of the loch from the falls of Brander, relieving the sunless slopes of Creag an Aonaidh.

Eas na Brogie   NN 191 517

This fall in Glen Etive is a great curiosity occurring in Dalness Chasm, the prominent rift beneath Stob na Broige, the peak of the shoe, which is the culmination of Buchaille Etive Mor above Glen Etive. At one point there is a fall of 90 metres in a chimney 200 metres in height. The foot of the chasm can be approached by a recess 50 metres in depth.

Carlonan Linn see Salmon Leap Falls, River Aray.

Eas a' Chaorainn   NM 817 110

A prominent fall on a wooded hillside above Loch Melfort on the A816. It is rather spoiled by the corrugated iron hangars which make a foreground for it.

Eas na Circe   NM 996 438

This cascading torrent has been used as the basis for a pleasant Forest Walk beside Loch Creran.

Falls of Cladich   NN 101 208

The indefatigable waterfall enthusiast, the Hon Mrs Sarah Murray, remarked on this fall which she heard rather than saw on her way from Loch Awe to Inveraray. It is on the burn above Cladich, reasonably close to the road, but rather difficult of access. There is a grand 15 metre fall at the head of the gorge. The fall was the subject of a painting exhibited at the Royal Scottish Academy in 1848 by John Wilson.

Connel Falls see the Falls of Lora

Eas Corrach   NM 512 456

The twisting fall occurs on the Allt Lon Biolaireich not far above its confluence with the Aros. There are two falls of about four metres at an angle to one another which are perfectly proportioned and very pretty.

Eas Criarachain   NM 476 196

Coastal waterfall in Mull which drains a sump near Carsaig. Its name means the fall of the marsh, literally, of the place like a sieve.

Falls of Cruachan   NN 079 270

These famous falls are now dominated by the Cruachan pumped storage hydro-electric power scheme. They are harnessed by a great dam which can be reached, with considerable

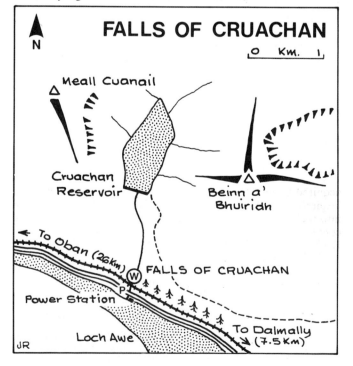

exertion, by following the banks of the stream from the Loch Awe-side road, or with less effort, by the hydroboard road. The falls, of the 'hanging valley' type, are close to the station and are still well worth seeing in spate. The dam, the falls, the underground power station and the forebay of the tailrace on Loch Awe are premier tourist attractions.

Eas na Dabhaich   NM 540 219

The cliffs at Carsaig are the highest in Scotland apart from the remote cliffs of Hoy and Foula. They are composed of Liassic sediments topped by lava and there are numerous waterfalls which plunge over the cliffs from the West. Eas na Daibhaich is close to the little settlement in Carsaig Bay consisting of an upper fall of about 70 metres and a series of cascades of about 20 metres.

Dalness Chasm see Eas na Broige

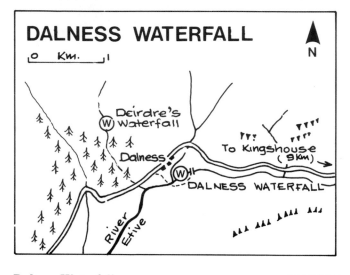

Dalness Waterfalls   NN 171 511

The falls on the Etive at Dalness, the field of the waterfalls, are the first real obstacle for salmon and they are decisive, for no fish ascend the river beyond them. The falls themselves are six metres high and stand in an impressive gorge the walls of which are 12 metres high. Above them the river flows over two or three rocky steps leading up to the main fall, and water to supply the Lodge is abstracted in a conduit from this point. Glen Etive is virtually unspoilt, desolate, yet impressive. From Dalness the view of Stob na Broige (Buchaille Etive Mor) and Stob Dubh (Buchaille Etive Beag) the two graceful peaks which dominate the valley is too foreshortened to have its maximum effect and the foothills of Clachlet are without distinction. Nevertheless Dalness Lodge is attractively situated. The Dalness Estate was the first mountain property to be acquired by the National Trust for Scotland in 1937 under the inspiration P J H. It was added to Glencoe which had passed into their hands in 1935 and marked a major departure in the conservation of mountain country. The estate includes the Buchailles and Bidean nam Bian. The Lodge itself is at the roadside where two famous passes cross to Glencoe. The falls are on the river immediately below it and there is a bridge downstream of them providing easy access.

Glendarroch Falls   NR 851 861

These are 'whisky' falls above the Glendarroch Distillery at Ardrishaig.

Deirdre's Waterfall   NN 161 517

This is the splendid hanging valley waterfall above Glen Etive where it is joined by Glen Fhaolain beneath Bidean nam Bian. There is generally sufficient water in the Allt nan Easain, the burn of the waterfalls, to make this fall, which takes three turning leaps as it tumbles down the mountainside, attractive. In *Highways and Byways in the West Highlands* Seton Gordon (1935) describes the scene:

> Where the river Etive turns abruptly from west to south-west was Deirdre's home, on the grassy slope that rises from the south bank of the river. Here was her grianan, or sunny bower, and the small peak of Stob Grianan perhaps commemorates the place. The hillsides are dark and frowning and hard to climb. Across the river from the grianan a waterfall of great height leaps from the mists. Here Deirdre roamed the hills with Naoise.
>
> At night the distant murmur of the great waterfall lulled her to sleep; she awoke to see the sun golden upon Buchaille Etive Mor.

> Glen Etive!
> There I built my first house;
> Lovely its woods after rising.

Douglas Falls   NN 060 047

South of Inveraray the little river Douglas flows in a series of cascades, the most prominent of which is nearly impassable for salmon. Below the main road (A83) there is a charming eighteenth century single-arched bridge.

Easain Duibh   NN 231 086

Bealach an Easain Duibh, the pass of the place of the black waterfalls, is the true name of the defile universally known as the 'Rest and be Thankful' under Beinn an Lochain between Arrochar and Inveraray. The waterfall which gives its name to the place is below Loch Restil on the Butterbridge side of the pass. It is a pleasing eight metre fall where the little river tumbles attractively over open rocks.

Easan Dubha see Falls of Orchy

Glen Dubh Falls   NM 968 419

These falls occur beside an enchanting forest walk in the Barcaldine Forest, Loch Creran. The first falls occur on the little river Teithil, and there are further falls higher upstream, notably Eas Garbh (*NN 011 429*).

Sput Dubh   NM 519 545

The waterfall which tumbles over black rocks into Tobermory Harbour is called Black Spout. It used to provide fresh water for sailing ships.

Eas Dubh (Inverglen)   NN 099 019

A local fall, providing a short excursion for visitors to Strachur.

Eas Dubh (Ross of Mull)   NM 445 194

One of the more prominent falls of the cliffed coast of the Ross of Mull

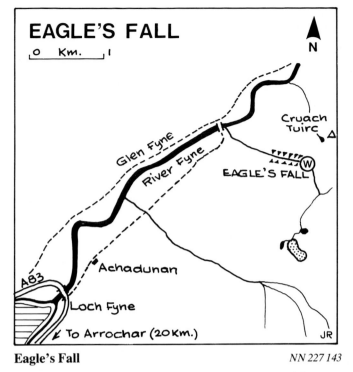

Eagle's Fall

NN 227 143

This fall in Glen Fyne is seldom visited, yet it is one of the most impressive natural features in Argyll and, if it were in a more accessible place, it would be considered a significant curiosity, not to be missed. This, of course, adds to its present charm. Access to the glen is by an estate road which leads through the farmyard of Achadunan to open country. The principal hill in these parts is Ben Buie, but it cannot be seen and the peak which dominates the view is Cruach Tuirc which will remind visitors familiar with the Lake District of Eagle's Crag in Borrowdale, an assertive little hill of great character. The road runs towards it and just before the bridge over the Fyne a spectacular hanging waterfall is seen descending from a perfect truncated valley on the skyline. Nowhere is the effect of over-deepening by a glacier more splendidly illustrated. The birch-filled ravine falls 150 metres. This is *Eas an Tuirc* (*NN 221 145*). At its head is a fine unsupported fall, of perhaps 50 metres, Black Linn. It is possible to follow either bank of the ravine, but the linn is well hidden. The best view is probably to be had from the right bank. Above the Black Linn—which might be considered a singular attraction in itself—you come to a very fine rock gorge with extremely precipitous sides and realise that the adventurous business of reaching Eagle's Fall itself is only just beginning. Only by picking a way up the bed of the stream is it possible to reach the fall. It is formed where a tributary stream is precipitated over a sheer rock face into the gorge. It is a fine cataract of some 50 metres which falls 36 metres clear. The fall is attenuated because the stream is diverted to Loch Sloy but only in very dry weather is it likely to be found wanting. The gorge would be impenetrable in spate, except for a very determined party. If eagles no longer nest there, they ought to.

Loch Etive

Loch Etive is the most southerly of the great sea lochs on the West Coast which does not have a public road running along its shores. It is accessible to the walker, and from the sea. At one time there was a regular steamer service and the round, from Oban or Fort William, by Glencoe and Loch Etive was considered one of the very finest in the Highlands. At the present there are cruises from Bonawe. The upper loch is the heart of the parish of Ardchattan, the wild mountain country of which is dominated by Ben Cruachan to the South, Ben Starav to the North and Ben Trilleachan to the West. Close to Bonawe and two Esragans enter the Loch. There are two picturesque falls on the Esragan itself, Eas na Gearr and Eas Chrialet. On the lesser Esragan, the Blarcreen Burn, there are several falls, one of particular beauty (*NN 008 355*). North of Bonawe a track leads along the west bank of the loch to Loch Etive Head under Ben Trilleachan. About halfway along the loch the track crosses the Allt Easach before following the shore under the Etive Slabs. These are the spectacular granite blocks which, since the war, have yielded climbing routes of the first quality. The streams which tumble down these slopes are all fine mountain torrents. The most prominent and spectacular fall is *Eas Doire Donncha* (*NN 088 428*), the fall of the Grove of Duncan. On the opposite bank the principal tributary of the upper loch is the Kinglass which occupies the trench between Ben na Aighean and Ben Lunnich which leads to Loch Tull and Rannoch Moor. There are falls *The Falls of Glen Kinglas* (*NN 191 348*) in the upper part of this long glen. Parallel to Glen Kinglas is Glen Noe, the charming valley under Ben Cruachan. The grey peak rises steeply above the cascades on the burn about 1.5 km from its confluence with the loch, *The Falls of Glen Noe* (*NN 067 338*).

Eas Eunaich

NN 140 309

In wet weather this is the most spectacular mountain fall in Argyll. It is well seen across Loch Awe with Kilchurn Castle in front of it from the road to Inveraray. The proper name of the fall is Steallair Eunaich. It is well off the beaten track, so it is surprising to find that it is the subject of a detailed account in John Stoddart's *Remarks on the Scenery and Manners in Scotland* (1801). Stoddart calls it *Eass Uain*:

It had rained all night, and the streams, which streaked the surrounding hills with silver lines, were seen in all their pride. The largest of these, roaring down a heathy ravine in a hill, which faced us, rushed towards the River Stree (or rapid), which gives name to its glen. About the middle of its course, it formed a cascade, called Eas Uain, to which I had climbed alone, on the preceding day, and now revisited it with Mr Walker. This fall is one of the kind most common in mountainous countries; but it is an uncommon one of that kind. It is a mere rill sliding down a rock, scarcely visible in dry weather, but after rain appearing as a white stripe, at a great distance. It does not therefore, come upon the eye with the effect of sudden discovery; yet, after losing sight of it for some time, in climbing the mountain, you are surprised, on near approach, to find it so much magnified. There is a tremendous cleft, which like a wound in the mountain's side lays bare the rocky strata of which it is formed. When you stand in this chasm, its stony walls wholly shut out the prospect of the vale below, and you see nothing but water, shooting, as it were, from the clouds, into this dreary solitude. There are four falls, which when viewed from the bottom, in one line, with the breaks concealed, are truly magnificent; for their height cannot be less than two hundred feet. The two uppermost may be considered as one fall, to which when you ascend it forms a most impressive scene; the water gliding about halfway, obliquely, then dashing precipitately down, broken by the jagged rocks as it falls, and spreading below into a sheet as fine as spray. As a picturesque object, a waterfall is of no value, without suitable accompaniments; here was neither tree, nor shrub, nor were the rocks themselves varied in their forms; but their simple massiveness, and vast scale, gave them a sublimity, which, perhaps, the pen can but ill convey, and the pencil cannot convey at all.

Having won such praise it is a wonder that Eas Eunaich is not better known. It remains as remote and isolated today as when Stoddart visited it.

Euchar Falls   NM 831 205)

The little river Euchar drains Loch Scamma dale and discharges into Loch Feochan at Kilninver. It traverses a finely wooded glen which provides a route for the coast road (A816) to the Pass of Melfort. Below the site of Raera Castle, on the left bank of the stream, is a fine roaring salmon leap.

Eas an Fhir Mor   NN 207 513

The 'cascade of the great one, is 1.5 km above the falls at Dalness on the Etive. It is here as charming a mountain river as it would be possible to wish. A number of other falls and pools on the Etive above this are favourite picnicing spots for discriminating visitors. One of the falls, about 4.5 km above Dalness, is four metres high.

Eas Fors   NM 444 422

This is arguably the finest coastal waterfall in Scotland. It is also probably the easiest to see properly although, because the

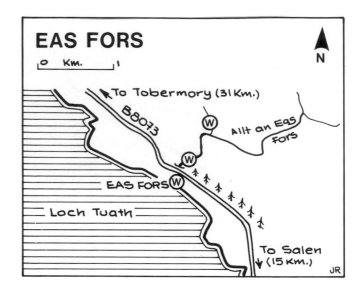

Eas an Fhir Mor, Glen Etive ('the cascade of the great one'). One of several excellent sites on the Etive for a refreshing picnic. OAT CARD COMPANY

greater part of it is situated below the road, it is frequently missed. The fall is situated on the north side of Loch Tuath, opposite Ulva in Mull. From it you look across Camas an Lagain, the bay of peace, to Ben More. A considerable body of water plunges 30 metres into a deep sea pool which is covered at high tide, but which can be reached at other times by paths which lead to the sea shore at a little distance from the fall. This is the *pièce de résistance* of the place, but immediately above the sea fall is a delightful apron fall of about eight metres, and above the road bridge, a double fall another eight metres in height. In a gorge a little distance above this there is another series of three falls which are also well worth seeing. The curious sounding name of the fall is a mixture of Gaelic and Norse elements, both of which mean waterfall. It occurs two or three times in Mull. Behind the sea fall there is an almost inaccessible cave where, it is said, a noted piper used to compose his tunes in secret.

Eas Fors   NM 423 497

Twin falls beside the by-road from Torloisk to Dervaig. They are some 12 metres in height and considerable in spate.

Eas a Ghaill   NN 215 265

Series of little falls in the woods below Socach.

Inverchorachan Falls   NN 230 174

In the upper part of Glen Fyne the river forms a series of charming cascades, the highest of which has holly trees at its foot, and wonderfully transparent mountain water falls about five metres over some bold rocks in beautiful woods.

Inverinan Falls   NM 988 176

One of several walks from Inverinan is called the Waterfall Walk. Unlike many forest walks it follows a mountain path through deciduous woodlands at first. The walk leads to precipitous little falls which are well set on the River Fionan.

Easan Labhar   NM 531 418

The noisy waterfalls, Easan Labhar, are above Loch na Keal in Mull.

Falls of Aray, *near Inveraray, in an area being transformed by new plantations.*
DAVID I HARVIE

White Fall. *Remote fall at the head of Glen Roy.* HAMISH BROWN

Coire an Lochan, *Ben Finlay, at the head of Glen Creran. Beautiful stopping place for the adventurous hill-walker. (left)* HAMISH BROWN

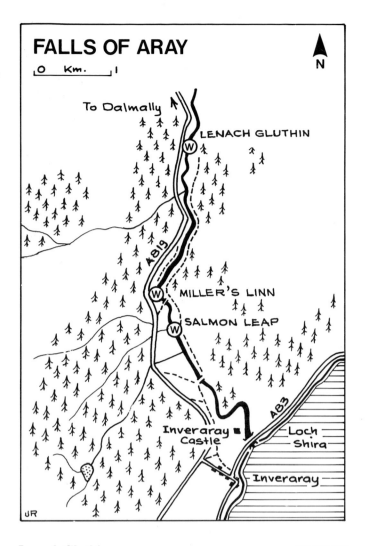

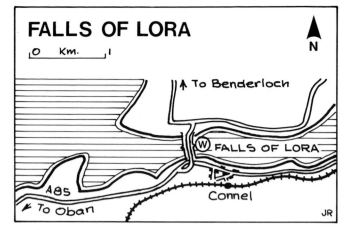

Lenach Gluthin
NN 088 128

The uppermost, and most impressive, of the Falls of Aray: a broken down bridge close to a cottage on the A819 marks the site of the falls which are, in all, some 25 metres in height. The fall consists of three main leaps in a savage little den overhung with old trees. The Aray is gradually being transformed by new plantations. Old ways beside the river are somewhat overgrown, but the fall provides a fine climax to a walk beside the river from the castle. For those who come by road there is a good view from above the principal fall on the right bank of the river, but everyone who visits the falls should cross the suspension bridge and view the falls from the left bank. In spate it is easy to see how the falls got their name which means 'the angry slurp'. In other conditions the falls are very picturesque and have a good claim to be the most aesthetically satisfying in the West of Scotland.

Falls of Lora
NM 911 345

These unique falls occur at the mouth of Loch Etive not far from Oban. The ebbing tide which issues from the loch forms the falls when it rushes over a rocky bar. They are 1.5 metres in height at spring tides, and the mass of water, 200 metres wide, which falls over the bar is very considerable, exceeding that of any other fall in Britain. At other times the falls may be found disappointing, but the water at the bar is always agitated.

The crossing of the old Connel Ferry was a dramatic experience requiring consummate skill on the part of the boatmen. However, they knew how to make the most economical use of the currents, and the crossing was usually accomplished safely enough in spite of appearances. It is said that one startled visitor, seeing the saltwater cataract, asked the ferryman if boats were ever swept over it, and their occupants lost. 'No,' replied the dry Highlander, 'They are never lost. The bodies always turn up in the next bay, or near Dunstaffnage.'

The little boats were succeeded by a steamer and, in 1903, by the cantilever bridge which remains one of the most outstanding engineering works in the highlands. The bridge [1901], for which Sir John Fowler was also the consulting engineer, is a copy of the Forth Bridge.

The falls, sometimes known as Connel Falls, get their much more widely-known name from the various references to them in the Ossianic poems published by James Macpherson.

Lussa Falls
NR 775 857

Above Kilmichael Glassary of Inverlussa in Knapdale.

Eas Meirlach see The Robbers' Waterfall

Pass of Melfort

With the building of the Oude Dam the character of the Pass of Melfort, which used to constitute one of the attractions of the journey from Oban to Lochgilphead, has been irreparably altered. Baddeley describes it as 'a deep, narrow ravine finely flanked by rock and wood, and quite the bonne bouche of the journey.' The pass, now deprived of water in most conditions, used to have a number of attractive falls. Eas Tarsuinn (*NM 841 152*) is the subsidiary ravine which joins the pass below the dam and still has water in it. The Hydro Board has provided access to the old pass at the dam and it makes a pleasant walk.

Miller's Linn
NN 086 110

On the Aray, about 2 km from Inveraray, quite close to the A819. It is above a recently established trout farm, the water for which is taken from the river just above the falls. A series of cascades over broken rocks catch the sun, and have considered charm on a fine day. The whole fall is about five metres high.

Eas Mor
NM 983 103

The great fall on the Kames River, Loch Awe.

Eas Mor (Ross of Mull)   *NM 466 230*

Fall above Loch Scridain.

Eas Mor   *NM 824 023*

Beyond Carnasserie Castle and above Loch Craignish in Lorn.

Eas Morag   *NN 240 274*

This is the singularly beautiful little waterfall on the Eas Daimh which drains into the Lochy and adds interest to what is otherwise a rather dull stretch of the A85 Ben Lui, which is generally considered to be the most beautiful mountain in the Southern Highlands, is so close to the pass that it overshadows it and cannot be seen properly. Nevertheless, Glen Lochy is a good starting point for the ascent of Ben Lui, the path to which passes close to this fall, which is named after Duncan Ban MacIntyre's girl-friend, or so it is said. Close to the fall is a stone 'Clach na h-Uruisg' where the Uruisg of Ben Laoigh (Lui) was often seen to be sitting. It was his job to prevent the water from falling too quickly over the fall.

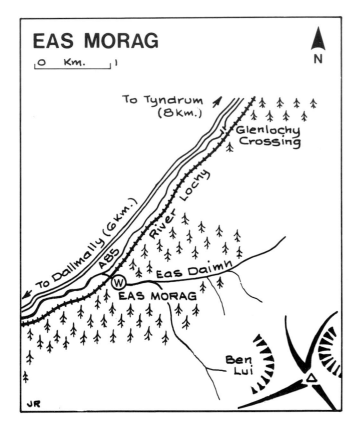

Eas a Muillinn-Luaidh   *NM 851 135*

A fall of 12 metres at the outfall from Parson's Loch north of Kilmelford. Its complicated name means fulling mill fall.

Falls of Orchy   *NN 242 321*

Glen Orchy is somewhat off the beaten track, being neither on the way to Oban nor on the way to Fort William from Glasgow or Edinburgh. Nor are there any striking mountains in its immediate vicinity. The valley nevertheless has a commanding pastoral quality and it is tempting to linger beside its salmon pools on a fine day. The lowest of the falls *Eas Urchaidh* (*NN 242 321*) is a complex of cascades beside a rather unprepossessing Forestry Commission bridge. These falls, 11 kilometres from Dalmally, are five metres high and they provide a formidable obstacle for fish, although a rough salmon ladder has been blasted out of the rock. The bridge provides a fine vantage point for watching the activity in the water at the right season. Not far above these falls but further from the public road (B8074) is *Eas a' Chathaidh* (*NN 247 330*), three metres high. The prettiest falls are 3 kilometres further on, 5 kilometres from Bridge of Orchy. These are the Black Falls, *Easan Dubha* (*NN 266 356*) where the river tumbles over grey rocks with open slabs which are just two metres high. This is generally a friendly place, but warning notices remind visitors that the falls are dangerous in spate and have been the site of at least one serious accident.

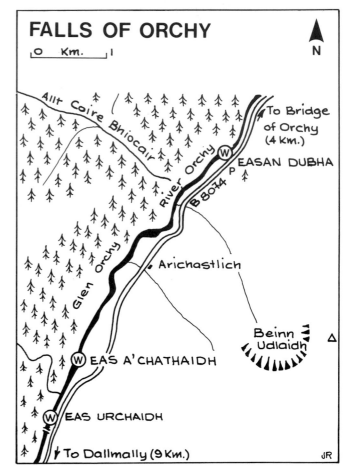

The Robbers' Waterfall   *NN 139 450*

Perhaps the most interesting in Argyll. It got its name either from the possibility that a herd of cattle might easily be concealed in the twisting gorge at its foot (a possibility which must have been realised more than once), or because it was a favoured resting place for cattle reivers above the lonely head of Loch Etive commanding a hidden pass leading to the south. The fall is approached from the farm by the track which leads to Ben Starav. This crosses the burn, but keeps away from it until the fall is reached. The fall has two distinct personalities. A tributary burn joins the Allt Mheuran in a charming series of

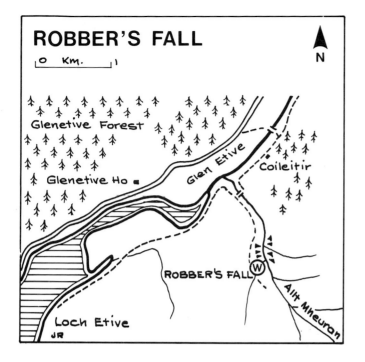

ROBBER'S FALL

It is a lovely glen, wilder and much shut in as you advance, with fine rocks appearing through the grassy hills, and thickly wooded at the bottom. We passed two farms, and then went up to where the glen closes, and on the brae there is a keeper's cottage, just above which are the remains of a house where Rob Roy lived for some time concealed, but on suffrance. His army of followers were hidden in Glen Shira. We got out here to look at some fine falls of the river Shira, a linn falling from a height to which footpaths had been made.

The scene is much as it must have been, although the amount of water in the river is now affected by the Hydro Board. To see the falls it is essential to go after heavy rain. The falls commence below the confluence of the main stream and the Brannie Burn.

In addition to its associations with Rob Roy and Queen Victoria the glen is the scene of episodes in the novels of Neil Munro.

Eas Stocair

A remote mountain fall, the fall of the trumpeter, on the Allt an Lon Biolaireich, a tributary of the Aros.

Falls of Glen Strae   NN 166 312

Glen Strae is a fine, wild glen at the head of Loch Awe. Like many another such place geologists would describe it as a 'glacial trough' and it is a characteristic of glacial troughs that their floors are stepped. Where the Strae is joined by its principal tributary, tumbling down the hillside from Ben Donachain there are considerable falls on both the Strae and its sister stream. The Strae itself falls over the site of a little gorge into the bed of the smaller burn. The falls are broken, but about six metres in height.

Tailor's Leap   NN 013 265

Three kilometres up Glen Nant there is a well-known picnic site beside the river at the Tailor's Leap. It is said that a tailor had an illicit still on a tributary burn where it plunges over a twelve metre fall. In Gaelic the fall is called *Eas na Coarach Duibhe*, the fall of the black sheep. He leaped across the Nant when pursued by excisemen. A little further up the river is Eas nan Clag (*NN 013 265*), the noisy fall.

Torness Falls   NM 648 324

Considerable fall on the rumbustious little river Lussa above Loch Spelve in Mull.

Eas an Tuirc see Eagle's Fall

Eas nan Uircean   NM 983 084

A fall of 20 metres on the Allt Garbh above the forest village of Eredine on Loch Awe.

Eas Urchaidh see Falls of Orchy

open cascades of two metres, two metres and six metres, the last being a charming curtain fall which descends into a pool which is a ford on the path. The main stream then plunges 15 metres into the sinister gorge below in an awe-inspiring double fall. The ford is one of the most enchanting places on a Scottish mountainside. From the fall there are superb views of the Bidean nam Bian Massif and the remote mountain passes across which the Glencoe villagers fled after the massacre. The setting of this impressive fall in the remote Etive deer forest is most attractive. There is a further fine waterslide higher up the Mheuran which is marked on some maps as the *Robbers' Waterfall* (*NN 143 444*).

Gleann Salach

This is the name given to the glen which links Barcaldine and Bonawe. There is a major fall, *Eas Mor* (*NM 967 403*), on the Dearg Abhainn and a further fall, *Eas a' Choin* (*NM 965 411*) on a tributary.

Salmon Leap Falls   NN 088 107

These low falls are the first to be encountered in the walk up the Aray from Inverary Castle. The river is regulated by a number of little salmon weirs below the falls. Above the Aray is Duniquoich, the sharp little hill with a watch tower which can be reached from the falls.

Falls of Shira   NN 143 160

Glen Shira is generally visited on account of Rob Roy's Cottage. Queen Victoria ascended the glen twice on her visit to Inverary in 1875:

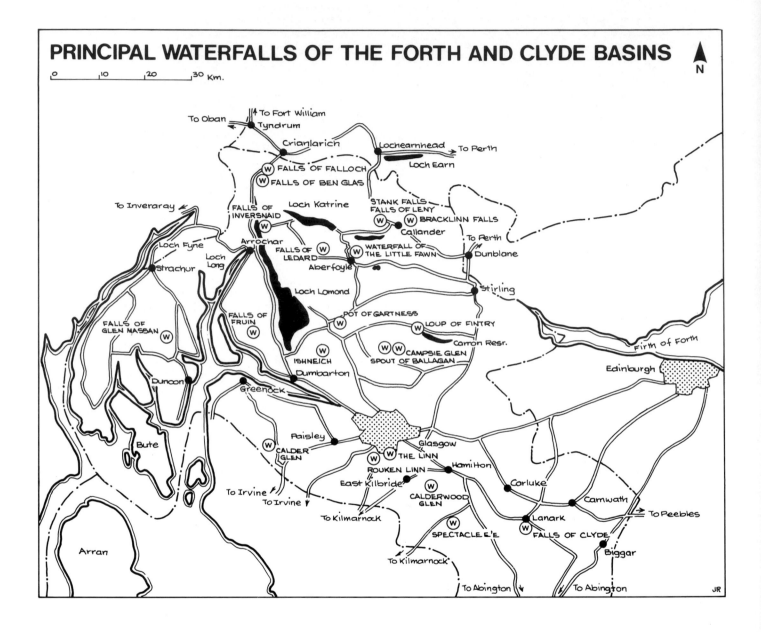

PRINCIPAL WATERFALLS OF THE FORTH AND CLYDE BASINS

N

0   10   20   30 Km.

To Oban
To Fort William
Tyndrum
Crianlarich
Lochearnhead
To Perth
Loch Earn
(W) FALLS OF FALLOCH
(W) FALLS OF BEN GLAS
To Inveraray
STANK FALLS
FALLS OF LENY
Loch Katrine
FALLS OF INVERSNAID
(W) BRACKLINN FALLS
(W)
Callander
To Perth
Loch Fyne
Arrochar
Loch Long
FALLS OF LEDARD (W)
WATERFALL OF THE LITTLE FAWN
(W)
Dunblane
Strachur
(W)
Aberfoyle
Stirling
Loch Lomond
FALLS OF GLEN MASBAN (W)
FALLS OF FRUIN (W)
POT OF GARTNESS
(W) LOUP OF FINTRY
Firth of Forth
(W)(W) CAMPSIE GLEN
SPOUT OF BALLAGAN
Carron Resr.
(W) ISHNEICH
Dumbarton
Edinburgh
Dunoon
Greenock
Bute
Paisley
(W) CALDER GLEN
Glasgow
(W)(W) THE LINN
Hamilton
ROUKEN LINN
Corluke
To Irvine
East Kilbride
(W) CALDERWOOD GLEN
Camwath
To Irvine
To Kilmarnock
Lanark
To Peebles
(W)
(W) FALLS OF CLYDE
SPECTACLE E'E
Biggar
Arran
To Kilmarnock
To Abington
To Abington

JR

FORTH AND CLYDE BASINS

Principal Falls

Outstanding Falls	Touring Centre
Falls of Clyde	Lanark

Significant Falls

Falls of Glenmassan	Dunoon
Falls of Falloch	Loch Lomond
Falls of Ben Glas (The Grey Fox)	Loch Lomond
Falls of Inversnaid	Loch Lomond
Pot of Gartness	Loch Lomond
Loup of Fintry	Fintry
Spout of Ballagan	Strathblane
Campsie Glen	Strathblane
Stank Falls	Callander
Bracklinn Falls	Callander
Falls of Ledard	Aberfoyle
Waterfall of the Little Fawn	Aberfoyle

Interesting Falls

Ishneich	Loch Lomond
Rouken Glen	Glasgow
The Linn (Cart)	Glasgow
Calder Glen	Lochwinnoch
Calderwood Glen	East Kilbride
Spectacle E'e	Strathaven
Falls of Glenfruin	Loch Lomond
Falls of Leny	Callander

Also recommended:

Spout of Ballochleam	Kippen
Gleniffer Linn	Paisley
Milton of Callander Fall	Callander
Rob Roy's Cave Fall	Balquhidder
Whistler's Glen	Helensburgh
Black Linn of Blairvaich	Aberfoyle

Waterfalls in the Forth and Clyde Basins

The Forth and the Clyde are intimately linked. The two basins make up the geographical heartland of Scotland. In the geological epoch immediately before our own it is probable that the Forth drained much of what is now part of the Clyde basin. The boundaries between the two are indistinct. For the purposes of this survey the Carron is included, but the Devon, very much a river of the East, is excluded. Cowal is included, but the Aray and the little rivers of Kintyre are excluded. The basins of the Clyde and the Forth comprise the old counties of Lanarkshire, Renfrew, Dunbartonshire and Stirlingshire and not much else.

The Clyde, as befits the most considerable river of the West coast, has several notable waterfalls. The Clyde Basin is, however, most remarkable for the romance and infinite variety of the falls on burns tributary to the main stream. The river rises in the Southern Uplands, its southern tributaries draining the Central Lowlands. The Leven, surging five miles from Loch Lomond to the Clyde, drains a basin including Strath Endrick and parts of the Southern Highlands. Old Red Sandstone gives rise to substantial gorges. There are waterfalls in Glasgow parks visited by mums pushing prams in the afternoon, and remote mountain falls in hidden highland glens visited by but a few walkers in a year. Fine linns are characteristic of the basaltic lavas of the Kilpatrick Hills, the Campsies and the Renfrewshire Heights.

The mighty Clyde itself falls more than 60 metres in four cataracts which, in spate, surpass all other waterfalls in Scotland in the combined fury of their falling waters. The Wordsworths visited the Falls of Clyde, the Falls of Falloch and the Falls of Inversnaid. Beside Dundaff Linn David Dale and Richard Arkwright built New Lanark, harbinger of the Industrial Revolution. At Gallangad beside a waterfall 'Black Knee' MacGregor began a wild adventure with a great white bull. If Bonnington Linn is a prosaic name for a waterfall, there can be no doubt that the Loup of Fintry, the Spout of Ballagan and Muckle Alicompen are names to conjure with.

The highest waterfall in the Clyde Basin is the Ben Glas Fall at the head of Loch Lomond; the Falls of Clyde have the greatest discharge. The Falls of Falloch, the Falls of Inversnaid and the Falls of Campsie Glen are the best known. The Spout of Ballagan and the Loup of Fintry are impressive falls which deserve to be more frequently visited. The Clyde Basin in respect of its waterfalls, as in other respects, sets standards for the rest of Scotland to emulate.

Beneath the frowning north face of the Fintry Hills is Flanders Moss. It is difficult to believe that the insignificant ditch which struggles across these flatlands is the mighty Forth. It constitutes unpromising material for waterfalls, and it is the principal tributaries of the main stream which drain areas of greater interest. Like the Clyde and the Tay, the Forth flows across the grain of the country and thus drains an area of highly contrasted rocks. The Falls of Leny, probably the most frequented of all falls, lie on the Highland Boundary Fault. The conglomerates of Old Red Sandstone age which make up the high ground between Callander and Crieff give rise to the furious Bracklinn Falls with their angular slabbed rocks. The basaltic ledges of the Fintry and Gargunnock Hills also cause falls.

Sir Walter Scott used both the Falls of Ledard and the Bracklinn Falls in his works, which accounts for the popularity of the falls to this day. In Carron Glen Home set his tragedy 'Douglas'. Near the Spout of Ballochleam, the Grahams and the Leckies fought a bloody battle at an unrecorded date. The upper part of the Forth Basin is rich in the lore of Rob Roy MacGregor and, high above Loch Voil, Rob Roy MacGregor's Cave is hidden by a curtain fall from behind which there is a stunning view. There may be comparatively few falls in the basin of the Forth, but very many of them are gems.

Annie's Linn — NS 518 737

There are really no grounds for including this fall in a survey of the waterfalls of the Clyde basin except that it figures on the six-inch map when many more impressive cascades are unnamed. The fall is on the burn beside the Windy Hill Golf Course between Hardgate and Milngavie on the edge of Douglas Muir. The insouciant little fall, two metres in height, is in a hawthorn dell at a bend in the stream.

Falls of Ardess — NS 364 991

Falls above Rowardennan beside the much-tramped footpath to Ben Lomond. There are two falls each of which is about two metres high.

Falls of Arnan — NN 308 189

These classic hanging waterfalls are somewhat obscured because the tourist's attention is distracted by the Ben Glas Waterfall opposite. In spate the Allt Arnan tumbles 30 metres in a fine cascade of white water above the Inverarnan Hotel.

Auchenlillylinn see Carron Glen

Auchentorlie Glen — NS 442 747

The centrepiece of Auchentorlie Glen is a fine series of three falls, 18 metres high. The glen is in neglected policies above the A82 at Bowling. A fall is visible from the trunk road, but it is well worth following the right-of-way above Auchentorlie House. The path crosses a rude stone bridge before the uppermost fall, *Bow Linn*, comes into view. The other two falls are below this and can only be seen by crossing the burn. There used to be a bridge but it has now gone. These double falls are highly attractive. The glen is of geological interest as unusual plant remains were found in the coal measures there. At the foot of the burn is Littlemill of Auchentorlie, a hamlet now swallowed up in Bowling, where one of the first whisky distilleries in Scotland was established. The original buildings remain.

Auchineden Spout
NS 503 785

The principal headwater of the Kelvin in the Allander valley is the Auldmurroch Burn. Beside it the cross-country route, from Halfway House (the inn at Carbeth described by Sir Walter Scott in *Rob Roy*) to the windy Kilpatrick Hills, climbs to the Burncrooks Reservoir. The countryside hereabouts is dominated by a rash of 1930s holiday shacks of the most basic kind. The encampment has a certain period charm about it, but it illustrates what a boon modern planning regulations are. Footpaths follow either side of the burn, and where it enters the old policies it falls ten metres in the splendid Auchineden Spout. This little-known fall deserves to be more widely appreciated.

Spout of Ballagan
NS 572 601

Above Strathblane is the Little Whangie, a rock cleft from the hillside like its better-known namesake on the Stockiemuir Road. Beyond the Church at Strathblane a well-marked footpath leads to it and, beyond the Little Whangie, to the Spout of Ballagan. This 21-metre fall is one of the three wonders of the Endrick basin, much visited in Victorian times. It displays a classic section of the calciferous sandstones called the Ballagan Beds. There is a fine building stone, Spout of Ballagan sandstone, at the top which is hard enough to cause the fall, and beneath it are alternating layers of cementstones and shales. It is possible to count a hundred layers of cementstone in 400 metres of strata. The fall is a scene of wild, romantic beauty. The burn, which comes down from Earl's Seat, hurls itself into this weird, cone-shaped basin, filled with trees, above Ballagan House. From the Spout it is possible to continue to traverse the hillside into Fin Glen (qv). The Spout of Ballagan is a Scottish Wildlife Trust nature reserve.

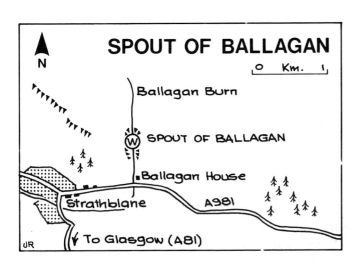

Spout of Ballochleam
NS 653 900

The six-inch map tells us that beside the lonely road to the Spout of Ballochleam¯ the Bealach (Pass) of the Leap – a bloody battle was fought. 'Brass, armour, spears and bones found here,' it proclaims. This marks the place where, at an unrecorded date, there was a conflict between the Grahams and the Leckies. The way to the pass is clear enough and the track goes over the pass to Cringate and the Loup of Fintry. At the edge of the plateau there is a cascade of forty-five metres where the Boquhan Burn tumbles over horizontally-bedded sedimentary rocks. Because it drains such a small basin at this point the fall is sometimes rather insubstantial, but the situation is very fine. It is the highest fall in the old county of Stirlingshire.

Sput Ban (Glen Falloch)
NN 314 232

The best way to the three peaks – Lui, Dubhcraig, and Oss – which dominate the country between the Falloch and the Loch Awe is by the Allt Fionne Ghlinne which can be followed to Loch Oss. Sput Ban is the splendid hanging valley waterfall seen in the upper part of this glen.

Sput Ban (Ben Lomond)
NS 364 997

The prominent rocky hill above the Rowardennan Youth Hostel is called Tom Eas, waterfall hill. It derives its name from Ben Lomond's finest waterfall Sput Ban. Indeed, Sput Ban is arguably Loch Lomond's finest waterfall, but it is curiously neglected. It forms a spectacular feature of the view of the Ben across the Loch after rain, and the path beside the fall constitutes by far the best approach to Ben Lomond, far superior to the ordinary route from Rowardennan, leading to a col between Ptarmigan and the Ben itself. The waterfall forms a major attraction during what is always the most tedious part of the ascent of any mountain, the initial business of gaining height. The fall tumbles 150 metres in a series of across mica schists. This gives the water in it a sparkling quality which is unmistakable. The upper cascade falls over the edge of the hill like spilt milk falling for about thirty metres in a waterchute. Below this the water is hidden in trees and in the bedding planes of the schists in which the stream has buried itself by relentless erosion. From the top of the fall there is a magnificent view of Loch Lomond with its islands of the Luss Hills and of the Arrochar Alps, less diffused than the same view from the top of the Ben.

Sput Ban (Stank Glen)
NN 565 116

A wild mountain fall above the main falls in Stank Glen on the way to Ben Ledi.

Sput Beag
NN 556 134

One of two falls on the Allt Mor above Loch Lubnaig, a suitable objective for a forest excursion.

Avon Linn
NS 674 415

Above Strathaven the Avon, main tributary of the Clyde, flows through exquisite pastoral scenery. Avon Linn is a complex river fall in two stages where the stream tumbles over open rocks. The linn, also called Arthur's Linn, is well-situated in a grassy gorge which can be reached by a footpath from the town, or by a footpath from the by-road at Linnbank.

Eas na Baintighearna   *NN 314 116*

The fall of the Proprietor's Lady is superbly situated on the lip
of the corrie of the same name on Ben Vorlich on the Allt
Ardvorlich. It is frequently prominent after rain and can be
seen from the A82.

Spout of Balbowie   *NS 643 869*

The B818 beyond Fintry crosses the Endrick by a charming
little bridge and turns a sharp corner to begin climbing towards
the Carron Forest, 2400 hectares of sprucewoods. The road
crosses the Cammal Burn at Broomhole Bridge where your
attention will be drawn to an ancient Graham Castle on a rocky
knoll and, above it, in a cleft in the twenty-metre lava bed
which forms a band across the hillside, to the Spout of
Balbowie.

Linn of Baldernock   *NS 591 759*

Like Annie's Linn this fall would not be noticed if it were
further from Glasgow. However, the fall is in an attractive dell,
has an imposing name and is the site of a limestone mine, which
facts amply justify its inclusion in this gazetteer. Baldernock is
some four kilometres from Milngavie and has an attractive
church and a picturesque old saw mill. Close to the hamlet are
The Auld Wive's Lifts, curious perched blocks on Craigmaddie
Muir. The falls occur in a well-wooded hollow which has been
safeguarded and improved by the Baldernock Amenity Society. The linn, together with its smaller companions, illustrates
perfectly the formation of waterfalls on rocks of differing
hardnesses. There are four tongues of dolerite, a tough
volcanic rock, intruded between sedimentary rocks including
limestone, sandstone and coal. Each band of dolerite is
represented by a fall where the softer rocks have been worn
away while the dolerite has proved much more resistant. The
principal fall is about four metres high and there is a cave
underneath it in limestone. This has been formed by mining by
the old 'stoop and room' method. An enchanting place for a
picnic on the right day.

The Ben Glas Waterfall   *NS 325 185*

The Devil's Staircase, is nearly always impressive. Situated on
the old march between Dunbartonshire and Perthshire and
constituting at 36 metres the highest fall in the former county
and in the new Dunbarton District, it was the fall beside which
the Wordsworths climbed out of the Vale of Awful Sound. It is
fed by a burn issuing from Lochan Beinn Chabhair which lies in
the peaty hollow beneath that peak which leads to Balquidder
and the Forth. In contrast to the Garabal and Arnan falls it is
enhanced by tree-clad slopes at its foot. The burn tumbles over
the edge of the moor in a broad cascade and, in spate, a
fountain of water is lifted across the face of the main fall. There
is a fine account of the fall in the West Highland Railway Guide
Book *Mountain, Moor and Loch* (1894):

> Down a narrow corrie fringed with birch and oak, from the
> crest of a hill rising steeply from the glen, a mountain
> torrent descends invisible until it suddenly breaks out of the
> face of a cliff in fine cascade like a huge vein of white quartz.
> It falls in three branches, two clinging round either side of a
> great projecting boulder spreading over the black rock like
> delicate lace while to the left a wide jet of foam flashes out,
> rushing down 'the Devil's Staircase' to join the other
> branches, the whole stream falling in a silver sheet into a
> basin about 120' below at the foot of the precipice. When
> the Lammas floods are on, in August, the force of the fall is

so great that the spray is sent seething up to a considerable
height, but so sheer is the fall of the water that down the
dark crag that it does not seem to move at all.

An alternative name for this impressive fall is the Grey Fox.
There is no finer excursion from the old posting inn at
Inverarnan than to climb up by the Ben Glas Burn into the
hollow which holds the lochan and then bear left to Ben Glas
itself. At its foot is Lochan a Chasteil, an enchanted rocky
place, commanding unrivalled views of the Vale of Awful
Sound.

Bennan Linn   *NS 516 516*

This tiny fall in the Renfrewshire Heights is said to resemble
the Fall of Foyers, although it is only three metres high.

Falls of Allt a' Bhalachain   *NN 286 040*

The aptly-named Buttermilk Burn tumbles from the Cobbler to
Loch Long. Beside it the path up the hill climbs steeply until it
reaches the corrie beneath the fantastic rock summits of Ben
Arthur. Here there are fine waterfalls which, unlike those
lower down, are unobscured by the spruce trees of the
Ardgarten Forest.

Black Linn of Blairvaich   *NS 453 997*

The Forth is here a lively mountain river which tumbles an
eight metre fall of the apron type after passing through a rock
gateway as high again. It is a remote isolated place reached
from either Kinlochard or Aberfoyle by the Pipe Track Road
which crosses the Duchray Bridge. Above the bridge on the
North side of the river the pipeline passes over its most
impressive aqueduct and just beyond this, if you are coming
from Aberfoyle, a fire break gives access to the Forth at the
Black Linn.

The fall is set in a natural birch wood, a pleasant change after
the rigid rows of conifers. Two particularly fine birches offset
the gateway through which the water pours into the linn.
Behind is Ben Lomond seen to great effect. The plunge pool is
inky black because of the dark slates which make up the river
bed. The fall occurs at the junction of these slates with schists.
It might be thought that this black river together with the
oppressive feeling which close ranked conifers can engender
would render the Black Linn of Blairvaich a sombre place.
However, the fact that the water soon breaks away from the
pool, rushing white again, over brighter rocks below together
with the airy perches that there are in the full face of the fall
make it a friendly place if there is any sun at all.

Black Linn see Calderwood Glen

Black Linn see Overtoun Glen

Black Mill Fall   *NS 719 785*

Fall in Kilsyth harnessed to an elaborate system of lades
serving old mills.

Black Spout see Fin Glen

Black Spout   *NS 610 863*

Above Fintry there is a prominent volcanic neck called

Dunmore, the site of an iron-age fort. Nearby, on Turf Hill, high above the road is Black Spout.

Blairessan Spout   *NS 527 867*

Beyond Killearn the A875 leads to Balfron. North of the village is the King's View which so charmed Edward VII who used to drive there from Duntreath when he stayed there to visit Mrs Keppel. It provides a first glimpse of the Highlands and of a corner of Loch Lomond across Strathendrick. Close to the King's View is Blairessan, supposedly the site of a battle between the Romans and the Caledonians. Blairessan Spout which gives the site its name is close to the village and can be reached by a beautiful avenue of trees above the splendid classical mansion house of Carbeth. The fall, on a tiny stream, is about five metres high.

Bonnington Linn see Falls of Clyde

Boquhan Glen (Killearn)   *NS 545 865*

One of the many attractions of this part of the world is the continued existence, *in situ*, of the old-fashioned finger posts at cross roads. A little distance beyond Killearn the traveller is informed with some exactness that it is five miles, 990 yards to Fintry. Just down the road is a bridge over a pretty dell with waterfalls in the woods. This is Boquhan Glen.

Boquhan Glen (Kippen)   *NS 664 938*

The Boquhan Burn which tumbles down from the Spout of Ballochleam reaches an old bridge at the entrance to Wright Park and tumbles over a five metre fall to enter Boquhan Glen. A characteristic Old Red Sandstone gorge, it was considered by the Victorians to resemble the Trossachs in miniature. At one point the gorge is so deeply incised that it is said to be like a Whale's Belly, at another is a Covenanters' Hiding Place. The main fall occurs below Auldhall.

Bow Linn see Auchentorlie Glen

Brackland Falls see Bracklinn Falls

Bracklinn Falls   *NN 645 085*

Bracklinn Falls are a short walk from Callander whence a pleasant hillside path leads to the falls. It was the alpine quality of the insubstantial wooden bridge above the roaring waters of the Keltie Burn which caught the imagination of Scott who was said to have ridden his horse at a gallop over the falls. His memorable line 'Brackland's thundering wave' popularised the falls. The bridge is now closed and, in dry weather, the falls are somewhat disappointing, but in spate they are very imposing. Bracklinn can also be visited from Wester Brackland. On this side of the Keltie a new forest road leads northward to the very fine *Eas na Caillich*, the witch's waterfall, where the burn plunges five metres under a bridge and then rushes through a narrowing of the stream to fall as far again in an even more imposing leap.

Browney's Linn see Calder Glen

Eas na Caillich see Bracklinn Falls

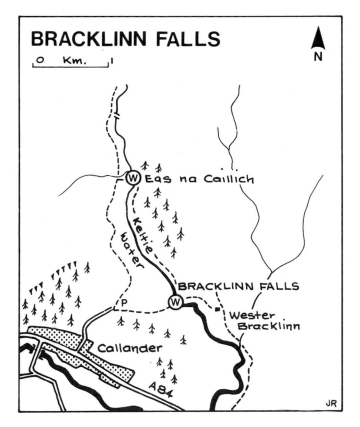

Bracklinn Bridge, near Callander. The bridge in this nineteenth century engraving is now closed.

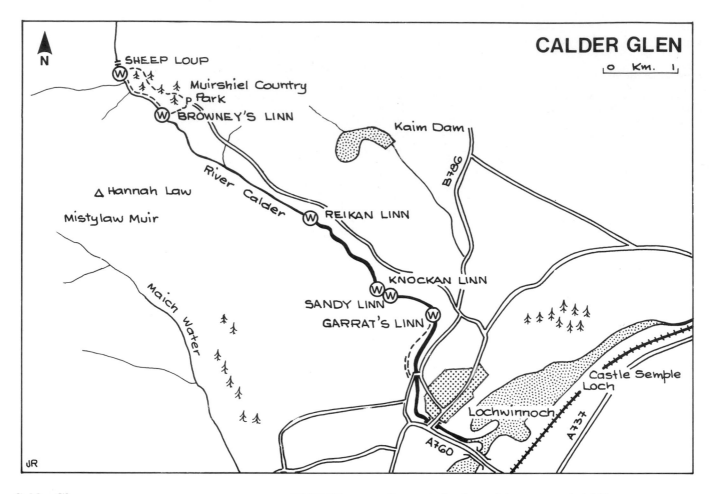

Calder Glen   NS 351 601

The Black Cart itself drains the Lochwinnoch corridor. Above Castle Semple Loch the principal feeder of the main stream is the River Calder. One of five rivers of this name in the Clyde Basin, it is the one without a soubriquet, for the others are the North Calder, the South Calder, the Rotten Calder and the Little Calder, a tributary of the Avon. *Calder Glen* is a long succession of very fine falls. It is the heart of the Clyde-Muirsheil Regional Park established by the old County Council and now administered by the Strathclyde Regional Council. At Brigend where the by-road from Lochwinnoch crosses the river is an attractive arched weir, six metres in height. Above it the Calder flows in a deep and, in places, dangerous gorge. In private ground on the right bank of the river are the remains of a cotton mill of interest to archeologists. Beside it is *Garrats Linn (NS 351 601)*. The series of falls beyond this includes *Sandy Linn (NS 345 602)* and, under the site of Cloak Castle, *Knockan Linn (NS 343 605)* where the Calder tumbles over broken rocks. *Reikan Linn (NS 334 613)* is further upstream, the most impressive of the falls. These falls are away from the road which leads to Muirsheil and are, in consequence, less frequented than *Browney's Linn (NS 313 628)* which is at the end of a short trail leading from the Visitor Centre at Muirsheil House. It is a pretty little fall, backed by rolling moorland. There is a further fall, *Sheep Loup (NS 309 634)* above the house which was the site of Muirsheils Mill. The regional park is full of interest and attractive leaflets describe ways through the woods and across the moors there.

Calder Glen is associated with possibly the greatest of the Renfrewshire poets, Alexander Wilson. In his extended poem 'Lochwinnoch' he describes Calder Glen (1789):

Low, at the foot of huge extended hills
Whose cloudy tops pour down unnumbered rills
And where loud Calder, rushing from the steep,
Roars to the lake with hoarse resistless sweep.

Calderwood Glen   NS 660 548

The Rotten Calder, a left bank tributary of the Clyde, is so named because yet another Calder unites at Torrance with the Rotten Burn. Below this confluence the river enters a fine sandstone gorge, the scenery of which is unsurpassed in an area where every glen has its supporters. Torrance, now a golf club and once the headquarters of the planners who invaded the green fields hereabouts to create the New Town of East Kilbride, is the site of a very charming nature trail. The visitor is conducted down into the gorge and, at one point, there is a fine fall of about 20 metres beneath which the trail passes the fall, on a miniscule tributary burn, is seen again on the return journey on the other side of the river. The nature trail is above the first of a series of substantial falls and rapids on the main stream in *Calderwood Glen*. Each of the principal falls is about five metres high and in spate they are impressive for the Rotten Calder is no minor hill stream, but a fully-fledged, fast-flowing river.

The Calderwood Estate is now one of the main suburbs of the New Town, fulfilling in every way the planners' garden city aspirations. It was for long the property of the Maxwells. Calderwood Castle, beside which the most impressive fall occurs, was pulled down as recently as 1952.

It is impossible to do justice either to the natural beauties of

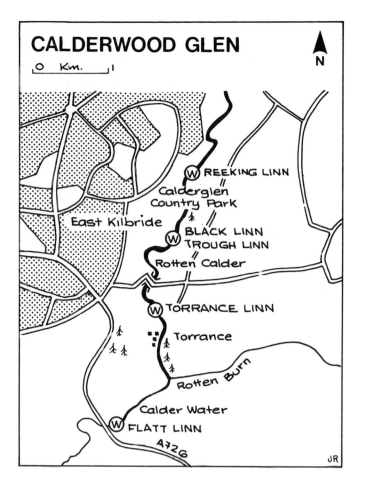

Calderwood in connection with this river, or to the taste and well-directed zeal of its present proprietor, Sir William Maxwell, Bart as displayed in his exertions to make the appear to the best advantage by the assistance of human art. It is sufficient to say that the highest expectations will not be disappointed.

Henry Moncrieff wrote this enthusiastic paeon to his parish in the New Statistical Account, and Calderwood Glen was for long a popular place of popular resort within easy reach of Glasgow. It now has purely local significance which is a pity. No one travelling to or from the Erskine Bridge on the A726 should omit Calderwood Glen. *Flatt Linn (NS 650 515)* is close to the road above Torrance. *Torrance Linn (NS 654 530)* is situated below the nature trail. Next come *Trough Linn (NS 657 539)* and *Black Linn (NS 658 541)* in the heart of the glen. Beneath Craigneth Castle, a ruin in a field reached from the road beneath Newhousemill and Crossbasket and perched dramatically above the rushing river in the sandstone gorge, are two falls the uppermost of which is called *Reeking Linn (NS 660 548)*. Immediately above General's Bridge at Crossbasket there is a final fall. Below the A776 the Rotten Calder occupies a fine, more open, gorge which gives the road a more dramatic aspect as it sweeps towards Blantyre with superb views of the dismantled viaducts of the Blantyre and East Kilbride Railway, their piers standing as monuments to a different age.

Spout of Calibae

NS 547 848

Above Boquhan Glen near Killearn there is a fine mountain fall in the Spout of Calibae. It can be reached by newly-built forest roads with grand views across Strathendrick to the

Highlands. The burn is one of several which drain the impressive north face of the Campsie Fells. There are two well-marked corries with fine headwalls and these give rise to magnificent wet-weather falls on the Balglass Burn and the Clock Burn.

Campsie Glen

NS 610 798

Campsie Glen typifies all that is best and worst in the many attractive glens in the Scottish Lowlands. It has long been a favourite beauty spot and it was one of the first glens to be opened up. There are nine distinct falls on Nineteentimes Burn, the main stream, with a total fall of 40 metres. The highest fall, however, occurs on a tributary, the Aldessan Burn, for *Craigie Linn (NS 609 799)* is perhaps twenty metres high. The Clachan of Campsie is a tiny hamlet north west of Lennoxtown, the centre of which is the site of the old church. The high railings of the churchyard, erected to deter body-snatchers in the eighteenth century, appear to block the way to the glen. The decayed tea rooms suggest that the place has been deserted for the beaches of Spain. Buses still use this place as a terminus, but few people arrive by this route. They now park their cars at the hairpin bend in the Crow Road above the glen. The Estate Office, too, is somewhat forbidding, but the way through is clear enough. In 1825 the then owner of the estate, John MacFarlane, opened it for the enjoyment of the local residents. Considering the obstructive attitudes displayed by some landowners a hundred years and more later, this was a liberal act on MacFarlane's part whose radicalism was to be confirmed some seven years later when he received a petition from the parishioners.

From the first the glen was a popular place of resort, not just for local people, but for folk from Glasgow. In view of the means of transport available in the early nineteenth century this is a testimony to the pulling power of waterfalls at the time. Excursions were the Regency equivalent of watching Rangers or Celtic today. It was this popularity which proved too much for the parishioners. They begged to draw MacFarlane's attention to:

> The advantage which is taken by many, and particularly by persons from Glasgow and other places at a distance, of resorting to your glens on a Sabbath for purposes of mere amusement, by which your parishioner petitioners conceive

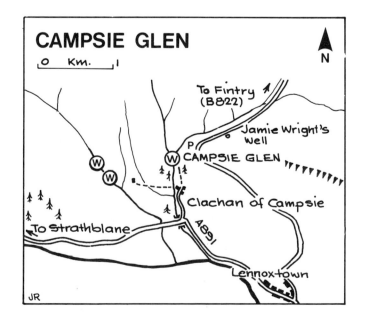

that the holy day is profaned and an example highly prejudicial to the morals of the young and inconsiderate of their neighbourhood is held out. But your petitioners would more especially beg leave to advert to a circumstance resulting from the advantage taken by some of resorting to the glens on a sabbath, which is that such persons are seen, in very many instances, returning to their place of abode in a state of intoxication; that rioting and quarrelling frequently takes place between them on the road, that fields are trampled down, cattle disturbed and the inhabitants of farmhouses and cottages frequently annoyed.

The petition concluded with a request to prohibit all access on the Sabbath so that the citizenry might be 'spared the contagious influence of profane and licentious example'. Only five tradesmen in the Parish did not feel sufficiently self-righteous to sign the petition. To his eternal credit MacFarlane refused the petition considering that, like many such outbursts nowadays, it did not reflect a true picture of the way in which most people behaved, but referred to the conduct of an unruly minority. In reply he stated that he would never dishonour himself or the religion to which he belonged by interfering with the enjoyment of the people who visited the glen.

Judging by the litter which mars the glen today, some visitors have lost nothing in either licentiousness or insobriety in comparison with their forebears. However, on a fine day the narrow wooded entrance to the glen at the foot of the sweeping grass slopes of Cort ma Law, 450 metres above, will distract attention from such unsightliness. Except in high spate the burn is friendly and the first fall *Lady's Linn (NS 610 798)* is soon seen on the left just beyond the site of the old bleachworks. It is no doubt named from its modest and charming character, or perhaps it was named after the wife of the Rev John Collins, murdered in 1848 and buried in the Kirkyard. His murderer, the laird of Balglass, coveted the Minister's wife and is said to have murdered her husband and robbed him of his watch to make it look as if he had been done for by a highwayman. He married the widow, and it was not until a number of years later that his new wife discovered him with the watch and found him out.

The next fall is *Jaws or Jane's Linn*. Immediately above this is *Craigie Linn* which has an unsupported drop of sixteen metres. To see this fall properly it is necessary to cross the stream, difficult in wet weather and dangerous in spate. In former times there was a footbridge at this point. Aldessan Burn is a relatively insubstantial tributary and it is only in flood that the fall and the succession of smaller falls above it can be seen to real advantage. The path up the left bank of the Glazert which we are following becomes rockier at the entrance to the gorge and there is a nameless fall of about five metres under the steep walls of the glen. The falls are formed by a number of complex geological factors which are admirably dealt with in the excursion guide *Geology of the Glasgow District*' edited by Brian Bluck (1973). Ahead the path appears to come to a halt at the face of a ten metre rock wall. *Darling Linn* can just be seen from this point. The fall is tucked away in a corner where a small branch joins the main stream. This fall is also about five metres high and was best seen from another footbridge, no longer extant. The rock wall is easily surmounted by natural and cut steps called Jacob's Ladder. This abrupt change from the deeply entrenched gorge to the V-shaped upland valley of the Nineteentimes Burn, the name given to the Glazert beyond this point, illustrates perfectly what the geomorphologists call a nick point. Below it the river is busy cutting back a deep gorge in an existing valley. Its power to cut back has resulted from a change in sea level which is now lower than it was when the original valley was formed.

The more open valley does not, however, mark the end of the falls – the best is yet to come. Round the corner is *Muckle Alicompen*, a substantial fall on the more open burn of about five metres. Beyond this is *Wee Alicompen*, the Niagara of Campsie Glen. It is a horse shoe shaped fall, and at most states of the river it is possible to walk behind a curtain of water which tumbles into a deep pool. The two falls are of about the same height and it is the friendlier aspect of the upper fall which probably gave rise to the soubriquet 'wee'. It is generally possible to cross the burn above Wee Alicompen to get the best view of the ten metre cascade above it. There is still more open country beyond and it is usual to follow the true right bank of the Nineteentimes Burn to the charming *Sheep Linn*, the last substantial linn on the burn. It is said that the burn got its curious name from the number of crossings between Campsie and Campsie Muir Toll. The burn can be conveniently crossed again at an intake below Jamie Wright's Well on the Crow Road (B822). The road is dangerous and walkers are advised to follow the old road above.

Campsie Glen is the outstanding attraction in these hills. It is readily accessible, and perhaps overtaxed. It is a good example of a place which was more cared about in Victorian times than it is today. It lacks the spectacular sense of high places which can be had in the Ochils, but it has undeniable charm.

Carron Glen
NS 756843

The little river which gives its name to the cradle of the Industrial Revolution in Scotland, the Carron Iron Works, rises in the Lennox Hills and follows a course of thirty-two kilometres to the Forth estuary. Its most notable feature is the Carron Valley Reservoir, one of the largest in Central Scotland, which now occupies the upper part of its basin, but below this, and above the little industrial towns of the estuary, is Carron Glen where the river leaps and bounds, tumbles over falls and rushes through narrows on its way to the sea. Nigel Tranter calls it phenomenal. *Auchenlillylinn Spout* is the uppermost fall which was transformed in 1801 by Robert Hill of Edinburgh. A rustic cottage was built on the margin of the deep fissure through which the waters of the Carron flow. 'The river, swollen by rains rushing forward, roaring, presented a magnificent spectacle from the dining room window.' Thus Hill must have felt well-pleased with his improvements. However, the New Statistical Account goes on to relate how, on one occasion, the stream 'struck the dining room window with its surge and, increasing in strength, burst through the window and, rushing into the kitchen, and cellar, made a new cataract over the rock adjoining the spout into the river'. One suspects that Hill may have found this a little close for comfort, although the writer does not tell us where Hill was at the time. Perhaps he was in Edinburgh. However, the Account goes on to illustrate the determination of these early improvers. Far from abandoning the site, Hill arranged for the channel to be excavated, and for the floodwaters to be led away through a culvert, facilitating access to the river through his policies. The remains of the cottage can still be seen and, although the reservoir prevents the river from displaying such a rate of discharge nowadays, the linn is still well worth visiting.

Below Auchenlillylinn Spout there are two other notable sites. The other marked waterfall is a little way downstream at *Tamarree Linn (NS 773 846)*. *The Lady's Leap*, immortalised in Home's *Douglas*, is near Denny.

This melodrama was very popular indeed from the middle of the eighteenth century until the middle of the nineteenth. Its heroine commits suicide at the climax of the play. The part has been played by famous actresses one of the first of whom was Sarah Siddons and one of the most recent Sybil Thorndike.

> She ran, she flew like lightening up the hill,
> Nor halted till the precipice she gained,
> Beneath whose low'ring top the river falls
> Ingulph'd in rifted rocks: thither she came,
> As fearless as the eagle lights upon it,
> And headlong down. . . .

Falls of Cart The Hammills) *NS 485 636*

In Paisley the Cart tumbles attractively over some huge rocks called the Hammills to form attractive waterfalls. The old mill there is now converted into a restaurant where good views of the Hammills may be had. John Wilson, a lifelong waterfall enthusiast, better known as Christopher North was bred here, as was Alexander Wilson whose poetry also reflects a love of waterfalls.

Above the Doune Motor Museum at Burn o'Cambus is a private mountain road which leads eventually to the pleasingly-named farm of Calziebohalzie. Beside the road is the Annet Burn which tumbles into the Teith in a series of cascades, the prettiest of which is called Cauldron Linn, about four metres in height.

Caldron Linn *NS 332 707*

This is a low fall of the apron type on the Gryfe in Renfrewshire. In the policies of the Duchal Estate there is a kenspeckle double fall of about four metres on the Gryfe near a notable motte.

Caulfield's Bridge Falls *NS 347 969*

These Loch-Lomondside falls are above the bridge on the old military road from Dumbarton to Inveraray which still stands beside the busy A82. They are hidden in a corner and may be easily missed, but they are well-worth seeking out as a wild mountain burn tumbles some 40 metres in a succession of helter-skelter falls. Caulfield, the successor to General Wade, built the road after the '45.

Eas Lochan a' Chroin *NN 622 155*

Fine mountain waterfall on a headwater of the Keltie under Stuc a'Chroin.

The Falls of Clyde

In spite of the many attractive falls already described in the Clyde Basin, the Falls of Clyde still occupy pride of place as the most considerable of all. They were, in flood, among the most substantial falls in Northern Europe and without parallel in Britain. Cauldron Snout and High Force in Teesdale approach them in majesty – for majesty was the word which Coleridge insisted should be applied to them – but the Falls of Clyde are the greatest falls on any main stream in the land. The Clyde Valley Electrical Supply Company harnessed the falls in 1926 and, since then, they have been much attenuated in ordinary weather except when, on four or six occasions a year, the South of Scotland Electricity Board arrange spates. These spates coincide with local holidays and are advertised in the press: on these occasions, the Falls of Clyde should not be missed. In wet

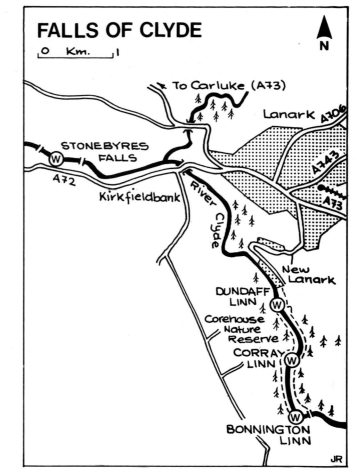

weather far more water than is required comes down the river in any case and, at these times, the falls can be seen in what approximates to their original state as well.

> Where ancient Corehouse hangs above the stream
> And far beneath the tumbling surges gleam,
> Engulphed in crags, the fretting river raves
> Chafed into foam resound his tortured waves.
> With giddy heads we view the dreadful deep
> And cattle snort and tremble at the steep,
> Where down at once the foaming waters pour
> And tottering rocks repel the deafening roar.
> Viewed from below, it seems from heaven they fell;
> Seen from above they seem to sink in hell;
> But when the deluge pours from every hill
> The Clyde's wide bed ten thousand torrents fill
> His rage the murmuring mountain streams augment
> Redoubled rage in rocks so closely pent.
> Then shattered woods with ragged roots uptorn
> And herds and harvests down the waves are borne
> Huge stones heaved upwards through the boiling deep
> And rocks enormous thundering down the steep
> In swift descent, fixed rocks encountering, roar,
> Crash, as from slings discharged , and shake the shore.

Thus John Wilson, the eighteenth century Lesmahagow poet, epitomises the Falls of Clyde, and, of all literary visitors to the falls, none have done it better. Smollett, Burns, the Wordsworths, Southey and Scott all knew the falls well. Gray, who has more claim than most to have led the way in establishing a taste for the countryside in the eighteenth century, considered the falls worthy of a Poussin and countless artists have made them the subject of pictures.

Turner is the most famous. His watercolour of Cora Linn derives from his Scottish Tour of 1801 and is not topographically accurate. In the foreground, giving scale to the dramatic scene, are a number of water-nymphs and the title of the picture refers to Akenside's poem 'Hymn to the Naiads'. Turner made a number of drawings of the fall culminating in that engraved in 1809 by Charles Turner. These works are all representational but at the end of his career Turner executed a fine oil painting of the Fall of Clyde (1835-40) which is impressionist in style.

The Falls also feature in William Combe's 'Doctor Prosody' a sequel to his much better-known 'Doctor Syntax' mocking the taste for the 'picturesque' in visitors. The good Doctor decides to make a sketch of the Falls of Clyde:

Now Prosody approaches near
The brink, with signs of awe and fear,
Though followed by his trusty suite,
Whom fear had also rendered mute;
Our Sage's picturesque taste,
However, banished from his breast
All thoughts of fear; with pencil ready,
He gan' to sketch with fingers steady;
Till losing all his wonted caution,
He tumbled from his horrid station;
His nether part the stream embraced,
The spray had reached his middle waist;
He hung like dangling pack of wool,
Above the horrid boiling pool.

One of his friends clung on to him and he was hauled back on to the bank. His other friend, Factobend, let the Doctor's coat tails slip from his grasp. In the Doctor's view this was deliberate and they fall out.

Henceforth thy friendship and thy courage
I hold not worth a mess of porridge

Other artists associated with the Falls of Clyde include Paul Sandby, the eighteenth century topographer, Joseph Farington (1747-1821), who first inspired Turner to visit the falls and Jacob More (1740-93) who painted well-known pictures of all three falls.

Bonnington Linn   NS 883405

The uppermost fall, *Bonnington Linn* (NS 883 405), should be visited first. The reason why the falls occur is complicated. It is almost certain that the Clyde once followed a more northerly course from above Hyndford Bridge. The Douglas was then a much longer river, joining the Clyde below Lanark. Where the post-glacial Clyde joined the course of the Douglas, a waterall was formed which has receded to form the gorge below Bonnington Linn. The fall thus formed is *Bonnington Linn*. Cora Linn is a similar fall formed at the point where the post-glacial Clyde joined its former course. Below Hyndford Bridge the Clyde flows gently between farmers' fields and turns abruptly to fall over the linn. The intake for the Power Station occurs here and, at low water, a good deal of bed rock is to be seen. The Clyde occupies a corner of the once impressive fall. In spate, Bonnington Linn is the widest of the Falls of Clyde and the wall of water is divided into two by a rocky island joined to the true right (east) bank by a bridge. The fall is about ten metres high.

Below Bonnington Linn is an impressive gorge, richly wooded. The Clyde sweeps quickly along, being confined at one point to a channel five metres wide, Wallace's Leap. The walls of this Old Red Sandstone gorge are 20 to 30 metres in height and a cave, difficult of access, is said to be the place where Wallace hid after his first serious encounter with the English. The woods on the banks are partly in the ownership of the Forestry Commission. The true left bank of the gorge is within the Corehouse Nature Reserve of the Scottish Wildlife Trust, and it is by this way that you will probably come if you wish to see Bonnington Linn before Cora Linn.

Cora Linn

is about a kilometre below Bonnington Linn. The river falls in three steps forming a rushing cascade; first there is a low fall, then, almost immediately, a second; next there is a slope beside which the spectator can stand in the midst of the linn, and, after thirty metres, the final fall. The whole cascade is set in a superb rock amphitheatre clothed with trees and ferns and, beside it at the top of a cliff, almost tumbling into the rushing water, Cora Castle:

Lord of the Vale! Astounding flood
The dullest leaf in this thick wood
Quakes – conscious of thy power:
The caves reply with hollow moan
And vibrates to its central stone
Yon time-cemented tower.

This was Wordsworth's apostrophe to Cora Linn. Dorothy Wordsworth tells of her feelings in her *Journal*. She was 'much affected by the first view' and goes on, 'The majesty and strength of the water, for I had never before seen so large a cataract, struck me with astonishment which died, giving place to more delightful feelings.' The place was first improved as long ago as 1708 when a pavilion with artfully-placed mirrors, which made it appear as if the water was falling onto the spectator, was first erected by Sir James Carmichael, then of Bonnington. The fall was rightly regarded as one of the wonders of Europe. Further improvements were made in 1829 when Lady Ross of Corehouse built the rustic staircase leading down to the falls.

Cora Castle, above the falls, is a ruined keep. The building is dangerous and, even if the roar of the falls has not succeeded in dislodging it, the depredations of time have led to its decay. Happily, it is not fenced off and a simple warning notice warns of the folly of exploration. It is associated with a princess of bygone days whose horse, startled by the noise of the mighty waterfall, leaped with its mistress into the abyss. She gives her name too to Corehouse, a fine house away from the river in the grounds of which this magnificent waterfall lies. By long tradition, the owners of the house have shared their good fortune with the public.

Dundaff Linn   NS 881422

The gorge below Cora Linn is even more impressive than that above it, its walls towering to 40 metres. Cora Linn is twenty five metres high. The third of the four Falls of Clyde, *Dundaff Linn* (NS 881 422) occurs at the foot of the gorge. It is a mere stripling, a broad, low fall of three metres. Beside it is a curious rock called Wallace's Chair:

Each rugged rock proclaims great Wallace fame
Each cavern wild is honoured with his name
Here, in repose, was stretched his mighty form
And there he sheltered from the night and storm.

Dundaff Linn makes a charming companion for its three greater brothers, but in one respect it exceeds them all in international reputation, for it was below Dundaff Linn that

David Dale and Richard Arkwright established New Lanark, for long the largest cotton mills in Scotland and the scene, between 1800 and 1824, of Robert Owen's famous co-operative. The first mill was built in 1785 where the fall provided by Dundaff Linn could drive Arkwright's machinery. Notable visitors to the mills in Owen's time included Southey who was critical of the co-operative but who greatly admired Owen, and the future Csar, Nicholas II, who, as Neil Munro observed in his book about the Clyde was studying ideals from which Russia seems to be even yet remote. The Grand Duke stayed at Braxfield, Owen's home, which was also where the hanging judge lived who was the model for Stevenson's *Weir of Hermiston*.

Stonebyres Linn   NS 852 441

Six kilometres below Bonnington Linn, reached from the A72. Dorothy Wordsworth considered it superior to Cora Linn, and other discriminating visitors since have endorsed her view although the fall lacks the romantic associations of the upper cascade. The river falls in three steps, more imposing than Cora Linn because they follow immediately upon one another. The apparent force of falling water that Stonebyres Linn demonstrates is thus much greater. The fall is caused by the belt of conglomerate in the red sandstone, relatively harder than the surrounding rock. In spate Stonebyres forms a barrier of falling water twenty four metres high. Below it is a deep salmon pool where, when the river is unpolluted, the restless fish must circle and fret, perhaps because none can ascend the river by this fall. Yet there are salmon in the upper Clyde and they have been seen jumping Dundaff Linn. The explanation is that the Clyde is linked with the North Sea through the Biggar Gap.

There was considerable lamentation when the Falls of Clyde were chosen as the site of the first major hydro-electric scheme in Scotland, but this was inevitable. Indeed the Falls provide the only site in Great Britain where hydro-electric power can be generated on any scale without storage. The works are now, fifty years after their completion, of some historical interest and do not obtrude. The falls drain a basin of 932 square kilometres where there is a comparatively low rainfall of 1092 millimetres. Bonnington Linn has a head of 57.5 metres.

The Falls of Clyde were visited long before Livingstone, who must have frequented these falls, visited the Victoria Falls and before the great waterfalls of the world were widely known. At that time they were looked upon as true giants. In 1926/27 the falls were undoubtedly diminished by the hydro-electric scheme. The Victorian and Edwardian travellers who would assiduously visit the falls were replaced by generations of tourists less concerned with what was, after all, a rather isolated attraction when there were many more accessible places supposedly richer in scenery than Lanarkshire.

The Falls are the scene of a new co-operative venture, the restoration by a Trust of the village of New Lanark. The new Clyde Walkway follows the right bank of the river. Lanark itself, dismissed by some writers as a dull place, is a fine market town, worth visiting, and there is a network of admirable footpaths and bridle roads nearby. Unless there has been exceptionally dry weather it is still possible to get some sense of the atmosphere of the falls which so delighted and amazed early visitors. 'No river ever found fairer way to the ocean' than the Clyde.

Clyde's Mill Fall   NS 812 489

After the Falls of Clyde the river flows through a contrasted district of pastoral charm called the Trough of Clyde. Southey was impressed with it and he asserted that no part of England, the Lake District alone excepted, was more lovely than the Clyde a few miles from Glasgow. Grand country houses like Maudslie Castle and Milton Lockhart are built across the river from the road between Hamilton and Lanark and they are connected to it by imposing bridges. There is no better place to appreciate the distinctive landscape of the Trough of Clyde than from the bridge to Milton Lockhart, a mid-nineteenth century imitation by the architect, Burn, of the old Bothwell Brig. Clyde's Mill Fall is where the broad river sweeps over broken rocks in a fine rapid.

Cochno Fall   NS 487 742

The Greenside Reservoir in the Kilpatrick Hills is drained by the Loch Humphrey Burn which, in spate, hurls itself with considerable force into a large pool from a height of about ten metres.

Corrie Spout   NS 676 789

High up on the southern face of the Campsies below the West Corrie Reservoir.

Craigie Linn see Campsie Glen

Craigie Linn   NS 474 605

Paisley, the *Glasgow Herald* has observed, has poets the way other people have mice. The best-known of them was Robert Tannahill and his favourite haunt was Gleniffer Braes. He loved the tiny linns there. The best-known falls occur on the Glen Burn, a tributary of the White Cart, where the local authority has established a fine nature trail linking the burn with the braes by the 'Tannahill Way'. Craigie Linn is the best known fall, although it is an insubstantial one, except in spate, but it enhances the park in which it is situated.

Falls of Craigton Burn   NS 517 773

Falls above the old toll bridge on the Stockiemuir Road in the Kilpatricks.

Darling Linn see Campsie Glen

Devol Glen

This splendid Renfrewshire glen is above Port Glasgow on the edge of Greenock. It commands magnificent views of the Firth of Clyde and the hills above Loch Lomond. At its head is a steep rock, Wallace's Loup, where the patriot is said to have jumped on horseback. Under it are two falls, comparable with many better-known, on an insubstantial stream. The lower, Ladies Linn, is some six metres high. The upper fall makes a splendid leap of thirty metres.

Downie's Loup   NS 706 931

This fall stands out above the villages of Gargunnock. The Gargunnock Burn tumbles down from the plateau in a series of cascades which, after rain, can be very impressive. The fall is reached by a track past a sawmill and through a pinewood. Downie's Loup. A 12 metre fall, is hidden from below.

Dualt Spout   NS 501 892

The Dualt Burn makes an aggressive leap of 20 metres on red sandstone in the old policies above Killearn House.

Eas Dubh   NN 552 033

Mountain fall in the Menteith Hills above Loch Drunkie.

Easan Dubh   NN 343 067

A fine hanging waterfall above Cailness on Loch Lomond.

Dubh Eas   NN 317 213

Dubh Eas is the site of the most considerable engineering work on the West Highland Line, the Dubh Eas Viaduct, a trussed viaduct 40 metres above the burn. It was one of the first structures to be built of concrete, but like many such early works it is disguised to look as if it were stone. There are two falls on the main stream, but those seen from the railway are on a tributary. It may be that the Dubh Eas got its name, the black fall, from the ribbon fall high up on the mountainside in Coire Ordrin which crosses a band of black rock.

Sput Dubh (Loch Ard)   NN 482 024

Above Drumlean at the foot of Loch Ard a steep ravine drops down from Creag Innish. This is Eas Chaimbeulach. From Drumlean a slate track climbs up beside before crossing it and the Eas Chiambeulach to reach an old quarry. The first burn encountered falls 60 metres in a series of cascades in a diamond-shaped wood. This is Sput Dubh, the black spout.

Sput Dubh (Glen Gyle)   NN 386 140

Mountain fall at the head of Loch Katrine above the farmhouse where in 1671 Rob Roy MacGregor was born. It can be reached either by the long road on the north bank of the loch along which a postbus runs, or from Stronachlacher. It is unaffected by the waterworks, but is a wet-weather fall.

Dundaff Linn see Falls of Clyde

Eaglesham Linn   NS 573 538

On the White Cart near Eaglesham House.

Earlsburn Falls   NS 712 874

Fine moorland falls, four metres high, on the back road from Stirling to Fintry. They occur at a road bridge which makes a pleasant stopping place under Earl's Hill.

Enoch's Linn   NS 579 498

In moorlands on a headstream of the Cart.

Eas an Eoin   NN 601 150

Mountain fall under Ben Each on the pass between Loch Lubnaig and Loch Earn.

Eas Eonan   NN 348 222

In the upper part of Glen Falloch the Eas Eonan joins the Falloch near Derrydarroch. There is a fine waterslide hidden in a corner which is 15 metres high.

Fairy Fall   NS 474 603

Tiny fall near Witch's Corner above Craigie Linn near Paisley.

Falls of Falloch   NN 338 208

The river Falloch tumbles down an attractive defile at the head of Loch Lomond. It rises between Ben a'Chroin and Cruach Ardrain above Crianlarich and the upper part of its course is across open moorland where there are a few remnants of the ancient Caledonian Pine Forest. The Glenfalloch estate became the property of Colin Campbell of Glen Orchy in the reign of James IV and the lower part of the glen is densely wooded. The trees were probably planted by Colin's son, Black Duncan of the Cowl, who was one of the first highland lairds to pay attention to the improvement of his estate.

Glen Falloch has been celebrated by many writers of whom Dorothy Wordsworth is perhaps the most famous. She gives a memorable account of her walk from the head of Loch Lomond to Glen Gyle, the birthplace of Rob Roy MacGregor, with her brother, William, and Coleridge:

> The most easy rising, for a short way at first, was near a naked rivulet which made a fine cascade in one place. Afterwards the ascent was very laborious being frequently almost perpendicular. Higher up we sat down and heard, as if from the heart of the earth, the sound of torrents ascending out of the long hollow glen. To the eye all was motionless, a perfect stillness. The noise of waters did not appear to come from any particular quarter; it was everywhere, almost, one might say, as if 'exhaled' through the whole surface of the green earth. Glen Falloch, Coleridge has since told me, signifies the hidden vale; but William says that if we were to name it from our recollections of that time we should call it the Vale of Awful Sound.

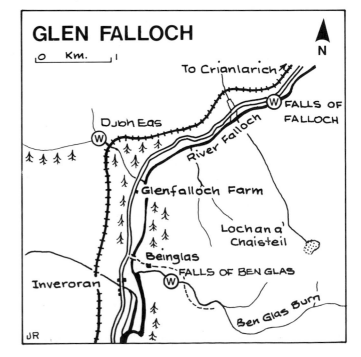

Falls of Leny, *near Callander, a dramatic introduction to the Highlands for the visitor arriving from the south.* PETER DAVENPORT

Falls of Inversnaid. Sir Walter Scott and Gerard Manley Hopkins have contributed to their fame. HAMISH BROWN

Falls of Falloch, Loch Lomond, celebrated by Coleridge and the Wordsworths. DAVID I HARVIE

There have been many changes since the Wordsworth's day, but Glen Falloch remains a valley of highly attractive waterfalls. At the foot of the glen is the Ben Glas Waterfall above Inverarnan, sometimes called the Grey Mare's Tail, or the Grey Fox. It is this cascade that Dorothy Wordsworth refers to at the beginning of the passage. Opposite are the Garabal Falls and the Falls of Arnan. In side glens are Dubh Eas, the Falls of

the Fionn Ghleann and Eas Eonan, but pre-eminently it is wild river Falloch itself which gives rise to the roar of waters.

The valley of the Falloch has always been a significant route between Loch Lomond and Breadalbane. It formed the route for the military road, built after the forty-five, between Dumbarton and Crianlarich. The river was canalised as far as Inverarnan as part of the coach route between Glasgow and Inverness. Passengers were conveyed by steamers into Glen Falloch at one time. In 1894 the West Highland Railway was built through the glen. In the twentieth century the motor traffic has rendered even the improved road one of the most unpleasant to negotiate in the Highlands at the height of summer, and at times it is the sound of articulated lorries which emanates from Glen Falloch nowadays. But it is surprisingly easy to get away from the din. Ben Lui, Ben Oss and Beinn Dubhcraig, considered by many to be the most attractive mountains in the Southern Highlands, stand at the head of quiet glens which branch off Glen Falloch.

Where the road begins to climb the glen it becomes confined beside the river and something of the falls may be seen, but the principal fall is not visible from the road. The hazel, birch, oak and alder woods and the clear waters of the river falling over grey-green mica schists present a fine picture at all seasons, but the falls are best seen in half-spate in golden autumn. Above the principal fall the river slides easily between grassy banks where there is a simple ford. Below this point the Falloch falls 100 metres to Loch Lomond in a succession of narrow gorges, low falls and water-chutes. At the principal fall the water plunges over a rock lip into a basin, the main stream falling ten metres sheer. This is Rob Roy country and the basin is dubbed Rob Roy's Bathtub. A smaller hollow, etched by a lesser arm of the stream in the wall of the basin is called Rob Roy's Soap Dish although it is unlikely that the famous cateran used that commodity when in these parts.

Sydney Tremayne, the Ayrshire poet who was a feature writer for the *Sun* and the *Daily Mirror*, echoes Wordsworth in his poem 'The Falls of Falloch':

> This white explosion of water plunges down
> With the deep-voiced rush of sound that shakes a city.
> A fine cold smoke drifts across dripping stone
> And wet black walls of rock shut in the scene.
>
> Now thought hangs sheer on a precipice of beauty
> Lifting with leaping water out from the rock.
> A gasp of time, flung clear in a weight of falling,
> Bursts like a bud above the deep pool's black
> Parted and curled back under by the shock
> Where light's bright spark dives to the dark's controlling.
>
> But the brilliance is not extinguished. The heart leaps up,
> The heart of the fall leaps up, an eternal explosion,
> Force without spending, form without fetter of shape.
> And at the pool's edge wavelets scarcely lap
> Where drifted spume clings with a soft adhesion.

Above this succession of falls there is another fall at a little distance. It is not above four metres high, but here the river narrows to such an extent that a horseman could leap across with ease. The fall is called Leum-an-t-Searrai the colt's leap. From it one may see the enormous power of the Falloch, and observe the way in which potholes are made in the river bed by the grinding action of boulders. Rob Roy's Bathtub is the product of the same kind of erosion.

The reasons why the Falls of Falloch occur are complicated. They almost certainly owe their origin to the occurrence of porphyritic dykes, walls of relatively hard rock, in the river bed. It is also probable that the gorge was deepened by meltwaters when the glaciers which used to occupy the Highlands retreated. Indeed, at one time the river probably flowed in the opposite direction, towards the Tay, and its course may be steep because it is so recent in geological terms.

At the Lower Falls of Falloch, the open falls where the glen is narrowest, the river drains a basin of some 56 square kilometres. It is an area of moorland underlain by impervious rocks with a heavy rainfall of between 2,000 and 2,500 millimetres annually. The discharge of the river Falloch thus compares with that of rivers with larger catchment areas, being almost as much as that of the Isla at Reekie Linn, nearly three times greater. The Falloch has a 'flashy' regime and work has been done to show that, in the West Highlands, in dry weather a burn may have one tenth of the water in it which it has in average conditions and that, when the ground is saturated, its discharge can rise to ten times the average (one hundred times greater than in dry conditions). These conditions can occur in even the driest months which, for the Falloch, are the six months from February until July. When the Falloch is in spate the narrow gorge above the falls fills up dramatically and the river becomes dangerous.

> The Glen narrowing, the river becoming more and more wild and rocky, running and roaming among alders and coppice woods, the hills landlocking the glen with less than half a mile interspace, the hills not very high, but much broken, their wildness a ragged wildness, I went into a field to my right and visited a noble waterfall. The trees are old and army, one on each side. The fall is one great apron with an oval pool at the bottom, but above it you look through a rocky stream with trees and bushes and the fall itself is marked by two great cauldrons delved out in the black rock down which it falls.

Coleridge was not always impressed by the scenery in Scotland but Glen Falloch clearly left a lasting impression on him.

It was at the Falls of Falloch that Bill Murray, the distinguished Scottish mountaineer, nearly lost his life. He tells the story in *Mountaineering in Scotland* (1962):

> On our way home we visited the Falls of Falloch, which were in full spate and a sight worth seeing. Above the topmost fall was a long narrow gorge through which the congested waters dashed foaming to leap with a thunderous roar into a rock cauldron. At one point the gorge was narrow enough to challenge one's sporting instinct. Was a leap possible? We measured it up. It would have to be a standing jump from spray-drenched rock. . . .
>
> One by one we jumped safely. The gut was narrower than it looked. We had been too impressed with the fury of the water. Thus I was just a trifle less careful in making the return jump; my foot slipped off the wet rock and down I went into the gorge.

He was swept over the falls and found it impossible to escape from the whirlpool at their foot. Nearing exhaustion he was finally carried out of the cauldron by an undercurrent.

An object-lesson for visitors to waterfalls.

Waterfall of the Little Fawn   *NN 522 016*

> How pleasing to my pensive mind
> The memory of thy bold cascade
> Thy green woods waving in the wind
> And streams in every vocal glade

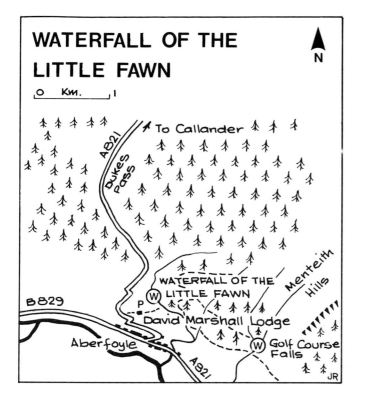

WATERFALL OF THE LITTLE FAWN

N

O KM. 1

To Callander

A821

Dukes Pass

WATERFALL OF THE LITTLE FAWN

Menteith Hills

P W

David Marshall Lodge

B829

Aberfoyle

A821

W Golf Course Falls

JR

Waterfall of the Little Fawn, Aberfoyle. Has also been known as the Grey Mare's Tail and MacGregor's Leap. Now reached by a short forest trail frequented by thousands of people annually, but the quiet gorge above the fall is little visited. LOUIS STOTT

William Richardson (1743-1814) lived in Aberfoyle and his poem 'Farewell to Aberfoyle' makes mention of this fall. The green woods he refers to were not those of the Forestry Commission, but otherwise things are probably much as they were. If the Falls of Ledard epitomise nineteenth century attitudes to waterfalls, the Waterfall of the Little Fawn epitomises those of the twentieth. Its name was imparted by the Forestry Commission. Locally it is known as the Grey Mare's Tail and one must be grateful to the Commission for reducing the number of falls called by this name. Between the wars the fall was known as MacGregor's Leap.

The Waterfall of the Little Fawn is close to the spectacularly-sited David Marshall Lodge on the Duke's Pass, the A821, above Aberfoyle. The Allt a'Mhangan, the burn from which the fall gets its name, is the brawling stream which runs beside the pass and turns away from it just before the descent into Aberfoyle begins. It forms several attractive cascades including an upper fall of about ten metres before it enters a wood of blackthorn, hazel, birch and willow before falling in an abrupt gorge, long known to botanists for its rich flora of mosses and liverworts. The burn turns a corner, Camadh Laidir, before tumbling over a broken 17-metre fall beneath the Lodge. It is reached by a much frequented forest trail from the information centre.

Across the river there is a footpath which leads to the head of the falls and connects with a network of forest paths accessible by cycle and on foot. A particularly attractive walk leads along the foot of the Menteith Hills above the outskirts of Aberfoyle. Above the golf course a path leads up the hill beside a little burn on which are *Golf Course Falls (NN 535 010)*. There are three or four pretty cascades. The path follows the burn through open woodland and eventually joins a forest road leading back to MacGregor's Leap. There are splendid views across the valley of the Forth from this elevated promenade.

Eas Fiadaich

NN 660 088

Mountain fall near Bracklinn on the Allt Ruith an Eas. The name means the fall of the deer.

Eas Fidhian see Eas Sneggan

Fin Glen

Fin glen is overshadowed in the popular imagination by the Spout of Ballagan and Campsie Glen which it lies between, but this pleasing, secluded valley should not be missed on that account. Its gathering grounds are in the heart of the Campsies under Earl's Seat, the highest point, and from Strathkelvin it has the appearance of a hidden valley concealing itself beside the open and more-inviting defile of Campsie Glen. For the discriminating hill-walker it provides a route full of interest. A rough track leads from the Clachan of Campsie to the open farmland above the well-wooded glen. The two principal falls are *Black Spout (NS 601 796)* and *White Spout (NS 599 799)*. Both are more considerable than those of Campsie Glen but are more open and lack the intimate charm of the falls in that glen. Two further falls are to be found in the densely wooded dell further up. It is possible to visit these from the same side of the burn but the better-defined track from Glenside provides an easier approach.

Loup of Fintry. When the river is full the fall is as broad as it is high.
HAMISH BROWN

Loup of Fintry

NS 661 861

Near the B818, the hill-road from Fintry to the Carron Valley, are some oddly-shaped boulders called the Gowk Stanes and beneath them is probably the finest waterfall in the old county of Stirlingshire, the Loup of Fintry. A broken-off noticeboard, either a welcome or an admonition, but no longer legible, indicates the start of a rough path to the breast of a hill where the pedestrian is opposite a dramatic 30-metre fall which tumbles towards him before the river turns away into a gorge at his feet. When the river is full the fall is as broad as it is high, but the water in the river is sometimes restricted because the Endrick has been diverted into the Carron Reservoir. However, there is no finer belvedere from which to view a waterfall in this part of the world.

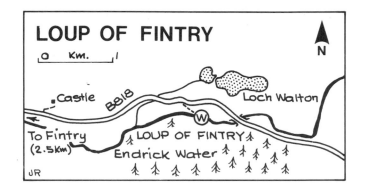

Falls of Fionn Ghleann
NN 327 222

The most attractive way from Glen Falloch to the three peaks of Ben Lui, Ben Oss and Beinn Dubhcraig is by the Fionn Ghleann. The going is wet at first, but there is a prominent rock step not far up the glen where twin falls make a picturesque mountain scene.

Flatt Linn see Calderwood Glen

Falls of Fruin
NS 306 865

The Fruin Water tumbles over a succession of rocks on the edge, the true geological edge, of the Highlands just below St Bride's Chapel at the entrance to the glen. The falls, a favourite bathing place, begin on Dalradian Schists and end on Red Sandstone. They are the subject of a splendid painting in the National Gallery of Scotland by John Milne Donald (1817-66).

Garabal Fall
NN 309 167

Garabal Hill, a site of special scientific interest, is a classic site for geologists, demonstrating, on a small scale, all the features of the great granite intrusions of the highlands. On the edge of it is the Garbh-uisge, the rough water, which falls into the trough occupied by Loch Lomond by a series of fine waterfalls, the highest of which is a fall of 20 metres, just above the West Highland line.

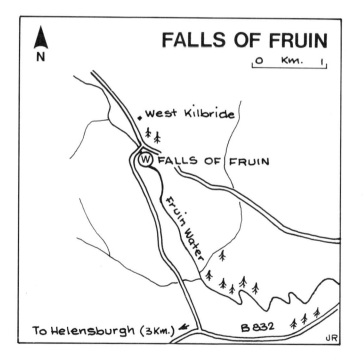

Garrat's Linn see Calder Glen

Pot of Gartness
NS 501 867

The River Endrick has great scientific interest. At its mouth is the Loch Lomond Nature Reserve where the Endrick meanders across its flood plain, famed for wintering wildfowl and passage migrants. The river has been the subject of exhaustive biological studies and there is even a book about the leaping behaviour of the salmon and trout at the Pot of Gartness. The

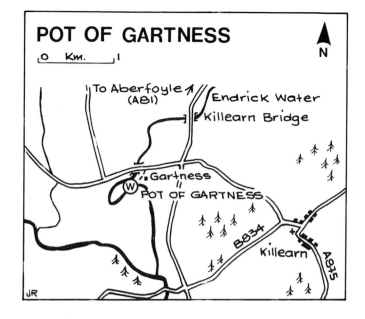

Buchanans, the Grahams and the Napiers who lived in Strathendrick and Strathblane, delighted in the rolling countryside beside the river at the foot of the Lennox Hills.

It should not be thought that these gentle valleys will have few waterfalls in comparison with the higher slopes of Ben Lomond and the Arrochar Alps. In fact the geology of this country is ideally suited to the development of falls. The foreland between Loch Lomond and the Lennox Hills consists of Old Red Sandstone while the hills themselves are made up of a succession of lavas and ashes, sandstones and mudstones, rocks of different hardnesses on which a succession of fine falls are developed. Because the hills are close to the cities of the central belt the lochans in them have been enlarged and new lochs have been built to supply water for industry and for domestic use. Nineteenth century writers thought that the abstraction of water from the Endrick had diminished the glory of the Loup of Fintry, but it is still impressive, except after drought.

The first fall on the Endrick is the renowned salmon leap, the *Pot of Gartness (NS 501 867)*. Only three metres high, it is superbly situated in the incised gorge of the river below the site of Gartness Castle. John Napier, who died in 1617, lived there. He was the inventor of logarithms, the decimal point, a primitive tank and a submarine. The Castle has long since disappeared, but stone from it was used in the construction of Gartness Mill which still clings to the banks of the river. This magnificent river fall is the subject of a poem by Maurice Lindsay:

> All the released collusion of wide rains
> twisted from ragged slopes in channelled rills
> plunges its whiteness, lunges towards the plains.
> Seawards the river spreads and over-fills,
> swirling against the sandy fringe of fields
> browed with loose meadow-grass and clutching sorrel
> as soil gives up its mould, cracks, crumbles, yields
> and clouds itself beneath some sucking whorl.

> In broad full-breasted surge the river rides
> tearing the earth-veined roots that bind its bed
> till boulders bend and fold its narrow sides,
> spume like an ocean's rears its spitting head,
> plummets the precipice and pounds the pool
> beneath, a boil of salmon pink with spawn,

a seethe of breathlessness, a steam of cool
precipitant force towards which these fish were drawn.

The fall lies at the junction of the Upper and Lower Old Red
Sandstone. It is reached from the bridge by a farm road which
leads to a flight of steps beside the fall.

Gilmour's Linn   NS 739 924

Six metre fall at the head of Touch Glen, the wooded beauty
spot near Stirling.

The Falls of Glenfinglas   NN 538 075

Above Brig o' Turk Glenfinglas has been transformed by
waterworks. The little river Turk still rushes down a fine gorge
where there are four low falls, the highest of which is four
metres. In spate the nineteenth century atmosphere of the
place may be recaptured, but the gorge is dominated by the
spectacular dam, 40 metres high, a little further up. In wet
conditions the spillway is a magnificent spectacle from the
gorge, a wall of white water reaching up to the skyline.
Beneath it there was a fine 20-metre fall which Sir Walter Scott
states was the hiding place of an outlaw who hid under a recess
behind the fall: it was quite inaccessible in spate and he was
sustained by provisions lowered to him from the precipice
above. Scott made the valley the setting of his weird ballad,
Glenfinglas. Calderwood (1921) states that four cascades in
Glenfinglas were impounded.

However, it is probably the falls lower down, still visible today,
which were the scene of one of the most famous seductions of
the nineteenth century. Probably the associations of the place
with Scott led the Ruskins and the brothers Millais to stay at
Brig o'Turk, the scattered village at the entrance to the glen.
John Everett Millais, a protégé of Ruskin's, he was anxious to
persuade the Pre-Raphaelites to be true to nature. Ruskin
made a famous sketch of the country rock. Millais determined
to paint a waterfall which would be the background to a
portrait of Ruskin and would be comparable with Turner's
treatment of waterfalls in the Alps and in Scotland. The picture
and the difficulty of its execution, the waterfalls and, above all,
the blossoming romance between John Everett Millais and
Effie Ruskin dominate the letters which the three wrote to
their family and friends in the late summer of 1853. At the
beginning of the holiday Millais was an admirer of Effie and
worshipped Ruskin; by the end of it he was complaining of
Ruskin and was hopelessly in love with Effie. When Effie left
Ruskin and married Millais the scandal which broke was the
greatest since Byron's day.

The portrait was abandoned in 1853 and finished in the
following year. Ruskin considered it very fine and it is one of
Millais' most famous works. Another picture 'The Waterfall'
which shows Effie sitting beside another spot on the Turk was
completed during the holiday. The atmosphere of the School-
teacher's house is captured in this letter from Millais to
Holman Hunt. It refers to his brother, William, and the
Ruskins:

> The last four days we have had incessant rain, swelling the
> streams to torrents. This afternoon we all walked to see
> some of the principal waterfalls which in colour resemble
> stout. The roads are deeper in water than the Wandle so we
> were walking ankle deep. The dreariness of mountainous
> country in wet weather is beyond everything. I have
> employed myself painting little studies of Mrs Ruskin whilst
> poor William has given way to whisky and execration . . . .
> Having the acquaintance of Mrs Ruskin is a blessing. Her
> husband is a good fellow, but not of our kind, his soul is

always with the clouds and out of the reach of ordinary
mortals. . . . I have a canvas and a box made in Edinburgh
to paint his picture portrait overlooking a waterfall. I think
it will be fine as it quite suits his character and the
background of the foaming water, rocks and clasping roots
look splendid behind his placid figure.

Gleniffer Linn   NS 435 600

The principal stream draining the Gleniffer Braes towards the
Black Cart is the Allt Patrick, or the Old Patrick Burn. It is
known locally as the Brandy Burn, and its head is the Dusky
Glen where there is a fine ten-metre fall, half-hidden in the
woods. Gleniffer Linn is described by the poet Hugh Mac-
Donald whose memory is celebrated with the monument at 'the
breast of the brae':

> At length we hear the roar of the waterfall, hidden in
> foliage, and half-drowning the song of the redbreast with its
> din. The water is dashed down in one white sheet which has
> a most pleasing effect as it is seen through its green veil of
> overhanging boughs.

Glengoyne Waterfall   NS 531 830

Many whisky distillers claim to take their water from falls
situated in the hills. The splendid distillery at the foot of
Dumgoyne extends this claim by displaying a waterfall on the
box in which their malt whisky is marketed. It is a fanciful
representation of the unprepossessing little fall in Distillery
Glen, but no matter, it is a fine walk up the brae to the fells
behind.

Falls of Glenkilloch   NS 477 580

This wee glen above the industrialised valley of the Levern
Water is a delight.

> Come my lassie, let us stray
> O'er Glenkilloch's sunny brae
> Blythely spend the gowden day
> 'Mang joys that never weary, O

Thus sang Tannahill and, if you climb up the brae past a
seemingly deserted mill, you are confronted by the falls of
Clyde in miniature, four metres, four metres and six metres in
height.

Falls of Glen Massan   NS 123 863

North of Dunoon is the most attractive glen in Cowal, Glen
Massan. The glen begins among the great trees of Benmore
and the clear waters of the river tumble splendidly beside the
road. Where the road climbs steeply the river flows through a
considerable gorge. There is no complete view of the falls,
which consist of a series of steps. The upper river is a gentle
stream. It falls three metres into a fine pool and then tumbles
into a sequence of potholes which illustrate the way in which
such falls are formed. The water is crystal clear in the
summertime and every detail of the river bed is visible. In
places the sides of two potholes have collapsed; elsewhere
there are natural arches. The brilliant water then falls five
metres down a further staircase. The *Falls of Glen Massan* are
quite the most picturesque river falls in the Clyde basin. It is an
idyllic place. Above these falls in the corrie where the river
rises is *Eas an Laoigh*.

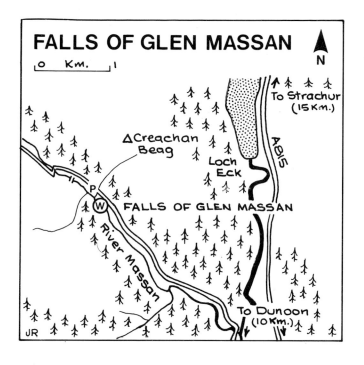

FALLS OF GLEN MASSAN

which runs diagonally across the hillside. From the fields the policies of Edinbarnet, a Victorian Baronial Mansion House are seen. Here the first rhododendron from the Himalaya was introduced by Hooker. Old vaults can be seen in the burial ground between Cochno and Edinbarnet and beyond these is *Lady's Linn (NS 502 742)* a fall in trees of some four metres. The most considerable fall on Jaw Burn is *The Grey Mare's Tail (NS 501 751)*. The burn, tumbling over lava beds, in spate forms an impressive continuous fall of about 3 metres. It is one of a number of falls in the vicinity of Glasgow thought to resemble greater falls. There is a miniature Fall of Foyers at Bennan and two series of little falls considered to resemble the Falls of Clyde. Before the reservoirs are reached there is an upper fall of some six metres. The open moorland beside the Jaw and Cochno Reservoirs is attractive, backed by the imposing little crag of Dunellan and, further away to the north west, Duncolm, the highest of the Kilpatrick Hills. Beneath Dunellan is Carnhowit, one of the lang cairns of the Clyde Group which give evidence of the occupation of the district in the third millenium BC. There are only two standing stones to be seen, but their situation is attractive and they can be reached by a circular walk crossing the causeway between the two reservoirs before revisiting the falls on the descent. The water scheme means that Jaw Burn is best seen after some rain, but the walk itself is always full of interest and the prospect, from Glasgow to the Lower Clyde, is fine.

Pot of Glenny
NN 568 025

Both Glenny and Aberfoyle feature in the military history of the district. They were the scene of a skirmish between the Appin Stewarts and the Earl of Menteith in the 1540s, and a hundred years later of a confrontation between Graham of Duchray and the Earl of Glencairn and General Monk's troops during Glencairn's rebellion. The fall is above the Lake of Menteith and the road to it commands splendid views of the lake with its abbey-on-an-island and of the mosses beneath the Campsie and Fintry Hills. It leads to a secluded valley in the Menteith Hills whence the stream is followed for about a kilometre to the head of a wooded rift about ten metres deep. This is the Pot of Glenny. A superb walk crosses the hills to Loch Vennacher, in the basin of the Teith.

Easan Grumach
NN 528 042

The gloomy waterfalls are in the shaded ravine on the Duke's Pass between Aberfoyle and the Trossachs from which splendid views of Loch Drunkie are obtained.

Eas Gobhain
NN 607 073

The waterworks at the foot of Loch Vennacher have destroyed the atmosphere of Coilintangle Ford, a once famous beauty spot, but the river runs over attractive rapids further down.

Grey Fox see Ben Glas Fall

Grey Mare's Tail see Waterfall of the Little Fawn

Grey Mare's Tail (Clydebank)
NS 501 751

Of all the glens in the Kilpatrick Hills that above Clydebank is perhaps the most frequented and the walk to Cochno Reservoir, Jaw Reservoir and Carnhowit is a favourite. It begins by following a private road in the policies of Cochno House, then a stile is crossed, and the path, a right of way, makes for a wood

The Ha' Glen
NS 543 407

Opposite Duntreath in the Blane Valley, where Edward VII's most discreet mistress lived, is the Ha' Glen where a series of falls is attractively set in a glen in the skirts of the hills.

Falls of Inverard
NN 501 014

In the Pass of Aberfoyle at the foot of Loch Ard. They are hidden in the woods below the stepping stones where the Avon Dhu, the infant Forth some say, creeps out of Little Loch Ard before rushing over two falls among rocks. Above the falls, on the way to the forest, is the site of the mill pond which fed the Corn Mill at the foot of the pass.

Falls of Inverbeg
NS 342 977

At the entrance to Glen Douglas just above the Youth Hostel at Inverbeg.

Falls of Inverlochlarig
NN 438 184

Above the farmhouse at the head of Loch Voil where the MacGregors lived for much of their lives.

Falls of Inversnaid
NN 338 088

> Farewell to the land where the clouds love to rest,
> Like the shroud of the dead, on the mountain's cold breast;
> To the cataract's roar where the eagles reply,
> And the lake her lone bosom expands to the sky
> (Scott; Rob Roy)

Inversnaid is the capital of the Rob Roy MacGregor country, so the falls there have been widely known since Scott's day. Tourists only have to walk a few steps to see them. Gerard Manley Hopkins (1844-89), on his only visit to Scotland – and that lasting for only a couple of days – found the place. Other poems of his draw inspiration from places in England and Wales, but 'Inversnaid' is among his finest. Its famous sprung

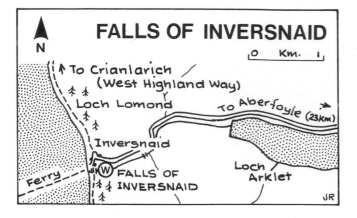

rhythm captures the pace of a falling mountain stream. In a letter, Hopkins describes Loch Lomond in the summer of 1881:

> The day was dark and partly hid the lake, yet it did not altogether disfigure it, but gave a pensive, or solemn beauty which left a lasting impression on me

The poem is dealt with in detail in a beautifully illustrated book, *Landscape and Inscape* by Peter Milward and Raymond Schoder (1975).

> This darksome burn, horseback brown,
> His rollrock highroad roaring down,
> In coop and in comb the fleece of his foam
> Flutes and low to the lake falls home.
>
> A wind-puff bonnet of fawn-froth
> Turns and twindles over the broth
> Of a pool so pitchblack, fell-frowning,
> It rounds and rounds Despair to drowning.
>
> Degged with dew, dappled with dew
> Are the groins of the brae that the brook treads through,
> Wiry heathpacks, flitches of fern,
> And the beadbonny ash that sits over the burn.
>
> What would the world do, once bereft
> Of wet and of wilderness? Let them be left,
> O let them be left, wildness and wet;
> Long live the weeds and the wilderness yet.

It is ironical that in 1907 one of the first hydro electric turbines was installed to provide electricity for the relatively remotely-sited hotel at Inversnaid. Seventy-five years later it became the projected site for a further scheme similar to those at Foyers and Cruachan. A storage reservoir would be built in the corrie between Creag a'Bhocain and Cruinn a' Bheinn, and power from the Grid would be used to pump water from Loch Lomond into it at night.

The Falls of Inversnaid were also radically affected by the Glasgow Waterworks. The Arklet Water on which they lie is now dammed to form Loch Arklet. In times of drought the burn has little water in it! In spate it trips down from the Garrison in splendid fashion.

Several writers, in addition to Scott and Hopkins, have found inspiration in Inversnaid. The American novelist Nathaniel Hawthorn was lavish in his praise of Loch Lomond in his *English Notebooks* (1871):

> Close beside the hotel of Inversnaid is the waterfall; all night, my room being on that side of the house, I heard its voice, and I now ascended beside it to a point where it is crossed by a wooden bridge. There is thence a view, upward and downward, of the most striking descents of the river, as I believe they call it, though it is but a mountain-stream, which tumbles down an irregular and broken staircase in its headlong haste to reach the lake. It is very picturesque, however, with its ribbons of white foam over the precipitous steps, its deep black pools, overhung by black rocks, which reverberate to the rumble of falling water.
>
> I rather think this particular stretch of Loch Lomond, in front of Inversnaid, is the most beautiful lake and mountain view I have ever seen. It is so shut in that you can see nothing beyond, nor would you suspect anything more to exist than this watery vale among the hills; except that, directly opposite, there is the beautiful glen of Inveruglas, which winds away among the feet of A'Chrois, Ben Ime, Ben Vane and Ben Vorlich,* standing mist-inwreathed together. The mists this morning, had a very soft and beautiful effect, and made the mountains tenderer than I have hitherto felt them to be; and they lingered about their heads like morning-dreams, flitting and retiring, and letting the sunshine in and snatching it away again.
>
> *Hawthorne renders these as 'Ben Crook, Ben Ein, Ben Vain and Ben Voirlich'

The reputation of Inversnaid was undoubtedly made by the Wordsworths who crossed the ferry to reach it. The ferryman's daughter made a lasting impression on Wordsworth, who celebrated her in one of his better Scottish poems, 'The Highland Girl'. It ends with a memorable evocation of the place:

> And these grey rocks; that household lawn
> Those trees, a veil just half withdrawn
> This fall of water that doth make
> A murmur near the silent lake;
> This little bay; a quiet road
> That holds in shelter thy abode
> In truth together do ye seem
> Like something fashioned in a dream.

Ishahallin see Ishneich

Ishneich   *NS 453 815*

Catter Burn is unprepossessing enough as it chatters along beside the twisting backroad between Croftamie and Gartocharn, but its tributaries are full of interest. Cameron Muir is the site of the cattle raid described by Nigel Tranter in *MacGregor's Gathering* after which a great white bull was driven up the side of Loch Lomond to their hiding place at Craigroyston. The scene of the raid was Gallangad Farm above Gallangad Burn which tumbles down to it from the moor. In private ground north of the farm is *Ladies' Linn (NS 443 827)*, and above it at the junction with the curiously-named Finland Burn, a further fall. The pearl of Gallangad Burn is *Ishneich*, the waterfall of the horse. It is in the highest part of the wooded glen on the edge of the moorland near the Lang Cairn. The fall possibly got its name from the old droving days for this now empty moor was an important highway for livestock being driven between the Argyllshire Highlands and Crieff and Falkirk where cattle and horses were sold in thousands. It is now in Forestry Commission property and the best approach to the fall is by the forest road from Cameron Muir. Where this road leaves the public road from Wester Cameron to Finnich Toll there is a rhyming gate.

> Be ye man, or be ye wummin,
> Be ye goin, or be ye cummin,
> Be ye early, or be ye late,
> Be ye share tae shut this gate.

ISHNEICH

0 Km. 1

N

Cameron Muir

To Alexandria (4km.)

Wester Cameron

Gallangad Muir △

Finland Burn

ISHNEICH

Chambered Cairn

Gallangad Burn

JR

During a drought Ishneich is a cascade, but in spate the burn hurls itself in a thirty metre waterchute over the lip of a wooded amphitheatre, from the right bank of which it is possible to obtain a grandstand view of the fall. It is in the same class as the Loup of Fintry and the Spout of Ballagan. The Lang Cairn, a neolithic chambered cairn, of considerable interest, is above the fall on the right bank. On the left bank below it, at the junction with Finland Burn, is a dun.

No visitor to Ishneich should omit to ascend the burn to the *Sheils of Gartlea Fall (NS 456 807)*, below the site of some old sheilings now gone. It commands a superb view of Loch Lomond and its islands and of the Bens of the Southern Highlands. It is more extensive than that from Duncryne which provides the finest immediate view of the loch from the South and more complete than the similar prospect from Auchineden, known as the Queen's View, on the A807. Below you is the fine five-metre fall just above a ford on the old drove road. The Knockupple Burn, the tributary which joins the burn at this point, is a succession of cascades. *Ishahallin (NS 450 797)* is the name given to the principal fall.

Jaw Linn see Campsie Glen

Jenny's Lum
NS 553 817

Fall on the cliffed edge of the Campsie Hills. It gets its name from the way in which the spray blows upwards in windy weather. It is a reasonably well known rock climb.

Knockan Linn see Calder Glen

Ladies' Linn (Gallanged Burn) see Ishneich

Ladies' Linn (Jaw Burn) see Grey Mare's Tail

Lady's Linn see Campsie Glen

Eas Lair

Wet weather fall above Rowcoish on Loch Lomond, well-seen from the A82 in the right conditions.

Laird's Loup
NS 701 804

The most remote source of the Kelvin is the Garrel Burn which falls 500 metres in two kilometres to the town of Kilsyth. The name is a corruption of Garbh Allt, rough burn. It has brought prosperity to Kilsyth for it was harnessed for water-power and its banks have always provided a place of recreation for the inhabitants. The burn rises on Laird's Hill and the most spectacular fall is Laird's Loup. There are coal seams in the sandstone of the gorge below the fall and a Covenanter's Cave, where a fugitive from the Battle of Kilsyth is said to have taken refuge.

Eas an Laoigh see Falls of Glenmassan

Sput Leacash
NN 657 088

Twelve-metre fall on the mountain burn below Wester Brackland near the Falls of Bracklinn

Falls of Ledard
NN 461 027

Above Loch Ard on the way to Ben Venue by the charming mountain path from the farm of Ledard, the visitor encounters the Falls of Ledard which so charmed Sir Walter Scott that he used the site in both *Waverley* and *Rob Roy*, 'a spot the recollection of which yet strikes me with admiration'. Beyond the farmhouse the path climbs up beside the burn until you reach the beautiful rock pool described by Scott. Nowadays you are greeted with an admonition. 'No swimming' says a rudely constructed notice board; this much frequented path skirts the farm's water supply.

The visitor who has read Scott may be surprised at the small scale of the falls and be tempted to doubt his arithmetic. No one will doubt his skill in describing the scene:

> The brook hurling its waters downwards from the mountain had in this spot encountered a barrier of rock over which it had made its way in two distinct leaps. The first fall, across which a magnificent old oak slanting out from the further bank partly extended itself as if to shroud the dusky stream of the cascade, might be twelve feet high; the broken waters were received in a beautiful stone basin, almost as regular as if hewn by a sculptor; and after wheeling around its flinty margin they made a second precipitous dash through a dark and narrow chasm at least fifty feet in depth and thence in a hurried, but comparatively more gentle course, escaped to join the lake.

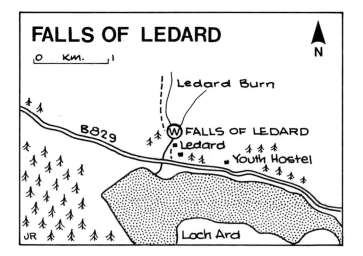

FALLS OF LEDARD

0 Km. 1

N

Ledard Burn

B829

W FALLS OF LEDARD

Ledard

Youth Hostel

Loch Ard

JR

That description from *Rob Roy* is mirrored by this from *Waverley*:

> The path ascended rapidly from the edge of the brook, and the glen widened into a sylvan amphitheatre, waving with birch, young oaks and hazels, with here and there a scattered yew tree. The rocks now receded, but still showed their grey and shaggy crests rising among the copse wood. Still higher rose eminences and peaks, some bare, some clothed with wood, some round and purple with heath and others splintered into rocks and crags. At a short turning in the path, which had for some furlongs lost sight of the brook, suddenly placed Waverley in front of a romantic waterfall. It was not so remarkable either for its great height or the quantity of water as for the beautiful accompaniments which made the spot interesting. After a broken cataract of about twenty feet the stream was received into a large natural basin filled to the brim with water which, where the bubbles of the fall subsided was so exquisitely clear that, although it was of great depth, the eye could discern each pebble at the bottom. Eddying round this reservoir the brook found its way over a broken part of the ledge and formed a second fall which seemed to seek out the very abyss; then wheeling out beneath from the smooth dark rocks, which it had polished for ages, it wandered murmuring down the glen forming the stream up which Waverley had just ascended.

Neither of the two accounts mentions the exquisite pale green colour imparted to the translucent pool by the slates which wall it. It is small wonder that people are tempted to swim in it.

Falls of Leny   *NN 593 087*

Of all the places where the visitor from the South can say to himself, 'At last I really am in the Highlands', the Pass of Leny is the most renowned. It is the site of a clan conflict between

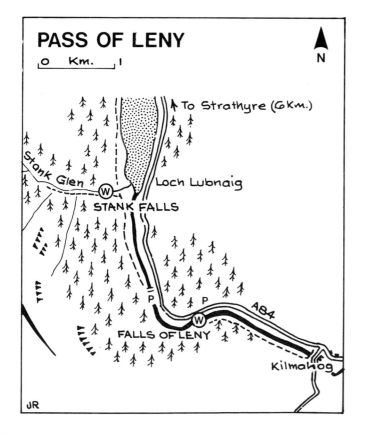

the men of Leny and the MacLarens, assisted by the ubiquitous MacGregors. There is nearly always a piper, suitably adorned beside the road in the summer months and the narrow defile is a busy place. However, arrangements have now been made to provide a car park and a guided walk to the falls, so it is less congested than it was. The river gorge is scarcely able to accommodate the river, let alone the old military road, the more modern road and the former Callander and Oban railway line which criss-crossed the rapids in such a dramatic fashion. To the West is Ben Ledi, and to the East the foothills of Ben Vorlich. The river falls in twin cataracts, five metres high, rushing over rough rocks and nearly always providing an abundance of white water. There is nearly always a considerable discharge because the falls lie immediately below Loch Lubnaig, so the river is generally full enough for the falls to be attractive.

The Linn   *NS 582 593*

The City of Glasgow's Linn Park takes its name from a fall where the White Cart tumbles over a teschenite sill of carboniferous age which is similar to that on which Cathcart Castle stands. *The Linn* is four metres in height, but it is impressive because the Cart is already a considerable stream at this point.

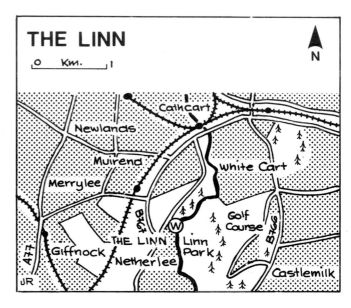

Lochar Linn   *NS 676 415*

A broken fall of six metres on a tributary on the Avon near Strathaven.

Locher Falls   *NS 401 647*

Falls on a tributary of the Gryfe at Lochermill on the A761 which occur on trap rocks which at one time yielded oil shale on a commercial basis. The two main cascades, 15 metres high, are in a pleasant wooded gorge.

Millholm Falls   *NS 704 444*

In the little town of Strathaven the Powmillan Burn falls headlong towards the Avon, almost surrounding the fifteenth century castle, stronghold of the Lords of Avondale, giving it

Falls of Inverbeg. At the entrance to Glen Douglas. OAT CARD COMPANY

an almost impregnable site. Millholm Falls are beneath the remaining tower. The two falls are said to have been called 'High Leddie' and 'Laigh Leddie' to distinguish between the class of lady who bathed there in the days before bathrooms were invented.

Milton of Callander Fall   NN 575 062

A good example of the kind of fall which attracted the Victorians but which is neglected nowadays. It is not very far upstream on the burn which tumbles down from Ben Ledi to Loch Vennachar beside Milton of Callander Farm. The principal fall, hidden in the woods is one of about 15 metres with two other falls above. One can see that it was sufficiently attractive to be, at six miles from Callander, a suitable place for the old coaches to stop.

Eas Mor (Loch Chon)   NN 411 050

This fall on Ben Dubh, the dark mountain wall above Loch Chon in the Trossachs, is a curiosity. It is well described in Campbell Nairne's informative book about the Trossachs when he refers to the vanishing waterfall of Loch Chon:

> In his description of Loch Chon, Graham (1806) mentions a spectacular cascade which could be looked for near the upper end of the lake. The existence of this cascade has been known locally for hundreds of years, yet it is rarely seen. The reason is that it appears only after a period of heavy rain. A mossy hollow on top of the mountain wall overflows and the water shoots down into the loch, a thousand feet below. Most of the fall is spray, but seen from a distance it is like a continuous white rope. After half an hour or so the cataract vanishes.

The peculiarity of the Loch Chon waterfall explains the blunder made by the seventeenth century antiquary and geographer Sir Robert Sibbald at the time when he was correcting and revising the district maps of Timothy Pont, the first projector of a Scottish Atlas. Sibbald, visiting the spot fifty years later, could find no waterfall and crossed out Pont's sketch. The original map was among Sibbald's papers acquired by the Advocates' Library in 1723 and the unfortunate erasure can still be seen.

Eas Mor (Cowal)   NS 129 826

Fall on a tributary of the Little Eachaig in Cowal.

MacGregor's Leap

Another name given, between the wars, to the Waterfall of the Little Fawn (qv) near Aberfoyle. It illustrates a strong propensity to trade on the name rather than any known associations with the famous Rob Roy.

Sput Mor   NN 558 136

Fall on the Allt Mor above the northern reaches of Loch Lubnaig.

Morag's Fairy Glen   NS 167 758

One of the natural attractions of the holiday resort of Dunoon is Morag's Fairy Glen, gifted to the town by Mr and Mrs George in 1929. It is pretty enough, although the very formal paths and fences detract somewhat from it. There are three groups of falls on the Berry Burn, the uppermost of which is eight metres high.

Old Mill Linn   NS 795 500

A characteristic little fall on Dalserf Burn, tributary of the Clyde, which joins that river where it flows through a relatively broad trench called the Trough of Clyde. The landscape is distinctive: orchards, market gardens, glasshouses, country houses and villages are all crammed into the trench. The burns which tumble down into the Trough have precipitous courses and are generally called gills and include Garrion Gill, Jock's Gill, Fiddlers' Gill and, best known, Gillytudlem, corrupted by Scott into Tillietudlem, where there is a splendid castle.

Overtoun Glen   NS 4 3 760

Above Dumbarton is the fine Victorian baronial mansion house of Overtoun, the policies of which were gifted to the town. It was built by James Smith, the Glasgow architect, of Spout of Ballagan sandstone. There are some fine falls in Overtoun Glen. Smith built the house for James White, later Lord Overtoun, who ran a Glasgow chemical factory and supported missions which ran Livingstonia in the Zambesi basin as a private colony. He was a man of enormous influence in Scotland and was a leading figure in the development of the railways in the district, as the style of the bridge which spans the burn suggests. Built in 1894 this bridge must be one of the most remarkable structures of its kind on private ground in Scotland.

The policies of Overtoun House have recently been improved and fine footpaths now lead up the glen. From a fine belvedere *Spardie Linn* is seen. Set below the house at the point where the Spout of Ballagan sandstone outcrops, it is a very charming double fall about ten metres high. The burn falls into an amphitheatre, rhododendron and tree-embowered. Dr Ian MacPhail suggests that the name is derived from Spairteadh, splashing. In Scots it means Sparrow's Linn. Donald Macleod, a nineteenth century Dumbarton poet celebrates the fall as follows:

> Nae son o' song has hymned thy praise,
> Thou pride o' a' the country round,
> Sae I'll to thee a song upraise
> While listening to thy thunderin' sound.
>
> Ye foamin' nurslin' o' the storm
> That rushest on, nor knowest rest,
> Since 'mang the muirlands ye were born,
> Aneath the Lang Craig's beetling crest.
>
> How grandly here your waters roar
> In ravin' madness o'er the linn,
> Wi' boilin', surgin', wild uproar,
> In awfu' loups mid spray and din.
>
> The bonny woods thick cluster roun'
> To weave their branches o'er thy head,
> And sing to thee a quiet tune,
> To soothe thy agonized speed.
>
> The wee birds here delight to dwell,
> And pipe thy praises to the gale,
> While neighbour birds the chorus swell
> And spread thy fame o'er hill and dale.
>
> The earliest flowerlets o' the spring
> Love to adorn thy rugged side
> And summer's bonnie bairnies cling
> Lang blushing on thy banks o' pride.

O Spardie, I ha'e lo'ed thee lang
 'Mid hallow'd mem'ries thou dost dwell;
I've crooned to thee this wee bit sang
 In token that I've lo'ed thee well.

Above the falls the burn runs through a gorge below the bridge referred to above. There are several fine cascades here. Beyond the House a well-marked path leads to the open moor beneath the Lang Craigs where, below a reservoir, is the *Black Linn* (NS 444 772).

Pig's Foot Falls   NS 413 054

Prominent falls on the steep slopes west of Loch Chon. After rain they form an attractive feature of the view from the charming by-road opposite.

Peggie's Spout   NS 678 821

Remote moorland fall in the hills above the Carron Reservoir reached by forest tracks.

Poachy Glen   NS 387 790

A sad place these days. At its foot is a scrapyard and an impressive little waterfall leaps into it. Above this a new road has been thrown across the burn, obscuring access to the glen. Before these assaults on its dignity, Poachy Glen was a notable place. The burn rushes down from Carman Hill, which commands splendid views of Loch Lomond and the Firth of Clyde, to the site of the Place of Bonhill, the Smollett family home before they moved to Cameron. Tobias Smollett refers to Poachy Glen in Humphry Clinker:

> Above that house is a romantic glen or clift of a mountain, covered with hanging woods, having at bottom a stream of fine water that forms a number of cascades in its descent to join the Leven; so that the scene is quite enchanting. A captain of a man of war, who had made the circuit of the globe with Mr Anson, being conducted to this glen, exclaimed, 'Juan Fernandez, By God.'

The captain was a friend of Smollett's who lived in Chelsea. Smollett edited Anson's Journal which is illustrated with prints of the waterfalls of the Pacific Island of Juan Fernandez.

Puck's Glen   NS 147 844

Opposite the entrance to the younger Botanic Garden at Benmore is Puck's Glen. There are a number of walks in the forest and a variety of ways of reaching the glen, the most usual way being the path from the car park. This path passes the ruins of Puck's House, a Victorian Folly, before dropping steeply into the rocky chasm. There are twelve little falls in this glen which shelters a wide variety of ferns and mosses in a damp environment.

Red Fall   NS 468 930

Fall in the moorlands beneath Conic Hill, so-called because it occurs on sandstone close to the Highland Boundary Fault. The walk to it from Moor Park commands really outstanding views of the islands of Loch Lomond.

Rob Roy's Cave Fall   NN 516 212

Almost every cleft in the rocks in Scotland is 'somebody's cave' and there is little actually to connect this splendid place with Rob Roy. It is said that he hid here, and he undoubtedly knew the place since he lived at Inverlochlarig. The fall is above Tulloch where a mountain burn runs over the entrance to a shallow cave. It is possible to enter the cave and look outwards through the curtain of water over Loch Voil. The cave is not obvious from below, but this spot is worth seeking out on a sunny day.

Rouken Glen   NS 549 579

The Auldhouse Burn falls through the Glasgow park which has most sense of the country about it, Rouken Glen. The burn provided power for the mills of Thornliebank, and there are the remains of an interesting water wheel to be seen on the Nature Trail in the park. In spate the burn roars through an entrenched gorge below the site of the house. At the head of the glen are Rouken Glen Falls, a series of impressive cascades of four metres, eight metres and 12 metres in height.

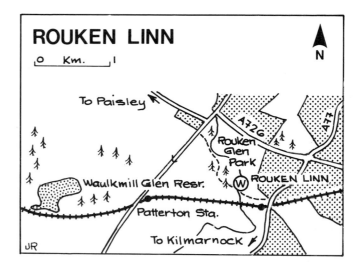

Ryatt Linn   NS 518 570

In the hills above Thornliebank on the Brock Burn, was the site of the first major water undertaking by the Corporation of Glasgow, the Gorbals Waterworks. The little fall is now situated between two large reservoirs.

Sandy Linn see Calder Glen

Sheep Linn see Campsie Glen

Sheep Loup see Calder Glen

The Slunger see Bonhill Falls

Eas Sneggan   NN 357 011

One of a number of torrents falling into Loch Lomond and visible, in spate, across the loch. This fall (Eas an Fidhian, on the old six-inch map) is above Ptarmigan Lodge near the West Highland Way.

Spardie Linn see Overtoun Burn

Spectacle E'e, in the Avon basin. These cascades were harnessed to drive water mills. GEOLOGICAL MUSEUM

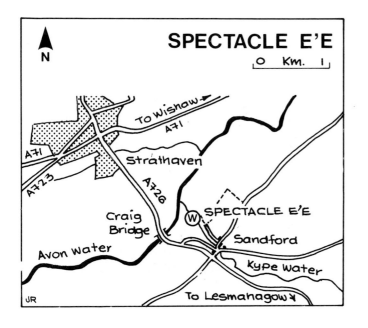

Spectacle E'e
NS 715 434

The most imposing fall in the basin of the Avon. The Kype Water falls into the Avon at the edge of the carboniferous lavas which make up the hill country beyond Strathaven and forms a series of picturesque falls culminating in a fall of 15 metres, Spectacle E'e. These cascades were harnessed at an early date to drive water mills, perhaps for the monks of Lesmahagow Abbey. Spectacle E'e Mill used to be called St Helen's Mill

> This mill, situated on the Kype, had a traditionary interest connected with it, which was that its thatched roof had been kindled by the heat of the suns rays through the eye, or lens of a pair of Spectacles—hence commonly known as Spectacle E'e Mill. The combination in this wee bosky dell of the mill, the waterfalls and jutting rocks, renders it quite a romantic nook, well calculated to give both inspiration to the artist and gladden the eye of the tourist   (Mary Gebbie (1879)).

It is difficult to believe today that, at the foot of this fall, there was room for a mill and its giant overshot waterwheel, but a careful examination of the ground will show both the artificial channels which were dug to conduct the water to the wheel and the foundations of the building. The fall is approached from the village of Sandford past Tweedie Mill, beside the uppermost of the falls and now restored to make a fine private house. A right of way, which was contested in 1937, leads down the true right bank of the Kype and the fall is seen round the corner. A better view is obtained from the opposite bank, and a grandstand view from the A726 on the edge of Strathaven.

Stank Falls
NN 577 105

Stank Glen above Loch Lubnaig is at the heart of one of the Forestry Commission's most successful schemes. It provides the most obvious route up Ben Ledi from the Pass of Leny. The path crosses the river and leads past a number of unprepossessing cottages towards the farm before a fine forest walk leads into the hills. The roar of the fall in spate is obvious enough, but it is hidden in trees until the last minute. The burn makes three impressive leaps of about eight metres each before taking a sheer leap over a 25 metre fall.

Stonebyres Linn see Falls of Clyde

Tammarree Linn see Carron Glen

Eas Thorr
NN 355 050

Moorland fall under the steeple of Ben Lomond.

Spout of the Three Marches
NS 471 785

Above the Burncrooks Reservoir in the heart of the Kilpatrick Hills is a tiny hidden waterfall on the boundary between three estates: Wester Cameron, Strathleven and Auchencek. The burn comes to life with a five metre leap.

Torrance Linn see Calderwood Glen

Trough Linn see Calderwood Glen

Eas Uilleann
NN 655 092

Honeysuckle Falls on the Brackland Burn tumble twelve metres in a tree-filled gorge. The walk to them can be combined with a visit to Bracklinn Falls on the Keltie.

Whinstone Linn

Fall above Old Mill Linn (q.v.) on the Dalserf Burn in the Trough of Clyde. Its name betrays the geological cause of the fall.

Whistler's Glen
NS 269 849

Smugglers' Glen above Rhu on the Gareloch is much obscured by the works of man. Had the West Highland Railway company been better financed there would, no doubt, now be a fine viaduct across the glen, but the burn was put in a culvert. The Navy have also built a housing estate there, but towards the hills the glen is just as attractive as ever it was. It is so-called because it was a tinkers' haunt where a look-out, the Whistler, was kept to warn of the approach of the excise men seeking their hidden stills. In the trees the burn runs over two ten metre falls on beautiful green schists. Scott exaggerates in his description:

> They came full in front of the fall which here had a most tremendous aspect, boiling, roaring and thundering with unceasing din into a black cauldron, a hundred feet, at least, below them which resembled the crater of a volcano (Heart of Midlothian).

Falls of White Cart see The Hammills

White Spout see Fin Glen

Spout of the White Horse
NS 432 796

The Carnock Burn joins the Blane near Killearn House above which is a remarkable sandstone gorge called Finnich Glen or Ashdown (Uisge Dhu) where cliffs tower above the water. Higher up is Auchencek, a now-ruined Scots Baronial mansion house improved by one MacNair who, although he was handicapped by deafness, showed conspicuous energy in building the house from which, it is said, there was one of the finest views in Europe—of Loch Lomond and its islands. There is a succession of falls on the burn which leads eventually to the Burn Crooks Reservoir. The building of the dam in 1914 for Clydebank put an end to a once-proud waterfall, the Spout of the White Horse. The name is, perhaps, a corruption of White Hawes where the old drove road crossed the burn.

Dundaff Linn, *the third of the four Falls of Clyde. Below this Linn Dale and Arkwright established New Lanark. (Opposite)* PETER DAVENPORT

Bracklinn Falls. *(Below)* HAMISH BROWN

Page 184 (Top)

Falls of Clyde, *Cora Linn (1801). J M W Turner's watercolour shows waternymphs inspired by Mark Akenside's poem 'Hymn to the Nyads'* LADY LEVER ART GALLERY

(bottom)

Falls of Clyde, *Bonnington Linn (1771). This painting is one of three studies of the falls by Jacob More.* FITZWILLIAM GALLERY

SOUTH WEST SCOTLAND

Principal Falls

Outstanding Falls	**Touring Centre**
Grey Mare's Tail, Moffat	Moffat
Falls of Glenashdale	Isle of Arran

Significant Falls	
Grey Mare's Tail, Talnotry	Newton Stewart
Grey Mare's Tail, Closeburn	Thornhill
Buchan Falls	Loch Trool
Falls of Garbh Allt	Isle of Arran
Stinchar Falls	Straiton

Interesting Falls	
Garpol Linn	Moffat
Falls of Minnoch	Loch Trool
Falls of Blackburn	Newcastleton
Glenmarlin Falls	Thornhill
Black Linn (Falls of Gogo)	Largs
Kelburn Falls	Largs
Spout of Garnock	Largs
Rossetti Linn	Straiton
Dalcairnie Linn	Dalmellington

Also recommended	
Falls of Struey	Isle of Arran
Eas Mor	Isle of Arran
Falls of Gairland Burn	Loch Trool
Dobb's Linn	Moffat
Crichope Linn	Thornhill
Tairlaw Linn	Straiton
Kirconnel Linn	Twynholm

PRINCIPAL WATERFALLS OF SOUTH WEST SCOTLAND

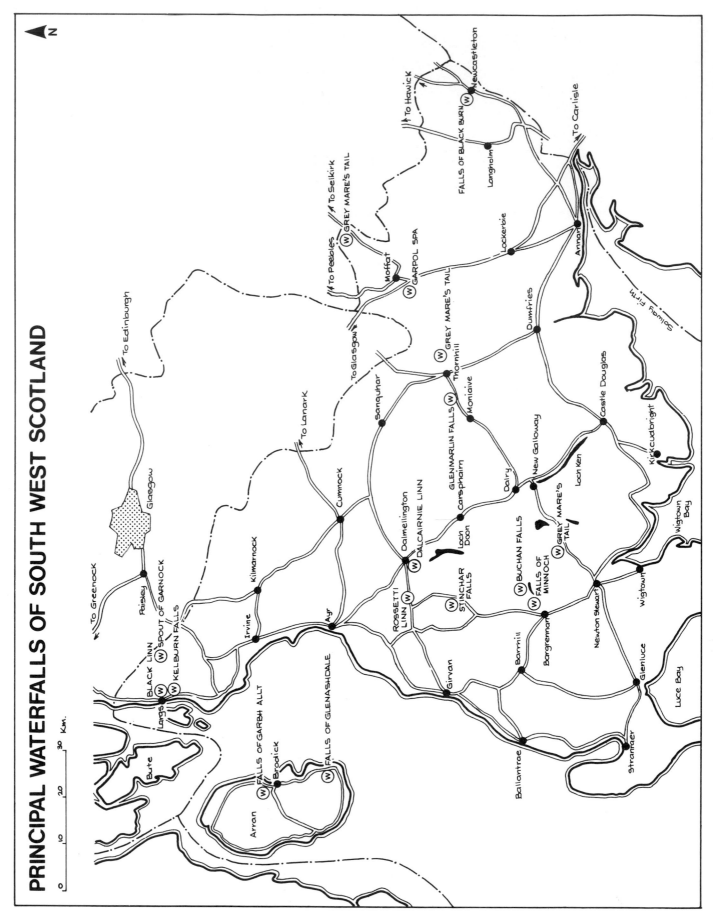

The Waterfalls of South West Scotland

Ye burnies wimpling down your glens,
Or foaming strang wi' hasty stens,
Frae linn to linn.

Robert Burns

Ayrshire and Arran combine landscapes from both the Highlands and the Lowlands. For many Arran is the epitome of Scotland: the uplands in the northern half of the island have all the more spectacular features of the North of Scotland, while the southern half displays the variety of topography characteristic of the Central Lowlands. In the north there are corrie waterfalls and rough glens with tumbling burns of clear water. In the south, volcanic rocks give rise to the highest falls in the Strathclyde Region, the Falls of Glenashdale.

In Ayrshire rolling, open country developed on Carboniferous rocks is combined with rugged moorlands around the granite complex of Loch Doon in the south and on the borders of Renfrewshire in the north. There are no great falls, but there are innumerable smaller falls which make attractive additions to Ayrshire dells. Ayrshire's rivers are limited in size, but the Ayr itself, the Doon, the Girvan and the Stinchar are renowned for their scenery. Burns was inspired by these rivers often enough and there are suitable tales attached to some falls. At Catrine, an industrial village in Central Ayrshire, one of the most significant early developments of water power took place. However, Ayrshire's most interesting waterfalls are in the fringing hills.

The Dumfries and Galloway Region embraces the basins of those rivers which drain into the Solway Firth; the Ayrshire Districts of Strathclyde embrace those which drain into the Firth of Clyde. Together they constitute a reasonably well-defined area which may be called South-West Scotland.

Of the Solway rivers the easternmost is the Border Esk with its tributaries; the most important of these is the Liddel which, at Penton Linns, forms a very beautiful river fall on the very border with England. Next is the Annan, the artery followed by the main road and the main railway from Carlisle to Glasgow. Then the Nith. Further west are the basins of the Dee, the Fleet, the Cree and the smaller Luce. The largest of these rivers is the Nith. Nithsdale combines the grandeur of finely delineated hills and an infinite variety of deciduous woodland.

The Nith divides two distinct types of scenery. To the North East are hills which are smooth, rounded eminences, clothed with grass or with heather, penetrated by deep valleys. To the South West are wild, rugged hills, associated with granitic intrusions, and culminating in the altered sedimentary rocks of the Merrick and Kells Ranges. Galloway has always been comparatively remote and isolated and has maintained its own traditions.

English visitors have always liked this part of Scotland which is associated with both Burns and Scott. It was, however, the countryside described by John Buchan and Dorothy L Sayers which drew visitors to Galloway in the 1930's. Both Dumfries and Galloway are closely associated with fierce adherence to the Covenants, which gives rise to various dramatic tales of fugitives, many of whom chose waterfalls as their hiding places.

There are many waterfalls in the region, most of which occur on the steep valley sides. Because the river basins are comparatively restricted in size there are few notable river falls. The best known fall is the Grey Mare's Tail, Moffat and, somewhat confusingly, there are four other falls in Dumfries and Galloway and one in Ayrshire with the same name. With impermeable rocks and heavy rainfall the region provides fine conditions for the development of falls.

Ayrshire and Arran

Crook of Ayr NS 594 256

Falls on the Ayr itself in Sorn Parish above the farm of Mid Heilar. The river occupies an incised meander where there is an island. There are falls above and below the Crook.

Black Linn see Falls of Gogo

Black Linn NX 368 955

Writing about the hydrology of the Parish of Barr in *The New*

Statistical Account the Reverend E B Wallace commented on the precipitate character of nearly all of the mountain burns there. He asserted that there would scarcely be one out of a hundred of them on which there was not a waterfall of some kind. Black Linn is the most impressive although its spectacular character is now masked by the lusty forest trees which clothe the steep slopes of the Stinchar valley. The Black Burn, between Black Row and the Stinchar Falls, cascades 50 metres in a hillside ravine with a single leap of 12 metres a short distance above its junction with the main stream.

Black Linn see Rossetti Linn

Capenoch Linn
NS 302 072

A little fall outside Maybole which has long been a popular objective for ramblers. The fall, pretty enough in its way, is situated under a low hill with a huge monument to the Fergusons on top of it and it is now somewhat marred by a scrapyard immediately above the place where the waters of the burn falls into a pretty wooded bower. From the top of the hill there is a view of Loch Spouts (NS 286 058) which is now a reservoir for Maybole impounded by a dam. Before the dam was built the burn which drained the the loch fell over a volcanic dyke in several places forming a number of low falls which gave it its unusual name. The little loch is interesting because it was the site of a crannog, an iron age lake dwelling.

Eas a' Chranaig see Falls of Glenashdale

Clashminnoch Falls see Loch Doon.

The Falls of Cleugh
NS 550 270

The little river Cleugh is a tributary of the Ayr which it joins between Sorn Castle and Sorn Church. It flows through a highly attractive glen which forms part of the policies of the Castle where there is a series of cascades which have been likened to the Falls of Clyde on a small scale. The Carboniferous Limestone charges the water which forms tuff which can petrify objects left.

Eas Cumhan
NS 011 219

Amphitheatre waterfall caused by a basalt sill in South Arran. The Levencorroch Burn crosses the two-metre sill to form a high twn fall. The underlying rocks are soft sandstones, shales and Keuper marls of New Red Sandstone age.

Levencorroch Burn is the burn of the rough half-penny land, a reminder of the fact that Arran was occupied by the Norsemen who used to describe the area of a piece of land according to its value in pennyweights of silver. Eas Cumhann means narrow falls.

Dalcairnie Linn
NS 465 043

Much noticed in early guide books when Dalmellington was considered to be something of a mountain resort. The fall is at a bridge where the burn turns a corner and hurls itself some twelve metres into a rocky pool. Because of its northerly aspect the fall looks somewhat menacing on a dull day.

Linn of the Darkness
NX 331 918

A remote fall on one of the headwaters of the Balloch Burn in a hillside ravine under Craigenreoch, the highest of the impressive group of hills west of the Nick of the Balloch road which crosses the Carrick Hills by a narrow ledge leading to a mountain pass. These Polmadie Hills have been forested since 1936.

Devil's Punch Bowl see Kilkerran Falls

Glen Diomhan
NR 922 470

From Catacol Bay, one of the fairest places in Arran, Glen Catacol leads inland. The brawling burn has a number of interesting features, but it is a tributary, the Allt Diomhan which makes the most interesting waterfalls. Where it joins the main stream it falls 60 metres in a series of cascades. Glen Diomhan has been a National Nature Reserve since 1956. Two

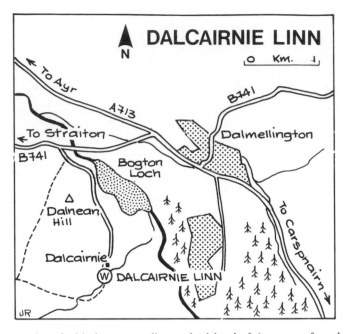

species of whitebeam peculiar to the island of Arran are found there.

Loch Doon

This is the largest loch in South West Scotland, a renowned beauty spot much altered by the Galloway Hydro Electric Power Scheme. South of it is the Dungeon, the name given to the remote granite upland between the Merrick and the Rhinns of Kells. The rivers—called Lanes—which drain this upland are sometimes wild, roaring streams with spectacular cascades. Elsewhere they are menacing, slow-flowing streams. Everywhere they are dangerous, and must be treated with respect. From Loch Doon a typical expedition into this isolated country is to Cove Macaterick, a cave now fallen in. On Elgin Lane, en route to Macaterick, are *Clashminnoch Falls (NX 452 904)*.

Fairlie Glen
NS 219 547

Above the Clyde coast resort of Fairlie in a pretty glen are the ruins of Fairlie Castle, a square tower built in 1521. Beneath the old keep there is an attractive fall.

Galloway Burn
NX 056 713

There are falls on the Galloway Burn which separates Galloway from Carrick.

Games Loup
NX 103 880

A coastal fall on the bold cliffs between Lendalfoot and Ballantrae in Carrick. Games Loup is close to Carleton Castle where the ballad May Cullean is set. Murray's Guide (1894) summarises it as follows:

> Here lived a baron who had a habit of frequently marrying and becoming tired of his wives, whom he despatched by pushing them from the top of the cliffs. Seven had already gone this way when May Cullean, the eighth wife, appeared on the scene, and was led out on to the rocks to perform the same ceremony.

The denouncement of the ballad come in the following lines:

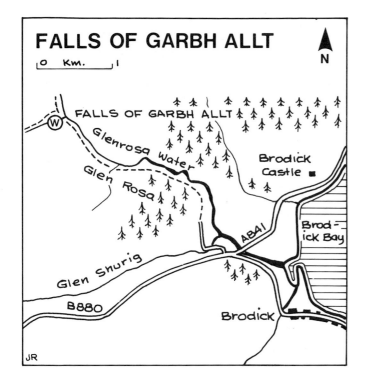

FALLS OF GARBH ALLT

Cast off your silken stays,
  For and your broidered shoon
For they are too fine and costly
  To rot in the salt sea foam

Cast off, cast off your Holland smock
  That's bordered with the lawn
For it is too fine and costly
  To rot in the salt sea foam.

O turn about thou false Sir John
  And look to the leaf o' the tree
For it never became a gentleman
  A naked woman to see.

He turned himself straight round about
  To look at the leaf o' the tree
She's twined her arms about his waist
  And thrown him into the sea.

Garbh Allt

NR 982 387

The most spectacular mountain falls in Arran are the cascades on the Garbh Allt on the edge of the National Trust for Scotland property which embraces the finest mountain scenery in the island. The Garbh Allt forms a hanging valley above Glen Rosa under the sharp granite peak of Ben Nuis. There is a small reservoir above the falls and a somewhat unsightly cast iron pipe provides a familiar landmark. The burn occupies a 'wild declivitous glen careering and leaping along a granite channel in a series of striking falls (*Ordnance Gazetteer*). In all, the falls are 150 metres in height. They make a very suitable objective for a short excursion into these famous island hills. However, hillwalkers will climb the path beside them, from which the coarse granite with its characteristic jointing can be particularly easily observed, as a prelude to the ascent of Ben Nuis and A'Chir.

Spout of Garnock

NS 287 609

The most imposing mountain fall in the Renfrewshire Heights.

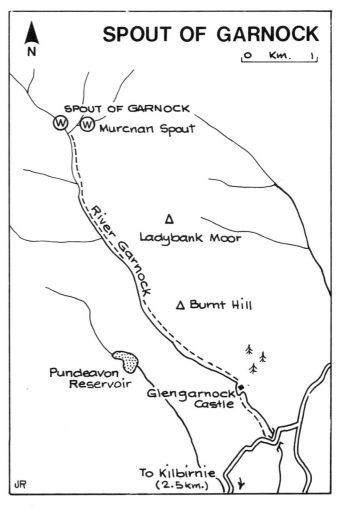

SPOUT OF GARNOCK

The lusty Garnock tumbles 12 metres into a rock basin in the remote moorlands approaching Misty Law. Not far away from the Spout of Garnock is Murchan Spout (*NS 290 608*) on a tributary. Both are caused by dykes. The Garnock valley provides a long but attractive route to the highest hills. The route begins below the ruined tower of Glengarnock Castle where there are also low falls (*NS 313 570*).

Grey Mare's Tail (Barr)

NX 269 956

This wet weather fall is well seen from the steep, winding road from Barr to Dailly aptly named The Screws. Its alternative name is The White Lady which is amply justified when the tumbling burn is full.

Falls of Glenashdale

NS 023 428

These falls, among the most imposing in Scotland, are the highest in the Strathclyde Region. In Murray's Guide they are called the Falls of Kiscadale—coffindale—and there is a ruined kirk at the foot of the glen where the dead were brought for burial, which explains this name. The name Glenashdale is tautological. It is a corruption of Easdale, a combination of Gaelic and Norse elements. The wooded glen is behind Whiting Bay and there are paths on both banks of the stream. That on the south bank is high above the stream, that on the north bank hugs the burn. In wet weather the glen path is muddy. The falls, which are 2.5 kilometres from the road, come into view soon enough at a point where the north bank

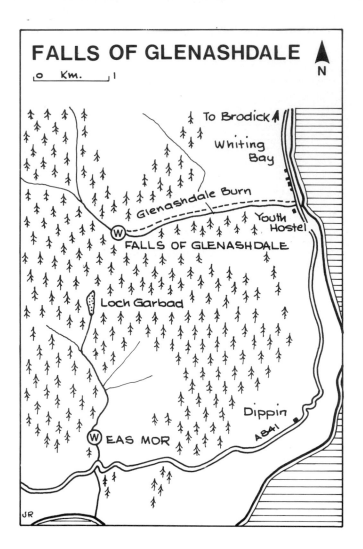

white cascades above and below the charming old bridge on the track to the Falls of Gogo. Some distance above the bridge is another fine fall, Maiden's Loup (NS 231 605).

Kelburn Falls   *NS 219 567*

The Clea Burn drains the lovely Kelburn Glen and forms two romantic waterfalls the lower one 15 metres high. Kelburn Castle, a fine house dating from various periods, is in a fine estate of which the glen is the heart.

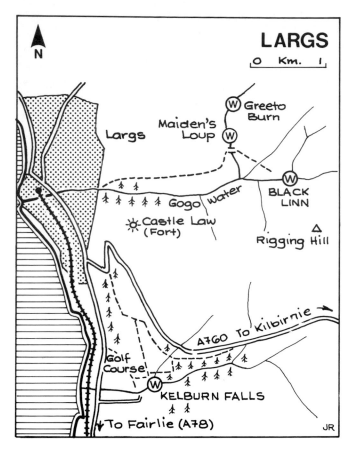

path forks, one branch going to the top of the falls, the other to the foot of the gorge. In spate it is possible to pass behind the main fall. The best point of view is a platform on the north bank. The burn makes a leap of between 12 and 15 metres, strikes a ledge and falls a further 32 metres. The fall is caused by a quartz-dolerite sill. The glen is very well wooded and it seems from above—and this is one of the few great falls where it is possible to get a good view from above of the face of the cataract—as if the water plunges into the trees. This accounts for the Gaelic name of the fall Eas a'Chrannaig, the fall of the plentiful trees. The gorge at the falls is 60 metres deep.

Falls of Gogo   *NS 237 594*

The Gogo is the more southerly of the two little rivers of Largs. It rises on Box Law and after gathering a number of moorland tributaries it enters a long, deep, steep-sided valley at the foot of which are attractive wooded grounds. At the head of the valley are the Falls of Gogo, 24 metres high. It is a long walk to reach them and the road to the shooting lodge marked on the map deteriorates after crossing the Greeto. On the right day, however, the walk to the falls with its striking views of the Firth of Clyde is highly enjoyable.

Greeto Falls   *NS 229 595*

The Greeto is a tributary of the Gogo, but it drains a larger basin. Where it joins its sister stream it forms a succession of

Kilkerran Fall   *NS 894 004*

Above the ruins of the old castle of Kilkerran there is a four metre fall of the Knockrochar Burn. The old castle is an interesting ruin worth seeking out. It is one of a number of outstanding buildings in the valley of the Water of Girvan. The mansion house of Kilkerran, some distance from the old castle, compares favourably with any of them and in its grounds is the Lady's Glen. Here Dante Cabriel Rossetti contemplated suicide. William Bell Scott in his *Autobiographical Notes* (1892) describes the occasion:

> Miss Boyd sometimes drove us about the country . . . One day she took us to the Lady's Glen, a romantic ravine in which the stream falls into a black pool round which the surrounding vertical rocks have been worn, by thousands of years of rotating flood, into a circular basin, called, as many such have been designated, the Devil's Punchbowl. We all descended to the overhanging margin of the superincumbent rock; but never shall I forget the expression of Gabriel's face when he bent over the precipice, peering into the un-

fathomed water in which sundry waifs flew round and round like lost souls in hell.

Rossetti stepped back from the brink.

Linn Dhu
NX 228 813

Fall on the Cross Water of Duisk, the principal tributary of the Stinchar.

Linn Spout
NS 283 485

Fall on the Caaf which rushes along in a series of rapids before falling over an eight-metre cascade.

Eas Mor
Ns 020 222

Waterfall in the Auchenhew Glen where the Allt Mor falls 30 metres into a rock basin. It is in a magnificent amphitheatre in the hills in a wood which occupies the floor of the glen. A brilliant rainbow hangs over the falls in certain weather conditions and services as a landmark for mariners.

Ness Glen

A fine example of a rock gorge, Ness Glen is magnificently situated at the foot of Loch Doon. Its beautifully-wooded, seemingly-straight sides are from 30 to 60 metres deep. It appears to be little wider than the little River Doon itself. Loch Doon is now diverted so that its waters fall into the Solway Firth via the Dee as part of the Galloway Hydro Electric Power Scheme. The dam above Ness Glen constructed in the 1930s replaced a scheme which had the reverse effect for, at one time, there were tunnels to reduce the level of the lake and prevent flooding. The narrow exit which favoured the building of the dam also favoured an original device used in an unsuccessful siege of Loch Doon Castle. In an effort to flood the island stronghold of Doon Castle a brushwood dam was built but it was swept away and the soldier who was building it was drowned. The fortress did not succumb to seige until it was shifted to its present site by the engineers.

Ness Waterfall
NS 411 214

A waterfall on the Water of Coyle in the grounds of a hotel, the Sundrum Castle, near Ayr. It is about two metres in height.

Penkill falls
NX 252 969

Fall of about four metres on the Penwhapple Burn above Penkill Castle, residence during the 1860s of Alice Boyd, mistress of William Bell Scott, a surly Pre-Raphaelite. In his biography of Dante Gabriel Rossetti (1960) Oswald Doughty describes a visit which the poet paid to the place when he was suffering from ill-health and in debt:

> Penkill Castle, he found, still preserved something of that mediaeval galmour dear to the Pre-Raphaelite heart. Despite seventeenth century additions and even modern restorations, its worn battlements, particularly on warm, autumn afternoons, invited the romantic dreamer looking out over the glen below beyond the quiet farmlands to the distant sea, to play with idle fancies, invent stirring legends, recall in pleasant, imaginative retrospect something of the pain and passion of the past.

It was on this visit that Rossetti contemplated suicide at Kilkerran (q.v.).

Ravenscraig Glen
NS 272 528

An attractive glen with pretty cascades on the South Burn, a tributary of Rye Water under Cock Robin Hill in the Cunninghame District.

Rossetti Linn
NS 391 053

Outside Straiton, the attractive Ayrshire Village on the edge of the Galloway Forest Park, is the Lambdoughty Glen. It is within the fine Blairquhan Estate and the woodlands there contrast with those of the Forest Park, representing a more generous spirit more in harmony with the landscape. An attractive nature trail, Lady Hunter Blair's Walk, leads up the glen. There are two falls on the burn. The first which the pedestrian following the path from Straiton reaches might be called *Lady Hunter Blair's Linn*. It is a gracious fall of some five metres. The upper fall, impressive in dark woods, is about ten metres high. It is called Black Linn and it is said locally that this was where Rossetti, haunted by insomnia and ill health and an alcoholic, contemplated suicide (see Kilkerran Falls and Penkill Falls).

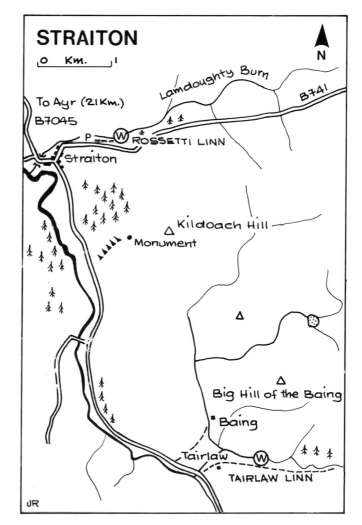

Glen Sannox

It is generally agreed that the glen occupied by the South Sannox Burn is one of the loveliest in Arran although its north-westerly aspect gives it a somewhat gloomy appearance at times. It is dominated by the incomparably graceful peak of Cir Mhor and the walk to its head takes the visitor into the very heart of the Arran mountains. The headwaters of the burn, which drain the corrie between Cir Mhor and the Castles, a favourite haunt for deer, falls in a series of waterfalls beside which there is a path leading to the col between the two peaks.

Stinchar Falls   *NX 371 963*

The little river Stinchar rises in the Awful Hand Range and reaches the Firth of Clyde at Ballantrae after some 40 kilometres. The upper part of its course is through the Carrick Forest and between the Shalloch Pass and Black Row, where it crosses the Southern Upland Boundary Fault and then follows it for some distance. The brawling mountain stream falls more than 150 metres in less than three kilometres. The uppermost falls are at Stinchar Bridge 8(NS 397 955) where there is a car park, and a waymarked forest walk leads downstream to enable the visitor to visit all of the falls. The prettiest are caused by a pophyritic dyke and are found just above a bridge on a forest road (*NX 384 970*). There is a picnic site here. The principal falls are further downstream. Beneath the abutments of an old bridge the Stinchar falls and there are further falls on the tributary which drains Linfern Loch. The river accomplishes the fall in four or five disjointed leaps, full of interest. Underneath the bridge when the river is low there are a number of potholes which illustrate perfectly the way in which these features are formed, for the huge boulders which have formed them are still in place in several instances. The Stinchar carries very little water in the summer and it is difficult to believe that the water is capable of shifting such rocks—the size of cannonballs—but in spate it is a different matter. The falls are now overshadowed by sprucewoods which clothe the steep slopes of the valley. The river is referred to by Burns in his famous song 'My Nanie O'

> Behind yon hills where Stinchar flows,
> 'Mang moors an' mosses many, O,
> The wintry sun the day has clos'd
> And I'll awa' tae Nanie, O.

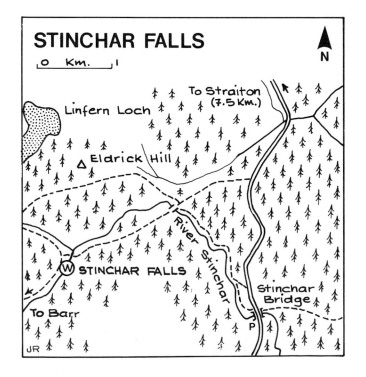

It was pointed out to him that the inclination of the English to pronounce the river's name as if it were written 'Stinker' rendered the verse somewhat inelegant, so Burns changed the river to the Lugar. This serves to remind us that the 'ch' sound is pronounced softly as in 'Church'.

Falls of Struey   *NR 993 203*

Arran has much in common with Skye and Mull from a geological point of view and it would be surprising if there was not at least one spectacular coastal fall. It is appropriate that Arran's falls should be close to Bennan Head, the southernmost tip of the island, and that the little river Struey, which drains a basin of only two square kilometres, should fall into the sea over cliffs 45 metres high to make an outstanding feature in the very heart of the Firth of Clyde. The river flows through a gorge cut in dolerite before falling over the cliff. It may be inspected from above and by following a rough path involving some scrambling to a wild shore from the foot of the cliffs. The footpath is 45 metres east of the burn and leads also to the Black Cave.

Southannan Glen   *NS 216 522*

Glen with cascades between Fairlie and West Kilbride where a notable house in the Italian style, now ruined, was built by Lord Eglinton. Lord Cockburn visited it and did not think much of it, but the Minister of the Parish wrote about 'a striking piece of Nature's work' in *The Old Statistical Account*. The principal fall of about 15 metres at the head of the glen is called *Biglees Fall*. It is now generally deprived of water by the reservoir, but the place is worth a visit because of the splendid views there are over the Firth of Clyde.

Tairlaw Linn   *NS 409 011*

By general agreement Tairlaw Linn is the finest single fall in the Galloway Forest Park. It is situated at the head of the forge above the old bridge across the Water of Girvan at Tairlaw about half way between Straiton and the Shalloch Pass on the Newton Stewart road. Kevan MacDowell asserts in *Carrick Gallovidian* that the name is Tairbealach Linn, the spray-enshrouded waterfall of the pass. It is caused by basaltic lavas of Old Red Sandstone age. The river flows through a fine old wood under the Big Hill of the Baing at this point. The Galloway Forest starts in earnest south of the road. The height of the fall is generally given as 18 metres but the uppermost fall, set in a beautiful rock amphitheatre overhung by spreading birches and distinctly difficult of access, is not more than 12 metres high, beginning with a very narrow fall, over which it is generally possible to step, set beside a group of pines. This is followed by a charming apron fall. The cascades culminate in a further narrow fall of bright water.

Tranew Linn   *NS 359 070*

This cascade is between Kirkmichael and Straiton on the Water of Girvan within the finely-wooded estate of Blairqhan. This superb mansion was built in the Tudor style in 1824 and it dominates the green valley between these two villages. C H Dick (1916) is enthusiastic about this part of Carrick:

> For a few miles beyond Kirkmichael as you go towards Straiton the way is enclosed among trees and runs high on the right bank of the Girvan, winding and doubling with surprises that fairly take your breath away, and giving now a lengthwise and now a broadside view of quiet pools and little

Tairlaw Linn. *On the edge of the Galloway Forest Park near Straiton.*
DAVID I HARVIE

cascades in the river. If the time of your travelling be early summer when the leaves are most delicate and the greens most vivid and the waters abundant and if the day be one of strong sunshine your journey will stand out among your memories of 'sweet wayfaring'.

White Water   *NS 025 422*

This is the everyday—and appropriate-name of the Corrie Burn in Arran. The rushing burn drains Corrie Lan under Goat Fell and provides a pleasing alternative route to the summit of that granite-block summit. The burn consists of a series of more or less attractive waterfalls and it stands out so clearly in spate that it can be seen far out to sea. It is characteristic of this wonderful island.

The Solway Basin

Aird Linn   *NX 815 923*

Aird Linn is a picturesque waterfall on the Shinnel Water in Upper Nithsdale. The fall is just below Tynron Manse on the by-road from Moniaive to Thornhill in a prettily wooded district under the termination of the fine range of hills between the Shinnel and the Scaur. At Tynron there is a National Nature Reserve, Tynron Juniper Wood, unmatched in the south of Scotland. The linn in overgrown woods is an imposing leap of eight metres.

Spout of Auchentalloch   *NX 666 566*

This pretty waterfall is not far from Twynholm in Kircudbright-shire close to the old military road between Gatehouse of Fleet and Castle Douglas. The Spout Burn drains a romantic den which makes a pleasing excursion.

Linn of Bargrennan   *NX 356 746*

This is the fall at the foot of the series which begins at Birch Linn on the Cree. The hamlet is call Clachaneasy, the hamlet at the waterfall, and it is near where the Minnoch joins the Cree. It was here on the back road, that Campbell, the artist-victim in Dorothy L. Sayers' *Five Red Herrings* was found. That author's atmospheric descriptions of the district will enhance any visit to the place. The Linn is some five metres in height.

Linn of Barhoise   *NX 339 624*

Modest falls on the Bladnoch near the farmhouse of the same name. Pretty enough and meriting a visit if you are in the area.

Loups of Barnshangan   *NX 192 650*

Falls on the Cross Water of Luce in the remote Wigtownshire countryside.

Beld Craig Linn   *NT 112 012*

Beld Craig gets its name from a magnificent overhanging rock at the head of an attractive cleft in the low hills south of Moffat. At the foot of the rock are some curious marks, the Devil's Hoof marks. The name is sometimes corrupted to Bell Craig. The fine little fall is reached from the Old Carlisle Road, a pleasing alternative to the A74. There is a likeable walk back to Moffat by Brakenside Farm and Dumcrieff affording a good view of the Meeting of the Waters where the Evan and the Moffat join the Annan.

Birch Linn   *NX 331 769*

Fall on the Cree near the Linn of Bargrennan(q.v.). Birch, that most graceful of all Scottish trees, is the most common tree found near waterfalls. It is surprising that this relatively unprepossessing little fall is the only one so-called. The fall, which is about four metres high, is reached by a farm track from Creebank on the A714. In the 1.6m reach between Carrick Burnfoot, 103 metres above sea-level, and the Linn, the Cree follows an outcrop of nearly vertical shaly rocks and the gradient is gentle, but between the Linn and Bargrennan Church there is a series of waterfalls which bring the stream to 41 metres above seas-level. The Upper Cree was once the true headwater of the Bladnoch: the elbow at Carrick Burnfoot represents, in geological terms, a comparatively recent change.

Falls of Black Burn   *NY 460 890*

These little-known falls near Newcastleton are reached from the farm of Blackburn near the road from Langholm. A family of goats inhabits the remote valley of this Border burn, adding considerably to its interest, but the approaches to this fall are attractive enough. First a low fall will be encountered and then Hog Gill Spout (*NY 462 892*) on a tributary. This is an eight metre fall of the apron type just out of sight of the main stream round a corner, but its roar can be heard from the Black Burn. The main falls, two pretty cascades of about ten metres, are reached next. They are the kind of fall which permits a full exploration, but they make their best impression at a little distance. It is unlikely that the modern visitor will share the reactions of the account written by the Minister of the Parish in 1845:

In this wild and romantic vale, nature appears in various

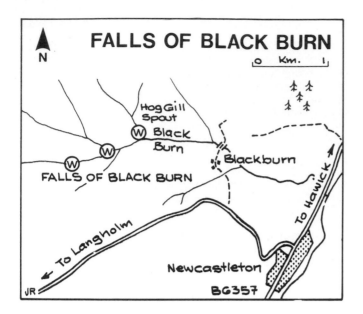

forms, now beautiful then awful, sometimes sublime, frequently terrible.

Above the principal falls there is a series of cascades and, on a tributary, Goat Linn (*NY 454 888*).

Black Linn see Grey Mare's Tail, Closeburn

Black Linn   *NX 369 788*

A two metre fall above a peat black pool on the Minnoch, a short distance above Stroan Bridge.

Black Linn   *NX 907 973*

Fall on Cample Water above Closeburn, less distinctive than the falls on Crichope Burn.

Black Water Falls   *NX 611 885*

Falls below the B729 at the Youth Hostel above the flooded Glenhoul Glen.

Black Water of Dee Falls   *NX 648 696*

The Forestry Commission have recently opened up some of their forest roads as 'forest drives'. The first, opened by the Queen in Jubilee Year, was the Raiders Road following the line of a chase in the novel by S R Crockett. There are attractive falls on the Dee just below the now disused railway viaduct on the Galloway line at the exit from Loch Stroan where the river tumbles about four metres in the metamorphic rocks at the edge of the granite. The granite itself forms the basis of Collin Falls (*NX 597 736*) above Loch Stroan where the river tumbles lazily over a variety of ledges at what is a favourite picnicking spot.

Bogle Linn   *NT 267 026*

Fall on the Moodlaw Burn, a tributary of the White Esk in the wilds of Eskdalemuir.

Falls of Buchan Burn   *NX 418 804*

The Buchan Falls are in the heart of the Galloway Forest Park. Where the cart track crosses the burn above Buchan Farm there is a faded inscription on the parapet of the bridge:

> Land of brown heath and shaggy wood
> Land of the mountain and the flood
> Land of my sires. What mortal hand
> Can e'er untie the filial band
> That knits me to thy rugged strand.

Scott's lines are nowhere more appropriate. The falls can be approached in two ways. Either by dropping from Bruce's Stone (where there is a car park) by the Scots Baronial farm to the bridge, or by following the track to the Merrick from Bruce's Stone and diverging to the right. The most attractive group of three falls cannot be seen from either the head or the foot of the burn which runs in a series of cascades 135 metres in height. Below a twisted oak the burn tumbles ten metres over abrupt, bleached rocks and then shoots through a waterslide which in most conditions is paralleled by a eight-metre fall. The two branches come together again to fall a further six metres. This combination of three falls is the heart of the place.

The Gaelic name of these falls is Eas Bothanach, the fall of the bothies (huts). Timothy Pont's map preserves the old Celtic name for Buchan Falls, Eas Buchany.

An attractive wooded dell leads to an open moor in which the falls are situated. Glen Trool is often likened to the Trossachs. The path to the falls forms part of a Forest Trail.

Falls of Buchan Burn*. Hanging valley falls above Loch Trool. From an old postcard.*

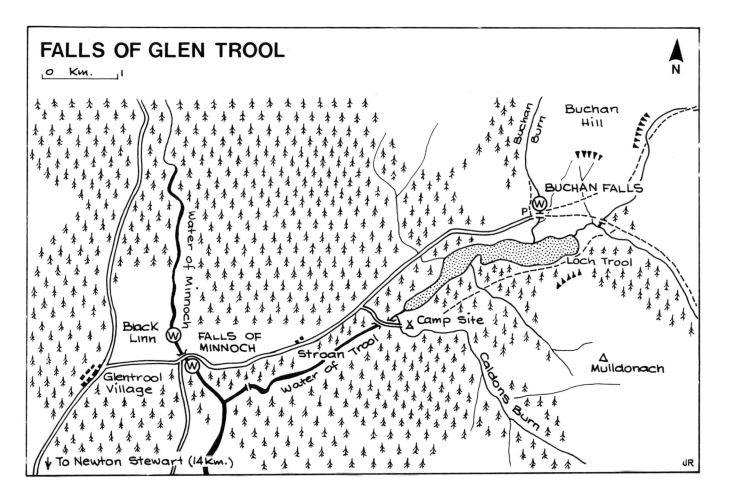

FALLS OF GLEN TROOL

0 Km. 1

N

Water of Minnoch

Buchan Burn

Buchan Hill

BUCHAN FALLS

P

Loch Trool

Black Linn

FALLS OF MINNOCH

Camp Site

Stroan Trool

Water of Trool

Caldons Burn

Glentrool Village

Mulldonach

To Newton Stewart (14 Km.)

JR

Buck's Linn   NX 607 798

A fall reached from the by-road which crosses the Craigshinnie Burn above Glen Lee. The house is said to be haunted by Lady Ashburton who is supposed to have poisoned her husband. The fall is in policies which have been laid out with paths and bridges.

Buck Loup   NX 490 722

Buck Loup is the attractive fall immediately above the road bridge at Talnotry on the A712 (The Queen's Way) which crosses the Grey Mare's Tail Burn. The fall is often mistaken for the Grey Mare's Tail itself which is, in fact, higher up on the same stream and hidden from view at the bridge. Buck Loup is ten metres in height and is between grassy banks overhung, in a pretty way, with a few trees. It can easily be reached from the car park at the foot of the hill.

Carron Linns   NS 874 000

The most splendid part of the railway journey from Dumfries to Glasgow is where the train crosses the Carron Water by a fine viaduct and climbs by a tunnel to the upper Nith. Almost all of the magnificent country seen is part of the Drumlanrig Estate, luxuriously wooded and dominated by the castle. At Carron Linns on the estate at the entrance to the wild Dalveen Pass a nature trail has been laid out beside the little river. The Carron Water falls over a succession of little sills in a red sandstone gorge. The scene is characteristic of Dumfries and Galloway. It reminds us that the word 'linn'—common

throughout South West Scotland—has three distinct uses. It means 'pool' and it is not difficult to see how this has been transferred to the fall above the pool. Linn is also used in the South West for 'burn'. The probable derivation of the word is from the Old English 'hlynn', a torrent. In Welsh the word can mean 'noisy'.

Cluden Leap   NX 940 793

The Cluden Water falls, picturesquely over successive shelves of new red sandstone at East Cluden where there is an interesting old mill which was the subject of a study by the Victorian photographer, George Washington Wilson.

Clugie Linn   NX 487 712

On Palnure Burn below the confluence with the Grey Mare's Tail Burn and below the A719 close to the Talnotry Camp site.

College Linn   NX627 902

On the Ken above High Bridge of Ken. The river has banked up with the building of the Kendoon Reservoir.

Craigie Linn   NX 535 352

On the Little Water of Fleet where it leaves the granits of the Cairnsmore of Fleet.

Crichope Linn   *NX 910 955*

A deep, narrow ravine in red sandstone—in this case desert sandstone of Permian age—which has delighted visitors over the years.

> The water in its passage over a hill of red sandstone, has in the course of ages cut a deep ravine so narrow that in many places one may leap across it. The sides of this ravine overhung by rich foliage, and presenting rocks of most picturesque forms, the noise and agitation of the water underneath produce a most imposing effect (*The New Statistical Account*).

The Linn was visited by Burns who was annoyed at his guide for continually telling him how wonderful the place was, the poet preferred to appreciate things for himself. Scott used the site in *Old Mortality*. At the entrance to the ravine there used to be a cave called the Elf's Kirk, but it was used as a freestone quarry. Its most notable associations are with the Covenantors and a narrow part of the Linn is called Barley's Leap. There is a Covenanters' Cave, and a rock in the ravine where a cobbler used to sit is still called The Souter's Seat. The pool below the waterfall is called Hell's Cauldron. On the edge of the ravine is a Hill Fort, 24 metres above the water and at the head is a further fall, the aptly named Gullet Spout (*NX 915 952*).

The Doaches   *NX 692 533*

This is the name given to the roaring cataract formed by the Dee at Tongland. Bridged by Telford, the site of a fine watermill, this series of river rapids presented a magnificent spectacle in spate. In spite of the fact that it broadened into what were in effect two lochs the Dee has always been a variable stream. It now forms part of a regulated system. The Tongland Power Station and Dam were completed in 1935. It has a catchment of 1023 square kilometres and a gross head of 35 metres. The discharge over the falls is now controlled by the South of Scotland Electricity Board.

> Its channel is extremely rugged. Its banks are richly wooded with oak, birch, elm elder (the bourtree), thorn and hazel. The current is, in some places, forced between perpendicular rocks 70 or 80 feet in height. It is boldest and most striking just before it joins the sea, and is seen to greatest advantage when swollen by the rains of autumn, or by the melted snows in spring. The best view of its impetuosity is commanded from an old two arched bridge a little above high water mark (*The New Statistical Account*).

The Doaches, famous salmon weirs. From an old postcard.

The Doaches are the salmon weirs which have long been erected in the Dee at Tongland. There is a detailed account of the weirs, and of the various methods used to catch salmon, in *The New Statistical Account*. 'Few objects can surpass in terrific grandeur this majestic river, when its torrent flood rushes along with appalling fury, like,' writes The Reverend John McMillan of Kircudbright, 'rolling masses of snow, forming a series of foaming cataracts, above which the sunbeams are reflected and refracted into mimic rainbows in the hovering spray.' The poet Alexander Montgomery, a contemporary of Shakespeare is thought to have been referring to the Doaches in the following lines:

> But as I looked me alane
> I saw a river rin
> Our o'er a steeple rock of stane
> Sine lichted in a lin,
> With tumbling and rumbling
> Among the rockis round
> Devalling and falling
> Into a pit profound.

Man's closest association with waterfalls has been as a fisherman. Salmon and sea trout have always been taken from Scottish rivers and they are nowhere easier to catch than at waterfalls. The best account of these fisheries is, perhaps, that of the Rev Dugald Stewart Williamson of Tongland in *The New Statistical Account* of 1843. He describes the Doaches, the elaborate salmon weirs on the Dee connected by stone batteries, and also the various methods used to take fish. Stake nets, erected at the mouth of the river, were common. Hang nets, or bag nets, drawn across the lower end of a pool were also used, but, in Tongland at least, most fish were taken by shoulder nets, 'a net fixed to a semi-circular bow of wood attached to a pole 20 feet in length'. The skill and strength required to take fish by this method can be appreciated if it is considered that, on one occasion, 35 salmon were taken with a single throw. Drag nets, worked by two men, were similar to shoulder nets. Other methods included draught nets, used in tidal pools, the gaff and the rod. Nothing if not thorough, the Reverend Williamson also describes grappling, the method used by poachers.

There is a fine passage in H V Morton's *In Scotland Again* describing a visit at night to the Doaches.

Linn of Deugh   *NX 807 908*

The Deugh, rising on Windy Standard, is the true headwater of the Dee, although the Deugh becomes the Ken before the Ken is usurped by the Dee. The Linn of Deugh, a roaring cataract beside the road from Carsphairn to Dalry, was a tourist attraction before the Galloway Hydro Electric Power Scheme. The riverine Loch Kendoon now occupies the gorge. Close to the Linn was the Tinker's Loup where a fugitive tinker leaped the Deugh.

Dobb's Linn   *NT 197 158*

This waterfall is a smaller version of the Grey Mare's Tail, Moffat, famous as a hiding place for Covenanters and because of its geological significance. The fall is hidden from the road (A708) where it crosses Raking Gill, but it is easily reached from this point. Because of its aspect it is often considered a dull place, but the site is full of interest. It is possible to walk to the fall from the Grey Mare's Tail, or to combine a day on the hills with a visit to both falls. The stream plunges down vertical Silurian grits in a series of steps and falls into a beautiful pool. Geologists visit this locality for the Ordovician and Silurian fossil graptolites—primitive forms of life which resemble quill pens—hence their name. They were discovered by Charles Lapworth and an inscription at the head of the pass reads

Birkhill Cottage where between 1872 and 1877 Charles Lapworth recognised the value of graptolites as a clue to the geological structure of these hills

The fall get its name from Halbert Dobson, the Covenanter. There is good description in Molly Clavering (1953) *From the Border hills*:

This wild and gloomy place, bleak even in the sunshine was the home during the Killing Times of two convenanting stalwarts Halbert Dobson and David Dunn, more commonly known as Hab Dob and Davie Din. They built themselves a cottage on the very edge of the cliff about 400 feet up, and with an overhang of another 200 feet of sheer rock above it. By day, or if danger pressed, they hid in a cave at the bottom of the Linn together with other fugitives who had sought refuge there, while one of their number kept a look out from Watch Knowe above.

Besides their earthly foes these two worthies had to contend with the devil in person who visited them nightly in their cottage and tried to terrify them into throwing themselves down the precipice. They finally routed him, armed with Bibles and rowan staffs and there is a rough but vivid rhyme telling how

Hab Dob an' Davie Dun,
Dang the De'il ower Dob's Linn

Habbie held him griff and rim
Till like a bunch o' barkit skins,
Doon flew Satan ower the linns

which can be read in Hogg's 'Mountain Bard'.

Dobb's Linn is part of the extensive National Trust for Scotland property which includes Loch Skene and the Grey Mare's Tail.

Dow Spout   NX 463 828

The most spectacular mountain waterfall in Galloway, in the remote heartland of the Galloway Hills on the east face of Craignaw. It is best seen from the Rhinns of Kells Road or the Garraries Forest Road at Black Hill of the Bush, but it is best reached from Glen Trool by Gairland Burn and Loch Valley (the curious name of this loch is a corruption of Bealach—a pass). A circular walk, 20 kilometres in length which will occupy a strong party all day, is described in the Galloway Forest Park Handbook. Dow Spout cascades 100 metres down the face of Craignaw.

Drumlanrig Waterfalls

In the splendid policies of Drumlanrig Castle woodland walks lead beside the Marr Burn. The chief attraction here is the magnificent woodland with fine Silver and Douglas Firs. The *Lower Falls of Marr Burn* (NX 848 991) are about two metres in height. The *Upper Falls* (NX 837 985), more difficult of access, are about four metres high. Beneath Drumlanrig the Nith is at its finest. A riverside path leads along the right bank to attractive rapids called *Duncan's Linn* (NS 858 004). Further north, towards Sanquhar, another attractive stretch of the same river, called *The Slunks* (NS 833 058), has a picnic site beside the A76.

Dunskey Glen

This waterfall is formed by a small stream called Auchtrematane Burn. When this stream is swollen with rains, it pours a copious torrent over rugged rocks into a narrow ravine, about 50 or 60 feet deep, whence it flows with a peaceful current for a quarter of a mile along the bottom of the glen, which opens out on to Port Kale Bay. The scenery about this cascade and from it to the sea is exceedingly fine. The rugged rocks near the waterfall are enriched with furze and heath, or overrun with ivy and honeysuckle; and the boldly sloping sides are well covered with thriving wood (*The New Statistical Account*).

Earlston Linn   NX 607 841

This fall is a shadow of its former self. C H Dick's description of the ways to it up the Ken from Allangibbon Bridge suggest that it must once have been a premier excursion, not to be missed. It could be reached by following either bank of the river, the left or east bank being the more attractive. There was a low fall at Fir Tree Island before the gorge was reached. The fall itself was spectacular, 'a roaring flashing waterfall where the whole river dashes through a very narrow cleft and spreads out fanwise over the rocks as it descends into a deep pool'. The Linn can still be reached in this way but the place is now occupied by Earlstoun Loch. At the fall itself there is still a considerable break in the passage of the Ken and the banks of the Ken are well wooded in parts. The fall and the loch take their name from the old Castle near the river, home of the Gordons.

Euchan Falls   NS 772 087

The Euchan rises in the hills between Carsphairn and Sanquhar and joins the Nith at Sanquhar Castle. It drains a wild moorland where a mineral spring once attracted tourists. Above Sanquhar it flows through a gorge called the Deil's Dungeon above which is a hill fort called Kemps Castle.

Falls of Gairland Burn   NS 417 804

This wild, cataracting burn is on the threshold of the Cauldron, the peat wasteland dotted with lochs which is the heart of the Galloway Hills. A path from Bruce's Stone keeps well above the burn itself at first. It is, none the less, the best way to visit this torrent which is a fine sight in spate.

Garpol Linn   NT 065 029

This linn is one of several close to Moffat which provided suitable short excursions for the tourists who came to 'take the waters'. At the head of the dell there was a mineral spring and above it is Auchen Castle, held on behalf of Bruce, which commands a fine view of the valley of the Evan Water now flanked by fine sprucewoods relieved by oak, beech and poplar. The ravine, with upper and lower waterfalls, is flanked by made paths and spanned by bridges. It is reached by going under the railway beyond Beattock. The modern baronial residence of the Youngers, Auchen Castle, is now an attractively set hotel seen from the A74.

Garroch Glen   NX 602 814

A footpath begins at the Allangibbon Bridge, Dalry, and winds over Waterside Hill to a footbridge beside an old watermill at the foot of Garroch Glen. Nowhere else is it possible to so

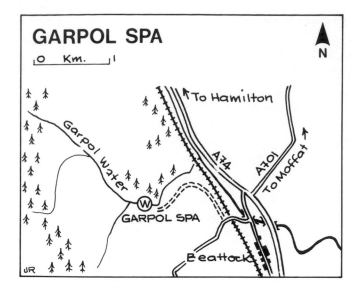

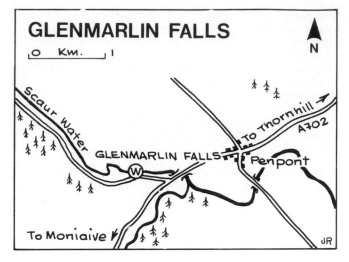

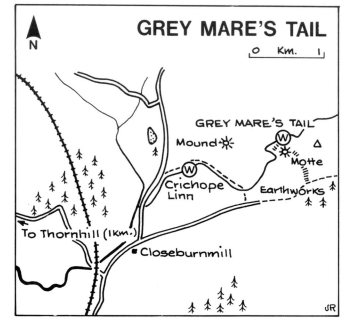

exactly capture the atmosphere of the valley of the Ken before the Galloway Hydro Electric Power Scheme. The wooded ravine occupied by the Garroch provides a very fine excursion.

Garwald Linns   NT 234 001

The principal tributary of the White Esk in Dumfriesshire, the Garwald rises on the southern slopes of Ettrick Pen in the heart of what was once the greatest forest in Southern Scotland. The aptly named stream—the rough burn—forms a magnificent waterfall.

> This linn is a long descent over a stony channel, sloping here and there precipitous, between rocky flanks, for the most part naked, but clothed at intervals with copse and brushwood; and forms now a cascade, now a capricious cataract and now a rushing rapid (*The Ordnance Gazetteer*).

Glencaird Linn   NX 369 790

A further low fall on the Water of Minnoch above the Black Linn and similar to it. It is reached by diverging from the Stroan Bridge Forest Walk.

Glenmarlin Falls   NX 833 944

Visitors to Scotland who have the good fortune to travel north by Nithsdale must first be impressed by the roaring river in Dumfries, but it will not be until they reach Thornhill that they will encounter the richness of Scotland's glens. No English great house is more imposingly situated in wooded parkland than Drumlanrig. At this point the Nith receives the united waters of the Scaur and the Shinnel and the discriminating visitor will be drawn to the place, 'so embellished with trees and cultivation as to be rife with picturesqueness and romance'. Thus the editor of *The Ordnance Gazetteer* describes the Scaur Water, the principal tributary of the middle Nith. There is a fine old bridge over the river near Penpont on the Pilgrims' Road to Whithorn and there is a magnificent gorge above this. The head of the falls is about a kilometre from the bridge and between this point and the bridge the river falls ten metres. These are the finest river falls west of the A74.

Grey Mare's Tail (Closeburn)   NX 922 959

This fall with a famous name is neither so high nor so impressive as the more widely known fall above Moffat. It is on Crichope Linn where the Linn Burn crosses the elusive Devil's Dyke, an earthwork of uncertain age and origin. There are a number of other earthworks, including a motte at the fall, which add interest to the parish. The approach to the fall is by the farm of Benthead above Crichope Linn (q.v.). It is hidden in an impressive amphitheatre of trees and is seen to be not quite vertical on close inspection. The height of the fall is about 30 metres and it merits a visit. Above the Grey Mare's Tail is another fall, Black Linn (*NX 926 961*) situated in a ravine.

The origin of the name 'Grey Mare's Tail' is of interest. Scott, in his notes for 'Marmion', states quite clearly that it is derived from the appearance of the Moffat fall and the upper fall in Moffatdale does have some resemblance to a horse's tail, drawn together at the top and spreading out below. This is not the case at Closeburn, nor elsewhere. However, it is such a descriptive name that it may well have been adopted to add interest to otherwise unnamed falls. There are six 'Grey Mare's Tails' in South West Scotland and there are 'Grey Mare's Tails' at Kinlochmore in Argyll, at Inverarnan and Clydebank in Dunbartonshire and at Aberfoyle in Perthshire.

In his book *Carrick Gallovidian*, in which there are a number of fanciful derivations, MacDowell gives the following account of the origin of the name:

This name is applied to various picturesque cascades or waterfalls throughout Galloway and its ancient division of Carrick, as well as in other parts of Pictish and Celtic Scotland. They are supposed to represent something like a grey mare's tail—but the true meaning is more beautiful. The supposition has arisen from the fact that the sound of the phonetic pronunciation is not altogether unlike that of the English 'grey mare's tail'. The place-name—and the picturesque description contained in it—are typically Pictish-Celtic.

Greith Mear Eas Tadh Ail means literally 'the glistening cascade rushing forth from the rocky ledge'. Here, in this place-name, is conveyed a vivid picture.

Grey Mare's Tail (Dundrennan)   NX 744 468

An unprepossesing little fall on the Abbey Burn, South of Dundrennan.

Grey Mare's Tail (Moffat)   NT 184 148

This is the most striking example of a hanging valley waterfall in the South of Scotland. The Tail Burn falls about 100 metres over the side of the glacial trough of Moffatdale. It forms a series of cascades culminating in a fine unsupported fall, the Grey Mare's Tail itself, one of the most renowned and most frequently visited in the whole of Britain. The fall deserves its reputation and it should not on any account be omitted from any itinerary in which it can reasonably be included.

The fall is above the main road from Moffat to Selkirk (A708) and a short footpath leads up the true right bank of the burn to the foot of the fall. Another path leads up the true left bank, much higher up the hillside, to reach the top of the fall and lead eventually to the remote Loch Skene. The main fall is seen to be in three parts and it is generally reckoned to be about 60 metres high. It plunges sensationally and its immediate environs are highly dangerous in wet conditions. The steep grassy banks look innocent enough but they should be treated with the greatest respect. The banks, which are treeless, might be thought to be dull, but are, in fact, extremely rich in wild flowers. The area is also the haunt of wild goats.

The place is steeped in associations. The Convenanters who hid at Dobb's Linn nearby undoubtedly knew the fall well. It is said that Claverhouse, the most hated of their pursuers, rode his coal black charger across the breast of Bran Law beside the fall 'where the descent is so precipitous that no mere earthly horse could keep its feet or merely mortal rider could keep the saddle' (Scott). Tradition has it that the horse was a gift of the Devil which enabled it to accomplish this feat. Scott's evocation of the the fall in 'Marmion' is fine:

> Where, deep deep down, and far within
> Toils with the rocks the roaring linn;
> Then, issuing forth one foamy wave,
> And wheeling round the Giant's Grave
> White as the snowy chargers tail
> Drives down the pass of Moffatdale

The Grey Mare's Tail is the property of the National Trust for Scotland who have placed information boards at the foot of the fall. The property comprehends a good deal more than the fall

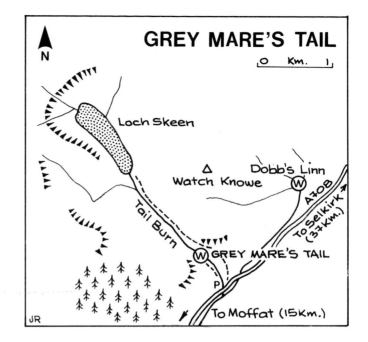

itself, stretching from the Birkhill Pass to Lochcraighead above Loch Skene along the ridge to White Coomb. These hills may be more often visited now than they were during the nineteenth century but they are lonely places. It is said that James Hogg borrowed a five pound note and, to his great chagrin, lost it during the course of a visit to Loch Skene. He found the same note 12 months later.

Grey Mare's Tail (Talnotry)   NX 491 726

This fall is no distance from the recently established forestry Commission camp site at Talnotry and from the car park on the A712 beneath Murray's Monument. It is nevertheless hidden from sight and Buck Loup, the fall below it, is frequently mistaken for the Grey Mare's Tail. The burn drains a considerable basin on the edge of the Lamlachan Hills. The cataract, 15 metres high, makes an impressive leap into a rock

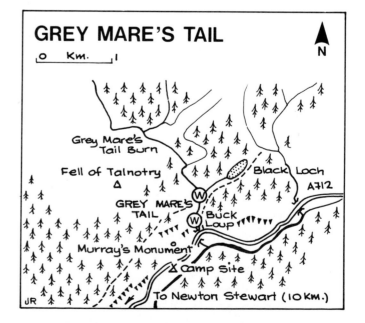

strewn pool. It is possible to reach the foot of the fall at the plunge pool in reasonably dry conditions.

It is almost certain that visitors to the Grey Mare's Tail will climb to the top of Talnotry Hill to the monument erected to commemorate the brilliant young scholar, Alexander Murray (1775–1813), the shepherd boy who became a professor of Oriental Languages at Edinburgh at the age of 36. Others will wish to see the Wild Goat Park established by the forestry Commission. The more energetic will follow the Commission's forest trail which leads from the road into the hills and back by the falls. Finally there is a grand walk by the Glen of the Bar beside Palnure Burn to the little port of the same name on the estuary.

Grey Mare's Tail, Wood of Cree   *NX 385 711*

Above the broad lower reaches of the Cree above Minnigaff where the salmon fishermen built the Cruives of Cree is the Old Wood of Cree, a natural oak wood on the edge of the conifers of the Galloway Forest Park. The Carnochan Burn which descends from Larg Hill forms this series of cascades just as it enters the old wood. There is a delightful walk to the open hillside from the little bridge at the foot of the burn.

Highlandman's Loup   *NT 093 071*

The mineral well at Moffat, patronised in Jane Austen's day by the most fashionable members of society, is some little distance from the spa town. Below the well, the Well Burn falls about 15 metres in a succession of little falls. About halfway down there is an anvil-shaped stone where it would be possible to leap across the burn. This must be the Highlandman's Loup.

Keltie's Linn   *NS 884 091*

At Keltie's Linn in the Enterkin Pass a minister and five Covenanters were rescued from captivity by a band of 12 local men under James and Thomas Harkness of Closeburn who attacked a company of dragoons and shot their commander, a Captain Keltie.

Holy Linn   *NX 655 808*

This attractive fall on the Garple is reached from the road from Dalry to Moniaive. A wood filling a deep glen is seen on the right. The fall is a sudden leap over a rock barrier into a basin forming a natural font. Congregations assembled here for worship in the days of the Covenanters and a rebel minister baptised children at the fall. Above it is the ancient Barscube Castle.

Kirkconnel Linn   *NX 674 612*

On Kirkconnel Moor north of Twynholm an infamous killing took place in 1685 when John Bell of Whiteside was barbarously murdered by a local laird. The martyr's monument can be visited en route to Kirkconnel Linn.

Loups of Kilfeddar   *NX 151 675*

Low falls in a rocky gorge on the Main Water of Luce.

Linn of Lairdmannoch   *NX 667 609*

A series of falls on the Tarff, 15 to 18 metres high, which are very impressive in spate.

Falls of Minnoch   *NX 371 785*

These falls are one of the focal points of the Galloway Forest Park now that the Forestry Commission have established a car park at Stroan Bridge. The falls are about two metres high, but the river tumbles under the bridge in a charming way and visitors need only walk a short distance to see the falls. The old estate woods at this point are interesting and the Commission has set up an attractive self-guiding forest trail leading to and from the falls.

Loch Neldricken   *NX 438 831*

On the west shore of Loch Neldricken north east of Loch Trool there is a menacing looking pool at the base of a waterfall which was chosen by S R Crockett as the site of a murder hole, where the bodies of murdered travellers were disposed of.

Penton Linns   *NY 431 774*

The Liddel Water, a tributary of the Esk, forms the boundary between England and Scotland and at Penton Linns, 4.8 kilometres from the confluence of the two rivers, is 'one of the most picturesque waterfalls in the Border Country' (Queen's Scotland). Above the fall are the ruins of Penton Mill and nearby is the site of the old station the Waverley line. The river sweeps under the charming early-nineteenth-century bridge across the Border and falls in a succession of broad cascades one and two metres high under a high wooded bank on the Scottish side. There is a terraced footpath along this bank and from it, it is possible to drop down to the river at various points. There is no finer crossing from England to Scotland than at Penton Linns.

Raehills Glen   *NY 069 935*

Situated above and below St Ann's Bridge on the A701, Raehills Glen is considered one of the most attractive of several river glens near Moffat. The Kinnel Water flows through a gorge below Raehills and the estate has laid out two nature trails which lead beside the river. The most notable feature is a three-ended bridge above a beautiful series of cascades, linked to one another in a series of steps which are the haunt of water-loving birds. The river falls ten metres in these cascades. One of the falls in the policies of Raehills is called Wallace's Loup.

Roaring Linn   *NS 614 114*

An unremarkable linn on the Afton Water, a headwater of the Nith, in Ayrshire.

Routin Linn   *NX 885 797*

The Old Water drains a bigger basin than might be supposed before it joins the Cluden. Just above the confluence it falls steeply over heavily inclined rocks in a charming oakwood. Routin Linn consists of two cascades, six metres in combined height, situated under the road bridge. From the bank below the bridge the two falls are seen through the arch. Towards Dumfries is Irongray Church where there is a memorial to Helen Walker, the prototype of 'Jeanie Deans'.

Glen of Spottes   *NX 804 673*

A pretty fall in a densely wooded glen above Haugh of Urr. It is about eight metres in height, of the apron type. Above the fall is an old mill, and an ivy-covered early chapel.

Tarras Water

This impetuous tributary of the Border Esk falls in a succession of cascades and passes through a romantically wooded glen close to Langholm. It is said that anyone falling into the burn will not drown for before this fate overtakes them their brains will have been dashed to pieces.

Wamphray Glen   *NY 127 964*

The Wamphray Burn drains a charming hidden valley in the foothills south of Moffat. The tiny church perched on a knoll is above the gorge crossed by a frail wooden bridge. The Kirk is almost dwarfed by the huge monuments in the kirkyard of which perhaps the most interesting is an open vault belonging to the Rogersons. John Rogerson who lived from 1741 to 1821 was the first physician to His Majesty the Emperor of Russia.

The falls are below the bridge and are most conveniently reached from the tiny by-road which leaves the Old Carlisle road at Pamlaburn Farm. The principal fall is a cascade of about four metres called *Dubs Cauldron* (*NY 127 964*). Two other amusingly named falls are *The Washing Tub* (or Washing Pan) and *The Pot*. All three are set in woods of creeper-covered trees beside steep grassy banks of great charm, a world away from the buzz of traffic on the busy A74.

Wellburn Spout   *NT 248 040*

A distinctive fall on the Fingland burn in Eskdalemuir Parish. It is 17 metres high.

Grey Mare's Tail, Moffat. Highest fall in the Borders and the most striking example in the South of Scotland of a hanging valley waterfall. HAMISH BROWN

Dobb's Linn. *Noted for its primitive fossils and as the hiding place of a famous Covenanter.* LOUIS STOTT

Explanation of the Tables

The tables list waterfalls in the river systems within which they occur in accordance with their geographical proximity to one another. The following information is given:

Reference Number
Each fall is given a reference number based on the hydrometric area in which it is situated. A further explanation of the numbering system is given below.

Name of Fall
The most commonly used name is given. Gaelic names are used in accordance with their spelling on the Ordnance Survey Map. If the fall does not have a name, the name of the stream on which it occurs is given.

Grid Reference
The full grid reference, including the two grid letters is used. Map references are explained on all Ordnance Survey Maps, and the references provide an index to the 1:25,000 and 1:10,000 maps. Generally falls on right bank tributaries are listed before those on left bank tributaries and where two falls occur on the same stream the fall furthest downstream is identified first on the grounds that it is likely to be the first to be encountered.

Area of Basin
The area of the river or stream above the fall is given in square kilometres. This provides a guide to the discharge of water in the fall. As a general rule falls which drain basins of less than 10 square kilometres are likely to be substantially impaired in dry weather.

Height of Fall
Where available the height of the fall is given in metres. This figure is much more difficult to determine than might be supposed and there are substantial variations in guide books. Almost all falls are successions of closely linked cascades. In some cases there is a single leap – the 'unsupported' part of the fall – which is sufficiently distinctive to be measured by itself, and this is what is meant by the height of the fall. The combined heights of cascades are asterisked in the tables.

Classification
The comparative interest of falls is indicated as follows, but the classification is subjective and the omission of a particular fall should not be held to reflect adversely upon it:

*** Outstanding falls; meriting a visit on their own account; of national importance;
** Significant falls; well worth visiting; of regional importance;
* Interesting falls; meriting a visit if in the locality; of local importance.

Map Number
The sheet number of the Ordnance Survey 1:50,000 map is given. Where the fall is named on the map the number is asterisked.

Access
A brief description of the most convenient route(s) is given indicating the road number and, generally, the town or village.

Access Class (Grade)
The following classification sums up the character of the approaches to the fall:

i Access by clearly marked footpath, generally a guided walk or nature trail;
ii Access by a reasonable path, less than two kilometres from a public road (up to four kilometres there and back); paths may not be cared for, or adequately protected throughout;
iii Falls more than two kilometres from a road, routes may not follow paths and some ability at route finding may be required;
iv Falls situated in grounds to which the public are not normally allowed access;
v Remote falls involving practiced route finding; and the exercise of common sense with regard to suitable weather conditions and with respect to adequate equipment.

River Systems

In the tables of waterfalls the numbering system adopted by the Water Resources Board for its Hydrometric Areas is used. Since the system is based on the rivers of the island of Great Britain it has some inconsistencies when used for Scotland by itself:

1 **Wick Group** Langwell; Wick
2 **Helmsdale Group** Helmsdale, Brora and Fleet
3 **Shin Group** (Kyle of Sutherland) Carron, Einig, Oykell, Cassley, Shin
4 **Conon** Allt Graad; Conon, Bran, Orrin, Blackwater, Meig
5 **Beauly** Glass, Farrar, Cannich, Beauly
6 **Ness** Ness, Loch Ness, Loch Oich, Garry, Moriston
7 **Findhorn Group** Lossie, Findhorn and Nairn
8 **Spey** Spey, Avon, Dulnain, Nethy, Feshie, Calder, Truim
9 **Deveron Group**
10 **Ythan Group** (Buchan) Ythan, Ugie
11 **Don** (Aberdeenshire)
12 **Dee** (Aberdeenshire)
13 **Esk** North Esk, South Esk; Bervie
14 **Firth of Tay Group**
15 **Tay** Tay, Dochart, Lochay, Lyon, Garry, Braan, Tummel, Isla, Ericht
16 **Earn**
17 **Firth of Forth Group**
18 **Forth** Forth, Teith, Leny; Allan, Devon
19 **Almond Group** (Lothians) Almond, Water of Leith, Esk
20 **Tyne Group** (Lothians)
21 **Tweed** Tweed, Ettrick, Yarrow, Teviot, Till, Whiteadder

77	**Esk** (Dumfriesshire) The Border Esk
78	**Annan**
79	**Nith**
80	**Dee** (Galloway)
81	**Cree Group** Luce, Bladnoch and Cree
82	**Doon Group** Doon, Girvan and Stinchar
83	**Irvine and Ayr** Irvine, Garnock and Ayr
84	**Clyde** Clyde, Avon, North and South Calder, Rotten Calder, Kelvin Black and White Cart
85	**Leven** (Dunbartonshire) Loch Lomond, Falloch, Endrick
86	**Firth of Clyde Group**
87	**Fyne Group** Aray, Shira
88	**Add Group** Euchar
89	**Awe and Etive** Orchy, Cladich, Avich; Loch Etive; Creran, Duror
90	**Loch Linnhe Group** Nevis, Leven (Kinlochleven), Coe

91	**Lochy Group** Lochy, Spean, Arkaig
92	**Loch Sheil** Morvern, Ardgour, Sunart, Moidart
93	**Loch Alsh Group** Carron, Elchaig, Sheil of Duich, Morar
94	**Loch Maree Group** Gairloch, Loch Broom
95	**Laxford Group** North West Ross and North West Sutherland
96	**Naver Group**
97	**Thurso Group**

The numbering system then goes on to take in the major island groups lying offshore, including, for example, The Isle of Wight, and the Isle of Man.

104	**The Kintyre Group** Arran, Kintyre, Jura
105	**Inner Hebrides** Mull, Rhum, Skye
106	**Outer Hebrides** Harris, Lewis
107	**Orkney**
108	**Shetland**

Numbering System used in the Tables

South East Scotland: The Borders and the Firth of Forth
Tweed (21); Lothians (17.2, 19, 20); Fife (14, 17.2); Devon Basin (18, 2).

South East Highlands: The Basins of the Tay and Earn
Earn (16); Tay (15.1), Almond (15.2), Braan (15.3), Tummel and Garry (15.4), Lyon (15.5), Isla and Ericht (15.6).

North East Scotland
Angus Glens (13), Dee, Don and Deveron (9, 11, 12); Buchan (10); Spey and Findhorn (7, 8); Ness (6).

Northern Highlands
Beauly (5); Ross and Cromarty-Lochcarron and Applecross (93.3), Torridon and Loch Maree (94), North West Ross (95, 1), Easter Ross (4); Sutherland and Caithness-Assynt and Edrachillis (95, 21), North West Sutherland (96), Caithness (97.1), East Sutherland (2), Kyle of Sutherland (3).

West Highlands
Skye and Lochalsh-Lochalsh (93.2), Skye (105.1); Lochaber-Glencoe/Glen Nevis (90), Great Glen/Glen Spean (91), Morvern/Sunart (92), Morar, Knoydart, Glenelg (93.1); Argyll and Mull-Loch Fyne (87), Knapdale/Mid Lorn (88), Loch Etive/Loch Awe (89.1), Upper Lorn (89.2); Mull (105.2).

Forth and Clyde Basins
Firth of Clyde (86), Loch Lomond (85, 1), Strathendrick and Strathblane (85.2), Lower Clyde (North Bank) (85.3), Lower Clyde (South Bank) (85.4), Upper Clyde and Tributaries (85.5); Leny Basin (18), Callander and the Trossachs (18), Middle Forth and Tributaries (18); Carron Basin (17.1).

South West Scotland
Ayrshire (82, 83), Arran (104); The Border Esk (77), The Annan Basin (78), The Nith Basin (79), The Galloway Dee (80), The Cree Group (81).

Sizes of River Basins

Square Kilometres

1 – 3 sq km:	Small mountain burn; eg Eas Coul Aulin
3 – 5 sq km:	Mountain burn; eg An Steall Ban
5 – 10 sq km:	Large mountain burn; eg Eas Fionn
10 – 25 sq km:	Mountain river; eg Falls of Torridon
25 – 50 sq km:	River in Small Glen; eg Falls of Balgy
50 – 100 sq km:	River in Glen; eg Linn of Quoich

Falls of Orchy:	200 sq km
Falls of Foyers:	275 sq km
Falls of Moriston:	400 sq km
Falls of Clyde:	950 sq km

Abbreviations

C	Coire	FW	Forest Walk
Ch	Choire	HB	Hydro Board
CP	Car Park	LRT	Land Rover Track
E	Eas (ED Eas Dubh)	NTS	National Trust for Scotland
EK	East Kilbride	P	Pass
ER	Estate Road	Sp	Spout
F/Fs	Fall/s	SWT	Scottish Wildlife Trust
FP	Footpath	Tr	Trail
FR	Forest Road	WH	West Highland
FT	Forest Trail		

Heights of Falls

Approximate Equivalents

Feet	Metres	Feet	Metres
10	3	50	15
12	4	60	18
15-18	5	80	24
20	6	90	27
25	8	100	30
30-36	10	120	36
40	12	132	40
		150	45
		200	60

Borders and Firth of Forth

Tweed

Ref. No.	Name of Fall	River or Burn	Map Ref	Area	Height	Class	Map	Access	Grade
21.01	Stichill Linn	Eden	NT 705 375	30	12	*	74	from B6364	ii
21.02	Hownam Salmon Leap	Kale	NT 777 666				80	Hownam; by-roads	iii
21.03	Roaring Linn	Jed Water	NT 678 134				80	A68	ii
21.04	Kaim Linn	Jed Water	NT 680 134				80	A68	ii
21.05	Robert's Linn	Slitrig Water	NT 538 026				80	B6399	ii
21.06	Wolcleughhead Fall	Wolcleughhead Burn	NT 330 088	12	8		80	Robertton; (B711)	i
21.07	Rhymer's Glen	Huntley Burn	NT 527 328				73	B6360	ii
21.08	Corbie Linn	Long Philip Burn	NT 448 295				73	FP from Selkirk	iii
21.09	Kirkhope Linns	Ettrick Water	NT 383 239				73	B7009	ii
21.10	Dow Linn	Henderland Burn	NT 229 236				73	A708: by-road Talla	iii
21.11	Cowie's Linn	Eddleston Burn	NT 234 513	30	12	*	73	A703	iii
21.12	Crooked Jock	(Lyne Water)	NT 139 528				79	FP from West Linton	ii
21.13	Carlow's Linn	Tweed	NT 097 243				72	A701	ii
21.14	Witches Linn	Talla Reservoir	NT 132 202				78	Talla Reservoir	ii
21.15	Gameshope Linn	(Talla Reservoir)	NT 131 191				78	Above Witches	iii
21.16	Talla Linns	(Talla Reservoir)	NT 137 202				78	By-road Talla	ii
21.17	Lamb's Burn Falls	Lamb's Burn	NT 568 589				74	FP from Al	iii
21.18	Tower Dean Falls		NT 785 702				67	From Al	iii

Lothians

Ref. No.	Name of Fall	River or Burn	Map Ref	Area	Height	Class	Map	Access	Grade
20.01	Linn Dean Cascade	Tyne	NT 465 598				66	A68	iii
20.02	Linton Linn	Tyne	NT 592 771				67	In East Linton	ii
19.01	Cramond Fall	Almond	NT 186 765		2		66	In Cramond	i
19.02	Grotto Waterfall	Almond	NT 169 752	369			66	Cramond Brig; A90	iii
19.03	Jaw Linn	Linhouse Water	NT 063 631				65	By-road Livingston	ii
19.04	Roslin	Esk	NT 274 625			*	66	By-road B704	iii
19.05	Habbies Howe Fall	Logan Burn	NT 183 618	4	40*		66	FP Glencorse	iv
19.06	Falls of Monks Burn	Avon	NT 181 573				66	A702	ii
17.2.05	Linn Mill Fall	Avon	NS 912 722				65	In Avonbridge	ii
17.2.06	Linn Mill Fall	Linn Mill Burn	NT 104 706				66	By-road S. Qu'ferry	ii

Fife

Ref. No.	Name of Fall	River or Burn	Map Ref	Area	Height	Class	Map	Access	Grade
17.2.01	Fordel Waterfall	Keil Burn	NT 148 851				66	By-road from A92	ii
17.2.02	Starley Burn Fall		NT 227 858				66	From Aberdour	iii
17.2.03	Groupie Craigs Falls		NT 250 912				66	In Kirkcaldy	iii
17.2.04	Keil Den	Keil Burn	NO 412 029	65	15	*	66	From Lundin Links	i
14.01	Dura Den Falls	Ceres Burn	NO 416 142				59	SWT Trail from Ceres	ii
14.02	Craighall Den	Ceres Burn	NO 400 107				59	From Falkland	ii
14.03	Maspie Den		NO 235 068				59	From Falkland	iii
14.04	Arraty Den	Eden	NO 220 075				59	From Kinnesswood	iii
14.05	Glen Burn Falls	Eden	NO 189 059				58	From Kinnesswood	iii

Devon

Ref. No.	Name of Fall	River or Burn	Map Ref	Area	Height	Class	Map	Access	Grade
18.2.01	Falls of Knaik	Knaik	NN 831 111				57	From Braco A822	ii
18.2.02	The Loup	Wherry Burn	NS 801 997				58	Bridge of Allan	ii
18.2.03	Menstrie Glen (10)	Menstrie Burn	NS 848 974			*	58	FP to Dumyat	ii
18.2.04	Alva Glen (8)	Alva Burn	NS 885 977			**	58	From Alva; A91	iii
18.2.05	Craighorn Spout	Glenwhinnel Burn	NS 885 988	2	18		58	From Alva Glen; A91	ii
18.2.06	Silver Glen (4)	Silver Burn	NS 891 977				58	From Alva; A91	iii
18.2.07	Mill Glen (6)	Mill Glen	NS 912 977			*	58	From Tillic'ltry; A91	ii
18.2.08	Sochie Falls	Burn of Sorrow	NS 960 944				58	Dollar Glen	ii
18.2.09	Hempy's Falls	Burn of Care	NS 962 992				58	Dollar Glen; A91	ii
18.2.10	Craigmean Falls	Burn of Care	NS 961 994				58	Dollar Glen	iii
18.2.11	Cauldron Linn	Devon	NT 005 988	100	24	**	58	Devonshaw; or A91	iii
18.2.12	De'il's Mill	Devon	NT 016 997				58	At Rumbling Bridge	v
18.2.13	St Serf's Falls	Devon	NN 998 032				58	A823	ii
18.2.14	Black Linn	Devon	NN 993 042				58	A823	ii
18.2.15	Linn Mill Fall	Black Devon	NS 926 929				58	A977	ii

South East Highlands: Tay and Earn Basins

Earn Basin

Ref. No.	Name of Fall	River or Burn	Map Ref	Area	Height	Class	Map	Access	Grade
16.01	Dornock Mill Fall	Earn	NN 884 185				52	By-road from B8062	ii
16.02	Falls of Turret	Turret	NN 839 243	24	10		52*	SWT Trail nr Crieff	ii
16.03	Falls of Barvick	Barvick Burn	NN 850 245	8	150*	*	52*	By-road from Crieff	ii
16.04	Falls of Keltie	Keltie Burn	NN 862 253	20	20		52	By-road from Crieff	iii
16.05	Falls of Monzie	Shaggie Burn	NN 885 253	8	16		52*	By-road from Crieff	ii
16.06	Sput Rollo	Lednock	NN 729 284				52*	By-road from Comrie	ii
16.07	Deil's Caldron	Lednock	NN 767 235	64	10	*	52*	SWT Trail by Comrie	ii
16.08	Eas an Aoin		NN 736 247				52	Dunira Policies	iv
16.09	Falls of Glentarken	Tarken	NN 668 252	15	12		52	Glentarken Farm	ii
16.10	Falls of Beich Burn	Beich Burn	NN 694 145	15	15		51	Lochearnhead	iii
16.11	Sput Dubh (Glen Ogle)	Burn of Ample					51	Glen Ogle; A84	v
16.12	Falls of Edinample	Artney	NN 602 225	16	20		51*	By-road Loch Earn	ii
16.13	Sput a' Chleibh		NN 733 177				52*	Glen Artney	ii
16.14	Falls of Allt Ollach	Allt Ollach	NN 584 261	6	18	*	52	Glen Artney	ii
16.15	Eas nan Lub	Strath a' Ghlinne	NN 679 171				57	Upper Glen Artney	iii
16.16	Falls of Ness	Machany Water	NN 885 157				58	FP from A823	ii
16.17	Kincardine Glen	Ruthven	NN 000 000				58	From Auchterarder; A9	ii
16.18	Jenny's Gush	Dunning Burn	NN 028 124				58	From Dunning	ii
16.19	Humble Bumble	Water of May	NO 063 161				58	By-road from B935	iv
16.20	Linn of Muckersie	Water of May	NO 073 158				58	By-road from B935	ii
16.21	Dron Waterfall		NO 136 151				58	Dron	ii
16.22	Nethy Linns		NO 153 158				58	From Abernethy	iii

Tay (Trunk Stream)

Ref. No.	Name of Fall	River or Burn	Map Ref	Area	Height	Class	Map	Access	Grade
15.01	Campsie Linn	Tay	NO 124 340	4590	2		52	A93; Stanley	ii
15.02	Falls of Dochart	Dochart (Tay)	NN 571 323	220	10	*	51*	In Killin	iii
15.03	Falls of Tyndrum	Cononish (Tay)	NN 345 287		5		50	A82	ii
15.04	Eas Anie		NN 289 284				50	FP to Ben Chuirn	v
15.05	Birnam Falls	Inchewan Burns	NO 016 406				53	FP from old A9	i
15.06	Falls of Balnaguard	Balnaguard Burn	NN 940 510				52*	FP from B898	ii
15.07	Falls of Moness	Urlar Burn	NN 852 474	25	15	**	52*	SWT Tr. Aberfeldy	i
15.08	Falls of Camserney	Camserney Burn	NN 814 497				51	From A827	ii
15.09	Falls of Aldavalloch	Allt Beallach	NN 784 453				51	By-road from Kenmore	iii
15.10	Falls of Acharn	Burn of Acharn	NN 758 430	16	15	**	51*	Ardeonaig	i
15.11	Falls of Dovecraig	Kidd Burn	NN 530 598	15	30	*	51	A827; FP to B. Lawers	ii
15.12	Dubh Eas	Lawers Burn	NN 676 408				51	By-road from Killin	iii
15.13	Falls of Lochay	Lochay	NN 543 351	125	10		51	By-road from Killin	ii
15.14	Falls of Kenknock	Lochay	NN 469 364				51	From A84	ii
15.15	Falls of Auchessan	Allt Essan	NN 446 282				50		iii

Almond

Ref. No.	Name of Fall	River or Burn	Map Ref	Area	Height	Class	Map	Access	Grade
15.16	Buchanty Spout	Almond	NN 932 283	117	4		52	B8063	ii
15.17	Falls of Milton Burn	Milton Burn (Almond)	NN 963 308				52	B8063	iii
15.18	Falls of Braan	Braan	NN 997 412	200	25	**	52*	A822; Rumbling Bridge	iii
15.19	Hermitage Falls (2)	Braan	NO 005 416			**	52	NTS Trail from A9	i

Tummel and Garry

Ref. No.	Name of Fall	River or Burn	Map Ref	Area	Height	Class	Map	Access	Grade
15.20	Black Spout	Edradour Burn	NN 954 578	7	36	*	52*	FP from Pitlochry; A9	ii
15.21	Linn of Tummel	Tummel	NN 907 600				52*	NTS Tr. Tummel Br.	i
15.22	Eas Chiabhlain	Tummel	NN 731 592				52	B8019	ii
15.23	Dunalastair Falls	Tummel	NN 721 591	600	5		52	B8019	iii
15.24	Linnie Chumhan	Innerhadden Burn	NN 670 568				42	FP from old A9	ii
15.25	Allt Mor Falls	Allt Mor	NN 662 589				42	Innerhadden; by-road	ii
15.26	Killichonan Falls	Killichonan Burn	NN 548 583				42	In Kinloch Rannoch	ii
15.27	Falls of Gaur	Gaur	NN 465 558	236	20		42	B846	iii
15.28	Easan Torra Mhoir	Abhainn Duibhe	NN 462 558				42	From Gaur Power Stn	iii
15.29	Allt Coire Easain Fs	(Corrie Ba)	NN 257 489				41	From Ba Bridge	v
15.30	Falls of Garry	Garry	NN 793 657				43	A9; Struan	ii
15.31	Falls of A. Eachain	Allt Eachain	NN 920 630				43	A9; NTS Centre	ii
15.32	Falls of Urrard	Allt Girnaig	NN 925 650	60	12	**	43	ER from A9	ii
15.33	York Cascade	(Tilt)	NN 874 662				43	Blair Castle; A9	iii
15.34	Falls of Fender	Fender	NN 880 667	25	25		43	By-road Old Blair	iii
15.35	Falls of Tilt	Tilt	NN 938 746				43	Glen Tilt	iii

South East Highlands: Tay and Earn Basins (continued)

Ref. No.	Name of Fall	River or Burn	Map Ref	Area	Height	Class	Map	Access	Grade
15.36	Falls of Tarf	Tarf	NN 982 796	57	60	**	43*	Glen Tilt	v
15.37	Falls of the Bruar	Bruar	NN 818 663	66	60	***	43*	A9; Calvine; CP	iii

Lyon

Ref. No.	Name of Fall	River or Burn	Map Ref	Area	Height	Class	Map	Access	Grade
15.38	Sput Ban	Lyon	NN 728 476	–	–	–	51	By-road Fortingall	ii
15.39	Brig o' Balgie Falls	Lyon	NN 577 467	–	5	–	51	By-road Fortingall	iii
15.40	Fs of Allt Da-ghob	Lyon	NN 536 453	161	20	–	51	By-road Fortingall	ii
15.41	Eas Mor	Allt Da-ghob	NN 696 471	15	–	*	51	By-road Fortingall	ii
15.42	Eas Phealaidh	Inverinan Burn	NN 653 475	–	–	–	51	By-road Fortingall	iii
15.43	Falls of Milton Roro	Allt a' Chobhair	NN 623 466	–	–	–	51	By-road Fortingall	ii
15.44	Falls of Mton Eonan	A. Bail a' Mhuilinn	NN 572 462	–	–	–	51	By-road Fortingall	ii
15.45	Conait Falls	Conait	NN 520 458	–	–	–	51	By-road Fortingall	iii
15.46	Eas nan Aighean	(Loch Lyon)	NN 425 430	–	–	–	50	Upper Glen Lyon	v
15.47	Eas Eoghannan	(Loch Lyon)	NN 424 422	–	–	–	50	Upper Glen Lyon	v
15.48	Eas Fhuiren	(Loch Lyon)	NN 398 445	–	–	–	50	Upper Glen Lyon	v
15.49	Fs of Keltneyburn	Keltney Burn	NN 773 497	44	20	*	52*	B846; Coshieville	ii

Isla and Ericht

Ref. No.	Name of Fall	River or Burn	Map Ref	Area	Height	Class	Map	Access	Grade
15.50	Canness Glen	Isla	NO 206 770	–	–	–	53	FP Glen Isla	v
15.51	Reekie Linn	Isla	NO 255 537	152	24	***	53	B954 from Alyth; CP	ii
15.52	Slug of Achrannie	Isla	NO 278 528	160	24	–	53	From Reekie Linn	iii
15.53	Loups of Kenny	Meglam	NO 278 332	–	–	–	53	By-road from Alyth	ii
15.54	Linn of Keith	Ericht	NO 178 457	420	3	*	52*	In Blairgowrie	ii

North East Scotland

Angus Glens

Ref. No.	Name of Fall	River or Burn	Map Ref	Area	Height	Class	Map	Access	Grade
13.01	Loups of Noran	Noran Water	NO 543 351	–	–	–	54	By-road from A94	ii
13.02	Fs of Drumly Harry	Noran	NO 452 624	50	18	*	54	Glenquiech; from A94	iii
13.03	Bachnagairn Fall	South Esk	NO 242 747	25	18	–	44	Glen Clova	ii
13.04	Falls of Corrie Fee	Fee Burn	NO 242 796	–	–	–	44	Glen Clova	iii
13.05	Loups of Edzell	Westwater	NO 573 689	100	4	–	54	By-road Edzell; CP	v
13.06	Loups of Esk	North Esk	NO 593 717	300	5	–	54	B966; Gannochy Bridge	ii
13.07	Falls of Unich	Water of Unich	NO 385 800	25	20	**	44*	Glen Esk	iii
13.08	Falls of Damff	Water of Unich	NO 385 792	20	24	–	44	Glen Esk	iii
13.09	Falls of Mark	Water of Mark	NO 394 833	–	–	–	44	Glen Esk	v
13.10	Gracie's Linn	Water of Tarff	NO 488 807	–	–	–	44	Glen Esk	iii
13.11	Den of Fenella	(Glen Ogilvy)	NO 880 798	–	–	–	45	A92; Crawton	iii
13.12	Buckie Den	(Den of Kellie)	NO 771 665	25	21	–	54	A92	ii
13.13	Devil's Cauldron		NO 694 524	10	9	–	54	A928	iii
13.14			NO 387 459	6	6	–	54	A92	ii
13.15	Arbirlot Falls		NO 601 405	–	–	–	54	B9127	ii

Dee

Ref. No.	Name of Fall	River or Burn	Map Ref	Area	Height	Class	Map	Access	Grade
12.01	Corbie Linn	Crynoch Burn	NO 860 998	–	–	–	38	A943	ii
12.02	Linn of Sheeoch	Burn of Sheeoch	NO 742 908	–	–	–	38*	A957	iii
12.03	Falls of Feugh	Water of Feugh	NO 701 950	–	–	*	38	A943 Bridge of Feugh	ii
12.04	Slog of Dess	Burn of Dess	NJ 567 004	25	4	–	37	By-road from A93	iii
12.05	Falls of Fungle		NO 520 963	–	–	–	37	Aboyne; Fungle Road	ii
12.06	Linn of Tanar	Water of Tanar	NO 385 890	–	–	–	44	Mounth Keen	iii
12.07	Vat Falls	Burn o' Vat	NO 425 995	72	12	–	44	A97; CP	v
12.08	Linn of Muick	Muick	NO 332 895	–	–	**	44	By-road; Ballater	ii
12.09	Piss o'Ch. Bhoidheach	A. Choire Bhoidheach	NO 231 835	–	–	–	44	Dubh Loch; Loch Muick	v
12.10	The Stulan	(Loch Muick)	NO 256 824	5	50	*	44	Loch Muick	ii
12.11	Glas Allt Fall	Glas Allt	NO 271 830	–	–	–	44	Above Loch Muick	iii
12.12	Falls o' the A. Dearg	Alltan Dearg	NO 287 836	–	–	–	44	Above Loch Muick	iii
12.13	Falls o' Piper	Crathes Burn	NO 253 965	20	20	–	44	B976/A939	ii
12.14	Falls of Garbh Allt	Garbh Allt	NO 198 898	–	–	*	43*	A93; restricted times	ii
12.15	Linn o' Clunie	Clunie Water	NO 151 914	–	–	–	43	In Braemar	ii
12.16	Linn o' Callater	Callater Burn	NO 159 880	–	–	–	43	A93	ii

North East Scotland (continued)

Ref. No.	Name of Fall	River or Burn	Map Ref	Area	Height	Class	Map	Access	Grade
7.04	Falls of Feakirk	Divie	NJ 036 447	–	–	–	27	A940; Farm track	iii
7.05	Ess of Dorback	Dorback	NJ 008 460	–	–	–	27	By-road from A940	iii
7.06	Falls of Altnarie	(Findhorn)	NH 931 391	5	28	**	27	Dulsie Bridge	ii
7.07	Falls of Torgarrow	Leonach Burn	NH 921 391	50	20	–	27	Dulsie Bridge; ER	ii
7.08	Ess of Glenlatterach	Leonach Burn	NJ 194 534	10	15	–	28*	A941; WB road	ii
7.09	Dun Cow's Loup	Lossie	NJ 197 554	–	–	–	28	B9010	iii
7.10	Ess of Auchness	Burn of Auchness	NJ 114 490	5	12	*	28*	By-road; B9010	iii

Ness Basin

Ref. No.	Name of Fall	River or Burn	Map Ref	Area	Height	Class	Map	Access	Grade
6.01	Falls of Reelig Glen	Moniak Burn	NH 558 419	–	–	–	26	FT; off former A9	ii
6.02	Fs of Douchfour Glen	Douchfour Burn	NH 603 385	–	–	–	26	A82	iv
6.03	Aberiachan Falls	Aberiachan Burn	NH 563 349	–	–	–	26	By-road (steep) A82	ii
6.04	Falls of Divach	Divach Burn	NH 494 272	12	30	**	26*	FW; by-road from A82	ii
6.05	Corrimony Falls	Enrick	NH 373 291	30	30	*	26*	FP; Corrimony; by-road	v
6.06	Falls of Allt Guish	Allt Guish	NH 475 212	2	30	–	34	A82	v
6.07	Falls of Allt Sigh	Allt Sigh	NH 454 192	35	20	*	34	A82; FP from YH	v
6.08	Falls of Moriston	Moriston	NH 422 164	391	8	–	34	A82; Invermoriston	ii
6.09	Falls of Allt Eiric	Moriston	NH 359 156	–	–	–	34	A897; LB	iii
6.10	Doe Falls	Doe (Moriston)	NH 403 128	–	–	–	34	A897	iii
6.11	Easan Ban	Allt an Eoin	NH 251 106	–	–	–	34	A897	iii
6.12	Steall Ban	Allt na Steall Ban	NH 055 126	–	–	–	33	A87	v
6.13	Allt a' Mhuilinn Fs	Allt a' Mhuilinn	NH 405 128	–	–	*	34	A82; Lay-by	iii
6.14	Falls of Farigaig	Farigaig	NH 541 244	–	–	–	26	By-road from B852	ii
6.15	Torness Falls	Farigaig	NH 579 270	–	–	–	26	A862	ii
6.16	Lower Fall of Foyers	Foyers	NH 497 294	275	30	***	34*	B852; FP to Green Pt	v
6.17	Upper Fall of Foyers	Foyers	NH 497 199	269	10	–	34	B852; by-road to Br.	iii
6.18	Whitebridge Falls	Breinag	NH 485 149	–	–	–	34	B862	ii
6.19	Falls of Fechlin	Fechlin	NH 495 143	–	–	–	34	By-road B862	iii
6.20	Calder Falls	Abercalder Burn	NH 571 183	19	24	–	35	From Errogie; B862	ii
6.21	Black Falls	River E	NH 545 140	10	25	*	35	LRT from Garthbeg	v
6.22	Knockie Falls	Allt Luaidhe	NH 442 140	–	–	–	34	Knockie Lodge; Ford	iii
6.23	Eas Mac Eoichd	(Loch Tarff)	NH 414 141	–	–	–	35	B862	iii
6.24	Doe Falls	Allt Doe (Loch Ness)	NH 411 084	20	30	–	35	B862	iii
6.25	Falls of Tarff	Tarff	NH 450 027	30	–	–	34	From Glendoe; B862	ii
6.26	Culachy Falls	Connachie Burn	NH 376 058	–	–	–	34	Corrieyairack Pass	iii
6.27	Bird Fall	(Loch Oich)	NH 355 091	3	30	–	34*	FR from Forest HQ	ii
6.28	Fs. of A. na Cailliche	Allt na Cailliche	NH 273 002	5	40	**	34	FW; A87	i
6.29	Falls of Garry	Garry	NH 228 006	386	4	–	34	A87	ii
6.30	Falls of A. Ladaidh	(Loch Garry)	NH 229 007	–	–	–	34	By-road A87; FR	iii
6.31	Eas Allt a' Mheil	A. a' Mheil (L. Quoich)	NH 042 023	–	–	–	33	By-road A87	ii
6.32	Eas Coire nan Camh	(Loch Quoich)	NG 977 045	4	30	*	33	By-road A87	ii

Northern Highlands

Beauly Basin

Ref. No.	Name of Fall	River or Burn	Map Ref	Area	Height	Class	Map	Access	Grade
5.01	Falls of Kilmorack	Beauly	NH 493 443	875	6	–	26	A831	iii
5.02	Eilanaigas Falls	Beauly	NH 469 422	–	–	–	26	A831	iii
5.03	Culligran Falls	Farrar	NH 377 401	294	5	*	26	Gated HB road; A831	ii
5.04	Deanie Falls	Farrar	NH 330 395	250	2	**	26	Gated HB road; A831	iii
5.05	Eas a' Mhuillidh	Allt Coire Mhuillidh	NH 280 389	–	–	–	25	Gated HB road; A831	v
5.06	Eas Sgaile	Allt Uchd Rhoda	NH 256 397	–	–	–	25	Gated HB road; A831	ii
5.07	Falls of Monar	Garbh Visge	NH 218 391	129	5	–	25	Gated HB road; A831	ii
5.08	Eas a' Chraisg	Glass	NH 382 342	–	–	–	26	By-road to Tomich	iii
5.09	Falls of Glassburn	Glassburn	NH 368 345	–	–	–	26	A831	iv
5.10	Easan Fhithich	Cannich	NH 318 321	186	10	–	26*	By-road from Cannich	iii
5.11	Eas Maol Mhairi	Cannich	NH 323 183	183	6	–	26*	By-road from Cannich	iii
5.12	Tomich Falls	Affric	NH 320 294	–	–	–	26	By-road to Tomich	ii
5.13	Badger Fall	Affric	NH 308 285	195	10	**	25*	HB road; FP	ii
5.14	Dog Fall	Affric	NH 288 283	190	10	***	25*	HB Road; Forest Walk	i
5.15	Falls of Fiadh	Abh. Gleann nam Fiadh	NH 206 242	–	–	–	25	Loch Benevean	ii

12.17	Breakneck Falls	(Corrie Kander)	NO 197 812	–	–	–	43	Jock's Road	v
12.18	Eas nan Meirleach		NO 132 785	–	–	–	43	A93	iii
12.19	Eas Allt a' Chlair	Allt a' Chlair	NO 118 897	–	–	–	43	By-road Linn of Dee	ii
12.20	Linn o' Corriemulzie	Corriemulzie Burn	NO 112 892	5	15	–	43*	By-road Linn of Dee	ii
12.21	Linn of Quoich	Quoich Water	NO 111 912	65	8	*	43*	By-road; Linn of Dee	ii
12.22	Eas Eidh	Ey	NO 088 863	–	–	–	43	Inverey; by-road	iii
12.23	Falls of Connie	Allt Connie	NO 085 892	–	–	–	43	FP from Inverey	iii
12.24	Falls of Lui	Lui Water	NO 067 900	66	12	*	43	By-road; Linn of Dee	ii
12.25	Falls of Derry	Derry Burn	NO 043 942	–	–	–	43	Glen Derry; L. of Dee	iii
12.26	Fs o'Derry Ln. Vaine	(Glen Derry)	NO 024 987	–	–	*	43	Derry Cairngorm	v
12.27	Falls o'C. Etchachan	(Coire Etchachan)	NO 019 994	–	–	–	43	Loch A'an Fr G. Derry	v
12.28	Linn o' Dee	Dee	NO 062 895	–	–	*	43*	By-road fr Braemar	ii
12.29	Chest o' Dee	Dee	NO 013 886	–	–	–	43	Larig Ghru Path	iii
12.30	Lochan Vaine Falls	(Lochan Vaine)	NN 960 983	–	–	–	43	Angel's Peak	v
12.31	Falls of Dee	Dee	NN 944 991	–	–	**	43*	Garbh Coire	v

Don and Buchan

9-11.01	Den of Craig	Burn of Craig	NJ 471 248	–	–	–	37	A97/B9007	ii
9-11.02	Rootie Linn	Fordean Burn	NJ 756 272	–	–	–	29	Track from Fyvie	ii
9-11.03	The Loup	(Tor of Troup)	NJ 832 621	–	–	–	29	By-road from Pennan	iii
9-11.04	Falls of Tarnash	(Isla)	NJ 443 490	–	–	–	28	FP from A97	ii
9-11.05	Linn of Keith	Isla	NJ 428 511	–	–	–	28	In Keith	ii
9-11.06	Cullen Falls	Burn of Deskford	NJ 504 667	–	–	–	29	From Cullen	ii
9-11.07	Linn of Deskford		NJ 511 618	–	–	–	29	Kirktown of Deskford	ii
9-11.08	Linn of Rannas	Burn of Rannas	NJ 465 644	–	–	–	28	By-road from A898	ii

Spey

8.01	The Linn	(Den of Garbity)	NJ 308 522	–	–	–	28	B9015	ii
8.02	Linn of Rothes	Burn of Rothes	NJ 258 484	–	–	–	28	A941	iii
8.03	Linen Apron	Dullan Burn	NJ 324 382	4	10	–	28	NT from Dufftown	ii
8.04	Linn of Ruthrie	Lour	NJ 266 418	27	8	*	28	A95; FP	ii
8.05	Laggan Falls	Laggan Burn	NJ 234 417	–	–	–	28	B9102; Archiestown	ii
8.06	Shepherd's Linn	Burn of Balintomb	NJ 183 428	–	–	–	28	B9102	ii
8.07	Poolflasgan Fall	Knockando Burn	NJ 183 428	–	–	–	28	B9102; Knockando	ii
8.08	Falls of Livet	Livet	NJ 215 260	–	–	–	36	B9008	ii
8.09	Linn of Brown	Burn of Brown	NJ 125 205	–	–	–	36	A939	ii
8.10	Linn of Avon	Avon	NJ 175 073	–	–	*	36*	Inchrory	iii
8.11	The Flume	Garbh Coire	NJ 110 013	–	–	–	36	Beinn a' Bhuird	v
8.12	Feith Buidhe Catrct	Feith Buidhe	NH 995 015	2	250	**	36	Loch A'an	v
8.13	Garbh Visge W'fall	Garbh Visge	NH 997 014	3	30	**	36	Loch A'an	v
8.14	Dreggie Falls	Dreggie Burn	NJ 024 283	–	–	–	36	Grantown-on-Spey	ii
8.15	Dulnain Bridge Falls	Dulnain	NH 992 250	–	–	–	36	A95; Dulnain Bridge	ii
8.16	Ess of Duthill	Burn of Duthill	NH 929 278	–	–	–	36	B9007	ii
8.17	Nethy Rapids	Nethy	NJ 020 107	–	–	–	36	Ryvoan Pass	iii
8.18	Falls of Garbh Allt	Garbh Allt (Nethy)	NJ 014 035	–	–	–	36	The Saddle	v
8.19	Chriochaidh Falls	Allt Chriochaidh	NH 943 003	–	–	–	36	A9	iii
8.20	Easan C. an Lochain	Coire an Lochain	NH 943 003	–	–	–	36	Glen Einich	v
8.21	Easan nan Bruaich	(Glen Einich)	NH 924 018	–	–	–	36	Glen Einich	iii
8.22	Fs of C. Boga-cloiche	A. Coire Boga-cloiche	NN 912 999	–	–	–	36	Glen Einich	v
8.23	Fs of Coire Dhondail	Allt C. Dhondail	NN 925 979	–	–	–	36	Glen Einich	v
8.24	Falls of Coire Odhar	Allt Loch nan Cnapan	NN 913 874	–	–	**	36	Glen Einich	v
8.25	Fs of Badan Mosach	Allt Fhearnagan	NN 858 971	5	50	***	36	Achlean	iii
8.26	Falls of C. Garbhlach	Allt Garbhlach	NN 875 947	–	–	**	36	Glen Feshie	v
8.27	Falls of Slochd Beg	Allt Lorgaidh	NN 845 986	–	–	–	36	Glen Feshie	v
8.28	Falls of the Feshie	Feshie	NN 000 000	–	–	–	43	Glen Feshie	iii
8.29	Fs of Stron-a-Barin	F. Craoibh Chaoruinn	NN 871 888	2	36	–	43	Glen Feshie	v
8.30	Landseer's Falls	Allt na Leuma	NN 886 894	5	50	**	43	Glen Feshie	v
8.31	Falls of Eidart	Eidart	NN 914 886	–	–	–	43	Glen Feshie	v
8.32	Tromie Bridge Falls	Tromie	NN 788 995	–	–	–	35	B970	ii
8.33	Eas a' Choin Dubh	Allt Bhrodainn	NN 734 845	4	20	–	43	Glen Tromie	v
8.34	Falls of Calder	Calder	NN 701 994	–	–	–	35	By-road; Newtonmore	ii
8.35	Falls of Truim	Truim	NN 680 923	–	–	*	42	A9	ii
8.36	Cadha an Feidh	(Creag Dubh)	NN 669 957	–	–	–	35	A86	v
8.37	Easan Buidhe	Spey	NN 548 942	–	–	–	35	By-road from A86	ii
8.38	Falls of the Mashie	Mashie	NN 587 908	–	–	–	35	A86	ii

Findhorn Group

7.01	Falls of Achneim	Reireach	NH 839 483	–	–	–	27	Cawdor	iii
7.02	Little Ess	Findhorn	NJ 000 516	–	–	–	27	Forres	iii
7.03	Muckle Ess	Findhorn	NJ 002 520	–	–	–	27	Sluie Walks	iii

5.16	Sputan Ban	Allt Coulavie	NH 135 225	–	–	–	25*	Loch Affric	v
5.17	Guisachan Fall	(Abhainn Debag)	NH 290 249	6	12	–	25*	Estate rd fr. Tomich	ii
5.18	Pladda Falls	Eas Socach (Ab, Deabag)	NH 277 248	6	40	**	25*	Estate rd, fr. Tomich	iii
5.19	Eas Socach	Eas Socach	NH 285 230	–	–	–	25	Estate rd fr. Tomich	iii

Lochcarron and Applecross

93.3.01	Eas nan Cuinneag	Applecross	NG 897 412	–	–	–	24	from Applecross	v
93.3.02	F. of Coire na Poite	(Loch Kishorn)	NG 828 448	–	–	–	24	from Tornapress	v
93.3.03	Eas Ban (L. Kishorn)	Russel Burn	NG 815 410	–	–	–	24	from Russel	iii
93.3.04	Allt na Caillich		NG 869 407	2	60*	–	24	from A896	iii
93.3.05	Carnan Falls	Allt nan Carnan	NG 897 412	–	–	–	25	from Loch Carron	iii
93.3.06	Eas an Teampuil	(Loch Carron)	NG 953 422	–	–	–	25	from A890	v
93.3.07	Eas Ban (L. Carron)	Attadale	NG 963 383	–	–	–	25*	from Strathcarron	iii
93.3.08	Falls of River Lair	Lair	NG 992 490	10	200*	**	25	from Achnashellach	iii

Torridon and Loch Maree

94.01	Falls of Balgy	(Loch Damph)	NG 849 538	43	8	–	24*	A896; track	ii
94.02	Ben Damph Falls	Allt Coire Roill	NG 886 538	–	–	–	24	Torridon Hotel; A896	ii
94.03	Easan Buidhe	Torridon	NG 921 556	–	–	–	24	A896	ii
94.04	Eas Mor	Torridon	NG 930 561	–	2	–	25	A896	ii
94.05	Easan Dorca	Coulin	NG 013 525	–	–	–	26	A896/A890; Coulin P.	iii
94.06	Torridon Falls	A. Coire Mhic Nobuil	NG 869 573	22	8	**	24	By-road A896; CP	ii
94.07	Eas na Gaibhre	Craig	NG 784 640	–	–	–	24*	Craig YH	iii
94.08	Eas Bad a' Chrotha	Badachro River	NG 782 737	–	–	–	19	In Badachro	ii
94.09	E. Braigh Horrisdale	Abh. Br. Horrisdale	NG 817 684	–	–	–	19	Track B'chro/Tor'don	iii
94.10	Falls of Kerry	Kerry	NG 836 721	–	–	–	19	A832	ii
94.11	Flowerdale Falls	(Gleann a' Ghrobain)	NG 828 750	–	–	–	19	FP from Gairloch	ii
94.12	Easan Mor		NG 771 775	–	–	–	19	By-road; Gairloch	ii
94.13	Victoria Falls	Garbhaig	NG 894 711	18	20	**	19*	A832; FT fr Car Park	i
94.14	Falls of Talladale	Allt Strath Lungard	NG 918 673	–	–	–	19	A832	iii
94.15	Falls of Glen Grudie	Grudie	NG 938 612	–	–	–	19	Mountain Path A896	v
94.16	Steall a' Mhuinidh	Allt a' Mhuinidh	NH 024 648	3	90	*	19	Kinlochewe; A832	v
94.17	Eas Ban	(Loch Garbhaig)	NG 990 709	–	–	–	19	Letterewe	v
94.18	Letterewe Falls	Allt Folais	NG 951 716	–	–	–	19	Letterewe	v

North West Ross

95.1.01	Eas Dubh a G. Garbh	Inverinavie	NG 957 888	–	–	–	19	A832; FP	ii
95.1.02	E. V. Toll a' Mhadaidh	Visge T. a' Mhadaidh	NG 965 873	–	–	–	19	A832	v
95.1.03	Linne na Cloiche	Gruinard	NG 951 911	–	–	–	19	A832; FP to Sheneval	ii
95.1.04	Eas nan Sonn	Gruinard	NG 975 890	–	–	–	19	A832; FP to Sheneval	v
95.1.05	Coneasan	Gruinard	NG 987 868	–	–	–	19	A832; FP To Sheneval	v
95.1.06	Eas Ban	(Creag Rannich)	NH 097 773	–	–	–	19*	From Sheneval Bothy	v
95.1.07	Ardessie Falls	Allt Ardeasiadh	NH 053 859	15	20	**	19	A832	ii
95.1.08	Garbh Allt Falls	(Strath Beg)	NH 108 857	–	–	–	19	A832	ii
95.1.09	Corrie Hallie Fall	Dundonnell River	NH 123 847	–	–	*	19	A832	v
95.1.10	Dundonnell Falls	Dundonnell River	NH 120 818	–	–	–	19	A832	ii
95.1.11	Falls of Measach	Droma	NH 204 779	44	82	***	20*	A835/A832; NTS Walk	i
95.1.12	Falls of Strone	Abhainn Cuileg	NH 181 770	56	15	–	20	A832 or Braemore	iii
95.1.13	Eas an Villt Granda	Granda	NH 114 711	–	–	–	19	ER from A832	v
95.1.14	Eas Fionn	Lael	NH 232 835	10	12	*	20*	FP to Ben Dearg; A835	iii
95.1.15	Falls of Ness	Ullapool	NH 131 952	–	–	–	15	A835	ii
95.1.16	Eas Dubh	Ullapool River	NH 151 954	100	15	–	20	ER from A835	ii
95.1.17	Eas a' Chroasain	(Loch Achall)	NH 198 956	–	–	–	20*	ER from A835	iii
95.1.18	Eas na Baintighearna	Rhidorroch	NH 238 929	–	–	–	20	ER from A835	ii
95.1.19	Eas an-t-Sinidh	(Glen Douchary)	NH 256 927	–	–	–	20	ER from A835	iii
95.1.20	Falls of Kanaird	Kanaird	NC 211 025	–	–	–	15	ER from A835	iii
95.1.21	Cul Mor Waterfall	A.L. Dearg a'Chuill M	NC 153 104	–	–	–	15	From A835	v
95.1.22	Falls of Polly	Polly	NC 087 137	40	12	–	15	By-road fr. Lochinver	iii

Easter Ross

4.01	Eas an Tairbh	Edderton Burn	NH 684 838	–	–	–	21	From Edderton (A9)	iii
4.02	Eas a' Chonaisg	Glass	NH 557 683	72	12	*	21	By-road from Evanton	ii
4.03	Eas Poll a' Greusach	Allt nan Coarach	NH 556 681	–	–	–	21	By-road from Evanton	v
4.04	Falls of Rogie	Black Water	NH 445 584	310	8	**	26*	FW; A832; fr. S'peffer	i
4.05	Silver Bridge Falls	Black Water	NH 402 639	300	10	–	20	A835	ii
4.06	Eas Buidhe	Glasgarnoch	NH 356 702	–	–	–	20	A835	ii
4.07	Steall Coir Lair	(Loch Prille)	NH 288 815	3	150*	–	20	A835; remote	v

Northern Highlands (continued)

Ref. No.	Name of Fall	River or Burn	Map Ref	Area	Height	Class	Map	Access	Grade
4.08	(Muirton Falls)	Conon	NH 448 544	–	–	–	26	By-road from A832	ii
4.09	Falls of Conon	Conon	NH 386 578	387	12	–	26	By-road from A832	ii
4.10	(Achanalt Falls)	Bran	NH 309 619	–	–	–	20	A832	ii
4.11	Falls of Grudie	Grudie	NH 305 627	–	–	–	20	HB road from A832	iii
4.12	Black Falls	Meig	NH 360 561	–	–	–	26	By-road from A832	iii
4.13	Meig Falls	Meig	NH 216 515	–	–	–	26	By-road from A832	ii
4.14	Falls of Orrin	Orrin	NH 469 517	110	5	*	26*	By-road from A832	ii
4.15	Fs of A. L. Ghormlaich	Allt Loch Ghormlaich	NH 252 458	–	–	–	26	Glen Orrin	v
4.16	Swallow's Den Falls	(Rosemarkie Glen)	NH 725 584	–	–	–	21	Rosemarkie	ii
4.17	Eathie Fall	(Eathie Den)	NH 780 642	2	8	–	21	Eathie	iii

Assynt and Eddrachillis

Ref. No.	Name of Fall	River or Burn	Map Ref	Area	Height	Class	Map	Access	Grade
95.2.01	Falls of Kirkaig	Kirkaig	NC 113 177	115	18	***	15	From Inverkirkaig	iii
95.2.02	E. D. Vidh a' Ghiagell	Amhainn Mor	NC 211 122	50	5	*	15	A835; from Elphin; FP	ii
95.2.03	Eas Crom	Crom Allt	NC 230 078	–	–	–	15	Above Loch Urigill	v
95.2.04	Eas Tabhrain	Allt an Achaidh	NC 228 067	–	–	–	15	Above Loch Urigill	v
95.2.05	Eas na Saigh Caime	A. Poll an Droighinn	NC 264 220	–	–	–	15	Inchnadamph	iii
95.2.06	Eas Raigh am Sagart	Allt Claice Mor	NC 263 213	–	–	–	15	Inchnadamph	iii
95.2.07	Cnoc an Vamh Cascade		NC 276 206	–	–	–	15	Inchnadamph	iii
95.2.08	Ardvreck Falls	Allt Chalda Mor	NC 241 238	6	8	–	15	Ardvreck Castle	ii
95.2.09	Eas Clais an Easaidh	A. Clais an Easaidh	NC 054 301	8	15	*	15	From Clashnessie	ii
95.2.10	L. an Leathaid W'fall	(Loch an Leathaid)	NC 169 303	–	–	–	15	From Drumbeg	iii
95.2.11	Torgawn Falls	Allt a' Ghamhna	NC 212 320	12	30	–	15	By-road to Drumbeg	iii
95.2.12	Wailing Widow	Allt Cranaidh	NC 243 293	9	30	*	15	A894	ii
95.2.13	Eas a' Chual Aulinn	(Loch Glencoul)	NC 280 277	3	200	***	15	A894(FP);by bt K'sku	v
95.2.14	Eas an-t-Strutha Ghil	(Loch Glencoul)	NC 289 277	2	290	–	15	Glenbeg (L. Glencoul)	v
95.2.15	Eas Craig an Luchda	Amh Glinne Dubh	NC 311 330	–	–	–	15	Glendhu	v
95.2.16	Falls of Maldie Burn	Maldie Burn	NC 251 342	25	75*	*	15	Kylestrome; A894	iii
95.2.17	Eas Mor Gisgil	Allt Mor Gisgil	NC 181 417	30	50*	–	15	From Geisgill	iii
95.2.18	Eas Vaine	A. L. an Easain Vaine	NC 331 453	–	–	–	15	A838; Achfary	v
95.2.19	Easan Garbh Mor	Achriesgill Water	NC 269 528	–	–	–	9	A838; from Riconish	ii

North West Sutherland

Ref. No.	Name of Fall	River or Burn	Map Ref	Area	Height	Class	Map	Access	Grade
96.01	Foinaven Waterfalls		NG 353 483	–	–	–	9	Strath Dionard	v
96.02	Smoo Waterfall	Allt Smoo	NG 418 671	11	24	**	9	Durness	ii
96.03	Eas an-t-Strathain	Allt an-t-Strathain	NC 491 639	18	15	*	9	From Inverhope;by bt	v
96.04	Alltnacaillich	Allt na Caillich	NC 465 455	7	50	**	9	Fr Alltnacaillich	iii
96.05	Eas Choineas	(Glen Golly)	NC 409 446	–	–	–	9	Gobernuisgach Lodge	v
96.06	Coldbackie Falls		NC 615 600	–	–	–	9	A836; Coldbackie	ii
96.07	Falls of Borgie	Borgie	NC 648 545	–	–	–	10	Borgie Lodge	v
96.08	Easan Feidh		NC 586 252	–	–	–	10	Crask Inn; A836	v

Caithness

Ref. No.	Name of Fall	River or Burn	Map Ref	Area	Height	Class	Map	Access	Grade
97.01	Bridge of Forss Fs	Calder	ND 035 685	–	–	–	12	A836	ii
97.02	Westerdale Falls	Thurso	ND 130 520	–	–	–	11	B870	ii
97.03	Eas Glutha	Glutt Water	NC 987 341	–	–	–	11	ER Westerdale	v
1.01	Trollie Pow	Clyth Burn	ND 307 386	15	24	–	11	A9; Clyth	iii
1.02	Forse Waterfall		ND 221 336	–	–	–	11	A9	iii
1.03	Eas Poll an Damarin	Ousdale Burn	ND 075 185	6	30	–	17	A9	iii

East Sutherland

Ref. No.	Name of Fall	River or Burn	Map Ref	Area	Height	Class	Map	Access	Grade
2.01	Kildonan Falls	Helmsdale	NC 904 213	–	–	–	17	B872	ii
2.02	Falls of Clyne	Clyne Burn	NC 892 064	6	18	–	17	By-road from A9	ii
2.03	Kilcolmkill Falls	Allt Smeorail	NC 846 098	12	12	–	17	By-road from Brora	ii
2.04	Falls of Balnacoil	Blackwater	NC 802 113	–	–	–	17	By-road from Brora	ii
2.05	Dunrobin Falls	Golspie Burn	NC 835 013	18	10	–	17	NT from Golspie	i
2.06	Torboll Fall	Carnaig	NH 745 985	42	20	*	17	By-road fr the Mound	ii

Kyle of Sutherland

Ref. No.	Name of Fall	River or Burn	Map Ref	Area	Height	Class	Map	Access	Grade
3.01	Falls of Shin	Shin	NH 576 993	495	4	*	16	B804 from Lairg; FW	i
3.02	Invernauld Falls	Invernauld Burn	NC 502 016	–	–	–	16	A839	iii
3.03	Cassley Fs (Achness)	Cassley	NC 468 029	250	10	*	16	A837; Rosehall	ii
3.04	Glenmuic Falls	Cassley	NC 372 134	75	10	–	16	ER from Rosehall	ii

West Highlands (continued)

Ref. No.	Name of Fall	River or Burn	Map Ref	Area	Height	Class	Map	Access	Grade
93.1.06	Eas Cuingid	Allt Utha	NG 868 109	–	–	–	33*	ER from Arnisdale	v
93.1.07	Eas Donnchaidh	(Loch Hourn)	NG 794 119	–	–	–	33*	FR near Sandaig	iii
93.1.08	The Waterfall	Allt Mor Shantaig	NG 773 147	6	4	*	33	by-road from Glenelg	ii
93.1.09	Falls	Allt Mor Shantaig	NG 796 140	4	24	–	33	FR from Sandaig	iii
93.1.10	Eas Mor Chuil an Dun		NG 820 171	–	–	–	33	by-road from Glenelg	ii
93.1.11	Eas Mor (Bernera)	Amhainn Eilg	NG 814 215	–	–	–	33*	from Bernera	iii

Morvern and Sunart

Ref. No.	Name of Fall	River or Burn	Map Ref	Area	Height	Class	Map	Access	Grade
92.01	Ardtornish Falls	(Sound of Mull)	NM 701 430	–	–	–	49	FP Kinlochaline	v
92.02	Eas na Mucaireachd	Geal	NM 732 498	–	–	–	49*	FP from A884	iii
92.03	Falls of Kinloch	Kinloch	NM 671 556	–	–	–	49	from Kinloch	iii
92.04	Falls of Achleck	Allt na h-Airigh	NM 790 592	–	–	–	49	from A884	iii
92.05	Eas an Torra Bhain	(Loch Sheil)	NM 721 668	–	–	–	40*	from A861	v
92.06	Eas nan Laithanach	(Glen Hurich)	NM 808 689	–	–	–	40*	FR from Polloch	iii
92.07	Eas nan Leacan Mine	(Glen Hurich)	NM 839 709	–	–	–	40*	Coire nan Con	v

Glen Spean/Great Glen

Ref. No.	Name of Fall	River or Burn	Map Ref	Area	Height	Class	Map	Access	Grade
91.01	Eas nan Long	Lochy	NN 135 790	–	–	–	41	B8004	ii
91.02	Eas na Smuid	Spean	NN 296 809	486	8	–	41	From A86 in gorge	iii
91.03	Eas na Fhearna	Spean	NN 299 810	–	–	–	41	From A86 in gorge	iii
91.04	Inverlair Falls	Spean	NN 340 807	–	–	–	41*	FP from A86	ii
91.05	Eas Finnisg-aig	(Cour)	NN 196 763	–	–	–	41	FR Leanachan	iii
91.06	Eas Ban	Allt Coire Mhadaidh	NN 239 745	–	–	–	41		v
91.07	Eas Chlianaig	Allt Beinn Chlianaig	NN 276 793	–	–	–	41	From Monessie	iii
91.08	Falls of Tulloch	Treig	NN 358 797	–	–	–	41	by-road A86; Fersit	ii
91.09	Easan Mor	(Loch Treig)	NN 317 715	–	–	–	41*	on Stob Coire Easain	v
91.10	Easan Dubh	(Loch Treig)	NN 308 695	–	–	–	41*	Creaguainish	iii
91.11	Na-h-Easain	Allt Coire Easain	NN 236 720	–	–	–	41	Upper Glen Nevis	v
91.12	Eas Ban (Gulbin)	Abhainn Gulbin	NN 236 720	–	–	–	42		v
91.13	Pattak Falls	Pattak	NN 566 902	–	–	**	42	CP; A86	ii
91.14	Linn of Pattak	Pattak	NN 557 882	95	12	–	42*	FR from A86	iii
91.15	Steall a Phrionnsa	(Glen Roy)	NN 292 896	–	–	–	34	Glen Roy; CP	iii
91.16	Easan Bhrunachain	Roy	NN 322 900	–	–	–	34	Glen Roy	iii
91.17	Falls of Roy	Roy	NN 360 920	–	–	–	34*	Glen Roy	iii
91.18	Dog Falls	Burn of Agie	NN 393 896	–	–	–	34*	Glen Roy	v
91.19	White Falls	Roy	NN 396 933	–	–	–	34	Glen Roy	v
91.20	Falls of Mucomir	Lochy Cut	NN 182 838	–	–	–	41	by-road Loch Lochy	ii
91.21	Kilfinnan Fall	Kilfinnan Burn	NN 271 966	10	40	*	34*	FP to Ben Tee	iii
91.22	Falls of Achnacarry	Arkaig	NN 186 880	–	–	–	34		iv
91.23	Eas Chia-aig (Kaig)	(Loch Arkaig)	NN 175 888	20	18	**	34*	by-road; CP	ii
91.24	Eas Cheanna Mhuir	(Loch Arkaig)	NN 106 918	–	–	–	34	Loch Arkaig	iii
91.25	Eas Buidhe	Mallie	NN 098 874	–	–	–	41	Glen Mallie	iii
91.26	Falls	Shangan Burn	NN 130 795	–	–	–	41	by-road Banavie	ii

Glen Nevis/Glencoe

Ref. No.	Name of Fall	River or Burn	Map Ref	Area	Height	Class	Map	Access	Grade
90.01	Falls of Coe	Coe	NN 172 560	32	3	–	41	by-road A82	ii
90.02	Ossian's Showerbath	Allt nam Beathach	NN 140 559	–	–	–	41	FP to Bidean	v
90.03	Falls	Allt Coire Gabhail	NN 172 560	–	–	–	41	FP to Bidean	v
90.04	Glencoe Waterfall	Allt Lairig Eilde	NN 184 562	8	20	**	41	CP A82	ii
90.05	Grey Mare's Fall	Loch Leven	NN 187 625	7	45	***	41	NT from Kinlochmore	i/ii
90.06	McKay's Fall	Leven	NN 195 616	165	6	–	41	FP Kinlochleven	ii
90.07	Falls of Glen Righ	Amhainn Righ	NN 031 629	16	40*	*	41	FC Trail near A82	i
90.08	Roaring Mill	Water of Nevis	NN 121 740	70	2	–	41	by-road from A82; CP	ii
90.09	Eas an-t-Slinnean	Glen Nevis	NN 119 727	–	–	–	41	FP from Ft William	ii
90.10	Lower Falls of Nevis	Water of Nevis	NN 144 683	48	12	**	41	by-road from A82	ii
90.11	Eas an Tuill	Water of Nevis	NN 173 691	–	–	**	41	by-road from A82; CP	ii/v
90.12	An Steall Ban	Glen Nevis	NN 180 682	5	105	***	41	FP from Glen Nevis	iii
90.13	Na h-Easain	Water of Nevis	NN 223 693	–	–	–	41	FP from Glen Nevis	iii
90.14	Eas nam Fitheach	Glen Suileag	NM 027 813	–	–	–	41	FP from Fassifern	iii
90.15	Eas an Dubhaidh	Loch Eil	NM 959 799	–	–	–	40	FP from A830	ii
90.16	MacLean's Towel	Upper Loch Linnhe	NN 002 652	–	–	–	41	Above Corran Ferry	v
90.17	Eas a' Choin	(Loch Linnhe)	NN 008 562	–	–	–	41	FP from A828	iii

Loch Fyne

Ref. No.	Name of Fall	River or Burn	Map Ref	Area	Height	Class	Map	Access	Grade
87.01	Easain Dubh	(Loch Restil)	NN 231 086	2	8	–	56	A83	ii

Ref. No.	Name of Fall	River or Burn	Map Ref	Area	Height	Class	Map	Access	Grade
3.05	Eas na Gaibhre	Cassley	NC 395 136	–	–	–	16	From Glenmuic	v
3.06	Dykell Bridge Falls	Dykell	NC 382 012	200	4	–	16	A837; Dykell Bridge	ii
3.07	Dykell Falls	Dykell	NC 310 182	–	–	–	16	From Dykell Bridge	v
3.08	Einig Fall	Einig	NH 381 999	150	5	–	20	ER from Dykell Bridge	iii
3.09	Eas Morail	Carron	NH 514 926	–	–	–	20	By-road from Ardgay	ii
3.10	Gaim Eas	Carron	NH 487 915	–	–	–	20	By-road from Ardgay	ii
3.11	Eas a' Mhoulinn	Blackwater	NH 451 913	–	–	–	20	By-road from Ardgay	ii
3.12	Eas Charron	Carron	NH 459 888	85	6	–	20	By-road from Ardgay	ii
3.13	Eas nan Toll Dubha	Carron	NH 446 894	–	–	–	20	ER from Amat	iii
3.14	Eas Cnoc na Morar	Abhainn Gleann Mor	NH 401 861	–	–	–	20	ER from Amat	v
3.15	Eas Choul	Allt a' Chrom Villt	NH 311 832	–	–	–	20	ER from Strathvaich	v

West Highlands

Ref. No.	Name of Fall	River or Burn	Map Ref	Area	Height	Class	Map	Access	Grade
Skye									
105.1.01	Hallaig Waterfall		NG 593 387	–	–	–	24	Raasay	iv
105.1.02	Holm Waterfall		NG 517 510	20	27	–	23	by boat	v
105.1.03	Bearreraig Waterfall	(Stor Lochs)	NG 515 525	–	–	–	23	from A855	iii
105.1.04	Lealt Waterfall	Lealt	NG 516 603	13	60*	***	23	A855; CP	iii
105.1.05	Mealt Waterfall	Loch Mealt	NG 509 655	4	52	**	23	A855; CP	ii
105.1.06	Steall a' Ghreip		NG 462 731	–	–	–	23	N. of Floddigarry	iii
105.1.07	Peiness Rapids	Snizort	NG 424 462	–	–	–	23	by-road from B885	iii
105.1.08	Eas Tardil		NG 311 570	–	–	–	23	from Achabeg	v
105.1.09	Rory Mor's Nurse		NG 249 489	2	12	*	23	Dunvegan Castle	i
105.1.10	Eas Aboist		NG 157 518	–	–	–	23	from Loch Poolteil	v
105.1.11	Camas an-t-Sithean		NG 140 476	–	–	–	23	from B884	iii
105.1.12	Moonen Bay Fall	Moonen Burn	NG 156 458	1	105	–	23	by boat	v
105.1.13	Geo Mor Fall	Dibidal	NG 203 394	–	–	–	23	by boat	v
105.1.14	Eas Mor (Dibidal)	Dibidal	NG 210 413	–	–	–	23		v
105.1.15	Carbost Waterfalls	Carbost Burn	NG 373 310	–	–	–	32	in Carbost	ii
105.1.16	Eas Mor (A' Chaillich)	Huisgill Burn	NG 325 311	2	45	–	32	by-road from Carbost	iii
105.1.17	Eas Fitheach	(Loch Eynort)	NG 386 282	–	–	–	32	FW from Glen Eynort	ii
105.1.18	Falls of Greadaidh	Allt Coire Greadaidh	NG 410 224	–	–	–	32	Glen Brittle	ii
105.1.19	Eas Mor (Banachdich)	A. Coire Banachdich	NG 419 215	3	25	**	32	FP to Sgurr Dearg	ii
105.1.20	Mad Cataract	Allt a Chaoich	NG 483 196	–	–	–	32	seen from boat	v
105.1.21	Falls of A. na Feadon	Allt na Feadon	NG 603 158	–	–	–	32	seen from Ord	v
105.1.22	Eas Ban (Kyleakin)		NG 747 238	–	–	–	32		iii
105.1.23	Eas Bhradain		NG 533 265	–	20	–	32	on A850; CP	ii
105.1.24	Falls of A. Daraich	Allt Daraich	NG 470 263	–	–	–	32	from Sligachan	ii
105.1.25	Eas Ruadh		NG 494 310	–	–	–	23	from Sligachan	iii
105.1.26	Falls of G. Varragill	Allt Tota Thaoig	NG 474 401	–	–	–	32	from A850	iii
105.1.27	Eas na Coille		NG 494 310	–	–	–	32	A850	iii
105.1.28	Portree Waterfall	Cracaig	NG 486 439	11	6	–	23	In Portree	ii
Lochalsh									
93.2.01	Eas Mhic Gorraidh	Allt E. Mhic Gorraidh	NG 844 226	–	–	–	33*	from Ardintoul	v
93.2.02	Easan Mhic Gorraidh	Allt E. Mhic Gorraidh	NG 849 222	–	–	–	33*	from Ardintoul	v
93.2.03	Falls	Ling	NG 941 314	–	–	–	24	from Killilan School	iii
93.2.04	Falls	Elchaig	NN 982 272	70	15	–	33	from Killilan	iii
93.2.05	Eas Ban (Camasluinie)	Allt Mor	NG 942 278	3	30	–	33*	from Camasluinie	iii
93.2.06	Eas Ban (Elchaig)	A. Ban an Li-ruighe	NG 983 263	2	60	–	33*	from Killilan	v
93.2.07	Fall of Glomach	Amhainn Girsac	NH 018 256	20	112	***	33*	1) Killilan; 2(Morvich	v
93.2.08	Falls of Carnach	Allt Coire Easach	NH 032 273	3	60	–	33	from Carnach	iii
93.2.09	Fall	Amhainn Chonnig	NG 984 228	–	–	–	33	from Dorusduain	ii
93.2.10	Eas Ban (Dorusduain)	Allt Eas Bhain	NG 974 238	–	–	–	33	from Dorusduain	v
93.2.11	F. of Allt Grannda	Allt Grannda	NH 022 171	–	–	**	33	from Glen Lichd	v
93.2.12	Eas nan Arm	Sheil of Loch Duich	NG 993 132	23	15	–	33	A87	ii
93.2.13	Falls of Badicaul	An Garbh Allt (?)	NG 000 000	–	–	–	33	from Kyle	iii
93.2.14	Falls of Braeinthra		NG 866 316	–	–	–	25	from Strome Ferry	iii
Morar, Knoydart, Glenelg									
93.1.01	Falls of Morar	Morar	NM 788 034	166	4	**	40	A880	ii
93.1.02	Easan Buidhe	Guiserain	NG 788 034	–	–	–	33*	FP to Ladhar Bheinn	iii
93.1.03	Eas a' Chaorainn	Amhainn Beag	NG 792 039	–	–	–	33*	near Easan Buidhe	v
93.1.04	Eas an Fholaich	Allt C. Tor Asgaill	NG 803 031	–	–	–	33	near Easan Buidhe	v
93.1.05	Kinlochhourn Falls	Allt C. Sgoireadail	NG 961 067	–	–	–	33	by-road Loch Quoich	ii
87.02	Eas an Tuirc	(Glen Fyne)	NN 221 145	6	150	–	56	HB road from A83	ii
87.03	Eagle's Fall	(Glen Fyne)	NN 227 143	5	36	*	56	HB road from A83	v
87.04	Inverchorachan Falls	Fyne	NN 229 174	–	–	–	56	HB road from A83	iii
87.05	Shira Falls	Shira	NN 148 164	–	–	–	56	ER from, Inveraray	iii
87.06	Salmon Leap Falls	Aray	NN 088 107	–	–	–	56	From Castle Grounds	ii
87.07	Miller's Linn	Aray	NN 086 110	45	8	–	56	A819; FP from Castle	ii
87.08	Lenach Gluthin	Aray	NN 088 128	35	25	**	56	A819; LB; footbridge	iii
87.09	Douglas Falls	Douglas Water	NN 060 047	–	–	–	56	A83	ii
87.10	Eas Dubh (Inverglen)	(Eas Dubh)	NN 099 019	–	–	–	56	in Strachur	iii
Knapdale and Mid-Lorn									
88.01	Glendarroch Falls	Kilduskland Burn	NR 851 861	–	–	–	55	A83, in Adrisnaig	ii
88.02	Lussa Falls	Lussa	NR 775 857	–	–	–	55	Kilmichael	ii
88.03	Eas a' Chaorainn	(Loch Melfort)	NM 817 110	–	–	–	55	A816	ii
88.04	Eas na Caillich	(Loch Melfort)	NM 853 128	–	–	–	55	By-road Kilmelford	ii
88.05	E. Mhuillinn Luaidh	(Loch Melfort)	NM 851 135	–	–	–	55	In Kilmelford	ii
88.06	Eas Mor	(Loch Craignish)	NM 824 023	–	–	–	55	FP from C'nassery C.	iii
88.07	Euchar Falls	Euchar	NM 831 205	–	–	–	55	A816	ii
Loch Etive and Loch Awe									
89.01	Falls of Lora	Loch Etive	NM 911 345	–	–	*	49	Connel Bridge; A823	ii
89.02	E. na Coarach Duibhe	(Glen Nant)	NN 013 281	–	–	–	55	B845	ii
89.03	Eas nan Clag	Nant	NN 013 265	–	–	–	55	B845	ii
89.04	Falls of Brander	(Loch Awe)	NN 053 287	–	–	–	50	A85	iii
89.05	Falls of Cruachan	(Loch Awe)	NN 079 270	–	–	–	50	FP Ben Cruachan	iii
89.06	Steallair Eunaich	(Glen Strae)	NN 000 000	–	–	–	50	From The Castles	v
89.07	Falls of Strae	Strae	NN 166 312	24	6	–	50	Track from A85	iii
89.08	Eas Urchaidh	Orchy	NN 000 000	200	5	–	50	B8074	ii
89.09	Eas a' Chathaidh	Orchy	NN 000 000	200	3	–	50	B8074	iii
89.10	Easan Dubh (Orchy)	Orchy	NN 000 000	200	2	*	50	B8704	ii
89.11	Eas a' Ghaill	(Glen Lochy)	NN 215 265	00	5	–	50	From Socach	ii
89.12	Eas Morag	Eas Daimh	NN 241 275	4	8	*	50	A85; CP	iii
89.13	Inverinan Falls	Amhainn Dearg	NM 988 176	–	–	–	55	By-road to Avich; CP	ii
89.14	Falls of Avich	Avich	NM 966 140	24	12	*	55	FT from Avich	i
89.15	Eas Ban (Loch Awe)	–	NR 883 997	–	–	–	55	By-road from Ford	iii
89.16	Eas nan Vircean	Allt Garbh	NM 983 084	2	20	–	55	B840	iii
89.17	Eas Mor (Loch Awe)	Kames	NM 983 103	–	–	–	55	B840	iii
89.18	Falls of Blarghour	(Loch Awe)	NM 997 131	12	27	*	55	FP From B840	iii
89.19	Falls of Cladich	Cladich Burn	NN 101 208	00	20	–	50	From Cladich	iii
89.20	Falls of Glen Noe	Noe	NN 007 338	–	–	–	50	Track from Inverawe	iii
89.21	F. of Glen Kinglass	Kinglass	NN 191 348	–	–	–	50	Track Inveroran	v
89.22	The Robber's W'fall	Allt Mheuran	NN 139 450	7	25	*	50	Track to Ben Starav	iii
89.23	Deirdre's Waterfall	–	NN 161 517	–	–		50		v
89.24	Dalness Waterfalls	Etive	NN 171 511	100	6	*	50	By-road Glen Etive	ii
89.25	Eas na Bhrogieh	(Glen Etive)	NN 191 517	–	–	–	50	By-road Glen Etive	v
89.26	Eas an Fhir Mor	Etive	NN 207 512	–	–	–	50	By-road Glen Etive	ii
Upper Lorn									
89.27	Eas Mor (Upper Lorn)	Amhainn Dearg	NM 967 403	–	–	–	49	B845	ii
89.28	Eas a' Choin	(Glen Salach)	NM 965 411	–	–	–	49		iii
89.29	Glen Dubh Falls	(Glen Dubh)	NM 968 419	–	–	–	49	A828; FT	ii
89.30	Eas Garbh	(Glen Dubh)	NM 011 429	–	–	–	41	From Glen Dubh	iii
89.31	Eas na Circe	(Loch Creran)	NM 996 438	–	–	–	41	FT from A828	ii
Mull									
105.2.01	Torness Falls	Lussa	NM 648 324	24	6	–	49	FP from A849	ii
105.2.02	Eas na Dabhaich		NM 540 219	–	–	–	49	From Carsaig	iii
105.2.03	Eas Criarachain	A. an E. Criarachain	NM 476 196	–	–	–	48	From Boat	v
105.2.04	Eas Dubh	Allt an Fhir	NM 445 194	–	–	–	48	From Boat	v
105.2.05	Eas Mor	Allt an Fhir	NM 466 230	–	–	–	48	From A849	iii
105.2.06	Airigh na Casteal Fs		NM 466 230	–	–	–	48	LRT from B8035	v
105.2.07	Easan Labhar	Allt Easan Labhar	NM 531 418	–	–	–	48	B8073	iii
105.2.08	Eas Fors	(Loch Tuath)	NM 444 423	6	30	**	48	Below B8073	ii
105.2.09	Eas Fors	Ardow Burn	NM 423 497	4	12	–	48	By-road to Dervaig	ii
105.2.10	Sput Dubh		NM 519 545	–	–	–	47		iii
105.2.11	Lower Falls of Aros	Aros Burn	NM 515 540	8	8	–	47	FT from A849	ii
105.2.12	Upper Falls of Aros	Aros Burn	NM 516 535	8	12	*	47	FT from A849	i
105.2.13	Aros Fall		NM 520 535	–	–	–	47	Aros Park	ii
105.2.14	Eas Corrach	A. nan L. Biolaireach	Nm 512 456	12	4	–	48	By-road from Aros Br	ii
105.2.15	Eas an Stocair	A. nan L. Biolaireach	NM 507 447	8	15	–	48	By-road from Aros Br	iii

Forth and Clyde Basins

Forth: Leny Basin

Ref. No.	Name of Fall	River or Burn	Map Ref	Area	Height	Class	Map	Access	Grade
18.01	Invertochlarig Falls	Invertochlarig Burn	NN 438 184	00	10	–	56	by-road Loch Voil	ii
18.02	Rob Roy's Cave Fall	(Loch Voil)	NN 516 212	–	–	–	51	above Tulloch	iii
18.03	Eas an Eoin		NN 601 150	–	–	–	57	from Ardchullarie	ii
18.04	Sput Mor	Allt Mor	NN 558 136	–	–	–	57	From Strathyre	iii
18.05	Sput Beag	Allt Mor	NN 556 134	–	–	–	57	From Strathyre	iii
18.06	Stank Falls	Stank Burn	NN 577 105	4	50*	*	57	FR from A84	v
18.07	Sput Ban	Stank Burn	NN 565 115	–	–	–	57	Above Stank Falls	–
18.08	Falls of Leny	Leny	NN 593 087	191	5	*	57	A84; CP; FR	i/ii

Callander and the Trossachs

Ref. No.	Name of Fall	River or Burn	Map Ref	Area	Height	Class	Map	Access	Grade
18.09	Eas Gobhain		NN 607 073	–	–	–	57	By-road A821	ii
18.10	M. of Callander Falls	Milton Burn	NN 565 062	20	15	–	57	From A821	iii
18.11	Glenfinglas Falls	Turk	NN 530 035	–	–	–	57	From Brig o' Turk	ii
18.12	Sput Dubh	(Glen Gyle)	NN 387 197	–	–	–	56	ER Loch Katrine	v
18.13	Sput Ban (Ben Venue)		NN 472 056	–	–	–	56	On Ben Venue	iii
18.14	Eas Dubh	(Loch Drunkie)	NN 000 000	–	–	–	57	Callander/Menteith	–
18.15	Bracklinn Falls	Keltie Water	NN 645 084	26	15	**	57	CP; from Callander	ii
18.16	Eas an Caillich	Keltie Water	NN 639 101	24	10	–	57	by-road Callander	ii
18.17	Eas Loch a' Chroin		NN 622 157	2	100*	–	57	From Callandar	v
18.18	Eas Uilleam	Brackland Burn	NN 655 092	4	12	–	57	Wester Brackland	iii
18.19	Sput Leacach	Brackland Burn	NN 657 088	6	6	–	57	Wester Brackland	ii
18.20	Eas Fiadhaich	Allt Ruith an Eas	NN 660 088	10	4	–	57	Wester Brackland	iii
18.21	Caldron Linn	Annet Burn	NN 700 048	10	4	–	56	Above Burn o' Cambus	iv
18.22	Falls of Inverard	Avon Dubh (Forth)	NN 501 014	4	18	**	57	At Milton; B829	i
18.23	W. of the Little Fawn	Allt Mhangan	NN 522 016	–	–	–	57	FT David Marshall L.	ii
18.24	Golf Course Falls		NN 000 000	–	–	–	57	From Aberfoyle	ii
18.25	Falls of Ledard	Ledard Burn	NN 461 027	5	15	**	57	From Ledard; B829	ii
18.26	Eas Mor	(Loch Chon)	NN 411 050	–	–	–	57	FR from Frenich	ii
18.27	Pig's Foot Falls	(Loch Chon)	NN 000 000	–	–	–	57	FR from Frenich	iii
18.28	B. Linn of Blairvaich	Duchray (Forth)	NN 453 997	52	8	–	57	Pipe Track Road	iii
18.29	Pot of Glenny		NN 568 025	2	45*	–	57	From A81	iii
18.30	Spout of Ballochleam	Boquhan Burn	NS 653 900	10	5	–	57	Track to Cringate	iii
18.31	Boquhan Glen	Boquhan Burn	NS 664 938	1	60*	–	57	Kippen; A811	iii
18.32	Downie's Loup	Gargunnock Burn	NS 706 931	–	–	–	57	Gargunnock; A811	iii
18.33	Gilmour's Linn	Touch Burn	NS 739 924	–	–	–	57	By-road from A811	iii

Forth: Carron Basin

Ref. No.	Name of Fall	River or Burn	Map Ref	Area	Height	Class	Map	Access	Grade
17.01	Auchenlilylinn Spt	Carron	NS 756 843	40	6	–	57	Carron Bridge	ii
17.02	Tammaree Linn	Carron	NS 773 846	8	4	–	57	Denny	iii
17.03	Earlsburn Falls	Earl's Burn	NS 712 874	8	–	–	57	Stirling/Fintry road	ii
17.04	Peggie's Spout	(Carron Reservoir)	NS 678 821	–	–	–	57	FR Carron V. Forest	iii

Clyde: Firth of Clyde

Ref. No.	Name of Fall	River or Burn	Map Ref	Area	Height	Class	Map	Access	Grade
86.01	Morag's Fairy Glen	Berry Burn	NS 167 758	2	8	–	63	In Dunoon	i
86.02	Falls of Glenmassan	Massan	NS 123 863	20	12*	**	56	By-road from A816	ii
86.03	Eas Laoigh	(Glen Massan)	NS 104 896	–	–	–	55	From Glen Massan	v
86.04	Eas Mor	(Glen Lean)	NS 124 826	–	–	–	56	From B836	v
86.05	Puck's Glen	(Strath Eachaig)	NS 147 844	–	20*	–	56	A815; FT; Car Park	i
86.06	F. of Buttermilk Burn	Allt a' Bhalachain	NS 286 040	–	–	–	56	FP to The Cobbler	iii
86.07	Whistler's Glen		NS 269 849	2	–	–	63	From Rhu	ii

Clyde: Loch Lomond

Ref. No.	Name of Fall	River or Burn	Map Ref	Area	Height	Class	Map	Access	Grade
85.01	Falls of Falloch	Falloch	NN 338 208	20	10	**	56*	A82; NT (Central R.)	i
85.02	Eas Eonan	(Glen Falloch)	NN 348 222	–	–	–	50	A82; cross WHR	iii
85.03	Fionn Ghlinne Falls	Allt Fionn Ghlinne	NN 327 222	10	15	–	50	A82; FP to Ben Oss	iii
85.04	Sput Ban		NN 314 232	–	–	–	50	FP to Ben Oss	v
85.05	Dubh Eas	Dubh Eas	NN 317 203	22	15	–	50	HB road from A82	ii
85.06	Eas of Arnan	Allt Arnan	NN 308 189	7	30	–	56	A82; Inverarnan	iii
85.07	Garabal Fall	Srath Dubh Visge	NN 309 167	8	20	–	56	Ben Vorlich; A82	iii
85.08	Ben Glas Waterfall	Ben Glas Burn	NN 325 185	7	36	**	56	WHWay; FP to G. Gyle	iii
85.09	Falls of Inversnaid	Arklet Water	NN 336 088	25	15*	**	56	WHWay; boat	iii
85.10	Eas Thorr	(Loch Lomond)	NN 355 050	–	–	–	56	On Ben Lomond	v

Forth and Clyde Basins. (continued)

Ref. No.	Name of Fall	River or Burn	Map Ref	Area	Height	Class	Map	Access	Grade
84.37	Ryat Linn	Brock Burn	NS 518 571	–	–	–	64	By-road Barrhead/NM	ii
84.38	Rouken Linn	Auldhouse Burn	NS 549 579	10	12	–	64	Rouken Glen	i
84.39	Falls of Cart	White Cart	NS 485 636	–	–	*	64	In Paisley	i
84.40	The Linn	White Cart	NS 582 593	–	–	–	64	From Muirend	i
84.41	Benan Linn		NS 516 516	–	–	–	64	By-road from A77	ii
84.42	Eaglesham Falls	Earn	NS 573 538	4	10	–	64	Eaglesham	ii
84.43	Enoch's Linn	White Cart	NS 579 598	–	–	–	64	Over Enoch	ii

Upper Clyde and Tributaries

Ref. No.	Name of Fall	River or Burn	Map Ref	Area	Height	Class	Map	Access	Grade
84.44	Reeking Linn	Rotten Calder	NS 660 548	–	–	–	64	In EK; A776	ii
84.45	Black Linn	Rotten Calder	NS 656 541	–	–	–	64	In EK; A776	ii
84.46	Trough Linn	Rotten Calder	NS 657 539	–	–	–	64	From East Kilbride	ii
84.47	Flatt Linn	Rotten Calder	NS 654 530	–	–	*	64	In EK; A726	ii
84.48	Spectacle E'e	Kype	NS 650 515	30	15	–	72	Sandford; A726	ii
84.49	Avon Linn	Avon	NS 716 434	120	2	–	71	By-road from A726	iii
84.50		(Avon)	NS 674 415	–	–	–	71	By-road from A726	ii
84.51	Whinstone Linn	Dalserf Burn	NS 676 415	–	–	–	64	A72	ii
84.52	Old Mill Linn	Dalserf Burn	NS 797 502	–	–	–	64	A72	ii
84.53	Clyde's Mill Linn	Clyde	NS 795 500	–	–	–	64	A72	ii
84.54	Beggar's Falls	Nethan	NS 812 489	–	–	–	72	A74	v
84.55		Clyde-Falls of Clyde	NS 000 000	–	–	–	72*	From A72	iii
84.56	Stonebyre's Linn	Clyde-Falls of Clyde	NS 852 441	950	18	***	72*	In New Lanark	iii
84.57	Dundaff Linn	Clyde-Falls of Clyde	NS 881 441	932	3	–	72*	SWT NT; by-road A72	iii
84.58	Cora Linn	Clyde-Falls of Clyde	NS 883 413	932	26	***	72*	SWT NT; from N Lanark	iii
84.59	Bonnington Linn	Clyde-Falls of Clyde	NS 883 405	925	8	***	72*		iii

South West Scotland

Arran

Ref. No.	Name of Fall	River or Burn	Map Ref	Area	Height	Class	Map	Access	Grade
104.01	Easan Biorach	(Glen Diomhan)	NR 946 495	3	–	–	69	From Lochranza	ii
104.02	Glen Diochen Falls	(Glen Diomhan)	NR 922 470	3	60	–	69	From Catacol	iii
104.03	Fs of Kilmory Water	Kilmory Water	NR 972 225	2	45	–	69	From Kilmory	iii
104.04	Falls of Struey	Struey Burn	NR 993 203	–	–	–	69	From A841	iii
104.05	Eas Cumhann	Levencarroch Burn	NS 011 219	–	–	–	69	From A841	iii
104.06	Eas Mor	Allt Mor	NS 020 222	3	30	–	69*	From A841	iii
104.07	Glenashdale Falls	Glenashdale Burn	NS 023 428	6	45	***	69*	From Whiting Bay; FE	i
104.08	Garbh Allt Falls	Benlister Burn	NR 990 311	5	–	–	69*	From Lamlash; A481	iii
104.09	White Water Falls	Garbh Allt	NR 982 387	5	150*	**	69	Glen Rosa; FP B, Nuis	v
104.10	Falls of G. Sannox	Corrie Burn	NS 025 422	–	–	–	69	Goat Fell Path	v
104.11		Sannox Burn	NR 975 435	–	–	–	69	Path to Cir Mhor	iii

Ayrshire

Ref. No.	Name of Fall	River or Burn	Map Ref	Area	Height	Class	Map	Access	Grade
83.01	Kelly Glen	Kelly Burn	NS 198 684	–	–	–	63	FP from Wemyss Bay	ii
83.02	Black Linn	Gogo Burn	NS 237 594	3	10	*	63	Track from Largs	iii
83.03	Greeto Falls	Greeto Burn	NS 229 595	–	–	–	63	FP from Largs	iii
83.04	Maiden's Loup	Greeto Burn	NS 231 605	–	–	–	63	FP from Largs	iii
83.05	Kelburn Falls	Clea Burn	NS 210 567	7	15	*	63	Country Park; A78	i
83.06	Fs of Fairlie Glen	Fairlie Burn	NS 219 547	–	15	–	63	FP from Fairlie	iii
83.07	Southampton Glen	Glen Burn	NS 216 522	4	–	–	63	By-road from A78	iii
83.08	Linn Spout	Caaf Water	NS 283 485	20	8	–	63	FP from Dalry	iii
83.09	Ravenscraig Glen	South Burn	NS 272 528	–	–	–	63	By-road Dalry; ER	iii
83.10	Grip Linn	Water of Garnock	NS 291 594	–	–	–	63	FP to Hill of Stake	v
83.11	Spout of Garnock	Water of Garnock	NS 287 609	3	12	*	63	FP to Hill of Stake	iii
83.12	Murchan Spout	(Water of Garnock)	NS 290 608	–	–	–	63	FP to Hill of Stake	iii
83.13	Head Linn	Lugton Water	NS 342 452	–	–	–	64	A736	ii
83.14	Polbaith Falls	Polbaith Burn	NS 484 387	10	18*	–	70	A719; Polbaith Farm	iii
83.15	Cleugh Falls	(Ayr)	NS 550 270	–	–	–	70	B705;	iii
83.16	Crook of Ayr	Ayr	NS 594 256	–	–	–	70	By-road from B705	iii
83.17	Ness Fall	Water of Coyle	NS 411 214	50	2	–	70	By-road from B742	v

85.11	Easan Dubh	(Loch Lomond)	NN 343 067	–	–	–	56	WH Way	v
85.12	Eas Lair	(Loch Lomond)	NN 341 049	–	–	–	56	WH Way; (Roweoish)	iii
85.13	Eas Sneggan	(Loch Lomond)	NN 357 011	–	–	–	56	WH Way; (Ptarmigan L)	iii
85.14	Falls of Ardess	(Loch Lomond)	NS 264 991	–	–	–	56	Ben Lomond Path	ii
85.15	Sput Ban	(Loch Lomond)	NS 364 997	4	150*	–	56	On Ben Lomond	v
85.16	Red Fall	(Conic Hill)	NS 468 930	–	–	–	56	From Moor Park	iii
85.17	Eas na Baintighearna	(Ben Vorlich)	NN 314 116	–	–	–	56	Path to Ben Vorlich	v
85.18	Falls of Inverbeg	Douglas Water	NS 342 977	15	6	–	56	FP from A82	ii
85.19	Caulfield's Br Falls	(Loch Lomond)	NS 247 969	–	–	–	56	A82	ii
85.20	Falls of Glen Fruin	Fruin	NS 306 865	30	4	–	56	By-road from H'burgh	ii
85.21	Poachy Glen	(Vale of Leven)	NS 387 790	–	–	–	63	Renton/Alexandria	ii

Clyde: Strathendrick and Strathblane

85.22	Pot of Gartness	Endrick	NS 501 867	110	3	**	57	By-road from A81	ii
85.23	Spout of Blairessan	–	NS 527 867	–	–	–	57	FP from Killearn	iii
85.24	Spout of Calibae	Machar Burn	NS 547 848	–	–	–	57	Boquhan Glen	ii
85.25	Boquhan G. (Killearn)	Boquhan Burn	NS 545 865	–	–	–	57	By-road Killearn	ii
85.26	Black Spout	(Endrick)	NS 610 863	–	–	–	57	From Fintry; B818	iii
85.27	Spout of Balbowie	Cammal Burn	NS 643 869	–	–	–	57	B818	iii
85.28	Loup of Fintry	Endrick	NS 661 861	22	30	**	57	B818	ii
85.29	Ladies' Linn	Gallangad Burn	NS 443 827	–	–	–	64	By-road from A809	iv
85.30	Ishneich	Gallangad Burn	NS 453 815	10	30	*	64	FR Cameron Muir	iii
85.31	Ishahallin	Knockupple Burn	NS 450 797	–	–	–	64	FR; Cameron Muir	iii
85.32	S. of the White Horse	Burn Crooks	NS 482 796	–	–	–	64	Cameron Muir	v
85.33	S. of Three Marches	(Dumbarton Muir)	NS 471 785	–	–	–	64	Cameron muir	v
85.34	Dualt Spout	Dualt Burn	NS 501 802	4	10	–	64	A809	ii
85.35	Glengoyne Waterfall	(Distillery Glen)	NS 531 830	–	–	–	64	A81	ii
85.36	Jenny's Lum	(Campsies)	NS 553 817	–	–	–	64	A81	v
85.37	Ha' Glen Falls	(Ha' Glen)	NS 543 407	–	–	–	64	A81	ii
85.38	Spout of Ballagan	Ballagan Burn	NS 572 601	4	21	**	64*	A891	iii

Lower Clyde (North Bank)

84.01	Spardie Linn	Overtoun Burn	NS 423 760	5	8	–	64	NT from Dumbarton	ii
84.02	Black Linn	Overtoun Burn	NS 444 772	–	–	–	64	FP from Overtoun	iii
84.03	Bow Linn	Auchentorlie Burn	NS 442 747	–	–	–	64	FP from Bowling	ii
84.04	Cochno Fall	Loch Humphrey Burn	NS 487 742	–	–	–	64	FP from OK/Duntocher	ii
84.05	Duntiglennan Falls	Loch Humphrey Burn	NS 490 736	–	–	–	64	FP from Duntocher	iii
84.06	Ladies' Linn	Jaw Burn	NS 502 742	–	–	–	64	FP from Duntocher	ii
84.07	Grey Mare's Tail	Jaw Burn	NS 501 721	–	–	–	64	FP from Duntocher	iii
84.08	Annie's Linn	–	NS 518 737	–	–	–	64	Windy Hill Golf C.	ii
84.09	Craigton Burn Falls	Craigton Burn	NS 517 773	–	–	–	64	A809	ii
84.10	Auchineden Spout	Auldmurroch Burn	NS 503 785	5	10	–	64	A809; FP to Duncolm	iii
84.11	Linn of Baldernock	–	NS 592 757	–	–	–	64	By-road from M'gavie	ii
84.12	White Spout	Fin Burn	NS 599 799	–	–	–	64	FP from Clachan	iii
84.13	Black Spout	Fin Burn	NS 601 796	–	–	–	64	FP from Clachan	iii
84.14	Craigie Linn	Aldessan Burn	NS 609 799	2	16	–	64	FP Campsie Glen	ii
84.15	Lady's Linn	Nineteentimes Burn	NS 610 798	–	–	–	64	FP Campsie Glen	ii
84.16	James Linn	Nineteentimes Burn	NS 799 609	–	–	–	64	FP Campsie Glen	ii
84.17	Darling Linn	Nineteentimes Burn	NS 801 610	–	–	–	64	FP Campsie Glen	ii
84.18	Muckle Alicompen	Nineteentimes Burn	NS 802 613	9	8	**	64	FP Campsie Glen	ii
84.19	Wee Alicompen	Nineteentimes Burn	NS 802 614	–	–	–	64	FP Campsie Glen	ii
84.20	Sheep Linn	Nineteentimes Burn	NS 802 614	–	–	–	64	FP Campsie Glen	ii
84.21	Corrie Spout	Corrie Burn	NS 676 780	–	–	–	64	From Burnhead	iii
84.22	Laird's Loup	Kilsyth Burn	NS 701 804	–	–	–	64	FP from Kilsyth	iii
84.23	Black Mill Fall	Kilsyth Burn	NS 719 785	–	–	–	64	In Kilsyth	ii

Lower Clyde (South Bank)

84.24	Devol Glen	Devol Burn	NS 000 000	–	–	–	63	From Port Glasgow	ii
84.25	Caldron Linn	Gryfe	NS 332 707	–	–	–	63	By-road Kilmalcolm	ii
84.26	Locher Falls	Locher Burn	NS 401 647	–	–	–	64	A761	ii
84.27	Garrat's Linn	Calder	NS 351 601	–	–	–	63	From Lochwinnoch	ii
84.28	Sandy Linn	Calder	NS 345 602	–	–	–	63	From Lochwinnoch	ii
84.29	Knocken Linn	Calder	NS 343 605	–	–	–	63	From Lochwinnoch	iii
84.30	Reikan Linn	Calder	NS 334 613	–	–	–	63	By-road from B786	iii
84.31	Browney's Linn	Calder	NS 314 625	–	–	*	63	M'sheil Country Park	ii
84.32	Sheep Linn	Calder	NS 309 634	–	–	–	63	M'sheil Country Park	ii
84.33	Craigie Linn	Glen Burn	NS 474 605	1	8	–	64	B774; then NT	i
84.34	Fairy Linn	Glen Burn	NS 474 603	–	–	–	64	B774; then NT	i
84.35	Gleniffer Linn	Old Patrick Water	NS 435 600	6	10	–	64	Tannahill Way; B775	iii
84.36	Glenkilloch Falls	Witch Burn	NS 477 580	4	14*	–	64	FP from A736	ii

83.18	Dalcairnie Linn	Dalcairnie Burn	NS 465 043	9	12	–	77	By-road from A713	ii
83.19	Ness Glen	Doon	NS 477 027	–	–	–	77	By-road from A713	ii
83.20	White Spout	White Spout Lane	NX 467 933	–	–	–	77	FR Loch Doon	iii
83.21	Clashminnoch Falls	Elgin Lane	NX 452 904	–	–	–	77	From Loch Doon	v
83.22	Spout of Lumling	(Doon)	NS 276 133	–	–	–	76	By-road from Maybole	ii
83.23	Capenoch Linn	(Water of Girvan)	Ns 302 072	–	–	–	76	By-road from Maybole	ii
83.24	Penkill Falls	Penwhapple Burn	NX 252 969	–	–	–	76	B734	ii
83.25	Kilkerran Falls	Knockrochar Burn	NS 294 004	4	4	–	76	By-road to Barr	ii
83.26	TRanew Linn	Water of Girvan	NS 359 070	–	–	–	77	B7045	iv
83.27	Lady Blair's Linn	Landoughty Burn	NS 000 000	–	–	–	76	B471 Straiton; FW	i
83.28	Rossetti Linn	Lamdoughty Burn	NS 391 053	4	10	–	76	B471 Straiton; FW	i
83.29	Drunmore Linn	Baing Burn	NS 401 026	–	–	–	76	Shalloch Pass	iii
83.30	Tairlaw Linn	Water Of Girvan	NS 409 011	30	18*	*	77	Shalloch Press	iii
83.31	Games Loup	(Coast)	NX 103 880	–	–	–	76	A77	ii
83.32	Linn Dhu	Cross Water of Duisk	NX 228 813	–	–	–	76	A714 Barrhill	ii
83.33	Grey Mare's Tail	Pingerrach Burn	NX 269 965	–	–	–	76	By-road from Barr	iii
83.34	Linn of Darkness	Balloch Burn	NX 331 918	–	–	–	76	Nick of Balloch Pass	v
83.35	Black Linn	(Stinchar)	NX 368 955	2	12	–	77	FR from Barr	iii
83.36	Stinchar Falls	Stinchar	NX 371 963	18	15*	**	77	Shalloch Pass; FW	iii

Border Esk

77.01	Garwald Linns	Garwald Water	NT 234 001	–	–	–	79	B709; FP to Moffat	iii
77.02	Wellburn Spout	Fingland Burn	NT 248 040	3	17	–	79	B709	iii
77.03	Bogle Linn	Moodlae Burn	NT 267 026	–	–	–	79	B709	iii
77.04	Falls of Tarras Water	Tarras Water	NY 384 815	–	–	–	85	By-roads from Langholm	iii
77.05	Penton Linns	Liddel Water	NY 431 774	–	–	–	85	B6318	ii
77.06	Falls of Black Burn	Black Burn	NY 460 890	21	10	*	79	By-road Newcastleton	iii
77.07	Hog Gill Spout	(Black Burn)	NY 462 892	–	–	–	79	FP to Fs of Black B.	iii
77.08	Goat Linn	(Black Burn)	NY 454 888	–	–	–	79	FP to Fs of Black B.	iii

Annan Basin

78.01	Raehills Falls	Kinnel water	NY 069 934	–	–	–	78	A701; St. Ann's Bridge	ii
78.02	Garpol Linn	Garpol Water	NT 065 029	–	–	*	78	Crooked Road Beattock	ii
78.03	Falls of Wamphray G.	Wamphray Water	NY 127 964	40	4	–	79	By-roads from A74	iii
78.04	Beld Craig Linn	(Annan)	NT 112 012	–	–	–	79	FP from Moffat	iii
78.05	Highlandman's Loup	Well Burn (Moffat)	NT 093 071	–	–	–	79	FP in Moffat	ii
78.06	Falls of Carrifran Glen	(Carrifran Burn)	NT 150 143	2	45	–	79	A708	v
78.07	Grey Mare's Tail	Tail Burn	NT 184 148	5	60	***	79	A708; NTS CP; FP	i/v
78.08	Dob's Linn	(Moffat Water)	NT 197 158	2	40*	–	79	A708; FP	ii

Nith Basin

79.01	Cluden Leap	Cluden Water	NX 940 793	–	–	–	84	B729	ii
79.02	Routin Linn	Old Water	NX 848 797	20	6	–	84	By-road from B729	ii
79.03	Glenmarlin Falls	Scaur	NX 833 944	76	10	**	84	A702; bridge	ii
79.04	Aird Linn	Shinnel	NX 815 923	40	6	–	78	By-road from A702	iii
79.05	Black Linn	Cample Burn	NX 907 973	–	–	–	78	By-road from A76	ii
79.06	Crichope Linn	Crichope Linn Burn	NX 910 955	–	–	–	78	By-road from A76	ii
79.07	Grey Mare's Tail	Crichope Linn Burn	NX 922 959	5	30	**	78	FP above Crichope L.	iii
79,08	Black Linn	Crichope Linn Burn	NX 926 961	–	–	–	78	Above GMT (Closeburn)	iii
79.09	Falls of Marr Burn	Marr Burn	NX 848 991	4	6*	–	78	By-road from A76	i
79.10	Duncan's Linn	Nith	NS 858 004	–	–	–	78	By-road from A76	ii
79.11	The Slunks	Nith	NS 833 058	–	–	–	78	A76; CP	i
79.12	Carron Linns	Carron	NS 879 009	–	–	–	78	A702; CP	i
79.13	Dinabod Linn	Carron	NS 894 087	–	–	–	78	A702	ii
79.14	Keltie's Linn	Enterkin Burn	NS 884 091	–	–	–	78	Enterkin Pass	iii
79.15	Euchan Falls	Euchan	NS 772 087	–	–	–	78	By-road from Sanquhar	ii
79.16	Roarding Linn	Afton	NS 614 114	–	–	–	71	By-rd from New Cumnock	ii

Galloway Dee

80.01	Sp of Auchentalloch	Old Mill Burn	NX 666 566	–	–	–	83	A75; Twyholm; Fp	ii
80.02	Linn of Lairdmannoch	Tarff Water	NX 667 609	–	–	–	83	A762; FP	ii
80.03	Kirconnel Linn	Tarff Water	NX 674 612	–	–	–	83	A762; FP	ii
80.04	The Doaches	Dee	NX 000 000	–	–	–	83	Tongland; A762	ii
80.05	Blackwater of Dee Falls	Blackwater of Dee	NX 648 696	–	–	–	77	Raiders' Road; A762	ii
80.06	Collin Falls	Blackwater of Dee	NX 597 736	–	–	–	77	Raiders' Road; A762	ii
80.07	Dow Spout	Cooran Lane	NX 463 838	–	–	–	77	FR Black Hill/Bush	v

South West Scotland (continued)

Ref. No.	Name of Fall	River or Burn	Map Ref	Area	Height	Class	Map	Access	Grade
80.08	Buck's Linn	Craigshinnie Burn	NX 607 798	–	–	–	77	By-road A712/A762	iv
80.09	Holy Linn	Garple Burn	NX 655 808	25	12	–	77	A702; FP	iii
80.10	(Earlstoun Linn)	Ken	NX 607 841	–	–	–	77	A713	ii
80.11	(Blackwater Falls)	Blackwater of Ken	NX 611 885	–	–	–	77	A713	ii
80.12	(College Linn)	Ken	NX 627 902	–	–	–	77	B7000	ii
80.13	(Linn of Deugh)	Deugh	NX 607 908	–	–	–	77	B7000	ii
80.14	Grey Mare's Tail	Abbey Burn	NX 744 468	–	–	–	83	By-road Dundrennan	ii
80.15	Linn of Spottes	Spottes Burn	NX 805 673	–	–	–	84	By-road A75	ii

Cree Group

Ref. No.	Name of Fall	River or Burn	Map Ref	Area	Height	Class	Map	Access	Grade
81.01	Craigie Linn	Little W. of Fleet	NX 585 652	–	–	–	83	B796; FP to Burnfoot	iii
81.02	Clugie Linn	Palnure Burn	NX 487 712	–	–	–	77	A712; FP to Bargaly	iii
81.03	Buck Loup	Grey Mare's Tail B.	NX 490 722	5	8	–	77	A712; The Queen's Way	iii
81.04	Grey Mare's Tail	GMT Burn	NX 491 926	4	15	**	77	A712; FW	i
81.05	Grey Mare's Tail	Cardorcan Burn	NX 385 711	–	–	–	77	By-road A714; FR	iii
81.06	Falls of Gairland Burn	Gairland Burn	NX 417 804	–	–	–	77	By-road A714; FP	iii
81.07	Buchan Falls	Buchan Burn	NX 418 804	10	36*	**	77	FP to Merrick	ii
81.08	Falls of Minnoch	Minnoch	NX 337 772	–	–	*	77	By-road A714; CP	i
81.09	Black Linn	Minnoch	NX 369 788	–	–	–	77	By-road A714; CP	ii
81.10	Glencaird Linn	Minnoch	NX 369 790	–	–	–	77	By-road	ii
81.11	Linn of Bargrennan	Cree	NX 356 746	–	–	–	77	A714; Clachaneasy	ii
81.12	Birch Linn	Cree	NX 331 769	–	–	–	76	A714; FP Creebank	iii
81.13	Linn of Barhoise	Bladnoch	NX 339 624	–	–	–	76	B7027	ii
81.14	Falls of Physgill Glen	Physgill Burn	NX 428 362	–	–	–	83	By-road Whithorn	iii
81.15	Loups of Barnshangan	Cross Water of Luce	NX 192 650	–	–	–	82	Southern Upland Way	ii
81.16	Loups of Kilfeddar	Main Water of Luce	NX 151 675	–	–	–	82	By-road New Luce	iii
81.17	Falls of Dunskey Glen	Duchtriemakain Burn	NW 995 556	–	–	–	82	Southern Upland Way	iii

Glossary

Apron Fall Waterfall in which the water is supported by the rocks over which it falls.

Bridal Veil Fall The kind of fall found in the Alps in which the water vapourises before it reaches the ground.

Cap Rock A layer of relatively hard rock at the head of a waterfall which is worn away more slowly than the softer rock underneath, which it may overhang giving rise to a *Curtain fall*(qv).

Cascade Waterfall; usually a series of linked falls.

Cataract Waterfall; properly a considerable, and abrupt, fall.

Catchment The area drained by a river or stream.

Corrie (Coire) An armchair-shaped mountain hollow, the fundamental landform of a glaciated highland; falls occur at the *corrie headwall*, and at the *corrie lip* where the burn draining the hollow tumbles into the glen below by means of a *hanging valley*(qv).

Curtain Fall Fall of the kind in which the water forms a curtain in front of a cave hollowed out by the fall; sometimes it is possible to pass behind the fall.

Den A narrow valley or ravine, usually wooded; a dingle.

Discharge The volume of falling water in a waterfall, or in a river or stream at a particular place, measured in gallons, or in cubic feet per second, or in cubic metres per second (cumecs). Discharge is related to the extent of a river basin, but it also depends on geology, precipitation, abstraction and so on.

Dyke A vertical wall of rock of volcanic origin which can give rise to waterfalls.

Eas (Ess) Waterfall; a ravine occupied by a succession of falls; a torrent.

Fault A dislocation in the rocks which, by bringing hard rocks next to relatively soft rocks, can give rise to waterfalls. As falls migrate upstream the fault which gave rise to a particular fall may be located some distance below it.

Gorge A narrow, steep-sided part of a river's course, often formed by the retreat upstream of a fall; some more spectacular gorges have been formed by the meltwaters of glaciers.

Hanging Valley A tributary valley falling steeply into a main valley caused by the over-deepening of the main valley by glacial action, often occupied by falls, sometimes called *ribbon falls*.

Head The difference in height between the unbroken water above a waterfall and at its foot; the vertical difference in height between the intake and the outlet of a power station.

Igneous Rocks Hard rocks like granite or basalt, so-called because they originate from the Earth's molten lava.

Leap (Loup) Waterfall; particularly a salmon-leap; sometimes a narrow place, a 'strid'.

Linn Waterfall; strictly the pool below a waterfall; in southern Scotland often a stream as a whole; rarely, a gorge.

Metamorphic Rocks Hard rocks, either sedimentary or igneous, which have been changed by pressure or heat; slate and marble are examples.

Plunge Pool The pool at the foot of a fall, sometimes, in soft rocks, deeper than the height of the fall itself.

Pothole Circular hollows formed by the grinding action of boulders in a river bed; they give rise to such terms as *punchbowl* or *quaich*.

Precipitation Rain and snow fall, etc; measured in millimetres: Ben Lomond – 2500mm (100 inches) per annum is wet, Stirling – 1000 mm (40 inches) is relatively dry.

Rapids Where the water in a river falls forward in the bedrock without giving rise to an unsupported fall.

Ravine The steep-sided part of the course of a mountain stream; a narrow place; a gorge.

Regime The seasonal fluctuation in the volume of water in a river or stream; many Highland rivers are subject to sudden spates, hence they are said to have 'flashy' regimes.

Relief The lie of the land; relative differences in elevation.

River Basin The area drained by a river or stream the boundary of which is a **watershed**.

Run-off The surface water which discharges into a river.

Sedimentary Rocks Relatively softer rocks usually originally deposited on sea beds or in lakes; sandstones and limestones are sediments.

Sill A horizontal intrusion of volcanic rock which can give rise to a waterfall.

Slug A narrowing; the narrow part of a river's course.

Spout (Sput) Waterfall; in gaelic **Sput** and **Steall** both have this meaning.

View House A garden house built to provide a view of a fall.

Waterfall An unsupported fall, or steep cascade, of water in a river or stream; waterfalls 'migrate' upstream in the course of geological time until they are eventually eliminated. Two falls side-by-side are called **twin falls**, two falls in succession are called **double falls**, and so on.

Bibliography

Alexander, Henry (1928) The Cairngorms
Andrew, K.M. and Thrippleton, A. A. (1972) The Southern Uplands
Anderson, G. and Anderson, P. (1850) Guide to the Highlands and Islands of Scotland
Anderson, I.F. (1935) Scottish Quest
Anderson, R. (1900) Glen Feshie (Cairngorm Club Journal)

Baddeley, M.J.B. (1890–98) Thorough Guides to Scotland
Baker, Ernest A. (1923) The Highlands with Rope and Rucksack. (1932) On Foot in the Highlands
Barnett, T.R. (1946) The Road to Rannoch and the Summer Isles
Black's Guide (1861–1920)
Bluck, B. (1973) Geology of the Glasgow District
British Regional Geologies:
Pringle, J. (1948) The South of Scotland
MacGregor, A.G. and MacGregor, M. The Midland Valley of Scotland
Read, H.H. (1948) The Grampian Highlands
Phemister, J. (1948) The Northern Highlands
Brown, Hamish (1978) Hamish's Mountain Walk. (1982) Poems of the Scottish Hills
Brown, R.L. (1973) Robert Burns' Tours of the Highlands and Stirlingshire
Burns, Robert. Poems and Songs
Burton, John Hill (1864) The Cairngorm Mountains
Bremner, A. (1912) The Physical Geology of the Dee Valley

Calderwood, W.L. (1921) The Salmon Rivers and Lochs of Scotland
Cambridge County Geographies
Campbell, Alexander (1802) A Journey from Edinburgh through Parts of North Britain
Challinor, J. Dictionary of Geology
Clavering, M. From Border Hills
Cordiner, Charles (1780) Antiquities and Scenery of the North of Scotland. (1795) Remarkable Ruins and Romantic Prospects of North Britain
Cooper, Derek (1970) Skye
Cowper, C.N.L. (1973) Breeding Distribution of Grey Wagtails, Dippers and Sandpipers on the Midlothian Esk (Scottish Birds)
Crichton-Smith, Iain Selected Poems
Crowe, Sylvia (1958) The Landscape of Power
Curzon of Kedleston, Lord (1923) Tales of Travel

Darling, F.F. and Boyd, J.M. (1969) Highlands and Islands
Dick, C.H. (1916) Highways and Byways in Galloway and Carrick
Dixon, J.H. (1925) Pitlochry: Past and Present. (1928) Gairloch
Drummond, R.J. Forgotten Scotland
Duff, David (1968) Victoria in the Highlands

Eagle, D. and Garnett, H. (1977) The Oxford Literary Guide to the British Isles
Edlin, H.L. (1969) The Forests of Southern Scotland
Von Engeln (1952) Geomorphology
Eyre-Todd, George (1946) Loch Lomond

Firsoff, V.A. (1954) In the Hills of Breadalbane. (1965) On Foot in the Cairngorms
Fisher, James (1966) Shell Nature Lover's Atlas
Ford, A.N. (1946) The Firth of Clyde
Forestry Commission
Forest Park Guides:
Glen More (Cairngorms) Forest Park
Queen Elizabeth Forest Park
Argyll Forest Park
Galloway Forest Park
Border Forest Park

Geikie, A. (1865) The Scenery of Scotland
Gilpin, W. (1769) Observations on the Highlands of Scotland
Glasgow Museum and Art Gallery (1972) Scenic Aspects of the River and Firth of Clyde
Gordon, Seton (1925) The Cairngorm Hills of Scotland. (1948) Highways and Byways in Central Scotland
Graham, R.B. Cunninghame (1895) Notes on the District of Mentieth
Grimble, Augustus (1913) The Salmon Rivers of Scotland

Harker, A. (1941) The West Highlands and Hebrides
Hinxman, L.W. (1907) The Rivers of Scotland: the Beauly and the Conon (Scottish Geographical Magazine)
Hogg, James (1803) A Tour in the Highlands
Hodge, E.W. (1953) Northern Highlands
Holden, A.E. (1952) Plant Life in the Scottish Highlands
Holloway, James and Errington, Lindsay (1978) The Discovery of Scotland
Holmes, W.K. (1946) On Scottish Hills
Hopkins, Gerard Manley Poems
Humble, B.H. (1946) On Scottish Hills
Hume, John (1976) Industrial Archeology of Scotland

Irwin, David and Francina (1975) Scottish Painters

Johnson, Samuel (1775) Journey to the Western Islands of Scotland
Johnstone, G. Scott (1966) The Grampian Highlands (Geology). The Western Highlands (SMC)

Lang, Theo (1957) The Border Counties (Queen's Scotland)
Lindsay, Maurice (1964) The Discovery of Scotland, (1971) The Eye is Delighted. (1973) The Lowlands of Scotland: Edinburgh and the South. (1973) The Lowlands of Scotland: Glasgow and the North. (1974) Scotland: An Anthology
Lutyens, Mary (1967) Millais and the Ruskins

MacBeth, George My Scotland
MacCaig, N. and Scott, A. (1970) Contemporary Scottish Verse
McCormick, A. Galloway: the Spell of its Hills and Glens
MacCulloch, J. (1824) The Highlands and Western Islands
MacCulloch, D.B. (1971) Romantic Lochaber, Arisaig and Morar
MacDowell, J.K. Carrick Gallovidian
MacDonald, H. (1854) Rambles Round Glasgow
MacFarlane's Geographical Collections (1720)
MacGregor, M. and others (1972) Geological Excursion Guide to the Assynt District of Sutherland
McLaren, Moray (1965) Shell Guide to Scotland
MacLean, Alan Campbell (1972) Explore the Highlands and Islands
MacLellan, R. (1970) The Isle of Arran
MacLennan, R. (1925) Gaelic Dictionary
MacNally, Lea (1968) The Highland Year. (1972) Wild Highlands
MacPherson, James. The Poems of Ossian
MacNab, P.A. (1970) The Isle of Mull
Macrow, Brenda G. (1946) Unto the Hills. (1948) Kintail Scrapbook. (1956) Speyside to Deeside. (1969) Torridon Highlands
Maxwell, Gavin (1960) Ring of Bright Water
Mills, Derek and Graesser, Neil (1980) The Salmon Rivers of Scotland
Mitchell, G.H. and others (1960) Edinburgh Geology
Mitchell, Joseph Reminiscences of my Life in the Highlands
Mitchell, W.R. (1972) Highland Spring
Moir, D.G. (1975) Scottish Hill Tracks
Morton, H.V. (1929) In Search of Scotland. (1933) In Scotland Again
Munro, Neil (1907) The Clyde
Murray's Handbook for Scotland (1894)
Murray, Hon Mrs S. (1798) A Companion and Useful Guide to the Beauties of Scotland
Murray, W.H. (1951) Undiscovered Scotland. (1962) Mountaineering in Scotland. (1962) Highland

Landscape (1968) Companion Guide to the West Highlands. (1976) Highlands of Scotland (SMC)
Muirhead, Finlay (1927) Blue Guide to Scotland

Nairne, Campbell (1961) The Trossachs
National Trust for Scotland Various Guides to Nature Trails
Nethersole-Thompson, D. and Watson, A. (1974) The Cairngorms
New Statistical Account (1845)
Nicholaisen, W.F.H. (1957) The Semantic Structure of Scottish Hydronymy (Scottish Studies)

Old Statistical Account
Ordnance Gazetteer

Paton, T.A.L. and Brown, J.G. (1960) Power from Water
Pennant, T. (1771–75) A Tour in Scotland and the Western Isles
Peihler, H.A. (1934) Scotland for Everyman
Perry, Richard (1948) In The High Grampians
Prebble, John (1963) The Highland Clearances
Prentice, Robin and others (1976) The National Trust for Scotland Guide

Quigley, Hugh (1936) The Highlands of Scotland

Rashleigh, E.C. (1935) Among the Waterfalls of the World
Ramsay, Allan (1725) The Gentle Shepherd
Robertson, R. MacDonald (1935) In Scotland with a Fishing Rod. (1936) Angling in Wildest Scotland. (1948) Wade the River, Drift the Loch
Rodda, J.C. and others (1976) Systematic Hydrology
St John, Charles (1846) Wild Sports of the Highlands
Scott, Sir Walter (1814) Waverley. (1818) Rob Roy. (1818) Heart of Midlothian. (1831) Northern Lights
Scottish Development Department (1973) Measure of Plenty
Scottish Mountaineering Trust:
District Guides (1920–32)
Scottish Tourist (1832)
Scottish Wildlife Trust Various Guides to Nature Trails
Shairp, John Campbell (1888) Glen Dessary and Other Poems, Lyrical and Elegaic
Sissons, J.B. (1967) The Evolution of Scotland's Scenery
Simpson, W. Douglas (1959) Portrait of the Highlands
Smith, K. (1972) Water in Britain
Snoddy, T.C. (1966) Twixt Forth and Tay
Southey, Robert Tour in Scotland
Steven, Campbell (1968) The Central Highlands (SMC). (1970) Glens and Straths of Scotland. (1971) Enjoying Scotland
Steven, H.M. and Carlisle, A. (1959) The Native Pinewoods of Scotland
Stevenson, R.L. Kidnapped
Stuart, T.A. (1962) The Leaping Behaviour of Salmon and Trout at Falls and Obstructions
Swire, Otta (1963) The Highlands and their Legends
Swinburne, A.C. (1925–27) Complete Works

Taylor, W. (1976) Military Roads in Scotland
Thomas, John (1975) West Highland Railway
Thompson, Francis (1974) The Highlands and Islands
Tranter, Nigel (1957) MacGregors' Gathering. (1970) The Heartland (Queen's Scotland). (1972) The Eastern Counties (Queen's Scotland). (1974) The North East (Queen's Scotland). (1976) Argyll and Bute (Queen's Scotland)
Tremayne, Sydney Poems

Watson, A. (1975) The Cairngorms (SMC)
Watson, A. and Allen, E. (1984) Place Names of Upper Deeside
Watson, W.J. (1927) History of the Celtic Place-names in Scotland
Weir, Tom (1949) Highland Days. (1971) The Kyle Line. (1970–72) The Scottish Lochs. (1973) Western Highlands
Wittow, J.B. (1977) Geology and Scenery in Scotland
Wordsworth, Dorothy Recollections of a Tour made in Scotland
Wood, Wendy (1950) Moidart and Morar

Acknowledgements

I am grateful to the late John Fielden for inspiration, and to the Librarians of the Mitchell Library and Glasgow University for help; and to Leila Stott, to David Harvie and Brian Osborne, and to Colin MacLean for all sorts of assistance.

I was absolutely delighted when Jim Renny agreed to do the maps, and I am even more pleased with his results. All the errors in the spellings of Gaelic names are my own, but I am most grateful to Adam Watson for pointing out some of the mistakes in my manuscript.

For permission to quote extracts from their works I am grateful to Molly Clavering, Iain Crichton Smith, Maurice Lindsay, George Macbeth, Brenda G. Macrow, W.H. Murray, Sydney Tremayne, and Adam Watson; to A. Holden ('Plant Life in the Scottish Highlands'); Mrs Lucie J. Robertson (for an extract from 'Wade the River, Drift the Loch' by R. MacDonald Robertson); Dr H. Swire (for extracts from her books about Folklore by Otta Swire); to Messrs Chatto and Windus (The Hogarth Press) and Norman MacCaig in 'Riding Lights'; the National Trust for Scotland (NTS Guide by Robin Prentice and The Highland Landscape by W.H. Murray); Messrs Martin Secker and Warburg and Andrew Young in 'The Poetical works of Andrew Young'; Messrs Hodder and Stoughton (F.S. Smythe 'The Mountain Vision); Messrs Hutchinson and R.M. Robertson (his other books); Messrs Faber and Faber (The White Hind by Sir James Fergusson); Allen Lithographic (Twixt Forth and Tay by T.C. Snoddy); Messrs John Grant, Edinburgh (Road to Rannoch and the Summer Isles by T. Radcliffe Barnett) Messrs Batsford (The Highlands by Callum MacLean, Western Highlands by Tom Weir, and Highlands of Scotland by Hugh Quigley); and to Messrs Penguin Books (Ring of Bright Water by Gavin Maxwell). It seemed to me that what these many distinguished writers had to say about the waterfalls of Scotland ought to be collected in a celebration of them.

For illustrations I thank the British Geological Survey for photographs of Ben Nevis (p. 12) and Spectacle E'e (p. 180); Messrs D.C. Thomson for photographs from the Adam (pp. 76, 95) and Brydon (p. 22) Collections; the Librarian, Aberdeen University, for a photograph (p. 103) from the George Washington Wilson Collection; the Lady Lever Art Gallery for use of the J.M.W. Turner painting on p. 184; the Fitzwilliam Gallery for use of the Jacob More painting on p. 184; and Jim Renny and Hamish Brown for various notable modern photographs. I also much appreciate the enthusiasm which Colin Alston, Peter Davenport and David Harvie have for waterfalls, and it is only a regard for the solvency of my publishers that prevents me from including all of their pictures.

I am also grateful to the many people who have given me information about various falls, and to all those authors who have written about waterfalls before me whose allusions to waterfalls have illuminated my understanding and enjoyment of them.

Louis Stott

Index to Waterfalls

Except where there is need to distinguish between 'Waterfall' or 'Fall' and other terms, the words 'Fall, Falls, Waterfalls (of)' have in most cases been omitted as part of the place names in this index. Other terms (e.g. Linn, Sput, Loup, Eas) have been retained.

Illustrations are in italics.

Waterfalls are also listed in the Tables (page 203)